From Parent to Child

POPULATION AND DEVELOPMENT
A series edited by Richard A. Easterlin

previously published:

Fertility Change in Contemporary Japan
Robert W. Hodge and Naohiro Ogawa

Social Change and the Family in Taiwan
Arland Thornton and Hui-Sheng Lin

*Swing Low, Sweet Chariot: The Mortality
Cost of Colonizing Liberia in the
Nineteenth Century*
Antonio McDaniel

THE UNIVERSITY OF CHICAGO PRESS / CHICAGO AND LONDON

From Parent to Child

INTRAHOUSEHOLD ALLOCATIONS AND

INTERGENERATIONAL RELATIONS IN

THE UNITED STATES

Jere R. Behrman, Robert A. Pollak, and Paul Taubman

Jere R. Behrman is William R. Kenan, Jr., Professor of Economics
at the University of Pennsylvania. Robert A. Pollak is Hernreich
Distinguished Professor of Economics in the College of Arts and
Sciences and the John M. Olin School of Business at Washington
University in St. Louis. Until his untimely death in May 1995, Paul
Taubman was professor of economics at the University of Pennsylvania.

The University of Chicago Press, Chicago 60637
The University of Chicago Press, Ltd., London
© 1995 by The University of Chicago
All rights reserved. Published 1995
Printed in the United States of America

04   03   02   01   00   99   98   97   96   95   1   2   3   4   5

ISBN: 0-226-04156-5 (cloth)
ISBN: 0-226-04157-3 (paper)

Library of Congress Cataloging-in-Publication Data

Behrman, Jere R.
    From parent to child : intrahousehold allocations and
  intergenerational relations in the United States / Jere R. Behrman,
  Robert A. Pollak, and Paul Taubman.
        p.   cm. — (Population and development)
    Includes bibliographical references and index.
        1. Family—Economic aspects—United States.   2. Education—
  Economic aspects—United States.   3. Intergenerational relations—
  United States.   4. Nature and nurture.   I. Pollak, Robert A.,
  1938– .   II. Taubman, Paul, 1939– .   III. Title.   IV. Series:
  Population and development (Chicago, Ill.)
  HQ536.B43   1995
  306.87—dc20

Paul Taubman—our colleague, collaborator, and friend for three decades—died on May 4, 1995. We mourn his untimely passing, celebrate his achievements, and dedicate this book to his memory.

J.R.B.
R.A.P.

Contents

         Can the Effects Be Identified?
         JERE R. BEHRMAN

Part Four **Associations between Parental Income**   213
         and Child Earnings
10   Intergenerational Earnings Mobility in the United   215
         States: Some Estimates and a Test of Becker's
         Intergenerational Endowments Model
         JERE R. BEHRMAN AND PAUL TAUBMAN
11   The Intergenerational Correlation between   229
         Children's Adult Earnings and Their Parents'
         Income: Results from the Michigan Panel
         Survey of Income Dynamics
         JERE R. BEHRMAN AND PAUL TAUBMAN

Part Five **"Nature versus Nurture" in Schooling and Earnings**   243
12   On Heritability   245
         PAUL TAUBMAN
13   Is Schooling "Mostly in the Genes"? Nature-   249
         Nurture Decomposition Using Data on
         Relatives
         JERE R. BEHRMAN AND PAUL TAUBMAN
14   Measuring the Impact of Environmental Policies   269
         on the Level and Distribution of Earnings
         PAUL TAUBMAN

         References   287
         Author Index   303
         Subject Index   305

Introduction

In making decisions that affect their children's human capital and the distribution of inter vivos gifts and bequests, do parents act as though they were concerned solely with the distribution of wealth among their children? Or do parents act as though they were also concerned with the distribution of the separate components of wealth—human capital and nonhuman capital? Do parents allocate educational resources among their children as though they were attempting to maximize the return on investment? Do parents favor boys? Do they favor their first-born child?

How great is intergenerational economic mobility in the United States? How highly correlated is the schooling of parents and children? How highly correlated are their earnings? What underlies these intergenerational correlations? What is the relative importance of nature (i.e., genetic factors) and nurture (i.e., environmental factors)? How similar is the economic status of siblings?

These questions raise two distinct but related sets of issues: the measurement and explanation of similarity among siblings ("intragenerational linkages") and the measurement and explanation of similarity between parents and children ("intergenerational linkages"). We view intragenerational linkages as the result of parental decisions to allocate resources—especially educational resources—among their children. Thus, both intergenerational and intragenerational linkages are related intimately to the functioning of families.[1]

The magnitudes of intergenerational and intragenerational correlations suggest that what happens in families has important and persistent effects on the economic opportunities available to children and, thus, on the outcomes they experience as adults. In the United States intergenerational correlations in

---

1. The definition of "families" is contested. Nuclear families consist of parents and their children. In this book we do not distinguish between step- and natural parents or between full and other siblings. Nuclear families may be extended vertically (e.g., including grandparents in addition to parents and their children) or horizontally (e.g., including siblings of the household head or spouse, perhaps with their children), or both. Much of the economic literature treats the term "family" as if it referred to a nuclear family that constitutes a household. We follow this convention, commenting explicitly when we depart from it to discuss other types of families.

1

schooling attainment are of the magnitude of 0.3 to 0.4. Intergenerational correlations in earnings or income, based on data for several years, are of the magnitude of 0.4 or greater.[2] Same-sex sibling correlations in schooling and adult earnings over the 1978–87 decade in the Panel Study on Income Dynamics are about 0.5 for brothers, 0.4 to 0.5 for sisters, and 0.8 for identical twins.[3]

The study of intrafamily allocations among children and intergenerational linkages raises big questions with enormous implications for the functioning of families, the economy, and the state. Four examples illustrate this point. First, if intergenerational economic mobility is high, a child from a poor family has a reasonable opportunity to do well economically; if intergenerational mobility is low, a child's economic destiny is largely determined by the family into which the child is born. Participants are likely to view a socioeconomic system with low intergenerational mobility as unfair and unjust. Second, if, on the one hand, parents are concerned only about the distribution of wealth among their children, then, under certain assumptions, they provide each child with the wealth-maximizing level of schooling, investing in the schooling of each child until the marginal rate of return to schooling equals the market rate of interest. With well-functioning capital markets and with no externalities to investments in schooling, the wealth-maximizing level of schooling is efficient. If, on the other hand, parents care about the distribution of earnings among their children then, even with well-functioning capital markets and without externalities, investments in schooling are inefficient except in very special cases. Third, if schooling prices depend on ability (e.g., because of merit scholarships), then, under plausible assumptions, parental investments in their children's schooling are likely to be more unequal than they would be if all children in a family faced the same prices of schooling independent of their abilities. Thus, within-family schooling opportunities would be more equal—although not necessarily more efficient—if society were to prohibit merit scholarships or subsidize schooling prices for less able children. Fourth, intrafamily allocations and interhousehold transfers may blunt the effectiveness of governmental programs

2. Behrman and Taubman (1990, in this volume), Solon (1992), and Zimmerman (1992) present recent estimates with alternative controls for measurement errors. Earlier estimates for the United States and for European countries without such controls and generally based on only one year of observations average less than half of this magnitude, suggesting much greater intergenerational mobility; these earlier estimates are summarized in Becker and Tomes (1986) and Behrman and Taubman (1985, in this volume).

3. Mixed-sex sibling correlations for earnings from the Panel Study of Income Dynamics are much lower, but the interpretation of mixed-sex earnings correlations is difficult because of selectivity; see Behrman, Pollak, and Taubman (1995, in this volume), Behrman, Hrubec, Taubman, and Wales (1980), Altonji and Dunn (1991), Lykken, Bouchard, McGue, and Tellegen (1990), Jencks and Brown (1977), and Olneck (1977) for these and other intergenerational and sibling correlations beyond those cited in the previous footnote.

targeted toward particular household members (e.g., infants, preschool children, school-aged children, pregnant and nursing women, the elderly): Barro's (1974) notion of Ricardian equivalence extends well beyond macroeconomics.

As colleagues at the University of Pennsylvania we have worked together for more than a decade studying intragenerational and intergenerational linkages. We have published the findings from our collaborative research primarily as articles in scholarly economic journals. Although the individual articles can stand alone, this volume is more than a collection of scattered articles. By bringing our papers together in a single volume, we hope to convey a sense of why these issues are important and of what economists can contribute to the study of intragenerational and intergenerational linkages.

We begin this introduction by summarizing and synthesizing what we have learned. Then, since no research program takes place in a vacuum, we locate our work in the context of other research on intragenerational and intergenerational linkages. Finally, we conclude this introduction with brief summaries of the articles included in this volume.

Summary and Synthesis

The study of intrafamily allocations helps explain intragenerational linkages and, hence, the causes of the sib similarities and dissimilarities. Although genetic endowments (including sex) are basically beyond parents' control, parental allocations of educational and other resources to their children are affected by these endowments.[4] We develop a model of this intrafamily allocation process in which parents are concerned with the distribution of earnings among their children. Our assumption that parents are concerned with the distribution of earnings and not simply with income—the sum of earnings and income from transfers—leads to the "Separable Earnings-Transfers" (SET) model. We contrast the SET model with the "wealth" model of Becker and Tomes (1976).

The wealth model is the dominant paradigm economists use to analyze intrafamily allocation among children. In the wealth model, parents are concerned only with the total wealth of each child, not with its composition or sources; hence, they do not distinguish between "earned" and "unearned" income.

The SET model and the wealth model have different implications for the efficiency of parental investment in their children's human capital. The wealth model, as Becker and Tomes originally presented it, implies that parents' investments in their children's human capital are socially efficient provided there are well-functioning capital markets and no externalities: parents invest in the

---

4. Amniocentesis and similar tests make possible selective abortion based on some characteristics of the genetic endowment of a fetus, but such tests are too recent to affect those in our sample.

human capital of each child until the marginal rate of return to education is driven down to the rate of return on financial assets; any additional resources provided to children take the form of transfers (i.e., gifts and bequests).

Becker and Tomes assume that parents with more than one child have equal concern for all of their children; in the simplest version of the wealth model, this assumption implies that parents use transfers to offset fully inequalities in their children's earnings. Hence, the wealth model with equal concern predicts a pattern of unequal earnings, unequal transfers, and equal wealth. The data, however, show that for most households the absolute magnitudes of gifts and bequests are insufficient to offset fully earnings differentials among siblings.

Subsequent elaborations of the wealth model drop the assumption of equal concern and the assumption that the parents are rich enough and altruistic enough that they provide all of their children the wealth-maximizing level of schooling. The elaborated version of the wealth model implies that, if parents do not allocate "enough" resources to their children, then some children receive less than the socially efficient level of human capital, and those children receive zero transfers. The SET model does not imply that human capital investments are efficient, even with well-functioning capital markets and no externalities; nor does it imply that parents with equal concern for their children attempt to offset fully differences in earnings by allocating transfer unequally.

Data limitations make it difficult to distinguish empirically between the wealth model and the SET model. The dominant pattern for bequests—equal sharing among siblings—appears more consistent with the SET model than with the wealth model.

Using the SET model, we investigate whether intrafamily allocation compensates for or reinforces differences in children's genetic endowments and differences in nonfamily environment. For example, we investigate the sensitivity of these allocations to prices for education that may vary with the availability of merit-based scholarships. For the United States, we find that investments in schooling are not determined solely by efficiency or productivity concerns: equity also weighs heavily in intrafamily allocations. For rural India, a much poorer society, we find similar results for the allocation of nutrients among children during the surplus season when food is relatively abundant, but during the lean season when food is scarce allocation is determined almost entirely by productivity concerns.

Parents might provide unequal education to daughters and sons because their preferences favor children of one gender or because they know that the labor market rewards unequally women and men with the same ability and the same human capital. Our research shows that the preferences of parents in the United States do not favor sons over daughters; indeed, if anything, when marriage market as well as labor market returns are incorporated into the analysis, the empirical evidence suggests that parents' preferences give slightly more weight to daughters than to sons. These results contrast with our finding about the allocation of nutrients to sons and daughters in rural India.

Birth-order effects have been widely discussed in the biological, psychological, and popular literatures. Lower-birth-order children (i.e., older children) may benefit from developing in more adult-oriented environments and from teaching their younger siblings. Higher-birth-order children, however, may benefit from having more experienced parents. Casual observation (perhaps primarily by older siblings) suggests that the youngest child is often spoiled by excessive parental attention and indulgence. Finally, birth order may be related to health because of the relationship between birth order and mother's age, with less healthy children borne by very young and very old mothers.

Birth order may affect intrafamily allocation through preferences or through constraints. On the preference side, parents may fail to exhibit equal concern and instead favor the eldest or the youngest child. On the constraint side, parents with many children may allocate less to each child, and borrowing constraints may vary over the parents' life cycle, differentially affecting children of different birth orders. Turning to the empirical evidence, we find that intrafamily allocations favor children of lower birth order both for the United States and for rural India in the lean season. For the United States, we find that constraints are part of the explanation.

The United States has long been viewed as a society in which intergenerational linkages are relatively weak. For social scientists, this view is equivalent to the belief that the correlation between children's economic status and that of their parents is low in the United States compared with other societies. For those with a broader perspective, this view is fortified by de Tocqueville's well-known nineteenth-century observation about high intergenerational mobility, reinforced by Horatio Alger's stories and buttressed by the relative absence of families with long, conspicuous, dynastic histories of great wealth. Widely held myths suggest that the United States is a "land of opportunity" where a family can go from "rags to riches" in a single generation (and perhaps back to rags in the next). Other views and other myths suggest contrary conclusions. Many regard the intergenerational transmission of poverty as a reality, although there is little agreement on the causal mechanism. "Like father, like son" and "a chip off the old block" are also part of American mythology.

We characterize the similarity between parents and children in the United States in terms of educational attainment and income or earnings. We find that the intergenerational economic correlations are substantially higher than previously reported when we control for transitory fluctuations in earnings by using data for time spans longer than a single year. We find some evidence that borrowing constraints are important. Finally, we find that children's earnings are more closely associated with parental income during children's teenage years—a period when critical schooling decisions often are made—than with parental income during other periods.

We also investigate some of the factors that determine a child's economic success or, more precisely, the factors that influence the probability of economic success. In particular, we consider Fisher's (1918) model of the effect of genetics and environment on observed outcomes and show how to extend it within a latent variable framework using observed environmental indicators. We discuss the critical assumptions underlying "nature-nurture" decompositions and the limitations of such decompositions for predicting the effect of policy changes on the distribution of outcomes such as schooling or earnings. We present estimates of such decompositions for two generations in the United States, estimates that suggest that genetic variance accounts for over half of the variance in schooling. Furthermore, the contribution of genetic variance to the total is greater for the more recent generation than for their parents, apparently because the GI Bill allowed veterans of the Second World War relatively more equal access to postsecondary education than that experienced by their children. These results reinforce the implication of our SET model that programs such as guaranteed student loans at market interest rates may promote both efficiency and equity.

Our Research and the Literature[5]

Research does not occur in isolation, but reflects what others have done and are doing. The research we present in this volume has been profoundly influenced by Gary Becker, winner of the 1992 Nobel Prize in economics, whose imaginative and provocative models have become the lens through which economists view the family. We believe that we have gone beyond Becker's work by developing new theoretical models and by subjecting new and old models to more systematic empirical analysis. We view our work as "standing on his shoulders"—though at times he may view some of our explications, extensions, and critiques of his work as "standing on his toes." To place our work in context, we briefly review alternative approaches to the analysis of intrafamily allocation.

Predecessors. Three strands of literature provide the underpinning on which recent studies of intrafamily allocation among children rely. First, Becker's (1965) household production model raised economists' interest in what was happening within the household and provided a powerful framework for analyzing it. Second, articles by Becker (1967), Mincer (1974), and Schultz (1961) developed the "investment" framework for analyzing the determinants

5. Behrman (1995) provides a more extensive review of this literature.

of schooling, health, and other forms of human capital. These studies provided a systematic way of thinking about the determinants of human resource investments, although they did not explicitly consider intrafamily allocations among children. Third, the quantity-quality fertility articles of Becker and Lewis (1973) and Willis (1973) analyzed the simultaneous determination of parental consumption, the number of children, and the average quality of children in a family. The quantity-quality models analyzed these decisions in terms of parents' preferences and the constraints parents face, although they did not consider the allocation of resources among the children. To avoid discussing resource allocation among children, the quantity-quality model assumes—sometimes explicitly, more often implicitly—that all of the children in a family are identical. With identical children, the issue of compensating and reinforcing investments cannot arise.

Consensus Parental Preferences with Passive Children. The defining characteristic of consensus parental preference models is the assumption that the parents act as if they were maximizing a single utility function, subject to appropriate constraints.[6] Most consensus models treat parents' preferences as a primitive and make no attempt to derive them from the underlying preferences of husbands and wives. Following this tradition, we begin by assuming that the parents' utility function includes parental consumption and, for each child, the two sources of the children's income when they become adults: earnings, which depend on human capital, and transfers, which do not.[7] The parents' utility function should also include the number of children, but we omit this argument because we have nothing new to say about the determinants of family size. The parental utility function reflects the preferences of the parents, not the children, although the parents are assumed to be "altruistic" in the sense that their utility depends on their children's nonlabor income and earnings.[8]

---

6. The term "consensus" is borrowed from Samuelson (1956). Various terms are used in the literature to describe models in which a single preference ordering for the parents is assumed (as in Samuelson) or derived. Lundberg (1988) refers to the "family utility model"; Thomas, (1990), to the "common preference model"; and McElroy and Horney (1981), McElroy (1990), and Schultz (1990), to "neoclassical models." McElroy (1992) uses "altruistic models," which she advocates because Becker's altruism model is often invoked to justify a parental preference ordering. Bourguignon and Chiappori (1992) refer to McElroy's Nash bargaining models as having altruistic preferences because the utility of one household member depends on the consumption or utility of another.

7. We consider only transfers from parents to children, ignoring other intrafamily transfers and government transfers.

8. An alternative "altruistic" model assumes that the children's utilities enter the parents' utility function, but this specification raises awkward difficulties of cardinality and interpersonal comparability.

Following the literature, we assume away a number of complications. First, we assume that hours of work are exogenously determined.[9] Second, we assume that education is solely a means of securing higher earnings for the child. This rules out the possibility that a child's educational attainment is a consumption good for the parents, as in Pollak's paternalistic preferences model or that some children enjoy education more than others.[10] Third, we assume that human capital does not affect an individual's productivity within the household. Fourth, we assume that human capital investment decisions do not yield marriage market returns and thus ignore the possibility that individuals with more human capital do better in the marriage market.[11]

To determine the optimal level of parental consumption, of transfers to each child, and of human capital investment in each child, the parental utility function is maximized subject to two types of constraints: a budget constraint and an earnings production function for each child.[12] The budget constraint requires that the sum of the present values of parental expenditures on their own consumption, on transfers to their children, and on investments in their children's human capital not exceed their total resources. The earnings production

9. Models that treat both hours of work and human capital investments as endogenous are complicated. When human capital investments are exogenous, "full income" (or "full earnings") finesses the endogenous labor-supply problem. When human capital investments are endogenous, the finesse fails because the separation theorem no longer holds: human capital investment decisions and consumption decisions (e.g., decisions involving the labor-leisure choice and goods complementary to leisure) must be analyzed simultaneously, except in very special cases. The earnings corresponding to any human capital investment depend on the child's labor-leisure preferences, so that human capital investments (e.g., law school or medical school) are more attractive for children whose preferences place relatively more weight on consuming goods than on consuming leisure. Similarly, because the child's labor supply decision depends on wealth, the human capital investment and transfer decisions must be analyzed simultaneously. Pollak (1993) develops these themes.

10. In a model with household production, human capital should also enter the production function. One might further complicate the model by distinguishing among various types of human capital.

11. The analysis of marriage market returns is more complex and more model specific than our brief discussion in Berhman, Pollak, and Taubman (1986, in this volume) suggests. In the SET model, it is plausible that the child with more human capital will have better marriage market prospects. In the wealth model, if parents provide each child with the wealth-maximizing level of human capital and use transfers to offset fully any differences in earnings, then a more educated child will have higher expected earnings but may have no better marriage market prospects than a less educated sibling who receives the lion's share of parental gifts and bequests. In this wealth model scenario, which sibling has better marriage market prospects depends on second-order considerations such as the timing of transfers, divorce probabilities, and whether a divorced spouse has stronger claims against an ex-spouse's human capital than against the portion of the ex-spouse's nonhuman capital acquired through gifts, past bequests, and anticipated bequests.

12. Applications that include other human resource outcomes (e.g., health) as arguments of the utility function must also include the corresponding constraints (e.g., health production functions).

function gives the adult earnings of each child as a function of the child's endowments and human resources investments in that child. Endowments include genetically inherited characteristics that are rewarded directly or indirectly (i.e., through their interaction with human capital investments) in labor markets.

The traditional analysis assumes children are passive and denies them an independent role as decision makers. Becker (1974*b*, 1981) attempts to justify this denial in terms of his "rotten kid" theorem, arguing that parents can use transfers as a carrot or stick to induce even selfish children to conform completely to their parents' interests and desires. Thus, Becker contends, even a completely selfish child who is a potential beneficiary of parental transfers will act so as to maximize the income available to the altruistic parents. Becker assumes that the parents' preferences depend on their own consumption and on the child's utility, which, he assumes, is a function of the child's consumption; the child, in contrast, is selfish in the sense that the child's utility does not depend on the parents' consumption or utility. Finally, Becker assumes that the parents make positive transfers to the child (i.e., the parents optimal choice is an interior rather than a corner solution). Under these assumptions, the rotten kid theorem asserts that, if the child has available actions that affect the income of the parents, and if the parents make subsequent transfers to the child to maximize their own utility, then the selfish child's optimal action is one that maximizes total family income (i.e., the sum of parents' and the child's income) and, therefore, the one that maximizes the parents' welfare.

The conclusion of the rotten kid theorem may fail to hold for at least three reasons. First, as Hirshleifer (1977, 1985) points out, the parents must make their transfer after the child acts. Otherwise, the selfish child can maximize at the expense of the parents with impunity. Second, Bergstrom (1989) and Bernheim, Shleifer, and Summers (1985) point out that the conclusion may not hold if utility does not depend solely on transferable commodities. Third, Bruce and Waldman (1990) show that the conclusion may not hold in a two-period setting with savings because of what they call the "Samaritan's dilemma."

During the past decade, we and other researchers have used the consensus parental preference framework with unobserved heterogeneity in endowments to investigate intrafamily allocation. Important examples of such studies by others include: the investigation of the quality-quantity model using as a natural experiment the birth of twins in India by Rosenzweig and Wolpin (1980); the study of female-male infant mortality differentials in India by Rosenzweig and Schultz (1982); the exploration of the determinants of child health given learning about the child health endowments over time and intrafamily allocations in Colombia by Rosenzweig and Wolpin (1988); the study of intrafamily time

allocation in response to illness of an infant in Indonesia by Pitt and Rosenzweig (1990); and the investigation of the intrafamily allocations of nutrients,
health, and work effort in Bangladesh by Pitt, Rosenzweig, and Hassan (1990).
These studies demonstrate the usefulness of the consensus parental preference
framework for analyzing intrafamily allocations and the importance of controlling for unobserved heterogeneity in endowments: empirical results obtained without controlling for unobserved heterogeneity are often seriously
misleading.

In its general form, the consensus parental preference model places few restrictions on the allocation of human resource investments and transfers to and
among children. Two special cases of the consensus parental preference
model—the wealth model of Becker and Tomes (1976, 1979) and the separable
earnings-transfers (SET) model of Behrman, Pollak, and Taubman (1982, in
this volume)—make stronger assumptions and yield sharper conclusions.[13]
The wealth model and the SET model provide the basis for most of our analysis
of intrafamily allocations among children. Both the wealth model and the SET
model ignore the allocation of resources between parental consumption and
children: both models treat the total resources devoted to children as predetermined and examine the allocation of that predetermined total among children.
Both models assume that the parents determine the amount of schooling their
children receive: parents decide, children comply. Both models assume that,
because of unspecified contracting problems or poorly functioning capital markets, investments in the children's schooling are not necessarily carried to the
point at which the marginal rate of return on such investments equals the rate
of return on financial assets.

The wealth model and the SET model differ in their implications for whether
parents allocate resources to compensate for or to reinforce differences in their
children's endowments. In the wealth model, parents never provide any child
with more than the wealth-maximizing level of human capital; in the SET
model, parents may provide some or even all of their children with more than
the wealth-maximizing level of human capital.

Most analytical modeling and most of the better empirical work on intrafamily allocation among children has utilized the consensus parental preference framework. These studies have dealt with an ever-widening range of issues in more integrated ways with increasing sensitivity to estimation issues.
The best of them elaborate and test hypotheses about the role of unobserved
heterogenous endowments within the context of labor, product, and marriage
markets. Their results suggest that controlling for unobserved heterogeneity is

---

13. Becker (1981) and Becker and Murphy (1988) elaborate the wealth model, as do we in
Behrman, Pollak, and Taubman (1995, in this volume).

critical for understanding intrafamily allocations. Nevertheless, even the best of these studies impose strong assumptions as maintained hypotheses, although different studies impose different assumptions.

Consensus Parental Preferences with Active Children. We now discuss two models with consensus parental preferences in which the children are active, independent decision makers: "strategic bequest" models and "paternalistic preference" models.

Bernheim, Shleifer, and Summers (1985) develop a strategic bequest model in which parents influence the behavior of their children by conditioning bequests on their children's actions. The strategic bequest model begins by recognizing that children may take some actions that affect both their own and their parents' utilities (e.g., the attention that children provide to elderly parents by visits, telephone calls, etc.). Bernheim, Shleifer, and Summers assume that parents want more attention from each child than the child wants to provide. This implies that the amount of attention that a child would choose to provide without special incentives is not Pareto optimal. Suppose, however, that the parents can credibly threaten to disinherit the child; then the parents can offer the child the choice between a specified precommitted level of transfers combined with a specified level of attention, on the one hand, and disinheritance (zero transfers), on the other. With this threat, if it is credible, the parents can enforce a Pareto-optimal solution in which they obtain their chosen point on the Pareto frontier, subject to the constraint that the child can be made no worse off than with disinheritance. Bernheim, Shleifer, and Summers discuss a bequest rule that, they claim, constitutes a credible threat and leads to a Pareto-optimal equilibrium. Under the rule they propose, each child who provides the level of attention specified by the parents receives a positive bequest, while each child who fails to meet this standard is disinherited; the total bequest is divided among those children who have provided the specified levels of attention. If all children are disinherited by this rule, then the child who comes closest to meeting the standard receives the entire estate. Bernheim, Shleifer, and Summers recognize that the credibility of this strategic behavior depends on the presence of plausible alternatives to each potential beneficiary; hence, they argue, the threat is not credible when there is only one child.

Finally, Bernheim, Shleifer, and Summers suggest empirical tests to distinguish their model from alternatives: "First, evidence that the behavior of children is influenced by anticipated bequests would support the class of models in which bequests function as a medium of exchange. Second, evidence suggesting that parents successfully wield influence only when they have more than one credible beneficiary would support the particular theory of strategic influence just described. Third, evidence suggesting that parents care *directly* about some actions taken by their children would establish the *motive* for strategic as opposed to nonstrategic influence (as in Becker's rotten kid theorem)" (1985, pp. 1057–58, italics in original).

Exchange models, of which strategic bequest models are an important example, advance beyond the previous literature in two dimensions: first, they allow children's preferences to play a serious role in the analysis, and, second, they incorporate a broader notion of the goods involved in parent-child interactions (e.g., the attention that adult children provide to their parents). Yet the exchange models retain the other limitations that we discussed in conjunction with the consensus parental preference model with passive children. Furthermore, empirical analysis based on exchange models, unlike the best of the literature that assumes passive children, ignores heterogeneity in endowments. This failure to incorporate unobserved heterogeneity in endowments raises serious doubts about the empirical tests that Bernheim, Shleifer, and Summers and others, such as Cox (1987) and Cox and Rank (1992), interpret as supporting exchange models. The exchange literature is also silent on the determinants of human resource investments. Finally, the exchange models investigated thus far have been rigged to ensure that the parents obtain all of the surplus from their interaction with their children. Pollak (1988, in this volume) argues that, in the strategic bequest model of Bernheim, Shleifer, and Summers, if the parents lack an institutional mechanism that enables them to precommit to a particular bequest strategy, and if the parents would prefer to leave equal bequests to their children, then the threat to disinherit a child who fails to provide sufficient attention is not credible. Although there are legal instruments (e.g., irrevocable trusts) that may allow parents to make the required precommitments, a will that the testator can revise at any time is *not* a precommitment mechanism. Without a precommitment mechanism, however, the threat to disinherit one child in favor of another is credible only if the parents do not mind disinheriting one or more of their children: more formally, parents must be indifferent among divisions of their estate among their children that leave positive bequests to all children and divisions that disinherit one (or more) of their children. Thus, although the strategic bequest model of Bernheim, Shleifer, and Summers allows children to be active, the game they specify is rigged to give parents a decisive strategic advantage.[14]

Pollak (1988, in this volume) proposes a model of paternalistic preferences that, he argues, is consistent with some observations about parental-child interaction that appear to contradict the assumption of altruistic models that parents seek to maximize their children's resources (e.g., wealth, earnings, nonlabor income) or their children's utility. Pollak challenges the assumption that parents

---

14. An alternative bequest game in which children can form coalitions and precommit to providing little or no attention might have a very different equilibrium.

accept fully their children's preferences. In Pollak's model transfers are tied—parental resources have strings attached. For example, parents may be willing to pay for college tuition or the down payment on a house, but not for a Mercedes or a trip around the world. The tied transfers model assumes that the child's ability or willingness to untie transfers is limited, perhaps because of transaction costs or perhaps because the child recognizes that untying the transfer would be disadvantageous in the repeated game.

Models without Consensus Parental Preferences. Microeconomic theory traditionally has treated the household (or, more precisely, the parents) as a single economic entity with well-defined, consistent preferences. Thus, the household is assumed to maximize a utility function subject to appropriate resource and production function constraints. This traditional approach is being challenged increasingly by advocates of nonconsensus approaches to household behavior that treat the household (or, more precisely, the adults in the household) as distinct individuals with conflicting as well as common interests.

Nonconsensus approaches view household behavior as the outcome of a noncooperative or a cooperative game, although the game itself is often not fully specified. Advocates of nonconsensus approaches argue that the traditional consensus approach either ignores differences in the interests and preferences of the individuals who constitute a household or provides an unsatisfactory account of how such differences are reconciled. The weaknesses of the consensus approach are particularly evident in dealing with household formation and dissolution because these issues cannot be approached without recognizing that different individuals have different interests and preferences; but distribution within marriage raises similar difficulties, as does distribution between parents and children. Thus far, nonconsensus models have generally focused on interactions between husbands and wives rather than those between parents and children or among children.

Among nonconsensus models, a basic distinction is between those that are rooted in cooperative game theory and those that are rooted in noncooperative game theory. Cooperative models often allow only Pareto-optimal outcomes, while noncooperative models often allow nonoptimal outcomes. Chiappori (1988, 1992) and Bourguignon, Browning, Chiappori, and Lechene (1991, 1993) have developed nonconsensus models that assume household allocations are Pareto optimal, but they avoid specifying a particular bargaining game or collective decision process. Bourguignon and Chiappori (1992) conclude their survey of nonconsensus approaches, which they call the "collective" approach: "The collective approach described above is still in a preliminary stage. Several theoretical issues remain unsolved; and the empirical work only begins. We however believe that it constitutes a coherent and promising research program, which is likely to be pursued in the forthcoming years" (p. 9).

Manser and Brown (1980) and McElroy and Horney (1981) introduced non-consensus models of distribution within marriage that rely on the Nash bargaining solution, a leading solution concept from cooperative game theory. The Nash bargaining model generalizes the comparative statics of the consensus model by allowing changes in the "threat point" to affect household behavior. In the Nash bargaining approach, the threat point corresponds to the utility that each individual would obtain in the absence of agreement. In Manser and Brown and in McElroy and Horney, these threat points correspond to the utility of divorce, while, in the separate-spheres bargaining model of Lundberg and Pollak (1993), they correspond to a noncooperative equilibrium in marriage specified in terms of traditional gender roles (also see Ulph 1988). In the Nash bargaining solution, the surplus from cooperation is shared so that the household maximizes, subject to the appropriate constraints, the product of the gains to cooperation, where the gains are measured from the threat point. The result is a system of "demand" equations for goods and leisure that depend on prices, broadly defined, and on the resources that each spouse controls.

In her recent writings, McElroy (1990, 1992) emphasizes that individual nonearned income and "extrahousehold environmental parameters" (EEPs) shift the threat point. As examples of EEPs, she proposes "parameters that describe marriage markets, parameters that characterize the legal structure within which marriage and divorce occur, and parameters that characterize government taxes and government or private transfers that are conditioned on marital or family status" (1990, p. 567). McElroy (1992) summarizes the empirical tests of the bargaining model to date as including tests of across-equations restrictions (which she characterizes as "few and inconclusive") and single-equation tests (which she characterizes as having "produced strong results favoring the bargaining models"; pp. 11–12). We are skeptical of testing cross-equation restrictions (e.g., Slutsky symmetry conditions) because it is almost always possible to interpret any rejection of such restrictions as a rejection of the functional form assumptions that underlie the calculation of the partial derivatives on which the test is based. Thus, we find single-equation testing more promising. As examples of single-equation tests, McElroy emphasizes Schultz (1990) and Thomas (1990), both of which explore whether income is pooled within the household or whether, on the contrary, outcomes such as fertility, women's time allocation, nutrient intakes, and child health are affected by which spouse controls household resources. We have reservations, however, about interpreting Schultz and Thomas as conclusive rejections of the pooling hypothesis or the consensus model.[15]

---

15. Rejection of the pooling assumption of the consensus model is not equivalent to accepting any particular alternative (e.g., the Nash bargaining model), although McElroy seems to suggest the contrary. Bourguignon and Chiappori (1992) criticize McElroy on this point.

To test pooling, one would like to conduct an experiment in which extra resources were distributed randomly to husbands and to wives and then to observe whether the marginal propensities to use such resources differed depending on which spouse received the resources. Because experimental data are unavailable, both Schultz and Thomas use individual "unearned" income to test the pooling hypothesis. By using unearned income rather than earned income or total income, they hope to avoid the price (i.e., opportunity cost of time) effects that wages would represent.[16] This empirical strategy, however, requires assuming that unearned income is orthogonal to wages. Whether this assumption is satisfied presumably depends on the sources of unearned income. In the data used by Schultz (from Thailand) and by Thomas (from Brazil), the sources are largely pensions and social security, both of which are related to past wages. Income from assets may also reflect past wages if such assets were acquired with past labor earnings. Unearned income may thus represent labor market productivity associated with household activities pertaining to health, nutrition, fertility, and time allocations. If this is so, their results do not necessarily imply that shifting resources from husbands to wives would have a positive effect on, say, child health; it is possible that there would be no effect, and that their estimates reflect the fact that more productive women have healthier children. Thus, their results are not conclusive rejections of the pooling hypothesis.

We find attractive the emphasis of nonconsensus models on individual preferences and individual control over resources. On the basis of casual observations, this seems to us an important feature of intrafamily allocation in many societies. In the case of what Lundberg and Pollak (1993) call "divorce threat bargaining models," nonconsensus models integrate concern about intrafamily allocation with concern about marital dissolution. Despite these attractive features, however, the literature on nonconsensus models has important limitations. Most important, both the theoretical and the empirical studies in the nonconsensus literature ignore the role of unobserved heterogeneous endowments. Hence, the empirical results are inconclusive even on the topic on which most work has been done, namely, whether households pool income.

The past decade has seen substantial progress in the analysis of intrafamily allocation, and we are pleased that our work has contributed to that progress. Nevertheless, much remains to be done. The modeling framework that we use is static, assumes perfect foresight, and treats family structure and the number of family members as exogenous. The most promising directions for future research in this area move beyond these limitations by exploring intrafamily allocations in a dynamic framework, introducing uncertainty, and treating

16. Preference effects that alter time use raise similar problems.

family structure and family size as endogenous. Although much remains to be done to analyze theoretically and test empirically models of intrafamily allocations and intergenerational linkages that link behavior more closely to the socioeconomic environment and address issues of concern to policy, the time has come, we think, to bring our work together in a volume.

Brief Summaries of the Articles in This Volume

We divide the articles in this volume into five groups. Part 1 includes four articles that develop the "Separable Earnings-Transfers" model of intrahousehold allocations and present some applications. Part 2 includes three articles that consider other approaches to intrahousehold allocations—the wealth model, transaction costs, and tied parental transfers. Part 3 includes two articles that explore the interpretation of schooling effects in light of intrahousehold allocations. Part 4 has two articles that characterize intergenerational mobility as reflected in associations between parental income and child earnings. Part 5 includes three articles that consider "nature versus nurture" in schooling and earnings and the implications for estimating effects of observed family characteristics and policies.

Part 1. The "Separable Earnings-Transfers" Model of Intrahousehold Allocations

Chapter 1, "Parental Preferences and Provision for Progeny," develops a "separable earnings-transfers" (SET) model of parental allocation of resources among children and discusses its implications. Conditional on functional form assumptions, this study uses adult male sibling data to estimate some of the critical parental preference parameters of the model. The estimates suggest that parents may slightly reinforce endowment differences among their children but that they have substantial concern about the distribution of their children's earnings. The estimates indicate that parental preference parameters are far from those that would lead parents to maximize the sum of their children's earnings.

Chapter 2, "Family Resources, Family Size, and Access to Financing for College Education," uses the SET model to examine the implications for schooling attainment of college costs being dependent on child ability and past school accomplishment. It argues that such dependence implies greater variability in within-sibling schooling attainment than would be observed if all children in a family faced the same price for higher education. Within-sibling variances in schooling attainments are compared for two U.S. generations, one that benefited from the GI Bill and one that did not. Individuals in the generation that benefited from the GI Bill all faced the same prices for higher education; those in the generation that did not benefit from the GI Bill faced different prices based on ability and secondary school accomplishments. The intra-sibling variance in schooling attainment is greater for the generation that did not benefit from the GI Bill, confirming the equalizing effects of the GI Bill on schooling attainment.

Chapter 3, "Do Parents Favor Boys?" expands the SET model to allow for the possibility that parents' preferences do not exhibit "equal concern" for boys and girls and to include the expected earnings of a child's spouse in addition to the child's own earnings in the parents' objective function. Estimates for an adult, mixed-sex sibling U.S. sample suggest that, if parents' preferences depart at all from equal concern, they do so only slightly and in the direction of giving more weight to daughters than to sons.

Chapter 4, "Birth Order, Schooling, and Earnings," extends the SET model to include unequal concern by birth order. Empirical estimates for an adult sibling U.S. sample suggest that lower birth orders (i.e., older children) are favored. Analysis of bias suggests that the extent of trade-off in parental preferences between equity and productivity of their investments in their children is biased towards productivity if the estimation procedure fails to control for simultaneity.

Part 2. The Wealth Model, Transaction Costs, and Tied Parental Transfers

Chapter 5, "The Wealth Model: Efficiency in Education and Distribution in the Family," examines the implications of the "wealth model" of Becker and Tomes (1976) when parents are not rich enough and altruistic enough to provide each child with positive transfers. If parents allocate "enough" resources to their children, the wealth model implies that each child receives the wealth-maximizing level of education (i.e., the level at which the marginal rate of return equals the rate of return on financial assets). Additional resources for children are given as transfers. This study shows that, unless parents allocate enough resources to their children so that each child receives positive transfers, some children will not receive the wealth-maximizing level of education. The wealth model also predicts a range of parental resource levels within which some children in a family receive positive transfers while others receive zero transfers. The empirical evidence examined suggests that for the United States the predictions of the wealth model fail to hold.

Chapter 6, "A Transaction Cost Approach to Families and Households," extends and applies to families and households the "transaction cost" approach developed by Coase (1937), Williamson (1979), and others interested in analyzing the organization, structure, and behavior of firms. The transaction cost approach, which focuses on the difficulties of writing, monitoring, and enforcing contracts, helps explain which activities are performed by families and households and which are performed by the market or the state.

Chapter 7, "Tied Transfers and Paternalistic Preferences," develops and elucidates an alternative model of intrafamily allocation in which parents care how children use the resources that parents make available to them. Paternalistic preferences provide a rationale for parents "tying" transfers to uses the parents regard as desirable (e.g., education or a new house, but not travel or conspicuous consumption).

Part 3. Intrahousehold Allocations and Interpretation of Schooling Effects

Chapter 8, "Is Child Schooling a Poor Proxy for Child Quality?" develops the implications of the SET model and the wealth model for the common practice of interpreting schooling as an indicator of child quality. This study shows that the conditions under which schooling is a perfect indicator of child quality are highly restrictive, and that schooling may be an inverse indicator of child quality when parents are motivated strongly by equity concerns and use greater schooling investments to compensate for lesser endowments.

Chapter 9, "Schooling and Other Human Capital Investments: Can the Effects Be Identified?" develops the implications of the SET model and the wealth model for estimating the returns to schooling when parents make multiple investments in their children (e.g., in health and nutrition as well as in schooling). This study demonstrates that it may be difficult to identify the contribution to earnings of schooling alone and that most standard estimates of the returns to schooling are likely to be upward biased because they fail to control for nonschooling investments. It examines the conditions under which schooling may serve as a good indicator of the distribution of investments among children and, hence, permit estimates of parental preference parameters.

Part 4. Associations between Parental Income and Child Earnings

Chapter 10, "Intergenerational Earnings Mobility in the United States: Some Estimates and a Test of Becker's Intergenerational Endowments Model," contributes to the small number of estimates of intergenerational earnings mobility from annual data. It investigates whether there are diminishing marginal effects of parental income on child schooling as predicted by Becker. Contrary to the predictions of Becker's model, the marginal effect of parental income on child schooling is positive, not negative.

Chapter 11, "The Intergenerational Correlation between Children's Adult Earnings and Their Parents' Income: Results from the Michigan Panel Survey of Income Dynamics," investigates the sensitivity of estimates of intergenerational income-earnings mobility to the number of years of income observations used. This study finds much less mobility (much higher intergenerational correlations—about 0.4 instead of 0.2) when income is averaged over a number of years than when a single year is used. It finds significantly higher intergenerational correlations for blacks than for whites and lower correlations for females than for males.

Part 5. *"Nature versus Nurture" in Schooling and Earnings*

Chapter 12, "On Heritability," elucidates the assumptions that underlie estimates of heritability, or nature-nurture decompositions, and discusses what can and cannot be learned from such decompositions.

Chapter 13, "Is Schooling 'Mostly in the Genes'? Nature-Nurture Decomposition Using Data on Relatives," extends R. A. Fisher's method for decomposing phenotypic variances into genetic and environmental components when indicators of the environment are available. This study estimates the extended model with eight different kin relations and finds that the genetic variance underlies a large proportion of the variance in schooling in the United States.

Chapter 14, "Measuring the Impact of Environmental Policies on the Level and Distribution of Earnings," discusses the importance of controlling for unobserved endowments in assessing the effect of policies and provides illustrations of the importance of such controls using twins data.

Part One

The Separable Earnings-Transfers Model of Intrahousehold Allocations

1

Parental Preferences
and Provision for Progeny

Jere R. Behrman, Robert A. Pollak, and Paul Taubman

The general preference model provides a new framework for analyzing parental allocations of resources among their children. This paper develops the general preference model, emphasizing its implications for the distribution of educational resources among siblings and the implied distribution of lifetime earnings. It estimates a particular version of the preference model, using data on the education and earnings of adult male twins.

In the preference model, parental aversion to inequality in the distribution of wealth or earnings among their children plays a critical role. Parental preferences play no role in the conventional treatment of the determinants of education and earnings based on the standard investment model of human capital theory. Although the investment model is not, strictly speaking, a special case of the preference model, the implications of the investment model for the distribution of educational resources among children coincide with those of the preference model when parents have no aversion to inequality.

To estimate the preference model, we assume a particular specification of the parental utility function and interpret the observed distribution of earnings as the outcome of parental utility maximization subject to two constraints: the parental budget constraint and an earnings function which summarizes the relationship between earnings and schooling. We estimate the parameters of the parental utility function using a sample of adult male twins. Because the implications of the investment model for the distribution of educational resources among children are identical to those of the preference model when parents

Reprinted from *Journal of Political Economy* 90, no. 1 (February 1982): 52–73. © 1982 by The University of Chicago. All rights reserved.

Behrman's research was supported in part by a John Simon Guggenheim Foundation Fellowship and the National Science Foundation. Pollak's research was supported in part by the National Institutes of Health and the National Science Foundation. Taubman's research was supported in part by the National Science Foundation. We are grateful to Judith Goff for editorial suggestions and to Fred Slade for computational assistance. We have received helpful comments from participants in workshops at Chicago, Hebrew University, University of Pennsylvania, Tel-Aviv, Yale, the London School of Economics, and University of Nottingham and from an anonymous referee.

have no aversion to inequality, our estimates provide a test of the investment model against a more general hypothesis. We find that parents display significant aversion to inequality, and therefore we reject the investment model.

This paper is organized as follows: Section I presents the general preference model and discusses its relation to the conventional investment model. Section II develops a particular specification of the preference model and presents estimates of the parameters of the parental utility function and the earnings function. Section III is a brief summary.

I. Preference Models

Preference models are models of constrained utility maximization. Parental preferences—in particular, parental aversion to inequality in the distribution of wealth, bequests, or expected lifetime earnings among their children—play a central role in determining the distribution of educational attainments and earnings among siblings. In contrast, the standard investment model implies that parental preferences play no role in determining these distributions.

To introduce the preference model, consider a world in which bequests and inter vivos gifts are prohibited and earnings are the sole determinant of an adult's economic well-being. Suppose that expected lifetime earnings are determined by an individual's genetic endowments and education. Parents affect their children's economic status through the resources they devote to education, and we assume that parents provide all resources for their children's education. Parental expenditures on education increase a child's expected lifetime earnings but at a diminishing rate; hence, a given total of parental expenditure on their children's education determines a convex feasible set in the expected earnings space of their children. When children have different genetic endowments, this feasible set need not be symmetric around the 45° line.

Assume that parental preferences exhibit equal concern for all of their children, in the sense that the indifference map in the earnings space is symmetric around the 45° line. The form and parameters of the parents' utility function reflect their aversion to inequality in the distribution of their children's earnings. We treat children's expected earnings as if parents anticipated with certainty that they would be realized. Thus, for a given total expenditure devoted to children's schooling, the problem is one of utility maximization subject to a nonlinear and nonsymmetric constraint (fig. 1). Because the feasible set may be nonsymmetric, equal concern does not necessarily imply that parents will allocate educational resources so as to equalize their offsprings' expected earnings.

This section is organized as follows: Sections A and B describe parental preferences and the constraints on the maximization of parental utility. Section C presents two special versions of the general preference model, the separable

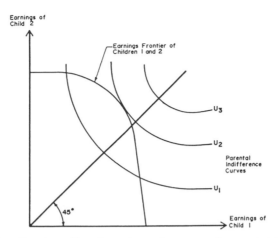

FIG. 1   Allocation of earnings with no bequests, equal concern, and a nonsymmetric feasible set.

earnings-bequest model and the wealth model. Section D contrasts the implications of two variants of the standard investment framework with those of the preference model. Section E discusses the conditions which determine whether parents adopt compensating or reinforcing strategies in distributing educational resources among their children.

A. Parental Preferences

We assume that parental preferences can be represented by a utility function $U(\mu, E_1, \ldots, E_n, B_1, \ldots, B_n)$, where μ denotes parental consumption, E_i, the expected lifetime earnings of the ith child, B_i bequests and inter vivos gifts to the ith child, and n the number of children.[1] Hereafter, we refer to E_i as "earnings" and B_i as "bequests." We ignore the sequential nature of these decisions and view the allocation problem in terms of a one-period planning model in which parents make a single, once-and-for-all decision over all the variables. Although the model could be generalized to treat the number of children as a decision variable, we treat family size as predetermined and interpret the utility function as conditional on the number of children.

To investigate the allocation of resources among children, we assume that this allocation is independent of parental consumption; that is, if the distribution $E^* = (E_1^*, E_2^*, E_3^*)$ is preferred to $\hat{E} = (\hat{E}_1, \hat{E}_2, \hat{E}_3)$ at one level of parental consumption, then E^* will be preferred to $\hat{E}$ at all levels of parental consumption. To insure this, we assume that in the parental preference ordering

1. The notion of parental preferences is problematic, but we follow the well-established custom of ignoring this difficulty.

the earnings of and bequests to children are separable from parental consumption. Parental preferences over the latter are reflected in the specific utility function $W(E_1, \ldots, E_n, B_1, \ldots, B_n)$, that we call the "parental welfare function":

$$U(\mu, E_1, \ldots, E_n, B_1, \ldots, B_n)$$

$$= V[\mu, W(E_1, \ldots, E_n, B_1, \ldots, B_n)]. \quad (1)$$

We assume that the parental utility function is quasi-concave, so the indifference curves have the usual shape. These assumptions are of little help in investigating the allocation of resources between parental consumption and children. They do, however, permit us to analyze the allocation of resources among children, without regard to parental consumption.

We say that parental preferences exhibit *equal concern* if the welfare function is symmetric in its treatment of all children—that is, if the parents are indifferent between permutations of the labels on earnings-bequests assignments among their children.[2] For example, suppose there are three children and they are all assigned identical bequests; then equal concern implies that the parents are indifferent between the expected earnings distributions (E_1, E_2, E_3) = (100, 400, 1,000) and (E_1, E_2, E_3) = (1,000, 100, 400); however, convexity implies that the parents prefer (E_1, E_2, E_3) = (500, 500, 500) to either of these distributions. Equal concern precludes favoring male children or the eldest or the most beautiful child. Since our empirical analysis is based on a sample of male twins, equal concern is plausible; throughout this paper we treat it as a maintained hypothesis.

Although equal concern rules out unequal treatment based on parental preferences which favor one child over another, it does not guarantee equal expected earnings. Differences in opportunities reflecting, for example, differences in genetic endowments may result in systematic differences in earnings among the children in a family. Figure 1 illustrates this possibility: Although the welfare function is symmetric, the feasible set is not, and the implied optimal solution (at the tangency) yields different earnings for the two children.

B. Constraints on Parental Utility Maximization

Parents face three types of constraints: the earnings function constraints, which relate each child's expected earnings to the child's genetic endowment, education, and other variables; a financial budget constraint; and a time budget con-

---

2. Equal concern, as we have defined it, also excludes from the parental welfare function asymmetries reflecting perceived differences in children's needs, or requirements, or in their tastes or sensitivities. It is debatable whether considerations of this sort should be excluded from a society's social welfare function, and even harder to justify their a priori exclusion from a parental welfare function.

straint. Although economists often stress the importance of parental time as a determinant of expected earnings, we ignore it in order to emphasize other variables.

The earnings function relates the expected lifetime earnings of the ith child (E_i) to the child's genetic endowment (G_i), schooling (S_i), and a vector of T other inputs specific to that child (X_i):[3]

$$E_i = E^r(G_i, S_i, X_i). \tag{2}$$

The earnings function is the same for all children in the rth family, since the child's genetic endowments appear as an explicit argument, but it may differ from one family to another. For the remainder of this discussion we omit the family superscript, r, from the earnings function and consider allocations within a particular family.

In the general preference model we distinguish between two financial budget constraints. The partial budget constraint contains only resources devoted to children. The complete budget constraint includes the variables in the partial budget constraint and also the parents' own consumption. The partial budget constraint is given by

$$\sum_{k=1}^{n} B_k + P_s \sum_{k=1}^{n} S_k + \sum_{t=1}^{T} P_t \sum_{k=1}^{n} X_{kt} = R^c, \tag{3}$$

where P_s is the price per year of schooling, which we assume is the same for all children and independent of the level of schooling attained; P_t is the price of the tth specific input; and R^c is the total value of resources devoted to children, including bequests. The complete budget constraint is $R^c + \mu = R$, where R is the parents' total resources; without loss of generality, we set the price of μ equal to one. One can imagine a world in which parents could require or children would agree to voluntary posteducation transfers of resources from one sibling to another to maximize the parents' welfare function. Although some such voluntary transfers do occur, we neglect them in our model. Becker and Tomes (1976, pp. S154–S155) discuss the implications of such transfers, while pointing out that agreements to make such transfers may be difficult to enforce. We assume that parents provide all resources for their children's education: children do not borrow from parents or from others, nor do they receive public or private scholarship aid. Violations of this assumption complicate the interpretation of our empirical results, but, because they bias our tests against the preference model (see Sec. IIB below), they do not prevent us from reaching strong and interesting conclusions.

3. We could generalize the model by including a vector of inputs consumed in common by all children in the family.

In both of these allocation problems, the appropriate budget constraint and the earnings function define a feasible set. Furthermore, under the plausible assumptions that the earnings function exhibits nonincreasing returns to scale and diminishing returns to schooling and the specific inputs, the implied feasible set is convex. Existence, uniqueness, and continuity of the solutions to the allocation problems follow from the convexity of the feasible set and the continuity and convexity of preferences.

C. The Wealth Model and the Separable Earnings-Bequest Model

We consider two alternative specifications of the parents' welfare function: the wealth model and the separable earnings-bequest model. Both presuppose that earnings and bequests to children are separable from parental consumption. The limited available evidence is mixed; we argue that the separable earnings-bequest model is as consistent with it as is the wealth model.

In the *separable earnings-bequest model,* earnings and bequests are independent in the sense that preferences among expected earnings distributions are independent of the distribution of bequests, and preferences among bequest distributions are independent of the distribution of expected earnings. This implies, for example, that bequests are not used to make up for the expected low earnings of a particular child by providing that child with an especially large bequest. In the separable earnings-bequest model, the parental welfare function is of the form:

$$W(E_1, \ldots, E_n, B_1, \ldots, B_n)$$

$$= W^*[W^E(E_1, \ldots, E_n), W^B(B_1, \ldots, B_n)]. \quad (4)$$

In the *wealth model,* parents are concerned only with the expected earnings-bequest combinations that achieve this wealth. Parents do not, for example, believe that, dollar for dollar, earnings are better than bequests because self-respect depends on earnings. In the wealth model, the parental welfare function takes the form:

$$W(E_1, \ldots, E_n, B_1, \ldots, B_n) = W(E_1 + rB_1, \ldots, E_n + rB_n), \quad (5)$$

where r is the interest rate.

We decompose the partial budget constraint in the separable earnings-bequest model and in the wealth model to illuminate their differences.

In the separable earnings-bequest model, the first stage allocates R^c between total bequests and total expenditures which affect earnings, while the second stage consists of two allocations: (*i*) bequests among children and (*ii*) expenditures which affect earnings among children:

$$\sum_{k=1}^{n} B_k = R^b, \tag{6}$$

$$P_s \sum_{k=1}^{n} S_k + \sum_{t=1}^{T} P_t \sum_{k=1}^{n} X_{kt} = R^e, \tag{7}$$

where R^b is the total value of bequests and R^e the value of resources devoted to increasing children's expected earnings. Since the bequest budget constraint, (6), is symmetric around the 45° line, equal concern implies that bequests are divided equally among children and are not used to counterbalance differences in earnings. Since the constraint in the earnings space need not be symmetric, the separable earnings-bequest model is compatible with differences in earnings.

In the wealth model, the first stage allocates R^c among children and the second allocates the resources devoted to each child between bequests and expenditures which affect earnings. If a child receives positive bequests, then the marginal returns to education for that child must equal the market rate of interest. This conclusion follows directly from the form of the welfare function: Since parents are concerned only with each child's wealth and since each child receives positive bequests, if these rates are unequal for any child, then the parents could increase the child's wealth by transferring resources from bequests to education or vice versa. If two or more children receive positive bequests, then these children must receive equal (expected) wealth since bequests fully counterbalance any differences in expected lifetime earnings and can be transferred from one child to another on a dollar for dollar basis. If no child receives positive bequests, then $R^c = R^e$, and the allocation of R^c in the wealth model is observationally equivalent to the allocation of R^e in the separable earnings-bequest model.

Since the wealth model and the separable earnings-bequest model are both special cases of the general preference model, it would be possible to estimate these two special cases and test them against the general model. Unfortunately, we cannot do this with our data since they do not record bequests. We can, however, assess the plausibility of the wealth model and the separable earnings-bequest model on the basis of the limited evidence available. Beyond causal empiricism, the evidence consists of studies by Smith (1975), Adams (1980), Menchik (1980), and Tomes (1981).[4]

---

4. The separable earnings-bequest model predicts equal bequests. The wealth model with positive bequests to more than one child predicts that bequests compensate fully for differences in earnings. See Appendix.

D. Comparison of Investment and Preference Models

The investment model represents the conventional framework for analyzing the determinants of expenditures on education and the resulting distribution of earnings.[5] Unlike the preference model, the investment model does not provide a complete framework for analyzing parental allocations of resources among children, for it is silent regarding the distribution of bequests among children and the allocation between parental consumption and expenditures on children. However, the investment model yields highly specific predictions about the total resources devoted to the education of children in a family, the distribution of these resources among the children, and the resulting distribution of earnings. The implications of the investments model for the distribution of educational resources among the children in a family are closely related to those of the separable earnings-bequest model with linear indifference curves. Because of this relationship, we are able to use our estimates of the preference model to test the investment against a hypothesis which is, in some respects, more general.

We consider two versions of the investment model. In the perfect capital market version of the investment model, children incur the costs of their own education and reap its benefits. Hence each child invests in education until the marginal return is equal to the market rate of interest. Thus, marginal returns to education must be the same for all children in all families. This conclusion also emerges in the wealth model when each child receives positive bequests.

In the imperfect capital market version of the investment model, children cannot borrow without limit against their future earnings at the market rate of interest, and the model identifies each child's borrowing opportunities with those of the parents. In effect, parents invest in the education of each of their children until the marginal return to education for each child is equal to the marginal rate at which the parents can borrow. Thus, although the marginal return to education is the same for all of the children in a family, it differs across families and need not be equal to the market rate of interest.

Since the investment models imply equal marginal returns to education for all children in a family, they also imply that parents allocate educational resources among their children so as to maximize the sum of earnings. Thus, the distribution of the observed total expenditure on education predicted by the investment model is identical to that predicted by the separable earnings-bequest model when the parental indifference map has linear indifference curves with a slope of minus one in the earnings space. That is, the parental

---

5. Becker (1975) is one prominent example of the investment model. In much other work, such as in Becker and Tomes (1976), the same author uses a preference model.

welfare function is given by:[6]

$$W^E(E_1, \ldots, E_n) = \Sigma E_k. \tag{8}$$

The investment model, unlike the separable earnings-bequest model, has precise implications for total resources devoted to children's education: It is the amount which equates marginal returns to education with the market rate of interest (in the perfect capital market version) or with the marginal rate at which the parents can borrow (in the imperfect capital market version). Thus, data on parents' marginal borrowing rates would enable us to distinguish between the separable earnings-bequest model with linear indifference curves and the imperfect capital market version of the investment model. Unfortunately, such data are unavailable. Therefore, our tests are based on the implications of the models for the distribution of the observed total expenditures on education.

E. Compensating and Reinforcing Strategies

We say that parents follow a *compensating* strategy if they devote more resources to increasing the earnings of a child with a smaller genetic endowment than to a child with a larger one; they follow a *reinforcing* strategy if they devote more resources to increasing the earnings of the child with the greater endowment; and they follow a *neutral* strategy if they devote equal resources to children, regardless of their different genetic endowments.[7] These definitions of compensating, reinforcing, and neutral strategies do not presuppose a particular model of resource allocation, and they accord with those used by Arrow (1971) and Becker and Tomes (1976). However, the parameters that determine whether parents adopt a compensating, reinforcing, or neutral strategy depend on the model employed. We illustrate this by comparing the wealth model with the separable earnings-bequest model, under the simplifying assumption that schooling is the only resource which affects children's earnings.

In the wealth model with positive bequests to all children, the parents' strategy depends solely on the properties of the earnings function and is independent of their aversion to inequality.[8] With positive bequests to all children, parents determine each child's level of schooling on efficiency grounds and allocate bequests to achieve an equal distribution of wealth. Since each child's education is pursued until its marginal return is equal to the market rate of

6. A Σ without indexes or limits of summation means $\Sigma_{k=1}^n$.

7. The labor market rewards many different skills and characteristics, each of which can have some genetic basis. "Genetic endowments" refers to the value of all these bases weighted by market prices.

8. See Becker and Tomes (1976), who translate the production function properties into differences in input shadow prices.

interest, whether the implied allocation of educational expenditures is compensating, reinforcing, or neutral depends solely on whether marginal returns to education are positively or negatively related to genetic endowments. If a greater genetic endowment implies a greater (smaller) marginal return to education, then the parents adopt a reinforcing (compensating) strategy. If genetic endowment and education do not interact in the earnings function, then parents adopt a neutral strategy.

In the separable earnings-bequest model, the parents' strategy depends both on their aversion to inequality and on the properties of the earnings function. This can be illustrated by a specific example in which parents maximize a constant elasticity of substitution (CES) welfare function,

$$W^E(E_1, \ldots, E_n) = \Sigma a E_k^c, \tag{9}$$

subject to a double logarithmic earnings function

$$\log E_k = \alpha_g \log G_k + \alpha_s \log S, \tag{10}$$

and the budget constraint

$$P_s \Sigma S_k = R^e. \tag{11}$$

The CES class of welfare functions provides a convenient example, since its members transparently exhibit the full range of inequality aversion—from the case of linear indifference curves (zero inequality aversion), through the Cobb-Douglas case (unitary inequality aversion), to the fixed coefficient case (infinite inequality aversion).[9] Solving for the equilibrium ratios of schooling and earnings from the first-order conditions, we find

$$\log \frac{S_i}{S_j} = \frac{\alpha_g c}{1 - \alpha_s c} \log \frac{G_i}{G_j}, \tag{12}$$

$$\log \frac{E_i}{E_j} = \frac{\alpha_g}{1 - \alpha_s c} \log \frac{G_i}{G_j}. \tag{13}$$

An examination of (13) indicates that, except in the Rawlsian case (i.e., $c = -\infty$), the child with the larger genetic endowment has larger earnings, since diminishing returns to schooling implies $0 < \alpha_s < 1$ and quasi-concave preferences imply $c < 1$. When $c < 0$, parents follow a compensating strategy and provide more schooling to the child with the smaller genetic endowments; yet in this case $[\partial^2 E(G,S)]/(\partial S \partial G) > 0$, so that in the wealth model with positive bequests, parents would follow a reinforcing strategy.

The implications of the various CES cases for the distribution of educational resources are easily determined.

9. Under our maintained hypothesis of equal concern, the only admissible linear indifference curves have a slope of minus one.

In the Rawlsian case (i.e., $c = -\infty$), the fixed coefficient indifference map implies that parents are unwilling to accept a small decrease in the expected earnings of the worse-off child to achieve a larger increase in the earnings of the better-off child. In this case, parents use education to equalize the earnings of their children, and this implies that they adopt a compensating strategy, regardless of the relationship between genetic endowments and marginal returns to education implied by the earnings function.

The Cobb-Douglas case is a limiting CES case as c approaches 0. In this case parents balance their preference for equality against the trade-off the earnings function offers them. If greater genetic endowments are associated with lower marginal returns to education, or if the marginal returns to education are independent of genetic endowments, then the parents adopt a compensating strategy. However, when greater genetic endowments are associated with higher marginal returns to education and these returns are sufficiently high, parents adopt a reinforcing strategy.

With linear indifference curves (i.e., $c = 1$), parents have no aversion to inequality and simply maximize the sum of their children's earnings. This calls for a reinforcing (compensating) strategy if the expected earnings function implies that greater genetic endowments are associated with higher (lower) marginal returns to education.

II. Empirical Analysis

We base our empirical analysis on the separable earnings-bequest model. We first discuss the specification that we estimate—the functional form of the parental welfare function for earnings and of the earnings function and the corresponding solutions to the constrained maximization problem (Sec. *A*). We then consider identification questions and present our empirical results (Sec. *B*).

A. *Specifications and Solutions*

The generalized CES welfare function for earnings is given by

$W^e(E_1, \ldots, E_n) =$

$$
\begin{cases}
\min \dfrac{E_k - b_k}{a_k}, & a_i > 0,\ E_i - b_i > 0,\ i = 1,\ldots, n;\ c = -\infty \\[2ex]
-\Sigma a_k(E_k - b_k)^c, & a_i > 0,\ E_i - b_i > 0,\ i = 1,\ldots, n;\ -\infty < c < 0 \\[2ex]
\Sigma a_k \log (E_k - b_k), & a_i > 0,\ E_i - b_i > 0,\ i = 1,\ldots, n;\ c = 0 \\[2ex]
\Sigma a_k(E_k - b_k)^c, & a_i > 0,\ E_i - b_i > 0,\ i = 1,\ldots, n;\ 0 < c < 1 \\[2ex]
-\Sigma a_k(b_k - E_k)^c, & a_i > 0,\ b_i - E_i > 0,\ i = 1,\ldots, n;\ c > 1.
\end{cases}
$$

$$\text{(14)}$$

Unlike the CES welfare function, the generalized CES need not be homothetic and thus allows parental preferences to depend on absolute as well as relative earnings.

With equal concern, we may set all of the a_k's equal to unity and all of the b_k's equal to a common value, b. Thus, with equal concern the generalized CES welfare function contains two independent parameters, which together reflect the parents' aversion to inequality in their children's earnings. If $c < 1$ we can sometimes interpret b as the minimum earnings which parents attempt to guarantee for each child. In these cases, it is only after each child had achieved this minimum that the parents trade off the earnings of one child against those of another, and it is only supernumerary earnings that are subject to such tradeoffs. However, if b is negative, this verbal interpretation is untenable, although the indifference map remains well behaved. If $c > 1$, we can interpret b as a bliss or satiation level of earnings. If $c < 1$, it reflects the parents' willingness to trade off the supernumerary earnings of one child against those of another, while if $c > 1$ it reflects their willingness to trade off the shortfalls from the bliss level.[10]

Different families may have different welfare functions, and these differences may be related systematically to socioeconomic or demographic characteristics. For example, there might be a positive relationship between the earnings floor or bliss point and variables that represent the parents' socioeconomic background. However, we do not explore these possibilities in this paper.

Our empirical work is based on a version of the double-log or Cobb-Douglas earnings function

$$E_i = \alpha_o G_i^{\alpha_g} S_i^{\alpha_s} \prod_{t=1}^{T} X_{it}^{\beta_t}. \tag{15}$$

If $\alpha_s + \Sigma_{t=1}^{T} \beta_t \leqq 1$, then the expected earnings function exhibits nonincreasing returns to scale in the purchased inputs. The partial double-log specification, in which $g(X, G)$ need not be multiplicative, is substantially less restrictive and provides an adequate foundation for our empirical work:

$$\log E_i = \alpha_s \log S_i + \log g(X_i, G_i). \tag{16}$$

The semilog or exponential expected earnings function is given by:[11]

---

10. The elasticity of substitution between supernumerary earnings of any two children is given by $\sigma = 1/(1 - \sigma)$.

11. In the semilog case, the efficiency condition implies that the ratio $(\partial E/\partial X_i)/(\partial E/\partial S_i)$ is equal to β_i/α_s. In this case, if all families have identical earnings functions and face the same prices, then prices must adjust so that $\beta_i/\alpha_s = F_i/P_s$ to achieve an interior solution. If prices are directly observed, they thus provide an immediate estimate of the ratio of the parameters of the earnings function.

$$E_i = \exp\left(\alpha_o + \alpha_g G_i + \alpha_s S_i + \sum_{t=1}^{T} \beta_t X_{it}\right). \tag{17}$$

In both the double-log and the semilog earnings functions, marginal returns to education are positively related to genetic endowments; hence, in the investment model and the wealth model with positive bequests, both of these forms imply that parents adopt a reinforcing strategy. The semilog specification is often found in the literature (e.g., Mincer 1974). For reasons discussed below, we base our empirical work on the double-log form.

We now examine the solutions to the separable earnings-bequest model corresponding to the generalized CES welfare function with double-log and semilog earnings functions. We treat schooling and genetic endowments as the only arguments of the earnings functions, both to simplify the notation and because we lack data on the other inputs.[12] To characterize the solutions, we form the Lagrangian expression

$$L(E_1, \ldots, E_n, S_1, \ldots, S_n, \lambda_o, \lambda_1, \ldots, \lambda_n)$$

$$= W^e(E_1, \ldots, E_n) + \lambda_o(R^e - p_s\Sigma S_k) + \Sigma\lambda_k[E_k - E(S_k, G_k)]. \tag{18}$$

The first-order conditions give:

$$\frac{W_i^e}{W_j^e} = \frac{E_s(S_j, G_j)}{E_s(S_i, G_i)}. \tag{19}$$

With the generalized CES welfare function, the left-hand side becomes

$$\frac{W_i^e}{W_j^e} = \frac{(E_i - b)^{c-1}}{(E_j - b)^{c-1}}. \tag{20}$$

For the partial double-log earnings function we have $E_s = \alpha_s(E_i/S_i)$. Hence, the first-order conditions imply

$$\frac{(E_i - b)^{c-1}}{(E_j - b)^{c-1}} = \frac{E_j}{E_i}\frac{S_i}{S_j}. \tag{21}$$

Taking logs of both sides and rearranging yields

$$(c - 1) \log\left(\frac{E_i - b}{E_j - b}\right) - \log\frac{E_i}{E_j} + \log\frac{S_j}{S_i} = 0. \tag{22}$$

12. If other variables of the earnings function enter in logarithmic form, the optimal allocation of these variables between any two children is proportional to the optimal allocation of schooling between the same two children. Therefore, our estimates about the effect of parental inequality aversion on the distribution of schooling among children also imply an identical effect on the distribution of other expenditures which enter into the double-log earnings function even though we do not have observations on such expenditures.

This is the form that we estimate below.

For the semilog earnings function the first-order conditions imply:

$$(c - 1) \log \left(\frac{E_i - b}{E_j - b} \right) + \log \frac{E_i}{E_j} = 0. \tag{23}$$

We cannot estimate this equation because we can obtain a perfect fit in any sample by setting $b = c = 0$.

B. Identification and Estimation

We estimate the parameters of the parental welfare function for earnings in the separable earnings-bequest model. We assume that all families in our sample have the same generalized CES welfare function for earnings and the same double-log earnings function.

The assumption that parental preferences are the same for all families does not imply that all parents with the same financial resources allocate the same amount to their children or that all families which devote the same amount to their children allocate it between earnings and bequests in the same way. Differences in children's genetic endowments imply differences in the constraints faced by such families, and such differences imply differences in optimal allocations. However, since our data do not report either parental consumption or bequests, we cannot analyze these differences empirically. Our data report earnings and schooling, and our empirical analysis is based on the separable earnings-bequest model, a specification which permits us to use these data to estimate the parental welfare function for earnings.

Our assumption that the welfare function for earnings is the same for all families does not imply that all families which devote the same resources to schooling allocate these resources among their children in the same way. Because children in different families have different relative genetic endowments, such families face different earnings frontiers, and these frontiers are more asymmetrical for families whose children have more varied genetic endowments.[13] It is these differences in the shapes of earnings frontiers across families which permit us to identify the welfare function for earnings (fig. 2).

Because we observe actual rather than expected earnings, we need a disturbance term in equation (21). The assumption that actual earnings (E_i^*) are related to expected earnings (E_i) by the logarithmic relation

$$\log E_i^* = \log E_i + u_i, \tag{24}$$

---

13. Behrman et al. (1980) present evidence that the relative genetic endowments vary considerably in our data set.

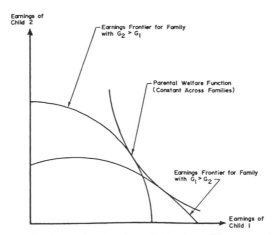

FIG. 2   Optimal allocation for two families whose children have different genetic endowments.

where u_i is an additive independent disturbance term, provides an approximate rationale for an additive disturbance term in equation (21).[14] Since we interpret our disturbance term as reflecting measurement error, our estimate of the coefficient $c - 1$ in equation (21) is biased toward zero.[15]

It might appear that the sums of the squared residuals could be minimized with respect to $\log (E_1/E_2)$, $\log (S_2/S_1)$, $\log [(E_1 - b)/(E_2 - b)]$, or any weighted combination of the three, and that different parameter estimates would correspond to every combination unless the fit were perfect. However, it is not possible to minimize with respect to $\log [(E_1 - b)/(E_2 - b)]$ because as b approaches $-\infty$ the variance of the dependent variable and hence the unexplained variable approach zero. Furthermore, since there are no coefficients for $\log (E_1/E_2)$ and $\log (S_2/S_1)$, minimizing the sum of squares in one of these directions yields the same parameter estimates as minimizing it in the other. It is these estimates which we report.

We use data for fraternal (dizygotic or DZ) white male twins from the National Academy of Science–National Research Council (NAS-NRC) sample to estimate the stochastic version of equation (21). These twins were born in the continental United States between 1917 and 1927, and both twins served in the U.S. military forces, primarily during the Second World War. Our sample con-

14. These results are only approximate because the b's in general are nonzero in eq. (21).

15. While the measurement error in E_i and E_j appears on both sides of the equation, the numerator and denominator terms are reversed. This implies negative correlation in the measurement error and yields the indicated results.

38   BEHRMAN, POLLAK, AND TAUBMAN

tains 914 fraternal pairs.[16] For schooling we use actual years of schooling.[17] For an individual's expected earnings we use his reported earnings in 1973, when the twins were between 47 and 57 years old.[18]

We estimate $c - 1 = -0.88$ (with an asymptotic t-value of -37.6) and $b = \$340$ (with an asymptotic t-value of 157.4). The estimate of c is 0.12 with an asymptotic t-value of 4.6.[19] This estimate is significantly different from zero and from one and lies between the linear indifference curves of the pure investment case and the translated Cobb-Douglas case.[20] The significance of the estimate of b suggests that the generalized CES welfare function provides a better specification than the homothetic CES. However, the estimated magnitude of b is too small to create much confidence in the minimum guaranteed lifetime expected earnings interpretation.

In our theoretical model, parents provide the resources for the education of their children. However, our empirical analysis is based on a sample of veterans, many of whom were eligible for GI Bill benefits, including funds for tuition and living expenses. Since individuals eligible for the GI Bill would presumably decide whether to obtain more schooling on the basis of their own benefits and costs, the availability of GI Bill benefits should cause the data to look more as if they were drawn from a world in which marginal returns to education were equated to the market rate of interest. Thus, our failure to take account of the GI Bill biases our results in favor of the investment model, which makes its rejection all the more striking.

16. For an extensive discussion of this sample, its origin, and its characteristics in comparison to the population of U.S. white male veterans of the same age cohort, see Behrman et al. (1980, chap. 5).
17. To the extent that actual schooling differs from schooling planned by the parents, there is also measurement error in this variable and, hence, an additional reason to add a disturbance term in eq. (21).
18. As is well known, human capital theory indicates that to adjust for the postponement of the receipt of earnings, annual earnings of the more schooled are higher in order to maintain the same present discounted value of lifetime earnings. We have recalculated our model adjusting the annual earnings back to lifetime earnings (at an assumed real interest rate of 5 percent per year). The estimates are not affected greatly by this change.
19. A referee points out that the wealth version of the preference model implies that inequality in earnings between siblings would be an increasing function of parental wealth, provided that low-income parents do not leave bequests. Using father's education as a proxy for parental wealth, we have split the sample into two groups: those for which father's education exceeds 10 years and those for which it is 10 years or less. For the first group the estimates of b and c are 334 and $-.10$, while for the second they are 292 and $-.13$. The magnitudes of these differences are small, and they are not significant at standard levels.
20. Measurement error in earnings causes our estimates of $c - 1$ to be biased toward zero because y_i is in the denominator of the dependent variable but in the numerator of the independent variable; hence, the unbiased estimates of the elasticity of substitution are smaller than these estimates indicate.

To illustrate the implications of these estimates, it is useful to have an estimate of the elasticity of earnings with respect to schooling, α_s in (10). Most estimates of this parameter suffer from an upward bias caused by the positive correlation between ability (based on unobserved genetic endowments and unobserved family environment) and schooling (e.g., Behrman et al. 1980).[21] By estimating an equation representing the difference in the expected earnings of pairs of identical (monozygotic or MZ) twins, we can control for genetic endowments and family environment. In terms of observable variables, the differenced earnings function is similar in form to equation (21), from which we estimate the parameters of the parental welfare function; indeed, the two relations are identical if $b = 0$. To identify the parameters of the parental welfare function, we used variations in the relative genetic endowments of pairs of fraternal twins across families. For identical twins there are no such variations, and hence we assume that stochastic differences in schooling trace out the earnings frontier.[22] We use data on the 1,021 pairs of identical twins in our sample to estimate α_s:[23]

$$\log \frac{E_1}{E_2} = \underset{(2.2)}{0.28} \log \frac{S_1}{S_2} + \underset{(1.3)}{0.014},$$

$$\bar{R}^2 = 0.004, \text{ SE} = 0.50, \ F(1,1019) = 5.0. \tag{25}$$

The overall relation and the estimate of α_s are significant at conventional levels. The estimate of the constant is not significantly nonzero even though the identical twins are ordered by their level of schooling, which suggests that omitted variables are not a major problem.

The significance of these estimates for family resource allocations can be illustrated by considering the solutions of equations (12) and (13). Since these equations are derived under the assumption that b is zero, the results are only approximate.

We have estimated $\alpha_s = .28$ and $c = .12$. With our estimated value of c, the right-hand sides of (12) and (13) are $.124\alpha_g \log (G_i/G_j)$ and $1.03\alpha_g \log (G_i/G_j)$. Suppose α_g and α_s were to remain unchanged but parents did not care about distribution of earnings among siblings, that is, $c = 1$. With $c = 1$, the

---

21. Suppose the earnings function for an individual in the rth family is: $\log E_i^r = a + b \log S_i^r + cA_i^r$, where $A_i^r = G_i^r + N^r + v_i^r$, where N is common environment and v is specific environment. If c is nonzero and A is omitted but correlated with $\log S$, then the estimate of b is biased. The implied within-pair equation for identical twins is $\Delta \log E^r = b\Delta \log S^r + c\Delta v_i^r$, and the estimate of b will be unbiased if Δv is uncorrelated with $\Delta \log S$.

22. Behrman et al. (1980) discuss the possible impact of measurement error on estimates in sibling models.

23. We assume that only schooling and genetic endowments enter in the earnings function since we do not have data on its other arguments.

corresponding numerical coefficients are both changed to 1.39. This effect of a unit difference in genetic endowments would be about 11 times as great for schooling and 1.3 times as great for earnings. The within-family standard deviation of schooling or earnings would be much greater if there were not parental aversion to inequality.

In his recent survey of sibling models, Griliches (1979, p. S61) speculates that ". . . families in fact act as (potential) income equalizers." Our results confirm his conjecture.

Our model is one in which schooling is endogenous. Hence, the effect of genetic endowments on the log of earnings has changed from α_g in equation (9) to $\alpha_g/(1 - \alpha_s c)$ in equation (12). Our estimates imply that the effect of genetic endowments on within-family resource allocation has only been raised by about 3 percent. If c were one and α_s unchanged, endogeneity would raise the coefficient by about 39 percent. Thus, in a world with no aversion to inequality or in a pure investment world, allocation of schooling expenditures would substantially reinforce differences in initial endowments.

III. Implications and Conclusions

Recent empirical studies have emphasized family background as a determinant of adult socioeconomic success, but they have generally been vague about resource allocation within families.[24] Recent theoretical studies, by Becker and Tomes (1976) and others, have developed models of resource allocation within the family. Although this theoretical literature often appeals to stylized facts, there has been little testing of specific hypotheses.

We analyze a general preference model of resource allocation among children and two special cases based on special assumptions about the form of the parents' welfare function. All of these models assume that parents have equal concern for all their children; that is, that the parental welfare function treats all children symmetrically. One special case—the separable earnings-bequest model—provides the framework of our empirical work. The separable earnings-bequest model does not imply that families which devote equal resources to schooling will allocate it among children in the same way, because differences in children's genetic endowments imply that different families face different earnings frontiers. Two versions of the standard investment model are closely related to the special cases of our preference model. The perfect capital market version is similar to the wealth model provided that bequests are positive, and the imperfect capital market version is similar to the special case of the separable earnings-bequest model in which parents have no aversion to inequality.

24. For examples, see Leibowitz (1977), Olneck (1977), and Behrman et al. (1980), and the references therein.

We define compensating strategies as those in which parents devote more resources to increasing the earnings of children with smaller genetic endowments than of children with larger endowments. In the wealth model whether parents adopt a compensating or a reinforcing strategy depends solely on the properties of the earnings function; if a greater genetic endowment implies a greater (smaller) marginal return to schooling, then the parents adopt a reinforcing (compensating) strategy regardless of their degree of inequality aversion. In contrast, with the separable earnings-bequest model, whether parents adopt a compensating or reinforcing strategy depends not only on the properties of the earnings function but also on parental preferences and, in particular, on their aversion to inequality. In the Rawlsian case of absolute inequality aversion, parents adopt a compensating strategy regardless of the properties of the earnings function. At the other extreme, with no inequality aversion, whether parents adopt a reinforcing or compensating strategy depends solely on the earnings function, just as in the wealth model. Between these two extremes, the properties of both the parental welfare function and the earnings function determine whether parents adopt reinforcing or compensating strategies.

Appendix

Smith (1975) analyzed data on a sample of 1,881 estates of whites filed for probate in Washington, D.C., during 1967. In the District of Columbia, an inheritance tax return must be filed if the estate exceeds $1,000. About one-half of the 1967 white descendents in Washington, D.C., did not file. The median net estate of those who filed was less than $24,000. While many of those who did not file undoubtedly had furniture and other goods whose value exceeded $1,000, Smith's data suggest that for many families bequests are insignificant. For parents who do not plan to leave bequests to their children, the wealth model is equivalent to the separable earnings-bequest model.

Menchik (1980) studied a sample of the largest 1 percent of estates filed for probate in Connecticut between 1931 and 1946. These may not be typical of the distributions made by less wealthy parents. Menchik (p. 310) found that, in families with two children, 62.5 percent receive equal bequests and that the average share going to the smaller or equal inheritor was 45 percent. For all families the coefficient of variation of within-family bequests is about .17, and Menchik concludes that bequests are not likely to attenuate greatly differences in earnings.

Both Adams (1980) and Tomes (1981) conclude that their studies support the wealth model. Both use "a 5 percent random sample of estates probated in the Cleveland, Ohio, area in 1964–65" (Tomes 1981, p. 939). Since the data do not include a measure of parental income, Tomes constructs one using his sample to estimate an income function for recipients (i.e., regressing recipient's

income on such explanatory variables as education). Assuming that the estimated coefficients apply to the earlier generation, Tomes substitutes parental
values of the explanatory variables into the estimated income function to obtain
a measure of parental income. Tomes finds that bequests are negatively related
to the recipient's own income, given parental income and other variables. However, the income variable for recipients refers to a single month, which is not
likely to be a very good proxy for permanent income. Furthermore the estimated coefficients on education and age (which Tomes reports in his notes to
table 1) are not consistent with those obtained by other investigators.

Adams (1980) used the Cleveland data to calculate the elasticity of bequests
with respect to parental wealth using a regression like Tomes's to obtain a measure of parental wealth. He also estimated a time-series model using deflated
mean estates and per capita income of the upper 1 percent of the population for
the period 1922–49. He concludes that earnings and bequests are not separable
in the parental utility function. His argument, as we understand it, rests on
improperly interpreting the symbol σ as both a correlation coefficient and an
elasticity. Since the separable earnings-bequest model is at least as consistent
with the available evidence as is the wealth model, we use the former as the
framework for our empirical analysis.

2

Family Resources, Family Size, and Access to Financing for College Education

JERE R. BEHRMAN, ROBERT A. POLLAK, AND PAUL TAUBMAN

Equality of opportunity is a widely shared goal, embraced by some as a means of achieving a more equal distribution of wealth, income, or earnings and by others as an end in itself. In this paper we focus narrowly on one component of equality of opportunity, equality of access to resources for financing college education, hereafter "equal access." [1]

Equal access prevails if all individuals, regardless of differences in family background and parental wealth, face the same marginal cost of resources for college. [2] Equal access requires no more than a student loan program that makes resources available to all high school graduates at the same interest rate, provided none of them can borrow elsewhere at a lower rate. With diminishing returns to schooling and equal access to resources, every high school graduate could and presumably would pursue further education until the marginal rate of return to schooling equals this interest rate. If this interest rate were no higher than the rate of return on financial assets and if parents and children were solely interested in expected wealth maximization, then neither parents nor children, however rich, would invest in education beyond the point at which the expected marginal return equaled the marginal cost of funds. (Some parents or children, however, may invest more to achieve nonmarket returns.)

Even with equal access and similar genetic endowments among children, family environment or family resources might make substantial differences in children's life chances. For example, inequalities in lifetime earnings might result from differences in family environment or resources available during childhood. Thus equal access does not imply equality of opportunity, and

Reprinted from *Journal of Political Economy* 97 (April 1989): 398–419. © 1989 by The University of Chicago. All rights reserved.

We thank two anonymous referees for excellent comments, the National Institutes of Health for research support, Judith Goff for editorial assistance, and Dick Voith and Myung Kang for excellent research assistance. The usual disclaimer applies.

1. Economists of widely different political and philosophical views have focused on equality of access (see Tawney 1961; Becker 1975; Okun 1975; Brittain 1978).

2. If the marginal cost of resources varies with the amount of schooling, then equal access requires that all individuals face the same cost schedule.

achieving equality of opportunity well might conflict with other widely shared values, such as family autonomy.[3]

To explore the importance of equal access, we compare the experience of World War II veterans, who were eligible for the educational benefits of the GI Bill, with the experience of the succeeding generation, who faced substantially less generous government programs for financing their college educations. Our analysis hinges on the relationship between sibship size, on the one hand, and sib schooling similarity and earnings similarity, on the other. In Section I we discuss previous work on equal access and on the interpretation of intrafamily differences in educational attainment. Section II presents a model of the determinants of schooling and examines its implications for intrafamily schooling differences; the model allows schooling prices to depend on abilities through the allocation of financial aid. In Section III we discuss the data and report our results. Section IV is a brief conclusion.

I. Background

Current loan programs provide students limited access to financing for their college education at market or below-market interest rates; scholarship and work-study programs also provide limited subsidies for college studies. Not long ago, however, the U.S. government had a program that gave a substantial segment of the male population equal access to resources for financing college education. It was called the GI Bill.

General Omar Bradley, the first post–World War II director of the Veterans Administration, summarized the provisions of the GI Bill and described its overwhelming impact on colleges (Bradley and Blair 1983). For married World War II veterans, the educational benefits in 1946 included a stipend of $90 a month ($65 a month for single veterans) and tuition of up to $500; to put these figures in perspective, annual U.S. per capita disposable income in 1946 was $1,124, and the University of Pennsylvania's undergraduate tuition plus general fee, which is comparable to Harvard's, was $495.[4] Thus eligible veterans

---

3. Some might be tempted to broaden the definition of equal access to include all human capital investment or even to equate it with equal opportunity by saying that children reared in environments that fail to foster emotional and cognitive development face a higher marginal cost of resources for investment in human capital than children growing up in more favorable environments. Expanded in this way, equal access is equivalent to a sociologist's, political scientist's, and philosopher's notion of equality of opportunity, but this expansion deprives the concept of its simplicity and empirical tractability. For references outside of economics, see Jencks et al. (1972).

4. The GI Bill also extended other benefits, including $20 a week while seeking a job, disability pensions, subsidized life insurance, free medical care for service-related health problems, and guaranteed loans for the purchase of homes, farms, and small businesses (Bradley and Blair 1983, pp. 451–62). Thus in many dimensions, Uncle Sam equalized the access of returning GIs; it did not, however, equalize opportunity because it did not eliminate the effects of differences in prewar family environment and resources or in wartime experiences.

making educational choices after World War II were far less dependent on their parents than they would otherwise have been, and far more of them than had been expected went to college.[5]

Behrman et al. (1980), using data on white male veteran twins, most of whom served in World War II, estimated how much the variation in resources and in family environment contributed to the variation in schooling, occupational achievement, and the natural log of earnings. These estimates were obtained using a latent variable methodology with cross-equation constraints. Some of these constraints, especially the identifying assumption that the expected value of the cross-twin correlation in the unobserved environment is the same for identical and fraternal twins, are controversial.[6] Using this identification assumption and a latent variable methodology, Behrman et al. estimated that unequal access accounted for a maximum of 12 percent of the variance in the natural log of earnings for the veterans sample.[7] They concluded that, for this sample, unequal access to resources for financing college education was a relatively unimportant source of earnings inequality. Unequal access, however, may have been much more important for those in the population not eligible for the GI Bill.

Family size may cause unequal access since parental expenditure per child is inversely associated with sibship size.[8] Because nonfamily financing is more costly than family financing, children from large families who must resort to outside financing pay more to obtain the same amount of education as children from small families. This constitutes unequal access.

In this paper we use a parental preference model to analyze the extent of sib schooling and earnings similarities in large and small families. We argue on theoretical grounds that a larger sibship size implies less sib schooling similarity unless there is equal access to financing, as there was for veterans eligible for GI Bill benefits. Our empirical results confirm our theoretical expectation. We also provide a rough estimate of how important unequal access would have been for World War II veterans in the absence of the GI Bill. Among white males, unequal access would have accounted for 25–30 percent of the variance

5. Bradley and Blair (1983, p. 451) report that in 1947 three-quarters of the students at Harvard and Stanford were World War II veterans.

6. Goldberger (1977b, 1978) emphasizes the crucial role of this assumption and claims that it is inappropriate; Taubman (1978a, 1981, in this volume) defends its use.

7. Section III and the Appendix provide details. The 12 percent figure is a point estimate that reflects all environmental sources of inequality, not just unequal access to financing. Behrman et al. point out that the true total proportion might be somewhat higher if transitory income were eliminated.

8. Children in large sibships receive less education and lower earnings than children in small sibships (see, e.g., Behrman et al. 1980). Economists often argue that parents with few children have substituted quality for quantity, where child quality is defined in terms of expenditures per child (Becker and Lewis 1973; Willis 1973).

in the natural log of earnings without the GI Bill, more than twice the estimate
of 12 percent with the GI Bill.

II. A Model of Sibship Similarity

Following Behrman, Pollak, and Taubman (1982, in this volume), we assume
that parents make all schooling decisions for their children and that parental
preferences are separable between the distribution of earnings among their
children and the distribution of other outcomes (e.g., property income or
health) that parents care about. We assume that the parental welfare function
for the distribution of earnings among the n_j children in the jth family is a
translated constant elasticity of substitution:

$$W(Y_{1j}, \ldots, Y_{nj}) = \left[\sum_{k=1}^{n_j} a_k (Y_{kj} - \mathrm{b}_k)^c \right]^{1/c}, \qquad (1)$$

where Y_{kj} is the expected earnings of the kth child in the jth family. The b
parameters reflect displacement or translation of the constant elasticity of substitution function from the origin; for earnings above these levels, parents are
willing to trade off the earnings of one child against those of another. The a
parameters are weights that the parents place on earnings above b. Although
the a's and b's may vary across children, reflecting unequal parental concern,
throughout this paper we assume equal parental concern for all children.[9] The
parameter c reflects parental inequality aversion. One extreme, $c \rightarrow -\infty$, is the
Rawlsian (Rawls 1971) or infinite inequality aversion case in which parents
value additional earnings only if they are received by the worst-off child. The
other extreme, $c \rightarrow 1$, is the zero inequality aversion or pure investment case
in which parents value the sum of their children's earnings but are unconcerned
with their distribution.[10]

The parental welfare function is maximized subject to two constraints: an
earnings production function and a partial budget constraint. We assume that
all human capital investments take the form of schooling and that the earnings
production function has a unitary elasticity of substitution:

$$Y_{kj} = \mathrm{d} S_{kj}^e G_{kj}^g, \qquad (2)$$

9. Empirical evidence suggests that equal concern is a good approximation; see Behrman, Pollak, and Taubman (1986, in this volume) and Behrman and Taubman (1986, in this volume) for
estimates implying that the effects of unequal concern associated with gender or birth order are
small in the United States.

10. Becker's model from his 1967 Woytinsky lecture (which is reprinted in the second edition
of his *Human Capital* [1975]) is consistent with a special case of the Behrman, Pollak, and Taubman preference model in which parental aversion to earnings inequality approaches zero.

where S_{kj} is schooling investment in the kth child in the jth family, G_{kj} is the predetermined endowment of this child, and e and g are parameters that lie between zero and one. The partial budget constraint is

$$\sum_{k=1}^{n_j} P(G_{kj})S_{kj} \leq R_j, \tag{3}$$

where R_j is the total resources devoted to investment in the jth family's children and $P(G_{kj})$ is the price of schooling. Behrman, Pollak, and Taubman (1982, 1986, both in this volume) and Behrman and Taubman (1986, in this volume) assume that schooling prices are independent of genetic endowments and identical for all children. Here we drop this assumption in order to represent the dependence of scholarship awards, subsidized loans, and work-study opportunities (all of which we hereafter refer to as "scholarships") on endowments. Figure 1 depicts the maximizing outcome at which an indifference curve of the parental welfare function is tangent to the earnings possibility frontier. The indifference curve is symmetric around the 45° line as a consequence of equal concern. With unequal endowments the earnings possibility frontier is skewed even if schooling prices are independent of endowments; we have drawn it on the assumption that sib 2 has greater endowments than sib 1, implying that sib 2 has higher earnings than sib 1 for any level of schooling.

The effect of an increase in sibship size on the variation in schooling is best understood by considering two polar cases: one in which there is only a "preference displacement effect," which implies that larger sibships are associated with less variability in education, and one in which there is only a "price effect," which implies that larger sibships are associated with greater variability in education.

The preference displacement effect arises because parental resources for schooling investment per child tend to decrease as sibship size increases, mov-

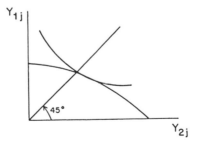

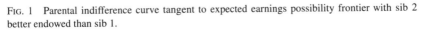

FIG. 1   Parental indifference curve tangent to expected earnings possibility frontier with sib 2 better endowed than sib 1.

ing the earnings possibility frontier toward the origin in figure 1. Because this places the tangency with the parental welfare function closer to the levels indicated by the b's and because parents make trade-offs among their children's earnings only above the b's, the preference displacement effect tends to reduce the variation in investment in schooling among the children in a family.[11] When the marginal schooling price is identical for all children in all families, the preference displacement effect by itself tends to lead to *greater* sib schooling similarity as sibship size increases.[12] Empirically, however, the values of b are very small for the two generations that we consider (Behrman, Pollak, and Taubman 1982, 1986, both in this volume; Behrman and Taubman 1986, in this volume), so the preference displacement effect is likely to be weak.

The price effect tends to cause sib schooling variability—and, therefore, earnings variability—to increase with sibship size.[13] Families with larger sibship size are more likely to be eligible for scholarships and thus more likely to face schooling prices that vary with their children's endowments. The price effect operates alone when the displacement parameters are zero; in this case the first-order conditions can be solved to obtain an explicit expression for the ratio of optimal schooling and earnings levels for sib 1 and sib 2:

$$\frac{S_{1j}}{S_{2j}} = \left(\frac{G_{1j}}{G_{2j}}\right)^{gc/(1-ec)}\left[\frac{P(G_{1j})}{P(G_{2j})}\right]^{1/(ec-1)} \tag{4}$$

---

11. Our interpretation of the b's as subsistence parameters rather than bliss points is equivalent to assuming that the parameter $c \leq 1$; for further discussion, see Behrman, Pollak, and Taubman (1982, p. 66, n. 13, also in this volume). Available empirical estimates suggest that c is close to zero (Behrman, Pollak, and Taubman 1982, 1986, both in this volume; Behrman and Taubman 1986, in this volume; Behrman 1988a, 1988b).

12. Our discussion assumes that intrafamilial variations in child endowments and thus in demand functions for schooling are independent of sibship size. There are, however, at least two reasons to expect wider diversity in the distribution of demand functions in larger families than in smaller. First, larger families are more likely to include children born to older mothers, and such children are more likely to have birth defects (see Behrman et al. [1980] for a discussion of this point and references to the literature). Although fraternal twins are born more frequently to older mothers, identical twins are not. Thus comparing identical and fraternal twins sheds some light on this possible source of greater demand diversity in larger families. In our twin sample, however, we find little evidence of greater demand diversity in larger families (see tables 5 and 6 below). Second, if there are liquidity constraints, families with more children are likely to have such children over more variegated parts of the life cycle income path and thus have more variation in the budget constraint than families with fewer children. This is one of the reasons that we focus on adjacent sib pairs in our regression analysis below.

13. We assume here that $c > -\infty$, so the preference functions are not at the Rawlsian extreme. When the b's are zero, $c = 0$ corresponds to the Cobb-Douglas case.

and

$$\frac{Y_{1j}}{Y_{2j}} = \left(\frac{G_{1j}}{G_{2j}}\right)^{g(1-ec)}\left[\frac{P(G_{1j})}{P(G_{2j})}\right]^{e/(ec-1)}. \tag{5}$$

These expressions imply that variations in sib schooling and earnings are greater when prices vary inversely with children's endowments. Increased sibship size does not result in more variation in schooling when the schooling price is the same for all children in the family and, a fortiori, when that price is the same for all children in all families.

III. Data and Estimates of Sibship Similarity and of the Impact of the GI Bill on Equal Access

In this paper we use two samples: the veterans sample of white male twins described in Behrman et al. (1980) and the sample of their adult offspring described in Behrman and Taubman (1985, in this volume).[14] The veterans sample is composed primarily of men who served in World War II or the Korean War. Most of these veterans were eligible for GI Bill benefits.[15] The veteran status of those in the offspring sample is not known. Some may have been eligible for the benefits available to those serving in the Vietnam War era, but—judging by the population as a whole—most were not.[16]

Offspring Sample

Our study requires accurate data on sibship size. In the veterans sample the sibship size classification is based on answers by both twins to questions on the number of older and younger sibs in 1940. In the offspring sample the sibship size classification is based not on *offspring* responses but instead on two separate responses by the *fathers*. In 1974 each father was asked to provide a list of all his children regardless of age. In 1978 or 1981/82 each father was asked

14. Both samples are above the U.S. average in earnings, education, and family environment. Both samples, however, yield earnings functions with slope coefficients similar to those obtained from random samples of the U.S. population (see Behrman et al. 1980; Behrman and Taubman 1985, in this volume).

15. Only the small number who were dishonorably discharged or did not serve during wartime were ineligible.

16. The veterans were born between 1917 and 1927. The earliest birth year of the offspring in our sample was 1939, and very few were born before 1945; hence, none of them were eligible for the Korean War GI Bill. Taussig (1974) compares the World War II and Vietnam War versions of the GI Bill and concludes that the World War II plan was more generous to veterans attending private colleges, while the Vietnam plan was more generous to veterans attending public colleges.

to provide the names and addresses of all his children over 18 years of age. The two lists are essentially consistent: almost all discrepancies between them could be accounted for by children who were reported in 1974 but who were not 18 when the second survey was undertaken. For the offspring sample, our sibship size classification misses children born after 1974, but we misclassify few families because of this since the youngest veterans at that time were 47 years old.

The well-known inverse relationship between years of schooling and sibship size might occur if children in larger families are less well endowed, if they receive less parental attention, or if they receive less parental financial aid per child. The offspring sample enables us to examine the relationship between parental financial aid and sibship size. Those offspring who went to college were asked the percentage of their educational financial support derived from each of five categories: work, scholarships, loans, parents, and other.[17] Although these data fail to indicate the level of college costs, they are nevertheless informative.

In table 1 we report estimates for males and females of the importance of alternative sources for financing college education. For both males and females, there are strong and statistically significant positive effects of sibship size on work and the use of loans, and a significant negative effect on parental aid even when we control for birth order, offspring's and parents' ages, mother's education, and parents' income. For males there is also a significant positive effect on "other," and for females a significant positive effect on scholarship aid. Thus for larger sibships, parental aid is less important and the remaining sources (including scholarship, loans, and work) are more important for financing both males' and females' college educations.

In table 2 we present means, within-family variances, and intraclass correlations (weighted by family size) in the offspring sample for years of schooling, expected years of schooling, and both of these adjusted for age, age squared, and gender using adjustment coefficients taken from ordinary least squares (OLS) regressions. The intraclass correlation is the portion of the total variance attributable to differences in family means. For this correlation we include only data for families from which two or more sibs answered the questionnaire. The responses show that many of these adults expect to obtain additional schooling and that those from larger sibships expect more additional schooling than those from smaller sibships. Thus our estimates may be sensitive to whether we base our analysis on expected schooling or actual schooling. To avoid biasing the

17. The responses for each category were coded in 10-point intervals. An analysis using midpoints of each group showed responses for nearly all respondents adding up to approximately 100 percent.

Table 1 Offspring Sample: Financing College Education

	MALES (N = 503)					FEMALES (N = 533)				
	Work	Scholarship	Loan	Parent	Other	Work	Scholarship	Loan	Parent	Other
Intercept	45.97	-4.54	27.10	7.23	37.91	68.75	22.53	52.16	-49.87	20.10
	(1.80)	(.25)	(1.80)	(.27)	(1.99)	(2.94)	(1.52)	(3.02)	(1.72)	(1.47)
Own age	.19	.12	-.047	-.87	.86	.05	-.32	-.15	-.19	.44
	(.44)	(.39)	(.15)	(1.98)	(2.71)	(.139)	(1.34)	(.54)	(.47)	(1.97)
Father's age	3.98	3.61	-6.42	6.94	-9.95	-5.31	2.15	-5.09	12.07	-5.15
	(.74)	(.96)	(2.03)	(1.25)	(2.48)	(1.34)	(.73)	(1.47)	(2.09)	(1.89)
Mother's age	-.71	-2.40	4.2	.74	-.76	-.18	-1.34	-1.32	2.43	.42
	(.35)	(1.66)	(3.46)	(.35)	(.50)	(.10)	(1.23)	(1.03)	(1.14)	(.42)
Birth order	-1.94	.68	.18	1.16	-.021	-.65	-3.17	-.94	3.12	.95
	(1.18)	(.59)	(.18)	(.68)	(.017)	(.44)	(3.36)	(.86)	(1.70)	(1.09)
Family size (number of sibs)	2.02	.48	1.19	-5.64	2.35	4.23	1.66	1.81	-6.70	-.47
	(2.01)	(.68)	(2.02)	(5.42)	(3.13)	(4.86)	(3.00)	(2.82)	(6.22)	(.94)
Mother's education	-1.64	.28	.13	1.25	.18	-.91	.15	-.38	1.19	-.070
	(2.84)	(.70)	(.38)	(2.09)	(.42)	(1.78)	(.48)	(1.02)	(1.86)	(.24)
Total family income	-.37	-.17	-.13	.65	-.013	-.23	-.076	-.14	.39	-.019
	(4.14)	(2.69)	(2.52)	(7.07)	(.19)	(2.60)	(1.37)	(2.10)	(3.57)	(.38)
$\bar{R}^2$	.082	.007	.052	.232	.050	.098	.032	.035	.178	-.0009

NOTE.—Absolute *t*-statistics are shown in parentheses below the point estimates.

Table 2   Offspring Sample: Summary Statistics on Years of Schooling
and Expected Schooling by Sibship Size

	SIBSHIP SIZE			
	One Child	Two Children	Three Children	Four or More Children
		Means		
Years of schooling	14.9	15.0	14.9	14.3
Years of schooling adjusted for age, age², sex	14.9	15.0	14.9	14.3
Expected years of schooling	16.1	16.1	16.0	15.6
Expected years of schooling adjusted for age, age², sex	16.1	16.1	16.0	15.6
		Intraclass Correlations		
Years of schooling	. . .	.226	.137	.037
Years of schooling adjusted for age, age², sex	. . .	.315	.191	.046
Expected years of schooling	. . .	.226	.137	.037
Expected years of schooling adjusted for age, age², sex	. . .	.220	.126	.037
		Standard Deviations		
Years of schooling	2.09	2.13	2.15	2.29
Years of schooling adjusted for age, age², sex	1.99	2.08	2.07	2.22
Expected years of schooling	2.25	2.29	2.30	2.48
Expected years of schooling adjusted for age, age², sex	2.17	2.28	2.28	2.47
		Sample Sizes*		
Years of schooling	168	887	1,169	1,762
Years of schooling adjusted for age, age², sex	167	887	1,168	1,759
Expected years of schooling	150	787	1,031	1,554
Expected years of schooling adjusted for age, age², sex	149	787	1,030	1,551

*Observations were eliminated if years of schooling are recorded to be less than one or more than 20.

analysis in favor of our hypothesis, we have used expected schooling as the dependent variable in the schooling regressions presented below.[18]

The first panel of table 2 indicates a drop in mean expected years of schooling as sibship size increases, although the difference between two- and four-or-more–child families is less than 5 percent. The second panel shows the intraclass correlations. All four series display similar patterns. When expected years

18. Estimates using actual schooling show the same general patterns but slightly greater differences with sibship size.

Table 3   Offspring Sample: Summary Statistics on Earnings by Sibship Size

	SIBSHIP SIZE			
	One Child	Two Children	Three Children	Four or More Children
	Means			
Earnings	14,072.4	15,240.3	14,979.6	13,414.6
Earnings adjusted for age, age^2, sex	16,051.1	17,175.2	17,460.8	15,516.8
	Intraclass Correlations			
Earnings	. . .	.010	.049	−.001
Earnings adjusted for age, age^2, sex	. . .	.057	.057	.010
	Standard Deviations			
Earnings	11,325.1	23,735.0	13,329.8	12,318.3
Earnings adjusted for age, age^2, sex	10,047.3	10,518.5	12,422.8	11,021.7
	Sample Sizes			
Earnings	159	835	1,112	1,663
Earnings adjusted for age, age^2, sex	140	699	958	1,423

of schooling are adjusted for cohort and sex, the correlation falls from .23 for two-child families to .04 for four-or-more–child families. The third panel contains estimates of the standard deviations, which generally increase with sibship size.

In table 3 we present the parallel analysis for earnings. Average adjusted earnings rise when we go from one- to three-child families and then decline more than 10 percent. With adjusted earnings data, the intraclass correlation falls when we go beyond the three-child family, while the standard deviations tend to rise with family size.

We turn next to regression estimates for the offspring. Table 4 presents OLS estimates for the offspring for expected schooling (pt. A) and for earnings (pt. B). The independent variables are, respectively, the expected schooling and the earnings of the next-older sib. We use the next-older sib rather than, say, the oldest sib in order to control better for factors such as family resources, which may vary over the life cycle, especially if liquidity constraints are binding. For the same reason we control for the age difference between adjacent sibs.[19] Sib similarity can be measured in two ways: by $\bar{R}^2$ or by the slope coef-

19. In alternative regressions the difference in age between the individual and the next-older sib is deleted, but its exclusion does not change the basic thrust of the results.

Table 4   Offspring Sample

Sample	Constant	Schooling of Next-Older Sib	Age Difference from Next-Older Sib	$\bar{R}^2$	Number of Observations
Two children	10.66	.36	−.30	.16	215
	(11.04)	(6.29)	(6.29)		
Three children	10.67	.37	.088	.15	421
	(13.68)	(7.97)	(2.00)		
Four children	9.84	.38	−.025	.14	350
	(11.84)	(7.42)	(−.51)		
Five or more children	9.64	.37	−.063	.13	486
	(13.77)	(8.49)	(−1.46)		
All	9.85	.39	−.014	.15	1,472
	(24.56)	(15.79)	(−.56)		

B.   EARNINGS SIMILARITY OF ADJACENT PAIRS AND SIBSHIP SIZE

Sample	Constant	Earnings of Next-Older Sib	Age Difference from Next-Older Sib	$\bar{R}^2$	Number of Observations*
Two children	12,391.5	.17	−899.7	.047	166
	(5.45)	(2.02)	(−2.30)		
Three children	16,885.9	.18	79.33	.029	358
	(9.73)	(3.19)	(.26)		
Four children	15,246.6	.13	−74.34	.015	293
	(10.11)	(2.08)	(−.26)		
Five or more children	12,192.8	.12	−596.1	.027	392
	(9.66)	(2.36)	(−2.57)		
All	14,069.6	.16	−342.2	.025	1,209
	(17.49)	(5.18)	(−2.35)		

NOTE—Single-child families are excluded. We have not reported regressions using the oldest sib as the dependent variable. Schooling is expected years of schooling. Absolute t-statistics are shown in parentheses below the point estimates.

*These differ from those in pt. A because of the few cases in which data are available on the oldest sib but not on the sib next in the birth order.

ficient on the next-older sib's expected education or earnings. The last row contains the results for all families from which two or more sibs responded to the questionnaire. For the whole sample the coefficient on the next-older sib's expected education is .42 and the $\bar{R}^2$ is .15, and the estimate on the earnings of the next-older sib is .16 and the $\bar{R}^2$ is .025.

We report separate estimates for sibship sizes of two, three, four, and five or more. The coefficients for the next-older sib are about .37 in all cases, though an F-test rejects the null hypothesis that all coefficients are the same. Another F-test indicates that the constant terms differ, but not the slope coefficients. However, the $\bar{R}^2$'s decline almost uniformly with sibship size, although the four-sib case is out of line for earnings. For earnings, the coefficient drops from

.17 to .12, and the $\bar{R}^2$ drops from .047 to .015 in the four-sib case. Covariance analysis tests strongly reject the null hypothesis of no difference in coefficients across sibship size groupings in both cases. For the offspring, sib schooling similarity and sib earnings similarity both fall with sibship size.

Veterans Sample

In part A of both tables 5 and 6, we present the estimates for the veterans sample for schooling similarity. Since previous research has indicated substantial differences in correlations between the identical and the fraternal twins, we

Table 5 Veteran's Sample, Identical Twins (OLS Regression)

	Mean Schooling	Twin's Schooling	Constant	$\bar{R}^2$	Number of Observations
No other sibs	14.5	.84 (20.3)	1.23 (1.93)	.74	144
One other sib	13.9	.83 (21.8)	1.07 (1.88)	.63	282
Two other sibs	13.6	.85 (23.7)	.95 (1.84)	.71	230
Three other sibs	13.2	.76 (17.1)	2.15 (3.42)	.72	118
Four other sibs	13.0	.85 (12.6)	.78 (.84)	.63	95
Five or more other sibs	12.2	.84 (16.5)	.73 (1.09)	.58	203
All identical twins	13.4	.84 (46.5)	.94 (3.60)	.67	1,072

B. SIB EARNINGS SIMILARITY BY SIBSHIP SIZE

	Mean Earnings	Twin's Earnings	Constant	$\bar{R}^2$	Number of Observations
No other sibs	19,114.3	.32 (8.19)	6,327.3 (5.45)	.32	144
One other sib	17,355.5	.50 (17.4)	2,625.6 (3.50)	.52	284
Two other sibs	17,905.1	.43 (11.8)	4,948.6 (5.42)	.38	230
Three other sibs	17,089.7	.52 (11.2)	1,482.2 (1.18)	.52	118
Four other sibs	14,782.9	.55 (9.29)	1,412.6 (1.16)	.48	95
Five or more other sibs	14,777.7	.27 (8.47)	5,583.9 (7.24)	.26	203
All identical twins	16,965.0	.42 (27.3)	4,084.5 (10.4)	.41	1,074

NOTE—Absolute t-statistics are shown in parentheses below the point estimates.

Table 6   Veterans Sample, Fraternal Twins (OLS Regressions)

	Mean Schooling	Twin's Schooling	Constant	$\bar{R}^2$	Number of Observations
No other sibs	14.5	.62 (8.26)	3.93 (3.34)	.46	82
One other sib	14.0	.74 (15.2)	2.01 (2.70)	.49	243
Two other sibs	13.7	.64 (13.2)	3.29 (4.52)	.46	206
Three other sibs	13.1	.81 (12.8)	.74 (.818)	.57	124
Four other sibs	12.6	.72 (9.95)	1.83 (1.81)	.53	91
Five or more other sibs	11.6	.71 (14.6)	1.39 (2.20)	.45	262
All fraternal twins	13.1	.76 (33.8)	1.38 (4.27)	.53	1,008

B.   SIB EARNINGS SIMILARITY BY SIBSHIP SIZE

	Mean Earnings	Twin's Earnings	Constant	$\bar{R}^2$	Number of Observations
No other sibs	17,239.1	.48 (6.97)	914.8 (.488)	.38	82
One other sib	18,957.2	.31 (9.03)	5,068.0 (4.86)	.25	244
Two other sibs	16,771.3	.31 (8.06)	4,861.6 (4.97)	.24	208
Three other sibs	14,951.1	.34 (9.36)	3,332.7 (3.62)	.42	125
Four other sibs	15,799.2	.45 (8.13)	2,385.4 (1.73)	.43	91
Five or more other sibs	12,916.6	.24 (8.68)	4,557.2 (7.74)	.22	263
All fraternal twins	16,023.0	.34 (21.1)	3,849.6 (9.33)	.31	1,013

NOTE—Absolute t-statistics are shown in parentheses below the point estimates.

have analyzed them separately, reporting the results for identical twins in table 5 and those for fraternal twins in table 6. In these equations the dependent variable is the education of the alphabetically first twin.

Consider first mean educational attainment. For both the identical and the fraternal twins, the larger the sibship, the smaller is educational attainment. The difference between no other sibs and five or more sibs is 15 percent for identical twins and over 20 percent for fraternal twins. This need not be due to wealth constraints since, as Zajonc (1976), Lindert (1977), and Birdsall (1979) have argued, the environment of a large family differs in a number of dimensions from that of a small family.

The remaining results in tables 5 and 6 can be described briefly. For the identical twins the slope coefficient estimates range from .76 to .85 and the R^2's range from .58 to .74. For the fraternal twins the respective ranges are .62 to .81 and .45 to .57. For fraternal twins the maximum slope coefficient is for three other sibs, while for the identical twins the maximum is for two or four other sibs. For fraternal twins the maximum value of R^2 is in the three-other-sibs cell, while for the identical twins the maximum is in the no-other-sibs cell. Although there is some tendency for sib schooling similarity to be less for the largest families (i.e., five or more other sibs or no other sibs) than for smaller families, the association of sib schooling similarity with sibship size is much weaker for the veterans than for the offspring.

A covariance test of all coefficients being the same rejects this null hypothesis in both tables 5 and 6. However, respecifying the equation to allow separate dummies for two, three, four, and five or more siblings and the interaction of each dummy with the twin's education yields no significant coefficients.

Part B of both tables 5 and 6 contains the corresponding results for the veterans' earnings. For the identical twins the slope coefficients are about .3 for the smallest and largest families and .43 to .55 for the rest. A similar pattern applies to the R^2's, with about .3 at the extremes and .38 to .52 elsewhere.

The results for the fraternal twins are slope coefficients that range from .24 to .38 for the five equations, but with that for four sibs about as similar as no other sibs and that for five or more sibs falling to .24. The R^2's range from .43 for four other sibs to .22 for five or more sibs.

For identical twins we accept the null hypothesis that all coefficients are the same. For fraternal twins the F-test is 21, which indicates a rejection of the null hypothesis. However, the only interaction term that is significant is the one for four or more siblings.

The Impact of the GI Bill on Equal Access

We now turn to an estimate of how much unequal access would have contributed to variation in schooling for the veterans without the GI Bill. We begin by representing earnings as the sum of two terms: the amount an individual with given endowments would receive with zero schooling investment (αG_{kj}) and the return on the schooling investment (the product $i_{kj} S_{kj}$):

$$Y_{kj} = \alpha G_{kj} + i_{kj} S_{kj}. \tag{6}$$

Equilibrium schooling in Becker's Woytinsky lecture model depends on an individual's endowments (G_{kj}) and on family wealth (W_j).[20] A linear approxi-

---

20. Endowments affect the demand curve. Family wealth may affect the marginal cost-of-funds curve (see Becker 1975).

mation to this relation is

$$S_{kj} = \beta G_{kj} + \delta W_j. \tag{7}$$

Substitution of (7) into (6) gives

$$Y_{kj} = (\alpha + \beta i_{kj})G_{kj} + \delta W_j. \tag{8}$$

The variance of the first-order Taylor series approximation at the means to (8) is given by

$$\sigma_Y^2 = (\alpha + \beta \bar{\imath})^2 \sigma_G^2 + \delta^2 \sigma_W^2 + (\beta \bar{G})^2 \sigma_i^2 + 2(\alpha + \beta \bar{\imath})(\beta \bar{G})\sigma_{Gi}, \tag{9}$$

where the bars denote mean values.[21] A reduction in the dependence of the marginal price of schooling on endowments causes both σ_i^2 and $|\sigma_{Gi}|$ to fall. If σ_{Gi} is positive, then such a reduction decreases the intrafamily variance of Y_{kj} and cross-twin covariances and cross-family variances in education and in earnings.[22]

In the Appendix we outline the statistical methods used in Behrman et al. (1980) to estimate the variance in genetic endowments for individuals (σ_G^2) and the covariance in environments across sibs (σ_{NN*}^2). Their estimates rest on the assumptions that the genetic endowment covariance is zero ($\sigma_{GN} = 0$) and that the expected value of the unobserved covariance of the twins is the same for identical and fraternal twins. They require data on the observed cross-twin covariances and on the value of a parameter λ, $0 < \lambda < 1$, which is a function of both the degree of assortative mating and the extent to which genetic effects are additive. The equations for σ_G^2 and σ_{NN*} are

$$\sigma_G^2 = \frac{\sigma_{YY*} - \sigma_{YY'}}{1 - \lambda} \tag{10}$$

and

$$\sigma_{NN*} = \frac{\sigma_{YY'} - \lambda\sigma_{YY*}}{1 - \lambda}, \tag{11}$$

where σ_{YY*} is the covariance in earnings between identical twins and $\sigma_{YY'}$ is the covariance in earnings between fraternal twins.

If the observed covariances, σ_{YY*}^2 and $\sigma_{YY'}^2$, are each reduced by the same amount because of the GI Bill, then the estimate of σ_G^2 would be unaffected, although its estimated *share* of σ_Y^2 would have been smaller if Y had varied

21. Within the family there are no covariance terms with W (σ_{GW}, σ_{iW}) since W refers to family wealth and is the same for all sibs.

22. If σG_i is negative but not too sensitive to the change in the dependence of the marginal price of schooling on endowments, this conclusion also holds.

Table 7   Veterans Sample, Both Twins in Navy:
Prewar and Postwar Schooling Equations

	PREWAR			POSTWAR		
	Constant	Twin's Schooling	$\bar{R}^2$	Constant	Twin's Schooling	$\bar{R}^2$
Fraternal	3.73	.67	.48	5.34	.57	.28
twins (N = 198)	(6.15)	(13.5)		(6.1)	(8.9)	
Identical	1.11	.91	.73	3.17	.76	.55
twins (N = 294)	(2.9)	(28.0)		(5.7)	(19.0)	

NOTE—Absolute t-statistics are shown in parentheses below the point estimates.

more. On the other hand, (11) implies that with the same equal reductions in observed covariances, the estimate of σ_{NN*}, the common environment, would become larger both absolutely and as a share of σ_Y^2.

To estimate the importance of the GI Bill in reducing unequal access, we need information on λ and on the magnitude of the changes in the observed covariances due to the GI Bill. In the simplest linear model, λ is .5. In the nonlinear latent variable model of Behrman et al. (1980), it is estimated to be .34.

We use two approaches to estimate the extent to which the correlations between the veteran twins' earnings were reduced by the GI Bill. The first uses pre-enlistment educational data for those veteran twin pairs for which both members served in the Navy. This sample is described in Behrman et al. (1980, chaps. 5–7).[23] It includes all pairs who answered the 1974 questionnaire (404 pairs) and a random sample of the remainder, for a total of about 1,200 pairs. Table 7 contains the sib equations for prewar and postwar schooling attainment for various groupings. The R^2's and slope coefficients are higher for prewar education than for postwar education for both sets of twins. The difference over time in the R^2's is about .2. For the sample for which we have both sets of educational data, we find a difference in R^2 of .18 for the identical twins and .20 for the fraternal twins. This suggests that the reduction in the variance common to members of the same family, and thus related to unequal access, due to the GI Bill is about .2 for both types of twins.

The second approach to estimating what the correlations would have been in the absence of the GI Bill begins by observing that the sib correlation in earnings is an upper bound for the father-child correlation in earnings (see

23. Although it would have been desirable to use Army and Marine as well as Navy files, it was not feasible to do so: 80 percent of the Army files were destroyed in a 1976 fire in the St. Louis Personnel Records Center; the Marine files are organized differently from the Navy files, and using them would have required costly retraining of the data extractors.

Behrman et al. 1980). An estimate of the latter may be suggestive of the former. Behrman and Taubman (1985, in this volume) obtain an estimate of .2 for the intergenerational earnings correlation.[24] There are, however, three problems with using this estimate. First, they did not control for genetic endowments. Second, the estimate is based on a single year of earnings or income data for each generation; average earnings or income data for several years would be more appropriate and would yield higher correlations.[25] Third, the average year of birth of the children in their sample is 1951; when these children reached college age in the late 1960s, several programs providing access to financing for college education were available to them that had not been available to nonveterans in the 1940s and 1950s—despite these qualifications.[26]

Both approaches suggest that the understatement of R^2 is approximately .2 or more. If λ is between .34 and .5, then the understatement of σ_{NN*} is about .10 to .13. Hence, our best estimate is that the Behrman et al. (1980) calculation of the contribution of unequal access to differences in earnings for the veterans is off by 100 percent for white males born between 1917 and 1927 who were not eligible for the GI Bill and for all white males born in that decade had there been no GI Bill. The substantial differences between the estimates obtained from the veterans sample and the offspring sample reflect the success of the GI Bill in providing World War II veterans with equal access to education.

IV. Conclusion

In this paper we have argued that unequal access to financing for college education is an important source of differences in educational attainments. We have developed a preference model relating sib schooling and earnings similarities to sibship size with and without equal access. With equal access the model predicts no systematic relationship between sibship size, on the one hand, and sib schooling and earnings similarities on the other. With unequal access the model implies a positive relationship between sibship size and sib schooling and earnings similarities if the preference displacement effect dominates, but a negative relationship if the price effect dominates. We have shown

24. Outliers, including individuals with less than 4 years of work experience and those with earnings below $5,000, were eliminated. See Behrman and Taubman (1985, in this volume) for details.

25. Behrman and Taubman (1990, in this volume) investigate this issue using the Michigan Panel Study of Income Dynamics.

26. An additional source of possible bias for our comparisons with the veterans sample arises from the fact that the veterans are all male while the offspring sample includes both males and females. To see whether gender affects our results, we estimated the relations in table 3 with additive and multiplicative parameters dependent on the gender of the children in each comparison. None of the coefficient estimates of the gender-dependent parameters is significantly different from zero.

that restricting earlier empirical work to World War II veterans, who were eligible for substantial educational benefits under the GI Bill, resulted in an underestimate of the importance of unequal access and, hence, of the differences in sib schooling and earnings similarities in large and small sibships that would have prevailed without the GI Bill. Two rough calculations suggest that the underestimate was on the order of 100 percent for earnings similarities for white males. The inverse relationship between sibship size and sib schooling and earnings similarities in the next generation suggests that even among white males there is substantial inequality of access to resources to finance college education. These calculations also imply that the U.S. government, through the GI Bill, provided eligible veterans with equal access to resources to finance college education, and as a result these veterans acquired substantially more human capital.

Appendix

To demonstrate the consequences of the reduction in βi_{kj} in relation (8), we must explain briefly how the Behrman et al. (1980) estimates were obtained. Behrman et al. show that to estimate a model using data on twins, identification can be obtained by assuming that the unmeasured environment is a latent variable affecting several observed phenotypes or endogenous variables. We can observe, however, the consequence of the missing βi_{kj} within a single-variable framework. For these purposes we are free to choose the units of the unobserved variables so that all coefficients are one and label $W_j + u_{kj}$ (where u_{kj} refers to random environmental effects that are not included in the expectation formulation of [8] above) as N_{kj}. With these conventions, a reduction in βi_{kj} implies a reduction in σ_G^2. We denote an identical twin by an asterisk and a fraternal twin by a prime. We calculate variances for all individuals and across twins. Under these assumptions, from equation (8) the expected value of the variance of Y is

$$\sigma_Y^2 = \sigma_G^2 + \sigma_N^2 + 2\sigma_{GN}. \tag{A1}$$

The expected values of the covariances across twins are

$$\sigma_{YY*} = \sigma_{GG*} + \sigma_{NN*} + 2\sigma_{G*N} \tag{A2}$$

and

$$\sigma_{YY'} = \sigma_{GG'} + \sigma_{NN'} + 2\sigma_{G'N}. \tag{A3}$$

Behrman et al. (1980) made several assumptions that we continue to make here: $\sigma_{GN} = \sigma_{G*N} = \sigma_{G'N} = 0$ and $\sigma_{NN*} = \sigma_{NN'}$. The first assumption is not required in principle in the multiequation latent variable model, but they were unable to obtain convergence with σ_{GN} as a free parameter. Moreover, they have shown analytically in their model that $\partial\sigma_G^2/\partial\sigma_{GN} = 0$ and that all the trade-off is with σ_N^2. The second assumption, however, is nontrivial: its implications and appropriateness are discussed in Goldberger (1977b, 1978), Taubman (1978a, 1981, in this volume), and Behrman et al. (1980).

We also make use of two additional facts: First, for identical twins the nonenvironmental or genetic endowments are identical so that $\sigma_{GG^*} = \sigma_G^2$, and, second, $\sigma_{G'G} = \lambda\sigma_G^2$, $0 < \lambda < 1$. These permit us to rewrite (A2) and (A3) as

$$\sigma_{YY^*} = \sigma_G^2 + \sigma_{NN^*} \tag{A4}$$

and

$$\sigma_{YY'} = \lambda\sigma_G^2 + \sigma_{NN^*}. \tag{A5}$$

Equations (10) and (11) are the solutions of (A4) and (A5) for σ_G^2 and σ_{NN^*}.

3
Do Parents Favor Boys?

JERE R. BEHRMAN, ROBERT A. POLLAK, AND PAUL TAUBMAN[1]

In many societies female earnings are found to be less than male earnings even after controlling for differences in work experience, hours worked, and human capital investments in schooling.[2] Although such differences are frequently interpreted as reflecting, at least in part, labor market gender discrimination, we remain agnostic about their underlying cause and refer to them neutrally as gender wage differentials. In many societies females also receive less investment in human capital than males.[3]

Within an optimizing model of parental allocation, systematic differences in human capital investments between the sexes may originate in at least three conceptually distinct ways. First, parents may respond to expected gender wage differentials in the labor market.[4] Second, parents may respond to systematic differences by gender in the price of human capital investments. Third, parental preferences may favor girls or favor boys in the sense that they value identical outcomes at identical cost more highly for one sex than for the other.[5] For the

Reprinted from *International Economic Review* 27, no. 1 (February, 1986): 31–52.

1. This research was supported by the NSF and the NIH. Richard Voith provided excellent research assistance. We are grateful to Judith Farnbach for editorial assistance and to Angus Deaton and Robert Willis for useful comments.

2. See Oaxaca [1973] for the United States and Birdsall and Sabot [1991], for Brazil, Nicaragua, Kenya and Tanzania.

3. Throughout most of the developing world, for example, primary schooling enrollment rates are less for girls than for boys, though the gaps have been narrowing (see World Bank [1984]). Schooling also is less for girls than for boys in many developed economies. In the U.S. sample on which our analysis is based, the mean schooling for girls is about 0.4 years less than for boys.

4. The difference between female and male human capital investment is often interpreted as reflecting parental responses to labor market gender wage differentials. For example, in a recent study of investment in children in India, Rosenzweig and Schultz [1982] emphasize this interpretation.

5. Our concerns and our terminology thus differ from those of Dawkins [1976, p. 132] who asks whether Selfish Genes will compel a mother to be "equally altruistic towards all her children" or to "have favourites" by which he means to "invest her resources unequally among her children." We interpret the question posed in the paper's title to refer not to unequal human capital investment regardless of its source, but specifically to unequal investment due to parental preferences exhibiting unequal concern.

purpose of this paper we say that parental preferences which are neutral between girls and boys exhibit "equal concern" and that preferences which favor
one sex or the other exhibit "unequal concern." How parents change human
capital investments in their children in response to changes in the gender wage
differential or in the price of human capital depends critically on the relative
importance of these three factors.

In this paper we undertake a theoretical and empirical analysis of the role of
parental preferences in general and unequal concern in particular in the allocation of human capital investments among children.[6] We begin by generalizing our earlier model of the allocation of human capital investments among
children (Behrman, Pollak and Taubman, [1982, in this volume], BPT) to incorporate the possibility that the returns to such investments may include not
only the child's own expected earnings but also the expected earnings of his or
her spouse.[7] Generalizing the original BPT model to include marriage market
outcomes is particularly important when comparing the determinants of human
capital investments and earnings for females and males, since the relative magnitudes of own earnings and marriage market returns for females and males
differ widely. The original BPT model is a special case of the generalized
model in which own earnings but not spouse earnings affect the allocation of
human capital investments among children. The generalized model thus reduces to the original one in two special cases: (1) when there is no assortative
mating based on schooling and, hence, expected spouse earnings are unaffected
by human capital investments and (2) when parents are concerned only with
the own earnings of their children and, hence, disregard the effect on expected
spouse earnings of the allocation of human capital investments.

Previous studies have not provided direct evidence about the extent to which
systematic patterns favoring males in such investments reflect parental preferences that favor males. Studies that make this claim—or the opposite one—do
so by *a priori* assumption, not by identifying empirically the role of such preferences. One major reason for this lacuna has been the absence of relevant data
on families with both female and male adult siblings. In this paper we introduce a major new data set on families with both female and male adult siblings.
We use it to estimate whether parental preferences exhibit unequal concern,
both under the original BPT model and under the generalized BPT model allowing marriage market returns. Our results indicate that the BPT model with

6. In a parallel study, Behrman [1988a] investigates the role of unequal concern in intrahousehold allocations in rural India using child health measures as outputs and nutrients consumed by
children as inputs.

7. This possibility has been emphasized recently by Behrman and Wolfe [1987] and Boulier
and Rosenzweig [1984].

unequal concern, generalized to allow marriage market returns, is more consistent with the observed experience of contemporary young adults than is the original BPT model.

1. A Generalized BPT Parental Allocation Model of Human Capital Investments with Assortative Mating

1.1. Wealth versus Separable Models

In most general models of parental resource allocation, each child's earnings and unearned income are arguments of the parents' utility function. Two particular specifications of parental preferences, the wealth model and the separable model, predominate in the economic literature on intrafamilial human capital investments. It is necessary to choose between these two models on the basis of indirect evidence because the lack of direct observations on adult outcomes other than income or earnings in most sibling data sets, including ours, precludes the direct testing of a model that encompasses both.

Becker and Tomes [1976] analyzed the wealth version of a preference model of parental investment in their children's human capital. Parents maximize a utility function which has as its arguments parents' consumption and the expected lifetime income of each child. Children's incomes depend on both their earnings and their returns on gifts and bequests from their parents. If there are diminishing returns to schooling and parents make gifts or plan to leave bequests to each child, then it is optimal for parents to invest in each child's human capital until the expected rate of return on human capital equals the market rate of interest and, at that point, to switch to gifts or bequests which are not subject to diminishing returns. Put another way, since parents are interested in the distribution of wealth among their children, they maximize total wealth by investing "efficiently" in human capital and then use gifts and bequests to achieve the desired degree of equity. Since earnings tend to vary considerably even among siblings of the same sex, parents who desire an equal distribution of income among their children must compensate for unequal earnings with considerable variations in gifts and bequests.[8]

In BPT, we proposed the separable earnings-bequest model as an alternative to the Becker-Tomes wealth-investment model [1976]. In the BPT model, par-

---

8. See, for example, Behrman, Hrubec, Taubman and Wales [1980], Chamberlain and Griliches [1975, 1977], and Olneck [1977] for evidence on realized variances in intrasibling earnings among adult males in the United States and Behrman and Wolfe [1984] for similar evidence for females in Nicaragua. Although expected differences may be less, the realized differences seem large enough to be accounted for by more than unanticipated events, particularly since substantial information is usually available about children's life-time earnings when parents make final bequest decisions.

ents are concerned not only with the distribution of wealth but also with the distribution of lifetime earnings among their children (say, because earnings confer self-esteem and social esteem). The BPT model assumes that children's earnings are separable from the other arguments of the parental utility function. In the BPT model, the allocation among children of investment in human capital (e.g., schooling) depends on the parameters of both the parents' utility function and the children's earnings functions. Since parents concerned about equity consider the distribution of gifts and bequests separately from the distribution of earnings, they may choose an equal distribution of gifts and bequests even though earnings are unequal. In the BPT model, the allocation of human capital reflects parental concerns about equity as well as efficiency and thus is efficient only in unlikely special cases.

Evidence to distinguish between the wealth model and the separable model is scanty, but arguments in support of both models have focused on the degree of equality in the distribution of bequests. Given the assumption that parents desire equality, the wealth model predicts an unequal distribution of gifts and bequests which compensates fully for the observed or expected inequalities in the distribution of earnings among siblings; the separable model is consistent with an equal distribution of gifts and bequests despite inequality in the distribution of earnings.

Although there are some data on the distribution of bequests among siblings, there is very little information on the distribution of gifts. Parents may give equal bequests but unequal gifts so that the sum of bequests and gifts is unequal among siblings. Becker [1981, pp. 188–9], in fact, claims that his Rotten Kid Theorem implies that bequests tend to be equal in order "to elicit the same amount of altruism from all older children," while gifts are used to compensate less-endowed children. But another implication of the Rotten Kid Theorem that Becker also notes is that parents want to delay contributions to children as long as possible in order to maintain control and induce rotten kids to act altruistically toward their siblings. This creates an incentive for parents to make bequests large relative to gifts. But if bequests are distributed equally, the larger bequests are relative to gifts, the less an unequal distribution of gifts can compensate for an unequal distribution of earnings by providing an unequal distribution of bequests plus gifts. Empirical evidence on the magnitude of bequests relative to gifts is very sketchy, but suggests that when bequests are fairly equal gifts generally are not large enough to compensate for inequalities in earnings.[9]

The available evidence on the distribution of bequests among siblings thus provides some indication of the relative merits of the wealth and the separable models. The first point that arises from reviewing this evidence is that be-

9. See Menchik [1980] and Behrman, Pollak, and Taubman [1988].

quests are unimportant for many families in the United States. On the basis of Blinder's [1973] estimates, for example, Becker [1981, p. 121] summarizes this evidence as implying that "less than 40 percent [of families in the United States] . . . invest significantly in their [children's] nonhuman capital." When there are no gifts or bequests, the wealth model and the separable model are equivalent. The second point concerns the minority of families for which bequests are significant. In BPT, we reviewed the evidence then available on the distribution of bequests and concluded that it is at least as consistent with the separable earnings-bequest model as with the wealth-investment model. Since then Menchik's [1988] re-examination of Tomes' [1981] analysis of the Cleveland probate data—which was the main empirical support for the wealth model—has provided additional support for the separability assumption.[10] In the light of this evidence we believe the separable model is more plausible than the wealth model although the available evidence is not absolutely conclusive. For the remainder of this paper, we adopt the separable model as a maintained hypothesis.

1.2. Human-Capital-Dependent Income

The discussion thus far has distinguished between earnings on the one hand and income from bequests and gifts on the other. In place of earnings, we now introduce a broader concept of human-capital-dependent income (HCD income). This replacement is appropriate if marriage market outcomes depend on human capital and if parents take account of marriage market outcomes in allocating human capital investments among their children. Both the Becker-Tomes wealth model and the BPT separable model can be generalized by recognizing that human capital investments affect marriage market as well as labor market outcomes. Generalizing the two models in this way does not, however, weaken the arguments for preferring the BPT separable model to the Becker-Tomes wealth model, so our analysis is based on the generalized BPT model.

---

10. Tomes [1981] analyzed a Cleveland probate sample in which estate information was obtained from a questionnaire administered to inheritors. Tomes found that inheritances reported in this sample related negatively to a measure of recipients' income and that the majority of estates gave unequal bequests to the children in a family. Subsequently Menchik [1988] drew a random sample from the same Cleveland probate population, and using the probate records themselves, found that 87% of the estates left to two or more children were divided evenly. Menchik's results raise questions about the reliability of the major empirical support for the wealth model. He conjectures that the finding of inequality in the data which Tomes used is due to measurement error in recalling bequests information in that sample, as opposed to the actual probate records which Menchik used. Unfortunately the information no longer exists to tie the sample which Tomes used back to the probate records so this conjecture cannot be tested.

Our generalization of the BPT model is based on this broader notion of the impact of parental investments in their children's human capital. Though this extension is straightforward, it has important theoretical and empirical implications, particularly for families with both female and male siblings. The generalized BPT model reduces to the original one if parents have a separable welfare function in their children's own earnings or if mating is not assortative on human capital investments. In Section 2, we test empirically whether our generalized model reduces to the original BPT model.

1.3. The Maximization Problem and Estimation Procedure for the Generalized BPT Model

Since the structure of the problem is the same in the generalized model as in the original one, we summarize it and refer the interested reader to BPT [1982, in this volume] for details.

Parents are assumed to have separable welfare functions defined over the expected HCD incomes of each of n children

$$w = W(Y_1, \ldots, Y_n) \tag{1}$$

where W is the parental welfare function, Y_i the expected HCD income of the i-th child, and n the number of children. These preferences are maximized subject to $n + 1$ constraints.

The first constraint is the partial nominal budget constraint that applies to family resources devoted to human capital investment (R). In anticipation of the empirical application in Section 2, we distinguish between investments in education (E_i) and other human capital investments (X_i); we assume parents face fixed prices for these investments (P_E, P_X) and that these prices are identical for all children:[11]

$$\sum_{i=1}^{n} (P_E E_i + P_X X_i) \leq R. \tag{2}$$

The remaining constraints are the n HCD income production functions, one for each child. The arguments of these HCD income production functions can be grouped into three categories. The first category includes those variables that determine the expected own-earnings of the i-th child (Y_i^0), such as education (E_i), other human capital investments (X_i), sex (S_i), and other genetic

---

11. Among the major private marginal costs of education are tuition, supplies, time of the children, and time of the parents. Probably the most troublesome of these in regard to the assumption of equal prices for boys and girls pertains to the cost of their time. For the generation under consideration in our empirical work, however, wages for school-age males and females did not differ nearly as much as for adults of previous generations, so this assumption is less troublesome than it might at first appear. Without this assumption, a_i/a_j would be replaced by $(a_i P_{Ej})/(a_j P_{Ei})$ in relations (15), (16), and (17) below.

endowments (G_i).[12] The second category includes those variables that determine the expected earnings of his or her spouse; these reflect the nature of the assortative mating process, the expected proportion of the i-th child's adult life that the spouse contributes earnings to the household, and the spouse expected earnings during the time that the spouse is making such contributions (Y_i^s). In addition to the factors that affect own earnings, these include the expected education (E_i^s), other human capital investments (X_i^s), sex (S_i^s), and endowments (G_i^s) of the spouse. The third category is the preference weight placed on the i-th child's spouse expected earnings (W_i^s). If this weight is 0, then the generalized BPT model reduces to the original BPT model and the expected spouse characteristics are irrelevant. Taking into consideration all of these arguments, we write the HCD income production function for the i-th child as

$$Y_i = Y_i(E_i, X_i, S_i, G_i, E_i^s, X_i^s, S_i^s, G_i^s, W_i^s). \tag{3}$$

Provided that this constrained maximization problem has an interior solution, the first-order condition for parental human capital investment in education of the i-th child is

$$\frac{\partial W}{\partial Y_i} \frac{\partial Y_i}{\partial E_i} - \lambda P_E = 0 \tag{4}$$

where λ is the family-specific Lagrangian multiplier for the partial nominal budget constraint that applies to resources devoted to investment in the human capital of the family's children. Expressing the first-order conditions in ratio form yields

$$\frac{\partial W/\partial Y_i}{\partial W/\partial Y_j} = \frac{\partial Y_j/\partial E_j}{\partial Y_i/\partial E_i}. \tag{5}$$

This ratio form, which includes neither the unobservable family-specific Lagrangian multiplier nor the usually unobserved price of schooling, corresponds to the usual tangency condition for a constrained maximum, i.e., the slope of the parental welfare function equals the slope of the HCD income possibility frontier for the i-th versus the j-th child (point A in Figure 1).

Since the right side of this equation depends on the endowments of the i-th and j-th children, the HCD income-possibility frontier varies among families even if they have the same partial nominal budget constraint in equation (2) and the same functional forms for equations (1) and (3). This variation in the HCD income-possibility frontier among families (or, for that matter, among pairs of siblings) permits identification of the slope of the welfare function (also see BPT [1982, in this volume]). Figure 2 provides an illustration in which the genetic endowments for child i relative to those of the j-th child are

12. Endowments include genetic and other factors that affect expected earnings but that do not enter the budget constraint. This usage seems consistent with Becker's [1981].

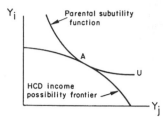

FIG. 1   Optimum parental intrafamilial allocation of human capital investments at point A.

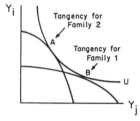

FIG. 2   Relative endowments for child I versus J higher in family 2 than in family 1.

higher in Family 2 than in Family 1. The slope of the welfare function is crucial because it characterizes the equilibrium efficiency-equity tradeoff and parental preference weights for the distribution of HCD income among their children.

Stochastic terms may enter equation (5) because of measurement errors and differences between actual and expected values of variables. For simplicity, we have written equation (5) without stochastic terms.

1.4. Specific Functional Forms for the Generalized BPT Model

In order to estimate identifiable parameters in the parental welfare function, we must make specific assumptions about the functional forms in relations (1) and (3).

For the welfare function in relation (1) we assume a generalized constant elasticity of substitution (CES) form

$$W(Y_1, \ldots, Y_n) = \sum_{i=1}^{n} a_i(Y_i - b_i)^c, \ (Y_i - b_i) > 0,$$

$$a_i, c > 0, \ -\infty < c \leq 1.\text{[13]} \quad (6)$$

13. In our description of the generalized CES welfare function we ignore the case

$$W(Y_1, \ldots, Y_n) = -\sum a_i(b_i - Y_i)^c; \ (b_i - Y_i) > 0, a_i > 0, c > 1.$$

This case is described in detail in BPT [1982, pp. 63–64]; we ignore it here to simplify the exposition. Our empirical analysis is compatible with this case but since our estimates clearly imply that $c < 1$, it is empirically irrelevant.

The first derivatives corresponding to this welfare function are given by

$$\frac{\partial W}{\partial Y_i} = a_i c (Y_i - b_i)^{c-1}. \tag{7}$$

The parameters $(b_1, \ldots, b_n)$ are "translation" parameters indicating any displacement of the CES from the origin. For levels of HCD income $(Y_1, \ldots, Y_n)$ above $(b_1, \ldots, b_n)$ parents are willing to trade off the HCD income of one child against that of another. The parameters $(a_1, \ldots, a_n)$ are "supernumerary weights" indicating the importance that parents give to each child's HCD income above $(b_1, \ldots, b_n)$. The parameter c reflects parental aversion to inequality in the distribution of supernumerary HCD income. We say that parental preferences exhibit "equal concern" for all children if the welfare function is symmetric in its treatment of all children so that the corresponding indifference map is symmetric around the 45° line (see BPT [1982, pp. 55–56; in this volume]). The generalized CES welfare function exhibits equal concern when the translation parameters for all children are equal to a common value (b) and the supernumerary weights for all children are equal to a common value (a). If all of the translation parameters are equal to a common value, but the supernumerary weight is higher for boys than for girls, then parents trade off HCD income among their children above b and value HCD income above that level more for boys than for girls. Figures 1 and 2 assume equal concern for the i-th and j-th children so the indifference curves are symmetrical around a 45° ray from the origin; Figure 3, in contrast, illustrates unequal concern with parental preferences favoring child j.

The role of the parental inequality aversion parameter (c) stands out most clearly when parental preferences exhibit equal concern. One extreme, $c \rightarrow -\infty$, is the "Rawlsian" or infinite inequality aversion case in which parents only value additional HCD income accruing to the worst-off child. The other extreme, $c = 1$, is the "linear" or no-inequality-aversion case: the indifference curves are straight lines and parents value all additional HCD income equally, independent of which child receives it and independent of the initial distribu-

FIG. 3   Unequal concern favoring child J.

tion of HCD income among their children.[14] Between them is an often used intermediate case in which $c = 0$—the "Cobb-Douglas" case.

Our proposed specification of the parental welfare function generalizes that in BPT in two ways: it replaces own earnings by the more general concept of HCD income and it allows unequal concern with parental preferences favoring girls or favoring boys. Our specification of the expected HCD income-generating function for the i-th child involves four steps. First, we posit that this income is a weighted average of own expected earnings (Y_i^0) and of spouse expected earnings, where the latter incorporates both the expected proportion of the i-th child's adult life that such earnings will be received (D_i) and the expected earnings of the spouse while they are received (Y_i^s).

$$Y_i = Y_i^0 + W_i^s(S_i)D_iY_i^s. \tag{8}$$

The weighting factor, W_i^s, is posited to depend on the sex of the i-th child. When W_i^s is 0, this formulation reduces to the original BPT model in which the parental welfare function depends only on the children's own earnings. When W_i^s is less than 1, parents consider their children's own earnings to be more valuable than spouse earnings.[15] When W_i^s is 1, parents consider their children's own earnings and spouse earnings to be perfect substitutes.

Second, we specify earnings production functions for Y_i^0 and Y_i^s. We adopt the Cobb-Douglas (i.e., unitary elasticity of substitution) earnings function and assume that the impact of gender on earnings is multiplicative:

$$Y_i^0 = \alpha(S_i)E_i^\beta X_i^\gamma G_i^\delta \tag{9}$$

$$Y_i^s = \alpha(S_i^s)(E_i^s)^\beta(X_i^s)^\gamma(G_i^s)^\delta. \tag{10}$$

This widely used and tractable form exhibits diminishing marginal returns to human capital investments in education when $\beta < 1$. The assumed multiplicative impact of gender differentials is the form normally found to dominate empirically.[16]

14. If the Y's were cardinal utilities, then the linear welfare function would correspond to the "utilitarian" case.

15. The parents may have these beliefs because own earnings confer self-esteem and social esteem, because the parents are risk averse and other HCD income sources are riskier than own earnings, or because they believe that distribution within the children's adult households will depend on the children's own earnings. Pollak [1985, pp. 598–605, in this volume] describes bargaining models in which distribution within the family depends on each spouse's own earnings and provides references to the literature. We refrain from making the weights functions instead of constants in the interest of keeping the model empirically tractable.

16. See the studies cited in footnote 1; these studies do not estimate earnings production functions, but they do find primarily a multiplicative effect of gender in semilog earnings functions with education and experience among the observable variables.

Third, we posit that the expected proportion of the i-th child's adult life during which he or she will have a spouse with earnings is a function of the gender of the child

$$D_i = \epsilon(S_i). \tag{11}$$

This specification allows this proportion to differ for females and males, as seems to be the case empirically in the U.S. and in most other societies.

Fourth, we hypothesize a simple assortative mating relation based on schooling

$$E_i^s = \eta(S_i)(E_i)^\sigma. \tag{12}$$

Since knowledge of potential mates is often obtained primarily through social contacts made in school, education plays a critical role in determining the marriage options open to an individual. Our specification of the assortative mating relation allows one of its key parameters to differ for females and males. Allowing this difference to appear as a multiplicative gender-dependent factor is less restrictive than it might seem. Maximization of the parental welfare function in the original BPT model with children's own earnings alone subject to the own-earnings production function and budget constraint implies

$$X_i = \frac{\gamma}{\beta} \frac{P_E}{P_X} E_i. \tag{13}$$

In this case education is a perfect proxy for other human capital investments since the expression $(\gamma P_E/\beta P_X)$ is the same for all children; hence, assortative mating on education is tantamount to assortative mating on all human capital investments undertaken by the parents.[17]

Next, we substitute (9)–(12) into (8) and take the partial derivative with respect to E_i

$$\frac{\partial Y_i}{\partial E_i} = (\beta Y_i^0 + W_i^s(S_i)\epsilon(S_i)\sigma\beta Y_i^s)/E_i. \tag{14}$$

Finally, we substitute (14) and (7) into the ratio of first-order conditions in (5) and rearrange terms to obtain

$$\frac{E_i}{E_j} = \eta_0 \left(\frac{Y_i^0 + \eta_i Y_i^s - b_i}{Y_j^0 + \eta_j Y_j^s - b_j} \right)^{c-1} \left(\frac{Y_i^0 + \eta_i \chi Y_i^s}{Y_j^0 + \eta_j \chi Y_j^s} \right) \tag{15}$$

---

17. In other cases education may be a less perfect—but still good—proxy for other human capital investments. See Behrman [1987b, in this volume] for more details.

where

$$\eta_0 = a_i/a_j$$
$$\eta_i = W_i^s(S_i)\epsilon(S_i)$$
$$\eta_j = W_j^s(S_j)\epsilon(S_j)$$
$$\chi = 1/\beta + \sigma.$$

With an appropriate stochastic specification and with data on sex, education, own earnings, and spouse earnings for families with both female and male adult siblings, estimates can be obtained of c, b_i, b_j, η_0, η_i, η_j, and χ. Although endowments other than sex play an important role in identifying the curvature of the parental welfare functions, a striking feature of relation (15) is that such endowments do not enter explicitly—which is fortunate since such endowments are generally not reported in available sibling data sets. The parameter η_i depends on the sex of the i-th child, because both the weighting scheme and assortative mating depend on the child's sex; the combination of these two dependencies, but not either one separately, can be tested empirically.

Although the supernumerary weights, $(a_1, \ldots, a_n)$, cannot be identified separately, the dependence of their ratio on the sexes of the i-th and j-th children can be investigated empirically to see if it depends on the sex of the children. Likewise the dependence of the translation parameters, $(b_1, \ldots, b_n)$, on the children's sex can be explored. Thus, whether parental preferences exhibit unequal concern can be determined from estimation of relation (15)— conditional on our assumptions about functional forms.

1.5. Implications of Gender Wage Differentials

One perhaps surprising feature of relation (15) is that gender wage differentials do not appear explicitly. This means that the parameters underlying these differentials, the α's in relations (9) and (10), cannot be estimated directly from relation (15).[18] It does not mean, however, that gender wage differentials leave the allocation of human capital investments unaffected: just as genetic endowments shift the income-possibility frontier, so do gender wage differentials.

Figure 4 illustrates this effect in the original BPT model in which HCD income includes only own earnings and in which parental preferences exhibit equal concern. The solid HCD income-possibility frontier represents a two-child family in which both children are males; it is tangent to the solid indifference curve at point A. Now consider an otherwise identical family in which

18. Of course relations (9) and (10) could be substituted into relation (15) to introduce the α's directly. But that also would introduce other unobserved endowments (G_i, G_i^s), so estimates of the parameters would be biased if endowments are associated with observed included variables.

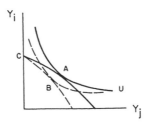

Fɪɢ. 4   Impact of comparative static change in sex of child ᴊ from male to female given sex wage differentials favoring males.

one male child, j, is replaced by an otherwise identical female child; suppose there is a gender wage differential so that $\alpha(S_i) > \alpha(S_j)$, and suppose total allocation of family resources to human capital investment in the children (R) is the same in both families. Under these assumptions the new HCD income-possibility frontier (indicated by the dashed line) lies everywhere interior to the old one except at the point C on the Y_i axis. The girl-boy family's HCD income-possibility frontier is tangent to the dashed parental indifference curve at B. At point B expected HCD income is less for both the i-th and j-th child than at A, the equilibrium point for the boy-boy family. Except in the extreme Rawlsian case in which the parental indifference curve is L-shaped along the 45° ray, the decline in HCD income is greater for the j-th child than for the i-th child because of the parental response to the less favorable labor market options facing females.

These notions can be illustrated algebraically for the simple version of the original BPT model in which the parental welfare function is not displaced from the origin so the translation parameters are 0. In this case, relations (9), (13), and (15) can be solved to obtain reduced-form expressions for the ratio of educational investment and the ratio of HCD income of the i-th child to the j-th child:

$$\frac{E_i}{E_j} = \frac{X_i}{X_j} = \left(\frac{a_i}{a_j}\right)^{1/(1-(\beta+\gamma)c)} \left(\frac{\alpha(S_i)G_i^\delta}{\alpha(S_j)G_j^\delta}\right)^{c/(1-(\beta+\gamma)c)}$$

$$= \left(\frac{a_i}{a_j}\right)^{1/(1-(\beta+\gamma)c)} Z^{c/(1-(\beta+\gamma)c)} \qquad (16)$$

$$\frac{Y_i}{Y_j} = \left(\frac{a_i}{a_j}\right)^{(\beta+\gamma)/(1-(\beta+\gamma)c)} \left(\frac{\alpha(S_i)}{\alpha(S_j)} \frac{G_i^\delta}{G_j^\delta}\right)^{1/(1-(\beta+\gamma)c)}$$

$$= \left(\frac{a_i}{a_j}\right)^{(\beta+\gamma)/(1-(\beta+\gamma)c)} Z^{1/(1-(\beta+\gamma)c)} \qquad (17)$$

BEHRMAN, POLLAK, AND TAUBMAN

Table 1   Dependence on Parental Inequality Aversion Exponents
for Relative Human Capital Investments and Relative HCD Income Distributions

Exponents of $Z=\left(\dfrac{\alpha(S_i)G_i^\delta}{\alpha(S_j)G_j^\delta}\right)$	$c=-\infty$ (Rawlsian case of only parental inequality aversion	$-\infty<c<0$	$c=0$ (Cobb-Douglas case)	$0<c<1$			$c=1$ (Linear case of no parental inequality aversion
				$c<c^*$	$c=c^*$	$c>c^*$	
For E_i/E_j in Relation (16) $c/(1-(\beta+\gamma)\,c)$	$-\infty$	$-\infty<,\ <0$	0	<1	1	>1	>1
For Y_i/Y_j in Relation (17) $1/(1-(\beta+\gamma)c)$	0	$0<,\ <1$	1		>1		>1

where Z is defined by

$$Z = \frac{\alpha(S_i)}{\alpha(S_j)}\ \frac{G_i^\delta}{G_j^\delta}.\tag{18}$$

These expressions show that the gender wage differentials, $\alpha(S_i)/\alpha(S_j)$, affect relative parental investments in human capital and relative HCD incomes in a manner exactly analogous to the relative earnings impact of endowment differentials, $(G_i/G_j)^\delta$. When the gender wage differential favors males, comparing the boy-boy family with girl-boy family is equivalent to investigating the effect of an increase in Z on these ratios.

The sign and magnitude of the exponent of Z is critical. If endowments are important (so $\delta > 0$) and if the earnings production functions exhibit nonincreasing returns to scale (so $\beta + \gamma + \delta \leq 1$), then the sum of the earnings elasticities with respect to the human capital investments is less than 1 (i.e., $\beta + \gamma < 1$).[19] This, together with the limit on the range of c to assure a maximum (i.e., $c \leq 1$), implies that the denominator in the exponents of (a_i/a_j) and Z is strictly positive. Other properties of these exponents depend critically on the extent of parental inequality aversion (c), as indicated in Table 1.

At the Rawlsian extreme ($c = -\infty$) parents are concerned only with equality. Thus they devote all of their human capital investments to the child for whom the combination of relative wage differentials and endowments otherwise would result in the lower HCD income; they pursue this strategy until their resources are exhausted or until equality in HCD incomes is achieved. In the Rawlsian case the distribution of parental resources between the i-th and

---

19. This is a sufficient, but not a necessary condition. Increasing returns to scale are admissible as long as $\beta + \gamma + \delta - 1 < \delta$.

j-th child is the same in the boy-boy family as in the girl-boy family provided the sign of $(Z - 1)$ is the same in both. If the sign of $(Z - 1)$ differs (e.g., because of sufficiently strong gender wage differentials favoring males), then the two families follow radically different strategies, with the girl-boy family investing only in the girl.[20]

Between the Rawlsian extreme and the Cobb-Douglas case ($-\infty < c < 0$), parental inequality aversion is strong enough that the child less favored by the combination of endowments and gender wage differentials receives greater human capital investments than the other child. This attenuates the relative HCD income impact of Z, but does not completely offset it. Comparing the boy-boy family with the girl-boy family, we find a shift in resources from the i-th to the j-th child, but there is a switch from the i-th child receiving more resources to the j-th child receiving more resources only if Z changes from less than 1 to greater than 1.

In the Cobb-Douglas case ($c = 0$), equity and efficiency concerns are balanced so that human capital investments are distributed independently of Z (e.g., the exponent in relation (16) is 0), and relative HCD incomes are proportional to Z (e.g., the exponent in relation (17) is 1). Comparing the boy-boy family with the girl-boy family, we find that resource allocation is identical; this implies a shift in the distribution of relative HCD income away from the j-th child and toward the i-th child proportional to the gender wage differential $(\alpha(S_i)/\alpha(S_j))$.

Between the Cobb-Douglas case and the linear extreme ($0 < c < 1$), parental concern for efficiency outweighs concern for equity. In this case parental human capital investments result in greater relative inequality in HCD incomes than would result directly from the endowment differences and gender wage differentials that are reflected in Z. That is, in these cases parents are so concerned with efficiency that they respond to endowment differences and gender wage differentials by investing so as to increase inequality of HCD income. Comparing the boy-boy family with the girl-boy family, we find that the value of Z is lower and the HCD income of the i-th child is higher. Whether this implies more or less HCD income inequality in the girl-boy than in the boy-boy family depends on whether Z moves closer to or further from 1.

On the linear side of the Cobb-Douglas case parents allocate human capital investments so that HCD incomes are distributed more unequally than they would be due to Z alone, but this does not imply that they invest more human capital in the child already favored by fortune in terms of endowment differences and the gender differential. Between the Cobb-Douglas and linear cases

20. See equation 18. It is possible that the endowment of the j-th child is larger than that of the i-th child, but the gender wage differential is large enough for $\alpha(S_i)/\alpha(S_j) > (G_j/G_i)^\delta$.

there exists a value of c, c^*, at which human capital investments are distributed exactly in proportion to Z:

$$c^* = 1/(1 + \beta + \gamma). \tag{19}$$

Given that $0 < \beta + \gamma < 1$, c^* can be bounded more narrowly to be between 0.5 and 1, with a value closer to 1 the smaller is $\beta + \gamma$.[21] For $0 < c < c^*$, human capital investments are distributed more equally than the impact of the endowment and gender wage differentials in Z (e.g., the exponent in relation (16) is less than 1), even though HCD income is distributed more unequally. For $c > c^*$, both human capital investments and HCD income are distributed more unequally than the factors in Z. Comparing the boy-boy family with the girl-boy family, the distribution of human capital resources depends on whether c is greater than, less than, or equal to c^*. When c is less than c^*, there is a relative shift in resources toward the j-th child (when c is greater than c^*, resources shift away from the j-th child; when $c = c^*$, there is no impact).

This discussion has focused on the original BPT model because explicit expressions cannot be derived for the generalized BPT model. Behavior in the generalized model can be discussed in general terms. First consider the case in which the weight on the spouse earnings (W_i) is 1, the proportion of the j-th child's adult life that he or she is expected to have an earning spouse (D) is 1, and assortative mating on human capital is perfect in the sense that $\eta(S_i)$ and σ in relation (12) both are 1. In this case, even if there are gender wage differentials, the HCD income-possibility frontier in the boy-boy family is identical to that in the girl-boy family: although own earnings are higher in the boy-boy family, the higher spouse earnings in the girl-boy family exactly offset this difference.

All other cases fall between this case and the original BPT model.[22] A lower weight on spouse earnings, a smaller proportion of the j-th child's adult life that he or she is expected to have an earning spouse, and a mating rule that is less assortative on human capital, all imply results closer to the original BPT model.[23] For these intermediate cases the flavor of the above comparisons of the boy-boy family with the girl-boy family on parental inequality aversion (c) and on the own earnings productivity of human capital investments ($\beta + \gamma$) is

21. That is, the less effect human capital investments have on earnings, the higher is the value of c^*.

22. We are assuming here that assortative mating on human capital investments is nonnegative. Were it negative, then the generalized BPT model could lead to a HCD income-possibility frontier inside of that for the original BPT model. Empirically, however, assortative mating on education is positive in all societies for which we have seen correlations.

23. The generalized BPT model reduces exactly to the original one if W_i, D, or assortative mating is 0.

similar, though the details hold more closely the closer the generalized BPT model is to the original BPT model.

1.6. Implications of Unequal Concern

Figures 1 and 3 suggest that the effect of unequal concern is to shift human capital investments away from children of the disfavored sex toward children of the favored sex. The shift in human capital investments shifts relative HCD income toward children of the favored sex, and the magnitude of this shift is larger the more effective are human capital investments (i.e., the larger is $\beta + \gamma$).

The dependence of parental resource allocation on the supernumerary weights (a's) favoring one sex appears to be positive in (16), but the extent of the dependence is not immediately obvious because of the induced change in the HCD incomes. For the original BPT model, however, the exact relation is clear from relation (15). The allocation of educational resources is positively associated with, but less than directly proportional to, the ratio of these weights in the generalized BPT model.

The dependence of parental resource allocation on the translation parameters can be seen by taking the derivative of relation (15) with respect to b_i:

$$\frac{\partial(E_i/E_j)}{\partial b_i} = -(c - 1)K \tag{20}$$

where K is positive. At the linear extreme parents do not care about distribution among their children; in this case c is 1 and this derivative is 0. Hence, in the linear case changing the displacement from the origin has no impact—hardly surprising, since in this case the parents do not trade off equity against efficiency. For all other admissible values of the parental inequality aversion parameter, this derivative is positive. Parents allocate more resources to a child of the sex with the larger translation parameter, because of diminishing marginal utility to supernumerary HCD income.

When parental preferences exhibit unequal concern (in either the supernumerary weights or the translation parameters), the increased resources devoted to children of the favored sex result in increased relative HCD income for that child in the generalized BPT model; unfortunately, we cannot express the general result in a simple and illuminating algebraic manner. For the simple version of the original BPT model in relation (17) (i.e., the version in which the translation parameters are 0), however, the exact impact of unequal concern manifested in the supernumerary weights is clear: relative HCD incomes change less than proportionately to the ratio of these weights, and change less, in relative terms, than the allocation of human capital. HCD income is less responsive than human capital because the earnings production function exhibits diminishing returns to changes in human capital inputs when endowments are held fixed (i.e., $\beta + \gamma < 1$). For the same reason, in the generalized BPT model the impact of unequal concern on the relative HCD incomes is less than proportional to its impact on the allocation of human capital.

2. Data and Estimates

2.1. Data

We use a new data set to explore the models of Section 1. These data include information on education, own earnings, and spouse earnings for 258 adult sibling female-male pairs who are offspring of the twins in the NAS-NRC Twin sample.[24] We assume that the education decisions were made entirely by the parents.[25] We use adjusted reported earnings to represent the expected earnings used by the parents in their human capital investment decisions. The adjustment is to correct for age differentials. We ran separate equations for each sex as a function of age and its square and then adjusted each observation for the impact of any age differential from the mean. The use of such adjusted observed earnings instead of unobserved expected earnings introduces measurement error which we assume results in a multiplicative lognormal stochastic term in relation (15).

The data are summarized in Table 2. For both education and own earnings the means are statistically less at the 5% level for female respondents than for male respondents. The mean spouse earnings are greater for female respondents than for male respondents, which is consistent with the hypothesis that the nominal income gains from marriage are greater for women than for men.

2.2 Selectivity Issues

One selectivity issue is whether the adult offspring in the NAS-NRC offspring data set are a random draw from their age cohort. This sample tends to be somewhat more educated and have higher earnings than a random sample. The more relevant question, however, is whether this sample results in structural estimates similar to those that would result from a random sample. Behrman and Taubman [1985, in this volume] estimate the rates of returns to education implied by the earnings functions using the larger sample of which the data set

---

24. For details concerning the NAS-NRC Twin sample see Behrman, Hrubec, Taubman, and Wales [1980]. For details concerning the larger offspring sample of about 4000 from which this special subsample was obtained, see Behrman and Taubman [1985, in this volume].

25. If the offspring made some of their own education decisions on the basis of investment calculations, then our estimate of c will be biased toward the linear case.

Table 2 Summary of Distributions of Own Earnings, Spouse Earnings
and Schooling for Male and Female Offspring Respondents

Sex and Variable	Mean	Standard Deviation	Standard Error of Means
Males			
Own Earnings	$20963	$12757	$836
Spouse Earnings	11404	7597	498
Education	15.13	2.36	.15
Females			
Own Earnings	12541	8160	479
Spouse Earnings	22797	15298	898
Education	14.69	2.25	0.13

for this study is a subsample. On the basis of their results, the answer to this question appears to be yes.

A further selectivity issue might appear to arise because we restrict our analysis to the subsample of individuals for whom we have reported earnings data both for themselves and for their spouses. This does not cause a selectivity problem akin to that discussed for female labor force participation by Heckman [1976] and others. In the usual selectivity problem, bias arises because the disturbance term in the earnings function is correlated with that in the labor force participation decision since characteristics like unobserved ability and motivation affect both relations. In the present context, although our data do not report such characteristics, we do incorporate their effects into the analysis through the endowments.

2.3. Bias

In our generalized BPT model, parents consider each child's earnings (or HCD income) and schooling to be choice variables. Behrman and Taubman [1986, in this volume] demonstrate that this induces an upward bias in the estimate of c and a downward bias in the estimate of the ratio of the α's, and show how to eliminate the bias; unfortunately at the time of this writing we do not have the necessary data to correct the bias so we present the biased estimates.

2.4. Testing for Unequal Concern in the Original BPT Model

The original BPT model is a convenient starting point. It is more straightforward and tractable than its generalization and it provides a basis for direct comparison both with the parental inequality aversion estimate for the previous generation presented in BPT [1982, in this volume] and with the estimates obtained from the generalized BPT model.

Table 3   Estimates of Original and Generalized BPT Intrafamilial Models without and with Parental Sex Preferences[a]

Model	Parental Inequality Aversion (c)	Supernumerary Weights (a_i)	Translation Parameters (b_i)		Spouse Weights $(\eta_i = W_i \varepsilon_i)$		$\chi = (1/\beta)+\sigma$	Residual Sum of Squares
		$a_i'^{SEX}$	b_i'	$b_i'^{SEX}$	η_i'	$\eta_i'^{SEX}$		
Original BPT								
Model (1)	.072 (.065)		−7955 (17754)					8.725
(2)	.036 (.010)							8.795
(3)	.069 (.079)	−.005 (.058)	−6663 (18377)	3819 (19000)				8.717
(4)	.033 (.011)	.011 (.016)						8.781
Generalized								
BPT Model (5)	.061 (.023)		906 (583)	2.33 (1.56)			.841 (.047)	8.551
(6)	.059 (.024)	−.104 (.063)	1570 (1046)	−1090 (1531)	4.54 (3.11)	−.716 (.706)	.787 (.065)	8.396

Asymptotic Correlation Matrix of Parameters in Row 6

	c	a'^{Sex}	b'	b'^{Sex}	η'	η'^{SeX}	χ
c	1.00						
a'^{Sex}	.01	1.00					
b'	.25	−.40	1.00				
b'^{Sex}	.29	.09	−.52	1.00			
η'	−.14	−.53	.80	−.60	1.00		
η'^{SeX}	.09	.79	−.73	.53	.92	1.00	
χ	−.12	.57	−.64	.57	−.74	.73	1.00

[a] Beneath the point estimates are the standard deviations.

The top of Table 3 gives estimates of the original BPT model for four cases. The first two rows assume equal concern: the second differs from the first in that the translation parameters—which are insignificant in the first—are constrained to 0. The next two rows are parallel, except that unequal concern is tested with regard to the supernumerary weights and, in the third row, the translation parameters. In each case in which parameters are tested for unequal concern, the test consists of positing that the parameter depends on the sex of the child.[26]

26. For example, we set $b_i = b_i' + b_i'' SEX_i$, where SEX_i is 0 for females and 1 for males.

The estimated magnitude of the parental inequality aversion parameter does not differ significantly among the alternative specifications. In each case it lies in the range 0.033 to 0.072. When the translation parameters are constrained to 0 (rows 2 and 4), the estimated value of c is significantly greater than the Cobb-Douglas value of 0 and significantly less than the estimate of 0.12 that we presented in BPT [1982, in this volume] for the previous generation. Nevertheless, all four estimates of c are close to our previous estimate, indicating surprising stability in parental inequality aversion across these two generations. Such a value of c implies substantial concern about equity (since it is significantly less than 1) and therefore challenges the Becker and Tomes [1976] wealth-investment model. All four estimates of c are significantly less than 0.5 and therefore significantly less than c^*, which implies that human capital investments are distributed more equally than is the impact of the endowments and gender wage differentials summarized in Z. Since c is on the linear side of the Cobb-Douglas (though not significantly so for the offspring generation unless the translation parameters are constrained to 0), relative HCD incomes are distributed less equally than the impact of the factors in Z.[27]

Now consider the estimates of the parameters indicating unequal concern. The estimates, based on the original BPT model, suggest that parental preferences exhibit equal concern; in all three cases the absolute value of the point estimate of a parameter associated with unequal concern is less than its standard error. Conditional on the assumptions underlying the original BPT model, therefore, the differential human capital investments and earnings by gender indicated in Table 2 do not reflect unequal concern, but only an optimizing response to gender wage differentials.

2.5. Testing for Unequal Concern in the Generalized BPT Model

The next part of Table 3 gives two estimates of our generalized BPT model in equation (15), the first with equal concern and the second allowing some parameters (a's, b's, η's) to depend on the sex of the child. The generalized BPT model with unequal concern is preferred to the original BPT model. An F test at the 5% level rejects imposing 0 restrictions on five coefficients in row (6) to obtain the original BPT model in row (1).[28] This test is of the composite hypothesis that parents take account of expected spouse earnings and that parental preferences exhibit unequal concern; both are required to reject restricting the coefficients to obtain the original BPT model of row (1). A test of restricting

27. The estimates of c may be biased upwards (see above). Such a bias would reinforce the conclusions in this paragraph since the estimated value of c would exceed the true value of c if there is such as bias.

28. F is 2.2, which is the critical value.

the coefficients in the generalized model with equal concern in row (5) to the original BPT model almost is rejected at the 5% level.[29] Thus, taken together the two generalizations of the BPT model proposed in this paper significantly improve our understanding of intrahousehold allocation of human capital investments.

The estimate of parental inequality aversion in the preferred model in row (6) is .059. This value is significantly greater than the Cobb-Douglas value of 0, and significantly less than the value of 0.12 we obtained for the previous generation with the original BPT model, although it is not significantly different from the other estimates in Table 3 for the offspring generation. It is significantly less than c^* in Table 1, once again, with the same implications as for the original BPT model.

The other estimates have much less precision and substantial correlation among them. The asymptotic correlation matrix of the parameters in row (6) is given in the bottom panel of Table 3; 13 of the 15 correlation coefficients (disregarding those involving c) have absolute values greater than 0.50. Such correlations make it difficult, for example, to untangle the true value of χ from that for η_i, although the point estimate obtained for the former is undoubtedly too low and that for the latter is possibly too high.[30] Similarly, the limited precision limits the conclusions that we can reach about the parental preference parameters. Judging by the ratios of the point estimates to the standard errors, the degree of unequal concern appears stronger for the supernumerary weights than for the translation parameters (the t values are 1.7 and 0.7, respectively). The direction of preference seems more definite: both of the coefficients are negative. Since the dichotomous variable for sex has a value of 1 for boys and 0 for girls, a negative sign means that parental preferences favor girls. Thus, unequal concern partially offsets the labor market incentives to invest more in boys.

3. Conclusion

In this paper, we have generalized the BPT model with unequal concern by dropping the assumption that parental preferences only value returns to edu-

---

29. F is 2.9, with a critical value of 3.0 at the 5% level. In contrast the value of F for restricting the parental preferences in the original BPT model in row (3) to obtain row (1) is only 0.1 (with a critical value of 3.0 at the 5% level) and the value for restricting the parental preferences in the generalized BPT model in row (6) to obtain row (5) is 1.7 (with a critical value of 2.6 at the 5% level).

30. Our point estimates of χ are less than the theoretical lower bound on this parameter: since the definition of χ is $(1/\beta) + \sigma$ where $0 < \beta < 1$ and $\sigma \geq 0$, the *a priori* lower bound on χ is 1, but our estimates are significantly less than 1. Our point estimates for η_i are possibly too high: provided the estimate of the product $\chi\eta_i$ is correct, an underestimate of χ implies an overestimate of η_i.

cation that accrue through the labor market, thus allowing for the possibility that parents also value returns that accrue through the marriage market. That is, in the generalized BPT model the relevant returns to education may include marrying a spouse with higher expected earnings. In this generalized BPT model we have investigated the role of parental preferences and of gender wage differentials on the allocation of human capital investments among children. Gender wage differentials favoring males, like differences in endowments favoring males, can have positive or negative effects on the resources allocated to human capital investments in males, depending on the values of the parameters in the parental welfare function.

Our empirical analysis indicates that gender wage differentials, like endowment differences, are mildly reinforced by the parental allocation of human capital investments. We also have found that marriage market outcomes are significant determinants of the allocation of human capital investments among children. In our empirical analysis we have dropped the assumption of equal concern—which served as a maintained hypothesis in the analysis of male twins in BPT [1982, in this volume]—in order to allow for the possibility that parental preferences may favor girls or favor boys. We have found no evidence that parental preferences favor boys: instead, our empirical analysis indicates that parental preferences either exhibit equal concern or slightly favor girls.

4

Birth Order, Schooling, and Earnings

JERE R. BEHRMAN AND PAUL TAUBMAN

Birth-order effects are posited by many to affect earnings and schooling. We show how such effects can be interpreted to shift either the earnings possibility frontier for siblings or parental preferences. We find empirical evidence for birth-order effects on (age-adjusted) schooling and on earnings for young U.S. adults, though the latter is not robust for all specifications. The examination of intrahousehold allocations suggests that these birth-order differences occur despite parental preferences or prices by birth order favoring later borns, apparently because of stronger endowment effects that favor firstborns.

Economists have become increasingly aware of the important role that childhood plays in conditioning adult socioeconomic success (see Easterlin 1973; Leibowitz 1974; Becker and Tomes 1976; Taubman 1977; Birdsall 1979; Behrman et al. 1980; Becker 1981; Behrman, Pollak, and Taubman 1982, in this volume; Behrman and Wolfe 1984). This awareness has led to intensified efforts to understand the nature of inter- and intrafamilial differences in observed investments—and in subsequent adult outcomes—among children. Models of intrahousehold allocation of such investments have been developed by Becker and Tomes (1976), Becker (1981), and Behrman et al. (1982, in this volume) that explain differences in investments and subsequent outcomes among siblings by differences in endowments and by the nature of parental preferences.

With a few exceptions (e.g., Lindert 1977; Birdsall 1979; Behrman 1988b) economists have not examined the differences in intellectual achievement, school attainment, or earnings by birth order in the family. This is surprising since it is widely believed that mother's time spent with children is an important determinant of child quality and since time budget studies show that the amount of mother's time spent with the children does not increase proportion-

Reprinted from *Journal of Labor Economics* 4, no. 3, pt. 2 (1986): S121–45. © 1986 by The University of Chicago. All rights reserved.

We thank NIH grant no. RO1 HD 16751 ("Family Effects on Child Development") for research support and Richard Voith for excellent research assistance. The usual disclaimer about responsibility applies. We wish to thank the participants (and particularly our discussant, Zvi Griliches) in the conference.

ately with number of children (e.g., Hill and Stafford 1974; Leibowitz 1974), a pattern that suggests that firstborns are treated preferentially.[1]

We suspect that the very limited research by economists on birth-order effects is due to comparative disadvantage and lack of data. On the one hand, psychologists are more familiar with IQ data that often include birth-order questions. Economists tend to be more interested in schooling and earnings or wages. While many large samples with information on wages and schooling are familiar to many economists, few include information on birth order.[2]

In this paper we make use of a new sample to examine, separately for males and females, interfamilial birth-order effects on schooling and earnings and birth-order effects on intrafamilial allocation. For this special sample we know the person's birth order because parents, who were studied earlier, provided us with a roster of their adult children. The sample also has the special adult sibling data required for our intrahousehold investigation.

I. Why to Expect Birth-Order Effects

In this section we consider biological and economic reasons why birth-order effects might be found. First, birth defects increase with mother's age at birth. Thus there is a tendency for later-born (higher-order) sibs to start life with lower genetic endowments. Second, the incidence of dizygotic multiple births increases with mother's age.[3] Twin children tend to be subject to more competition for biological support in the womb and for other support after birth because of the larger number of siblings, and they also tend to be higher in the birth order. Multiple births when the mothers are older also mean that such children are more likely to result in a family size above the desired level, with

1. Enough parental learning by doing or sufficient increasing returns to scale in parenting could be compensating, but it seems unlikely that these factors are large enough to offset completely the reported greater time spent with firstborn children. Initial explorations reported in Behrman, Pollak, and Taubman (1984), e.g., have not found evidence of important parental experience effects on child development for the same sample that we use below.

2. This is unfortunate since, in principle, it is not necessary to have expensive adult sibling samples to explore many dimensions of birth-order effects; a random sample of first-, second-, and nth borns would suffice. However, different family sizes may be associated with different social classes, which should be controlled along with family size to obtain the pure effect of birth order. The problems that arise from the lack of controls is one of the major issues raised by two psychologists, Ernst and Angst (1983), in their recent critique of studies that purport to find birth-order effects. Sociologists have done some studies. A recent effort with negative results is Hauser and Sewell (1985).

3. See Cavalli-Sforza and Bodmer (1971) or Behrman et al. (1980). In the latter study of a large U.S. sample of male twins, the fraternal twins average one-half sibs more than the identical twins.

a resulting need to readjust (down) investment strategies in the higher-order children while considerable investments already may have been made in the lower birth-order siblings. Third, in an uncertain world parents do not know the nature of genetic endowments of their prospective children,[4] and many parents have considerable uncertainty regarding the rewards to be obtained from having children. The first child may be very revealing to the parents. If parents get a bad draw or learn that they dislike parenting, they may choose not to have more children. Thus the offspring in an only-child family may be worse off from a genetic or an environmental viewpoint than first- or even later-born children in large sib groups, as is sometimes found in IQ studies (Zajonc 1976).[5] On the other hand, if the first child is a good draw and the parents continue to have further children, the draw on these children is not likely to be as good on average as for the first child.

Psychologists have provided additional theories. Firstborns, they argue, grow up in an adult-oriented environment and try harder to imitate their parents. Arguments of this sort date back to Galton (1874).

More recently, Zajonc (1976) and his colleagues have presented a more comprehensive "confluence" model to explain why birth-order effects for intelligence appear if subjects are tested at some but not at other ages. This theory might explain why firstborns in families of small sizes have greater teenage intelligence test scores than do only children.

Zajonc's model contains two essential ingredients: (1) one's own intelligence is influenced by the average family environment (the average intelligence of all the family members) and (2) older children learn more from teaching younger children than the younger children gain. The first element is used to explain a number of phenomena. For example, the average family environment declines with the birth of a new child who begins life as a blank sheet with intelligence (not IQ) of zero. This decline in the average family environment causes an immediate reduction in intelligence of older children. Zajonc's second element also explains why a child with younger siblings soon enters onto a steeper intelligence growth path and, as a teenager, scores higher than an only child.[6] Zajonc uses this model to explain why intelligence decreases with family size (adult intelligence is more diluted) and falls off sharply for last borns (there is no one younger to teach). These changes in the level and growth path of intel-

4. For a description of the randomness involved in the genetic inheritance process, see Behrman et al. (1980, chap. 4).

5. We ignore at this point the possibility that the parents can provide more resources to an only child.

6. This assumes that the larger family size in the second case does not cause the elder child in that family to have less resources than the only child.

ligence could affect schooling completed and adult earnings. It is interesting to note that Zajonc neither invokes optimizing behavior nor assumes that parents plan on how to space their children.

Economists, such as Birdsall and Lindert, use a human-capital, time-budget approach to explain birth-order effects. Time spent by mothers with children is thought to be important in increasing the capabilities of a child and in helping him or her to acquire more schooling. But time is not readily saved and transferred over years. Time-budget studies indicate that time spent per child decreases as number of children increases (see Hill and Stafford 1974; Leibowitz 1974).[7] The oldest child has some periods, particularly during presumably critical early years, when he or she has less competition for mother's time than do younger siblings. Lindert (1977) uses recent time-budget studies from the United States to explore schooling achievements of siblings born at the beginning of this century. Birdsall (1979) uses a similar framework to investigate more recent schooling achievements in Colombia.

Many economists also have suggested that investment in human capital can be inhibited by capital market imperfections. It often is argued that major advances in development occur when children are young. Young children in large families may reach crucial development points when parents have relatively low income and cannot borrow much. Alternatively, when the time comes to make a decision between more schooling and taking a full-time job, younger children may find that their elder siblings have depleted the family savings but are not willing or able to finance their younger sib's education. On the other hand, if there is a large gap in sibling ages, the younger sib may reach this decision point when the parents are closer to the peak of their earnings profile and may find it easier than do older sibs to finance additional years of schooling.

The household production approach provides other reasons for anticipating birth-order effects. With the possible exception of dealing with illnesses, we would expect parents to learn from raising older siblings to the benefit of younger ones much more than vice versa. Moreover, higher-order sibs generally are raised by more mature parents. Such considerations point to higher-order sibs having advantages, ceteris paribus, over lower-order sibs. In Behrman et al. (1984) we examine such possibilities and find age-of-parent effects apparently related to general maturity, but we do not find any effect of years of parenting experience.

If parents invest in children for insurance or for altruistic reasons that depend on the investment returns when the children become adults, it may be sensible

7. These studies and most arguments of this ilk ignore the possibility of joint products, i.e., that a mother can read a story to or can instruct more than one child simultaneously.

to favor lower-order children since the financial or psychic returns are more likely to be available when the parents are still able to enjoy them.[8]

Finally, the nature of parental preferences in combination with life-cycle timing phenomena may result in birth-order effects. For example, diminishing marginal utility with parenting may lead to preferential treatment of lower-order sibs—perhaps, particularly, of firstborns. On the other hand, higher-order sibs—particularly last borns—may be raised at a time when parents are more concerned about insuring perpetuation of the family across generations and less preoccupied about their own career development.

II. A More Systematic Model

The discussion of birth-order effects can be organized more systematically by expanding the Behrman et al. (1982, in this volume) intrahousehold allocation model, where we consider a 1-period problem in which parents maximize a utility function defined over their own consumption and the expected earnings capacity of each child. The earning capacity of each child depends on his or her endowments and human-capital investments, the earnings augmenting power of which is subject to diminishing returns. Parents face a money budget constraint in which their income equals the value of their consumption and expenditures on investment in children. This is because financial bequests and inter-vivos gifts are either so small as to be ignored, which holds for bequests from a majority of descendants (e.g., Blinder 1973), or they enter the parents' utility function separably from earnings.[9] Parental consumption also is assumed to enter into their utility function separably from the expected earnings capacity of the children.

The parental maximization problem, therefore, is to decide on the investments (say, schooling, S_i) in each of their n children to maximize the parental subutility function defined over each child's expected earnings (Y_i) in relation (1), subject to constraints provided by the earnings production function in relation (2) and to the partial budget constraint for total expenditures (T) for investment in schooling at the price (P_i^s) in relation (3). Earnings are a function of both human-capital investments (S_i) and initial endowments (E_i):

$$U = U(Y_1, \ldots, Y_n), \tag{1}$$

$$Y_i = Y_i(S_i, E_i), \tag{2}$$

$$\Sigma P_i^s S_i < T. \tag{3}$$

8. We thank our colleague, Edward Buffie, for suggesting this possibility.

9. This later assumption is not trivial but seems to be at least as consistent with available empirical evidence (particularly after the recent work of Menchik [1979, 1988]) as the nonseparable assumption favored by Becker and Tomes (1976).

Assuming that the functions have the standard desirable properties so that an interior maximum exists, the first-order conditions imply that

$$\left(\frac{\partial U}{\partial Y_i} \cdot \frac{\partial Y_i}{\partial S_i}\right) \Big/ \left(\frac{\partial U}{\partial Y_j} \cdot \frac{\partial Y_j}{\partial S_j}\right) = \frac{P_i^s}{P_j^s}. \tag{4}$$

The advantage for estimation of (4) is that the unobserved family-specific Lagrangian multiplier cancels out. With specific assumptions about the form of the utility function in (1), the earnings production function in (2), and the stochastic structure, (4) can be used to obtain estimates of critical parameters in the parental utility function. In Behrman et al. (1982, in this volume) we assume that (1) is a translated constant elasticity of substitution (CES) welfare function and that (2) is a quasi-Cobb-Douglas form:

$$U = \Sigma a_i (Y_i - b_i)^c, \tag{1a}$$

$$Y_i = S_i^\alpha f(E_i), \tag{2a}$$

where b_i are the translation parameters from the origin above which parents trade off expected outcomes among their children; c is the parental inequality aversion parameter for such trade-offs, with $c \to 1$ implying pure investment or utilitarian preferences with no concern about inequality and with $c \to -\infty$ implying Rawlsian preferences with concern only about the worst-off child; a_i are the supernumery parental preference weights; α is the elasticity of expected earnings with respect to schooling; i refers to the ith child; and f is a function of endowments (genetic and environmental). In this case, relation (4) becomes

$$\ln\left(\frac{S_i/Y_i}{S_j/Y_j}\right) = (c - 1)\ln\left(\frac{Y_i - b_i}{Y_j - b_j}\right) + \ln\left(\frac{a_i P_j^s}{a_j P_i^s}\right). \tag{4a}$$

One property of this explicit formulation is that the endowments (E_i) do not enter (4) directly. In Behrman et al. (1982, in this volume) we present estimates of equation (4a) using data for fraternal male twins. We assume that the parents have equal concern about the twins ($a_i = a_j$, $b_i = b_j$) and that they face identical prices for them ($P_i^s = P_j^s$).

Some of the critical features of birth-order effects can be clarified by the graphical representation in figure 1. This figure illustrates the Behrman et al. (1982, in this volume) model with equal concern, which is reflected in the symmetry of the parental preference curves around the 45-degree ray from the origin. The maximizing outcomes for Y_i and Y_j are given by the tangency of the parental preference curves with the expected earnings possibility frontier. Unless the parents have L-shaped preference curves this tangency generally is not located on the 45-degree ray from the origin even though the parents are assumed to have equal concern. The tangency is not on the 45-degree ray be-

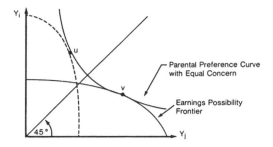

FIG. 1   Behrman et al. (1982, in this volume) intrahousehold allocation model with parental equal concern and alternative earnings possibility frontiers.

cause the earnings possibility frontier generally is not symmetrical around the 45-degree ray because of differential endowments or schooling prices between the ith and jth children. Such differentials permit estimation of the parental preference surface (conditional on the prior specification of the earnings production function); since these differentials vary across pairs of children, the tangencies of the earnings possibility frontiers for different pairs of children trace out the parental preference surface (e.g., the dashed line in fig. 1 indicates greater endowments and/or lower schooling prices for the ith child relative to the jth child than in the solid curve, with a tangency at u instead of at v). The Behrman et al. (1982, in this volume) framework can be extended to incorporate birth-order effects that alter either the earnings possibility frontier or parental preferences.

Birth-Order Effects and the Earnings Production Possibility Frontier

The solid earnings possibility frontier in figure 1 may reflect a number of birth-order effects, each now described, ceteris paribus. (1) If birth defects and multiple births are more associated with higher birth order, on the average, j refers to the lower birth order because of endowment differentials. (2) If parental time is critical in early child development, j refers to firstborns. (3) If unanticipated births cause the resource constraint per child to be tighter than previously anticipated for higher birth-order children, j refers to the lower birth-order child. (4) If there are Zajonc confluence effects, j refers to the lower birth-order children, particularly firstborns. (5) If the present discounted value of earnings is relevant because of insurance effects or because the parents will receive more satisfaction from actually seeing their children's successes, j refers to a lower birth-order child. (6) If household productivity in raising children improves either because parents learn by parenting or because of general maturity, j refers to the higher birth-order child. (7) If there are capital market imperfections and if typical life-cycle earnings paths constrain more severely investments in lower birth-order children than in higher birth-order children, j refers to the higher birth-order child.[10]

These considerations indicate how birth-order effects may alter the earnings possibility frontier among siblings to favor the jth child and, therefore, human-capital investments and earnings outcomes. However, these effects may be off-setting, with the first five increasing earnings possibilities relatively for the lower birth orders, while the last two increase such possibilities for the higher birth orders.

But this framework also points to the importance of the shape of the parental preference curves in determining the impact of birth-order effects on human-capital investments and of adult outcomes among children. If parental inequality aversion is limited (and the parental preference curves relatively flat), the maximizing allocations of human-capital investments reinforce birth-order effects. If parental inequality aversion is strong and the preference curves relatively sharp cornered, the opposite is the case.

These notions can be illustrated explicitly in the special case in which the parental subutility function in (1a) is not translated from the origin, the expected earnings production function is Cobb-Douglas, and all birth-order effects on the production of earnings for given schooling levels are collapsed into endowments (E_i):

$$U = \Sigma a_i Y_i^c, \tag{1b}$$

$$Y_i = S_i^\alpha E_i^\beta. \tag{2b}$$

Then the optimizing conditions can be solved to obtain

$$\frac{S_i}{S_j} = \left(\frac{a_i P_j^s}{a_j P_i^s}\right)^{1/(1-\alpha c)} \left(\frac{E_i}{E_j}\right)^{\beta c/(1-\alpha c)}, \tag{5}$$

$$\frac{Y_i}{Y_j} = \left(\frac{a_i P_j^s}{a_j P_i^s}\right)^{\alpha/(1-\alpha c)} \left(\frac{E_i}{E_j}\right)^{\beta/(1-\alpha c)}. \tag{6}$$

If there are no price differences across children and if parents have equal concern, the first terms on the right sides are equal to one. Under these assumptions, the birth-order productivity effects, operating through the relative endowments, depend on the elasticity of earnings with respect to birth-order effects (β) and schooling (α) and on parental inequality aversion (c). A critical value of the parental inequality aversion parameter in the Cobb-Douglas case

10. We are combining the differential budget constraints for different periods into the 1-period story of our model by changing the resources available over the parental life cycle for different children.

of zero, in which case schooling is equalized and relative earnings are proportional to $(E_i/E_j)^\beta$. If c is greater than zero, schooling ratios reinforce the birth-order effects so that the earnings ratio is even more unequal than it would be with birth-order effects alone (and no induced schooling investments). If c is less than zero, schooling is allocated to favor the child not favored by the birth-order effects.

A further extension of the Behrman et al. (1982, in this volume) model can test for Zajonc-type confluence effects insofar as they operate through cross-sibling schooling effects on the earnings production functions. For example, assume that the expected earnings of each child depends not only on one's schooling investment but also on that of siblings because of sibling interactions. In the two-sibling case, the quasi-Cobb-Douglas earnings production function becomes

$$Y_i = S_i^{\alpha_i} S_j^{\gamma_j} f(E_i). \tag{2c}$$

The ratio of the first-order conditions yields

$$\frac{P_2^s}{P_1^s} \left[\frac{a_1(Y_1 - b_1)^{c-1}\alpha_1 Y_1 + a_2(Y_2 - b_2)^{c-1}\gamma_1 Y_2}{a_1(Y_1 - b_1)^{c-1}\gamma_2 Y_1 + a_2(Y_2 - b_2)^{c-1}\alpha_2 Y_2} \right] = \frac{S_1}{S_2}. \tag{4b}$$

If there is parental equal concern across birth orders so that $a_1 = a_2$, tests can be conducted to see if the cross-sibling effect of the elder child's schooling on the younger child exceeds that of the younger child on the elder child (i.e., if $\gamma_1 > \gamma_2$).

Birth-Order Effects and Parental Preferences

Thus far we have assumed parental equal concern across birth orders. However, parents may prefer some birth orders over others because of diminishing marginal utility or because of life-cycle patterns in interests in child raising versus other activities. This implies parental preference curves that are not symmetrical around the 45-degree ray. Figure 2 gives an illustration of parental preferences for the child of birth order j.

Such parental unequal concern according to birth order can be represented by letting the supernumery weights (a's) or the translation parameters (b's) depend on birth order. Estimation of this model can test directly for parental preferences regarding birth order insofar as they affect human-capital investments or expected earnings for their children.[11]

---

11. Whether or not there are these birth-order effects, there may be birth-order effects regarding bequests. At least for high-income U.S. families, however, Menchik (1979) reports no evidence of such effects.

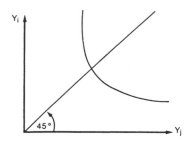

FIG. 2   Parental preference curve favoring jth born.

The effect of parental preferences favoring the jth child in the supernumery weights is immediately evident in (5) and (6): for a given effect of the endowment and price ratios, preference for a given birth order shifts both optimal schooling and earnings ratios to that child in less than direct proportion to the ratio of the preference weights. The shift is less in the earnings ratios than in the schooling ratios if the elasticity of earnings with respect to schooling (α) is less than one, as almost surely is the case if endowments are important in producing earnings (i.e., if $\beta > 1$). Note that such shifts occur for all degrees of parental inequality aversion. Even if parents are extremely inequality averse so that their preference curves are L-shaped, they may prefer one child over the other so that the loci of the L-shaped preference curves are not along the 45-degree ray but along a ray from the origin on the side of the 45-degree ray that pertains to the favored birth order.

Birth-Order Effects, Family Size, and Family Background

In their recent survey of birth-order effects, Ernst and Angst (1983) criticize many studies that fail to control for family size and family background. Higher birth orders, for example, are only observed for larger families that have different child quantity/child quality trade-offs. If so, then birth-order effects from interfamilial data may be reflecting only differential child quality/quantity shadow prices across families and not within family birth-order effects.

These considerations can be interpreted in figure 1. Family size and family background alter the location of the earnings possibility frontier for the ith versus the jth child. Ceteris paribus, this frontier moves to the origin with a larger or less well endowed household.

Taste Heterogeneity, Stochastic Considerations, and Biases

When the parents choose an allocation, they pick the ratios of both schooling and expected earnings. Suppose there is heterogeneity in tastes, with the average curve yielding A as a tangency in figure 3 but with a tangency for a par-

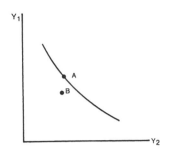

FIG. 3　Average outcomes and a deviation arising from random differences in utility or production function.

ticular family at B, at which point the second sib in the second family has less schooling and earnings than has the second sib in an average family. Now let us consider the bias obtained in an OLS (ordinary least squares) nonlinear regression. Consider the schooling ratio to be the dependent variable. Denote the natural logarithm of the ratio (with b subtracted from earnings) by small letters. Then the equation to be considered is $s_j = cy_j + w_j$, which is simply (4a) rewritten with the last term suppressed. The expected value of the least square estimate (for any value of b) is given by

$$\text{plim}(\hat{c}) = \frac{\text{plim } \Sigma s_j y_j}{\text{plim } \Sigma y_j^2} = \frac{\text{plim } \Sigma (cy_j + w_j) y_j}{\text{plim } \Sigma y_j^2}$$

$$= \text{plim}(c) + \frac{\text{plim } \Sigma w_j y_j}{\text{plim } \Sigma y_j^2}. \quad (7)$$

Now the w_j can be written as $u_j + v_j$, where v_j consists of measurement error arising, for example, from differences between lifetime expected earnings and the realization in any year and where u_j represents the error arising from taste heterogeneity. We make the standard assumption that v_j and y_j are uncorrelated. For (2b), each unit decrease in s_j caused by heterogeneity results in an α reduction in y. Thus plim $\Sigma w_j y_j = $ plim $\Sigma \alpha y_j^2$. Therefore, plim($\hat{c}$) equals $c + \alpha$ and is biased up. The variable α is no greater than one in this model; we have estimated it to be about .25 using data on identical twins.

There are two other cases to be considered. The first is where there is error in the income possibility frontier. However, if we still have the frontier, including errors tangent to the utility function, we merely observe points such as A and B in figure 3, and the same analysis goes through.

The second additional case arises because some groups of parents deviate from the "average" by preferring one birth-order position over another. The situation is shown in figure 4. The "error" still affects both s and y. Let an observed percentage change in a_i/a_j be denoted by Δ. Using (5) and (6), we

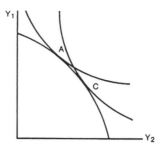

FIG. 4   Differences in choices arising from differences in preferences toward birth order.

note that a Δ change in a_i/a_j leads to an equilibrium change in y of $\beta\Delta$. Thus the plim $\Sigma w_j y_j = \beta \Sigma y^2$ and the plim of $\hat{c} = c + \beta$. No estimates of β are available, though from (2) it must be positive. If there are constant returns to scale in (2) and if α is .25, β would be .75.

It is possible to obtain unbiased estimates of the parameters if there are measures of the endowments. In such a case we can estimate equations (5) and (6). If the a's or the prices differ within a family, the estimated parameters can be solved for all the structural coefficients. Even if the a's and the prices are the same in a family, we can use the endowment coefficients to obtain an estimate of c. We are assembling data on test scores and grade point averages, which we will use in subsequent research to estimate this model.

III. The Data

Most data sets that have information on the completed schooling and earnings or wages of individuals have neither the individual's birth order nor the number of siblings. We have developed a data set that has this information plus data on some obvious controls, including parental education and income. As shown below, our sample is more educated and better paid than is the corresponding population. Nevertheless, we are not aware of any reason why we should expect differential bias to first- or nth-born individuals in this sample.

The data set that we use consists of the twins in the National Academy of Science/National Research Council (NAS/NRC) twin sample and their adult offspring. The twin sample is described extensively in Behrman et al. (1980). The offspring sample was collected in three stages. In 1977 a pilot project was conducted in which about one in seven twins in the NAS/NRC sample were mailed letters that explained the project, requested names and addresses of all adult offspring (including stepchildren and adoptees), and included a sample copy of the questionnaire. The offspring identified in this way were sent a letter and a questionnaire that was followed up twice if there was no response. The pilot project yielded 382 replies from offspring. A full-scale mail survey, fol-

Table 1 Means and Variances of Selected Variables in Offspring Sample

Variable	Number of Observations	Mean	Standard Deviation
Father's current wife is mother	3,668	.9	.3
Sex*	4,066	1.5	.5
Year of birth	4,061	1953.3	4.6
Schooling	3,986	14.7	2.2
Schooling of spouse	2,127	14.5	2.4
Schooling of father	2,804	13.4	3.1
Schooling of mother	2,811	12.7	2.7
1980 yearly earnings (in $1,000s)	3,768	14.3	15.8

*1 = male; 2 = female.

lowing the same methodology as in 1977, was initiated in 1981. In addition, 237 offspring who had not yet responded to the mail survey were interviewed in 1982 in a telephone survey with a shortened questionnaire. The offspring sample combines all three sources.

This paper uses data from about 4,000 offspring and their parents, with the offspring data collected mostly in 1981. Table 1 contains some summary statistics about the individual offspring whose responses are analyzed in this paper. The average age of the respondents is about 28, their average education is 15 years, and their average earnings are about $14,000 per year.

In the 1980 census the median education of people in the age range of 25–35 was 12.9 years, while in our sample the median education is 15 years. This suggests that the offspring are not a random draw from the population, which is not surprising since their fathers were somewhat above average in education and earnings (see Behrman et al. 1980, chap. 4). Moreover, it is not uncommon for mail surveys to be answered selectively. To examine the possibility of such selectivity, we calculated means and standard deviations for parents with offspring responding and for parents with no offspring responding. As is shown in table 2, the respondents tend to come from wealthier and larger families and to have more-educated mothers, but the differences are not large except for number of offspring.

The NAS/NRC twin sample for the respondents' parents is not a random draw of the population but yields regression results for individuals similar to those from random samples drawn in the same time period (see Behrman et al. 1980, chaps. 5–6). To examine whether this is the case for the offspring, we estimate a standard Mincerian semilog earning function for the responding male nonstudent offspring:

$$\ln Y = 7.80 + .082\ S + .15\ EXP - .0052\ EXP^2, \quad \bar{R}^2 = .23,$$
$$\quad (62.3) \quad (10.6) \quad (14.6) \quad (8.3)$$

Table 2   Selected Variables on Parents with Offspring Reporting
and Parents with No Offspring Reporting

Variable	Parents with Reporting Offspring		Parents with No Reporting Offspring	
	Means	Standard Deviations	Means	Standard Deviations
Education:				
Father	13.4	3.2	13.2	3.2
Mother	12.7	2.7	11.4	4.3
Earnings (in $1,000s)*	17.2	13.1	16.0	13.2
Age*	60.1	2.9	60.1	2.9
Hours normally worked*	44.5	11.6	43.3	12.9
Number of offspring of parents	3.1	1.5	2.7	1.6
Religion:				
% Jewish	5.5	. . .	4.9	. . .
% Catholic	24.5	. . .	24.2	. . .
% Protestant	67.4	. . .	67.5	. . .

*Fathers only.

where Y is earnings in 1981, S is years of schooling, *EXP* is current year minus year of first full-time work, and absolute t-values are given in parentheses under the point estimates. The coefficient on years of schooling is significant and similar in magnitude to those obtained in random samples in recent years (e.g., Lillard and Willis 1978). The experience variables have the expected signs and are significantly nonzero. Experience has its peak effect in about 15 years, which is younger than in many other samples. But, since the sample has mostly young people, it is not very appropriate for finding this peak.

For within-pair regressions and for estimated means we adjust our data for age or years of work experience. The adjustments are obtained from regressions on age and its square or on comparable variables for years of work experience and place, calculated for everyone at the sample mean. Both sets of regressions intermix life-cycle, secular, and cohort effects.

IV. Estimated Birth-Order Effects

In table 3 we present the years of schooling and natural logarithm earnings by birth order[12] and sex. We have excluded students and those children whose father's current wife is not the child's mother. The birth-order data are taken from a roster of names and birth dates of adult children provided by the father. The total number of children was checked against data on the number of children he had supplied in 1974 or earlier. Few errors were uncovered. If there was a discrepancy, we used the ordering and number given in the roster unless

12. Birth order is calculated without regard to sex. Thus, if the oldest-born male is the second child in the family, he is second born.

Table 3   Mean Offspring Education and Earnings by Birth Order and Sex*

	Average Schooling†	Number of Cases	Average Log Earnings‡	Number of Cases
Sex:				
Male	14.8	1,334	9.73	1,221
Female	14.5	1,559	9.34	1,179
Birth order:				
1	15.0	1,101	9.61	896
2	14.6	898	9.52	747
3	14.3	545	9.53	463
4 or more	13.9	349	9.38	294
Birth order (males):§				
1	15.1	519	9.80	477
2	14.7	413	9.73	377
3	14.5	254	9.71	238
4 or more	14.2	148	9.54	132
Birth order (females):§				
1	14.9	582	9.40	419
2	14.5	485	9.31	370
3	14.1	291	9.33	228
4 or more	13.7	201	9.25	162

*If father's current wife is not child's mother, the child is excluded. Students also are excluded.
†Adjusted for age differences.
‡Adjusted for experience differences. People with zero earnings are excluded.
§Birth order calculated regardless of sex of other siblings.

there were children young enough in 1974 not to be an adult at the time of the survey.

For males the average education declines from 15.1 to 14.2 as we move from firstborns to fourth or later borns. Using a *t*-test, the .8 years difference is significant at the 5% level. The decline in average earnings is even more pronounced, about 6% per position. These differences also are statistically significant.

For females the differences also are large. Firstborn women have 14.9 years of schooling, while fourth- or later-born females have 13.7 years. Restricting ourselves to working women,[13] we observe somewhat erratic declines of about 15% overall in the ln of earnings between firstborns and fourth borns (or more).

Individual Multivariate Estimates of Birth-Order Effects on Schooling and ln Earnings with Background and Family-Size Controls

Estimates of birth-order effects from individual data may confound birth order with family background and family-size effects. Therefore, in tables 4 and 5 we present alternative multivariate estimates for birth-order effects in years of

13. We note that labor force participation selectivity probably is not as great a problem with this cohort as with earlier cohorts since participation rates are much higher (76% for our sample).

Table 4 Individual Multivariate Regression for Birth-Order Effects on Years of Schooling*

	Males				Females			
	1	2	3	4	1	2	3	4
Intercept	-6.98 (2.30)	-4.85 (1.62)	-5.49 (1.77)	-4.04 (1.134)	-9.52 (3.67)	-6.28 (2.43)	-8.82 (3.37)	-6.00 (2.31)
Firstborn	1.17 (3.03)	...	.68 (1.55)	...	1.67 (5.69)	...	1.34 (3.83)	...
Second born	.81 (2.15)	...	.40 (.96)	...	.87 (3.05)	...	.58 (1.77)	...
Third born	.56 (1.50)	...	.24 (.61)	...	.53 (1.85)	...	.31 (.98)	...
Fourth born	.19 (.45)	...	-.030 (.070)	...	.31 (1.01)	...	.18 (.56)	...
Birth order	...	-.26 (4.08)	...	-.17 (2.45)	...	-.42 (7.63)	...	-.37 (5.47)
Age	.54 (2.90)	.52 (2.84)	.57 (3.07)	.55 (3.00)	.70 (4.50)	.66 (4.25)	.72 (4.64)	.67 (4.33)
(Age)²	-.0070 (2.16)	-.0067 (2.08)	-.0076 (2.34)	-.0072 (2.25)	-.011 (4.15)	-.011 (3.89)	-.012 (4.27)	-.011 (3.95)
Father's age†/10	3.47 (1.82)	3.11 (1.64)	3.07 (1.60)	2.76 (1.45)	3.30 (2.06)	2.83 (1.77)	3.14 (1.96)	2.70 (1.69)
(Father's age†)²/100	-.54 (1.74)	-.48 (1.57)	-.48 (1.56)	-.43 (1.42)	-.54 (2.13)	-.47 (1.85)	-.52 (2.05)	-.46 (1.78)
Mother's age†/10	1.51 (2.94)	1.53 (2.99)	1.29 (2.47)	1.32 (2.53)	1.99 (5.03)	1.96 (4.93)	1.88 (4.67)	1.88 (4.65)
(Mother's age†)²/100	-.16 (3.04)	-.17 (3.09)	-.14 (2.64)	-.15 (2.70)	-.17 (4.12)	-.16 (4.03)	-.16 (3.83)	-.16 (3.82)
Father's education	.16 (5.96)	.16 (6.05)	.16 (6.07)	.17 (6.15)	.16 (7.35)	.16 (7.25)	.17 (7.42)	.16 (7.30)
Mother's education	.056 (1.96)	.056 (1.96)	.054 (1.90)	.054 (1.91)	.086 (3.39)	.087 (3.42)	.083 (3.30)	.085 (3.35)
Parental family earnings	.013 (2.67)	.013 (2.70)	.014 (2.85)	.014 (2.85)	.017 (3.84)	.017 (3.82)	.017 (3.91)	.017 (3.86)
Catholic	.17 (1.12)	.17 (1.11)	.28 (1.73)	.27 (1.70)	-.20 (1.62)	-.17 (1.33)	-.13 (1.00)	-.12 (.89)
Jewish	1.20 (3.52)	1.20 (3.52)	1.16 (3.41)	1.16 (3.42)	.93 (3.53)	.94 (3.57)	.93 (3.52)	.94 (3.56)
Other non-Protestant	.021 (.028)	-.013 (.018)	.072 (.095)	.032 (.042)	.21 (.47)	.21 (.46)	-.21 (.47)	-.21 (.46)
Number of sibs + 1	...	...	-.11 (2.28)	-.099 (2.08)	...	...	-.071 (1.76)	-.048 (1.20)
R²	.221	.223	.225	.226	.304	.299	.305	.299
Number of observations	913	913	913	913	1,069	1,069	1,069	1,069

* Absolute t-values are given in parentheses beneath the point estimates.
† Measured at date of birth of the respondent.

Table 5 Individual Multivariate Regressions for Birth-Order Effects on ln Earnings*

	Males				Females			
	1	2	3	4	1	2	3	4
Intercept	3.15 (2.64)	3.26 (2.77)	3.51 (2.91)	3.44 (2.92)	2.69 (1.85)	3.00 (2.08)	2.96 (2.01)	3.16 (2.18)
Firstborn	.086 (.64)	...	-.047 (.30)	...	.25 (1.66)	...	.12 (.64)	...
Second born	.061 (.46)	...	-.051 (.35)	...	.085 (.58)	...	-.028 (.17)	...
Third born	.070 (.54)	...	-.015 (.11)	...	.21 (1.41)	...	.12 (.75)	...
Fourth born	-.005 (.033)	...	-.066 (.44)	...	.070 (.44)	...	.021 (.13)	...
Birth order	...	-.021 (.92)	...	.0039 (.141)	...	-.042 (1.53)	...	-.012 (.35)
Age	.23 (3.47)	.24 (3.57)	.24 (3.59)	.24 (3.68)	.30 (3.71)	.30 (3.67)	.31 (3.83)	.31 (3.78)
(Age)²	-.0030 (2.56)	-.0030 (2.64)	-.0032 (2.69)	-.0032 (2.77)	-.0047 (3.26)	-.0046 (3.20)	-.0049 (3.37)	-.0047 (3.30)
Father's age†/10	.54 (.80)	.52 (.78)	.42 (.62)	.42 (.62)	-.17 (.19)	-.17 (.19)	-.20 (.23)	-.22 (.25)
(Father's age†)²/100	-.11 (.96)	.10 (.93)	-.088 (.80)	-.088 (.80)	.054 (.391)	.055 (.40)	.057 (.41)	.060 (.44)
Mother's age†/10	.42 (2.17)	.43 (2.23)	.36 (1.84)	.37 (1.90)	.073 (.34)	.058 (.27)	.033 (.15)	.016 (.073)
(Mother's age†)²/100	-.049 (2.45)	-.050 (2.52)	-.044 (2.17)	-.045 (2.23)	-.00031 (.015)	-.0015 (.074)	.0031 (.146)	.0051 (.24)
Father's education	.012 (1.14)	.012 (1.16)	.012 (1.20)	.012 (1.21)	-.021 (1.67)	-.021 (1.68)	-.019 (1.58)	-.019 (1.57)
Mother's education	-.010 (.91)	-.011 (.94)	-.011 (.98)	-.011 (.99)	.035 (2.43)	.036 (2.47)	.035 (2.41)	.035 (2.44)
ln parental family earnings	.095 (1.66)	.095 (1.66)	.10 (1.76)	.10 (1.75)	.14 (1.94)	.14 (1.95)	.14 (1.83)	.14 (1.84)
Catholic	.047 (.83)	.045 (.79)	.077 (1.29)	.075 (1.25)	.080 (1.24)	.079 (1.23)	.11 (1.58)	.11 (1.58)
Jewish	-.19 (1.59)	-.19 (1.63)	-.20 (1.69)	-.20 (1.72)	.12 (.95)	.13 (.98)	.13 (.99)	.13 (1.02)
Other non-Protestant	.11 (.33)	.11 (.34)	.13 (.40)	.14 (.41)	-.12 (.40)	-.14 (.45)	-.15 (.46)	-.16 (.52)
Number of sibs + 1	...	...	-.029 (1.70)	-.028 (1.59)	...	...	-.029 (1.29)	-.029 (1.32)
R²	.177	.180	.179	.182	.062	.058	.062	.059
Number of observations	764	764	764	764	729	729	729	729

*Absolute t-values are given in parentheses beneath point estimates.

†Measured at date of birth of the respondent.

schooling and natural logarithm earnings for the offspring, separately, for males and females.

For family background we use the respondent's age, the age and education of each parent, paternal family earnings, and religion. Since we include these variables basically as controls, we do not discuss their coefficient estimates in detail here, but we do note a few major features. Parental family earnings have a significant effect at the standard 5% level[14] in the schooling relations but only at the 10% level in the earnings relations. The intergenerational earnings link, therefore, seems quite limited (see Behrman and Taubman [1985, in this volume] for an extensive exploration of intergenerational links). Likewise, parental education has strong effects in the schooling relations, but in the ln earnings relations only maternal schooling is significant only for females. The latter result may suggest some intergenerational bonding of females. Being Jewish significantly increases schooling but not earnings.[15] Finally, the quadratic in mother's age at time of birth of the respondents tends to have significant effects on schooling and males' earnings, but father's age at time of birth is not significant in most regressions. We interpret these results to be related to maturity and capital market imperfections and life-cycle income paths (for details, see Behrman et al. [1984]). That all the parental variables affect offspring schooling more than earnings reflects a fading of parental effects over the children's life cycle that also has been noted by Hauser and Daymont (1977), Behrman et al. (1980), and Behrman and Wolfe (1984).

We include two alternative representations of birth order: (1) dichotomous variables for being firstborn, second born, third born, or fourth born (with fifth or higher born the excluded category) and (2) a continuous variable with the value of the birth order (i.e., 1, 2, 3, 4, . . .). The first two equations for each sex in both tables contain these variables in addition to the family background controls discussed above and controls for the respondent's own age. They do not include the number of siblings (plus one) since, in a quality/quantity model, the number of siblings is determined simultaneously with the human-capital investment in the children. However, failure to control for family size may confound birth-order with family-size effects. Therefore, the additional equations in both tables include the number of siblings (plus one).[16]

14. We use this level below unless otherwise qualified.

15. In the twin-generation and in the NBER/Thorndike-Hagen sample (Taubman and Wales 1974), which contains men who were born at about the same time as were the twins, the Jewish subsample of the population had substantially greater than average earnings. The vanishing of prior earnings differentials has been observed when contrasting recent immigrants and subsequent generations (Chiswick 1983).

16. Sibs born since 1974 are probably missed in this court because of our data collection procedure, but this should be a very small number and probably had little effect on the environment of the older sibs of interest.

In the equations without the number of siblings, the dichotomous birth-order effects are significant for schooling for first- and second-born males and for the first three orders for females (with the last significant at the 10% level). The continuous birth-order variables are significant in both cases, indicating a decline of .26 years of schooling per unit increase in the birth order for males and a significantly greater (at the 10% level, $t = 1.7$) decline of .42 years of schooling per unit increase in the birth order for females. For ln earnings, in contrast, the coefficients are not statistically significant at the 5% level, though the coefficients of first- and second-born females are significant at the 10% level. Thus for these estimates it appears that again there is a pattern of birth-order effects fading over the life cycle, with somewhat greater persistence (as for maternal schooling) for females. Any birth-order effects appear to favor lower orders or firstborns, though these estimates do not provide guidance by which to select among the various proposed reasons why birth-order effects might make firstborns or the lower orders more productive.

Once the number of siblings is included, birth-order effects remain significant for schooling in the continuous case for both sexes and with dummy variable for females. With the dichotomous variables for females, being a firstborn is associated significantly with an additional 1.3 years of schooling, and being a second born is associated with a significant (at the 10% level) additional .6 years. With the continuous birth-order variable, each higher place in the birth order is associated with a significant decline of .37 years of schooling for females and of .17 for males. These effects appear to be quite robust since they persist with a large number of controls for family size and background. The coefficient of the number of children in the childhood family of the respondent is negative in all the estimates in which it is included, as the discussion above suggests it should be, but the effects are significant by standard tests only for schooling for males.

Several people have asked if the difference in results for birth order and for religion arises because we have used different samples in tables 4 and 5. To examine this possibility, we have reestimated the equations using only those people who reported both schooling and earnings. In these equations, which are not shown, there are small changes in coefficients, but the anomalies remain.

People also have asked if the residuals in the earnings and schooling equations are correlated. There is a statistically significant positive correlation for individuals, which is reduced in size but remains if we eliminate family means. The R^2 varies by equation but is in the range of .010–.025. This positive correlation is consistent with there being common omitted variables in both equations and with the allocation results summarized in (5) and (6).

Table 6 Sibling Estimates of Behrman, Pollak, and Taubman Parental Preference
Intrahousehold Allocation Model with Preference for Firstborn
in Supernumery Weights, Full Sample, and Various Subsamples by Sex*

Sample	Inequality Aversion (c)	Translation Parameter (b)	Birth-Order Effect on Supernumery Weight (a)	Number of Sibling Pairs
All pairs	.048	123	...	1,288
	(7.4)	(4.2)		
	.044	116	−.024	1,288
	(6.8)	(3.9)	(4.7)	
Male pairs	.050	173	...	396
	(4.3)	(3.0)		
	.048	174	−.025	396
	(4.4)	(3.0)	(2.6)	
Female pairs	.064	147	...	358
	(5.3)	(3.2)		
	.055	126	−.034	358
	(4.5)	(2.7)	(3.5)	
Mixed-sex pairs	.042	117	...	639
	(4.4)	(2.5)		
	.039	111	−.019	639
	(4.0)	(2.4)	(2.7)	

*For each sample the first estimate is for the Behrman et al. (1982, in this volume) model in equation (4a) with equal concern ($a_i = a_j$, $b_i = b_j$), and the second estimate allows for preference for firstborns, so $\ln[(a_iP_j^s)/(a_jP_i^s)]$ is represented by a dichotomous variable with a value of one if i is a firstborn and a value of minus one if j is a firstborn). Earnings are corrected for years of work experience, and education is corrected for age. The regressions are weighted so that each parental family is weighted equally. Absolute t-values are given beneath the point estimates.

Intrafamilial Estimates of the Behrman et al. Model without and with Birth-Order Effects

Table 6 gives sibling-pair estimates of the Behrman et al. (1982, in this volume) model in equation (4a) with equal concern and with firstborn preference in the supernumery parental preference weights (a's). The sample uses the greater of schooling or expected schooling for those who are still students. Similar results are found if current students are excluded. These estimates are given for all 1,288 adult offspring pairs for which the necessary data are available and for subsamples of pairs of males only, females only, and mixed sex in case there are interaction effects between birth order and sex.

These results are easily summarized. The estimates of parental inequality aversion (c) range from .039 to .064, with no significant difference, depending on which sample is used or on whether there is a birth-order control.[17] This

17. As discussed earlier, the estimates are biased up because of errors due to the joint determination of both schooling and expected earnings ratios.

range of values is significantly greater than the Cobb-Douglas value of zero and significantly less than the value of .12 obtained for the previous generation in Behrman et al. (1982, in this volume), though not very substantially different. Thus there is some evidence of a slight increase in parental inequality aversion across generations; for both generations the values are slightly on the utilitarian side of the Cobb-Douglas case.

The estimates of the translation parameters (b's) are significantly nonzero with means in the $111–$174 range, without significant differences among the estimates. Such values are very small and are significantly below the value for the previous generation in Behrman et al. (1982, in this volume) when adjusted for inflation.

Interestingly, all the estimates in table 6 suggest a significantly negative effect of being a firstborn. This contrasts with the significantly positive effect of being a firstborn in the individual schooling reactions in table 4. The birth-order effects in the estimates in table 6, as is indicated in relation (4a) above, could reflect either that parents prefer higher birth-order children over the firstborn in the sense that they weigh equal outcomes more for them (i.e., the a_i weights are greater) and/or that the effective schooling prices are higher for firstborns than for subsequent children (i.e., P_i^s is greater for firstborns).[18] The effective price for schooling might be higher for firstborns even if nominal schooling prices are constant, for example, if there are capital market imperfections and if life-cycle income paths imply a tighter resource constraint for firstborns than for later children.[19] Whatever the weights of preferences versus prices in these birth-order effects favoring later-born children over firstborns in terms of intrahousehold allocations, they apparently are outweighed by the various factors discussed in Sections I and II, resulting in firstborns having sufficiently greater endowments (in terms of relation [5]) so that they tend to have greater schooling (table 4).

Table 7 gives estimates of the Behrman et al. (1982, in this volume) model extension discussed with regard to relation (4b) above in which cross-sibling schooling effects are allowed. The sample in this case is 174 sibling pairs from two-children families for which schooling and earnings data are available for both sibs. Because relation (4b) is complicated and because in all the estimates we have explored the translation parameters (b's) are small, we have simplified

18. We cannot identify the relative contribution of these two factors to the negative birth-order effect.

19. The derivation of relation (4a), of course, is within a 1-period model that is, strictly speaking, not consistent with imperfect capital markets. The statement in the text, however, is meant to suggest that the effects of imperfect capital markets and typical, more severe resource constraints early in the life cycle can be approximated by higher effective schooling prices (in terms of forgone parental consumption) for firstborns.

Table 7 Sibling Estimates for Intrahousehold Allocation Model
with Schooling Confluence Effects for 174 Two-Sib Families*

Equation	Inequality Aversion (c)	Cross-Sib/Own Schooling Elasticity (γ/α)	
		Firstborn	Second Born
(1)	.026	...	...
	(2.3)		
(2)	.053	.327	.327
	(.002)	(.002)	(.002)
(3)	.031	.152	.126
	(.001)	(.0005)	(.0004)

*The first estimate is for the Behrman et al. (1982, in this volume) model, the second is for the schooling confluence case in which the ratios of the cross-sib to own schooling elasticities are constrained to be the same in relation (4b), and the third is for the schooling confluence case in which the ratios of the cross-sib to own schooling elasticities vary in relation (4b). In all cases, equal concern is assumed ($a_1 = a_2$, $b_1 = b_2$), the translation parameters are assumed to be zero ($b_1 = b_2 = 0$), and schooling prices are assumed to be identical for the two sibs ($P_1^s = P_2^s$). Absolute t values are given beneath the point estimates.

by assuming equal concern ($a_1 = a_2$, $b_1 = b_2$), no translation from the origin ($b_2 = b_2 = 0$), and no relation between birth order and schooling prices ($P_1^s = P_2^s$).

Since this is a much more limited sample than that used for table 6, in the first row of table 7 we present an estimate of parental inequality aversion for this sample with no cross-sib effects. This estimate is 0.26, which is significantly different from the Cobb-Douglas value of zero and is not significantly different from the estimates in table 6.

The second and third rows allow the cross-sib schooling effects to be non-zero; in the second row the ratio of the cross-sib to own schooling elasticity (γ/α) is constrained to be the same for the two sibs, but it is allowed to differ in the third row. The point estimates suggest that the cross-sib schooling effects may be important—from an eighth to a third of the own schooling elasticities, with that for schooling of second borns. The point estimates for parental inequality aversion are not very different from those in row 1 or in table 6. However, the correlations among the parameter estimates are so high (.99) and the standard deviations are so large that none of the point estimates have much precision.

V. Conclusions

In this paper we have examined birth-order effects on schooling and earnings. We have shown how birth-order effects posited by economists, psychologists, and others can be interpreted to shift either the earnings possibility frontier among siblings or parental preferences. After adjusting for age or work experience we show that there are differences by birth order in both schooling and ln earnings for young adults. The effects on ln earnings become statistically insignificant if there are controls for observed childhood family background characteristics. For schooling, however, the results persist even when we control for family background and family size. The examination of intrahousehold allocations suggests that these birth-order differences occur despite parental preferences or prices by birth order favoring later borns, apparently because of stronger endowment effects that favor firstborns.

Part Two

The Wealth Model, Transaction Costs, and Tied Parental Transfers

5

The Wealth Model: Efficiency in Education and Distribution in the Family

JERE R. BEHRMAN, ROBERT A. POLLAK, AND PAUL TAUBMAN

The "wealth model" of Becker and Tomes (1976) develops and explicates what is now economists' standard model of human capital investment and intrafamily allocation. The efficiency and distributional implications of this model, although distinct, are intimately related. The usual description of the wealth model is straightforward: altruistic parents provide children who have different abilities with different but efficient amounts of human capital, equating the marginal returns to investments in schooling with the return to financial assets; hence, sibs generally receive different earnings. The wealth model, it is said, implies that parents generally "reinforce" differences in their children's "endowments" by investing more in children with larger endowments and then use "transfers" (inter vivos gifts and postmortem bequests) to achieve their distributional objectives. For example, parents with "equal concern" for their children distribute transfers so as to equalize their children's wealth.

As Becker (1981) acknowledged, the wealth model's strong conclusions about efficiency and equity hold only if the level of resources devoted to children is sufficiently high: if parents are not sufficiently rich or sufficiently altruistic to provide all of their children with positive transfers, the wealth model does not imply that human capital investments are efficient. Yet the only alternative to the case in which all children receive positive transfers that Becker examines is the opposite polar case in which parents are so poor or so selfish that none of their children receives transfers. Thus, Becker's analysis of the wealth model does not exhaust its implications.

In this chapter we explore the neglected intermediate cases in which some children receive transfers while others do not. We show that the wealth model does not imply that parental investments in human capital necessarily reinforce differences in endowments. Furthermore, we argue that the distributional implications of the wealth model in the neglected intermediate cases are so im-

The authors thank NIH for support for this study, Judith Goff for editorial assistance, and participants in seminars at Boston University, Brown University, University of Delaware, University of Pennsylvania, Rutgers University, Stanford University, UCLA, Yale University, and Williams College for helpful comments.

plausible as to raise serious doubts about the model's validity. More specifically, we show that the wealth model predicts that, for some range of resources devoted to children, parents make positive transfers to some children and zero transfers to others. We argue that this pattern of transfers to children is inconsistent with the available empirical evidence for the United States, as well as with new evidence that we present.

I. Theory

In the one-child version of the wealth model, the altruistic parents' utility function is $U(\mu, W)$ where μ is the present value of parental consumption and W is the present value of the child's wealth. The child's wealth has two components: the present value of earnings (Y) and the present value of transfers (T), where transfers are the sum of inter vivos gifts and postmortem bequests. Present value calculations are based on a market interest rate (i) that represents the rate of return on financial assets.

The wealth model is a special case of a general altruistic model in which parents obtain utility from the present value of both each child's earnings and the transfers that each child receives. The wealth model owes its name to its assumption that earnings and transfers are perfect substitutes (i.e., only their sum enters the parents' utility function); this assumption is also made in some other altruistic models (e.g., Nerlove, Razin, and Sadka 1987). The separable earnings-transfers (SET) model that we proposed in Behrman, Pollak, and Taubman (1982, in this volume) is an example of an altruistic model that does not make this assumption.

We distinguish between the wealth model in which the parents' utility function depends on the child's wealth and an alternative altruistic model in which the parents' utility function depends on the child's utility. If the child's utility function remains fixed and depends only on the child's wealth, then the utility model reduces to the wealth model if we substitute wealth into the child's utility function. The utility model, however, raises awkward difficulties about cardinal utility even in the one-child case, difficulties that become apparent if we try to restate the model in terms of the child's preference ordering. With more than one child's utility entering the parents' utility function, issues of interpersonal comparability and the aggregation of preferences (as in Arrow's impossibility theorem) arise. To avoid these issues we follow Becker and Tomes and limit ourselves to the wealth model.

Earnings are determined by an "earnings production function" that relates the present value of earnings to the child's endowment (G), which is part genetic, and to human resource investments, hereafter "education" (E): $Y = f(G, E)$. We assume diminishing returns to education. We also assume that parents know their child's endowment when deciding how much to invest in the child's education. Letting R denote the resources devoted to the child, the resource constraint for the one-child family is: $E + T = R$.

The wealth model has strong implications for the allocation of resources between education and transfers. Parents who devote sufficiently high resources to their child invest in the child's education until the marginal rate of return to education (r) equals the market rate of interest (i); thus, parents provide the child with the wealth-maximizing level of education, which we denote by E^*. We denote the implied level of earnings by Y^*: $Y^* = f(G, E^*)$. After providing the wealth-maximizing level of education, parents provide additional resources as transfers. The story has a good Chicago moral: the child receives the socially optimal amount of education—no more, no less.

The conclusion that each child receives the wealth-maximizing level of education depends on the assumption that parents devote enough resources to each child. Parents who are insufficiently wealthy or insufficiently altruistic (i.e., those who fail to place "enough" weight on the child's wealth in their utility function) do not provide their child with the wealth-maximizing level of education. Becker and Tomes recognize this problem, and Becker discusses the issue in his *Treatise on the Family* (1981), where he cites research indicating that "less than 40 percent" of U.S. families make significant transfers to their children (p. 121). Becker and Murphy (1988) argue that these problems of poverty and selfishness can be overcome by public education.

This analysis of the determinants of children's education rests on two additional assumptions that we retain throughout this paper. First, like most of the literature, we ignore all uncertainty including that associated with returns to education. Second, we assume that parents determine the education received by their children and that parents cannot appropriate their children's earnings.[1] A model in which children are passive and parents make all educational investment decisions is consistent with the assumptions that children have no resources and cannot work or borrow to finance their educations.[2] Thus, even in the one-child case, the wealth model's conclusion that children obtain the wealth-maximizing level of education must be qualified to allow for boundary solutions resulting from insufficient wealth or insufficient altruism, for uncer-

---

1. We can replace the second assumption with the assumption that parents cannot borrow to finance children's education at the market rate of interest. If parents could appropriate earnings and borrow to finance education, then even completely selfish parents would provide each child with the wealth-maximizing level of education.

2. An alternative model is one in which children make all educational investment decisions and parents are passive; Becker's investment model can be interpreted as such a model. Allowing both parents and children to be active players in an allocation game yields a more complex model that has not yet been analyzed.

tainty, and for the complications that result from recognizing that children as well as parents are decision makers.[3]

The welfare conclusion that parents provide children with the socially optimal level of education requires an additional qualification: externalities may cause social returns to education to diverge from private returns in either direction. For example, a democratic society may benefit from having an electorate educated beyond privately optimal levels. In contrast, to the extent that education is simply a signaling mechanism, privately optimal levels may exceed socially optimal levels. Hence, the welfare conclusion should be restated: if private returns to education are equal to social returns, then the wealth model implies that parents provide their children with the socially efficient level of education.[4]

Three implications of the wealth model hold regardless of the number of children and regardless of the level of resources parents devote to their children. First, parents never provide transfers to any child receiving less than the wealth-maximizing level of education. If they did, the marginal returns to education would exceed the returns on financial assets, and parents could increase the child's wealth by reallocating resources from transfers to the child's education. Second, parents provide the wealth-maximizing level of education to any child receiving positive transfers. Thus, if all children in a family receive positive transfers, the wealth model implies that all receive the wealth-maximizing level of education. Third, parents never provide any child with more than the wealth-maximizing level of education. If they did, the marginal returns to education would be below the rate of return on financial assets, and parents could increase the child's wealth by reallocating resources from the child's education to transfers.[5]

New issues arise in the wealth model if parents have more than one child. Following Becker and Tomes, we assume that the parental utility function, $U(\mu, W_1, \ldots, W_n)$, is separable and write it as $U^*[\mu, V(W_1, \ldots, W_n)]$. We call V the *parental welfare function* to distinguish it from the U, the *parental utility function*.

---

3. We also assume that parents are the only source of transfers, and we ignore labor-leisure choices and taxes.

4. Under these assumptions, there is no efficiency justification for public subsidization of education for children whose parents are sufficiently wealthy and sufficiently altruistic.

5. Education above the wealth-maximizing level is possible in our SET model and in Pollak's (1988, in this volume) paternalistic preferences model. In the SET model, parents may invest in education beyond the wealth-maximizing level if, for example, they prefer that their children "earn" income rather than clip coupons. Even if parents provide one child with the wealth-maximizing level of education, they may provide more (or less) education to another child to obtain the earnings distribution they prefer. In Pollak's model, parents may invest beyond the wealth-maximizing level because they regard education as a "merit good."

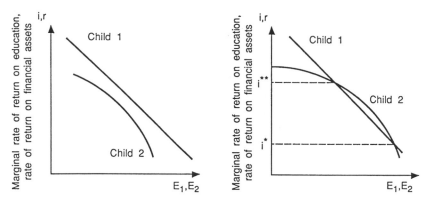

Fig. 1   Marginal returns to education schedules. *a,* With that for child 1 always above that for child 2. *b,* With two intersections, but earnings for child 1 always greater than for child 2.

For a given interest rate, we can rank children in terms of the resources required to give them the wealth-maximizing level of education, E_i^*. We say that child 1 is "more educable" than child 2 if more resources are required to provide child 1 with the wealth-maximizing level of education, that is, if $E_1^* > E_2^*$.[6] Two points require elaboration. First, if the schedule of the marginal returns to education for one child always lies above the corresponding schedule for the other child, as in figure 1*a,* then the identity of the "more educable" child is independent of the rate of interest. If these schedules intersect, as in figure 1*b,* child 2 is the more educable child for rates of return on financial assets between i^* and i^{**}, and child 1 is more educable for other rates of return; thus, if both children receive the wealth-maximizing level of education, which child receives more education depends on the interest rate. Second, if both children receive the wealth-maximizing level of education, the more educable child need not be the child with higher earnings: higher *marginal* returns need not imply higher *average* returns to education.

To examine the characteristics of the wealth possibility frontiers corresponding to different levels of resources devoted to children, we identify four successively greater resource levels. We let R_2^- denote the minimum level of resources required to provide the less educable child with the wealth-maximizing level of education: $R_2^- = E_2^*$. We let R_1^- denote the minimum level of resources required to provide the more educable child with E_1^*: $R_1^- = E_1^*$. Since child 1 is the more educable child, $R_2^- \leq R_1^-$. We let R^* denote the minimum level of resources required to provide both children with the wealth-maximizing level of education: $R^* = E_1^* + E_2^*$. Finally, we let R^+ denote the minimum level of

6. Thus, "more educable," as we use the phrase, means "more expensive" and need not coincide with "more able" in the ordinary language sense.

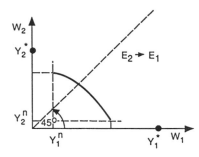

FIG. 2   Very low resource case

resources required to provide both children with the wealth-maximizing level of education *and* to have enough resources remaining to equalize the wealth of the children with transfers: $R^+ = E_1^* + E_2^* + |Y_1^* - Y_2^*|$, where $Y_i^* = F(G_i, E_i^*)$. Clearly,

$$R_2^- \le R_1^- < R^* \le R^{+}.[7] \tag{1}$$

These four resource levels enable us to distinguish five cases:

very low resources:	$R < R_2^-$,
low resources:	$R_2^- \le R < R_1^-$,
moderate resources:	$R_1^- \le R < R^*$,
high resources:	$R^* \le R < R^+$,
very high resources:	$R^+ \le R$.

As resources increase from the very low resource case to the very high resource case, there is a tendency to shift from additional investments in education to additional transfers. We have drawn the figures so that child 1, the more educable child, has greater earnings, except in figures 4*c,* 5*b,* and 6*b* (see below), where the more educable child has lesser earnings.

To identify the regions of the wealth possibility frontier in each case, we consider a sequence of families facing the same opportunities and devoting the same level of resources to their children: we first consider a family whose preferences favor the less educable child so strongly that it invests all resources in child 2, and then we consider a succession of families whose preferences are increasingly favorable to the more educable child until we reach a family that devotes all resources to child 1.

In the *very low resource case* (fig. 2), parents provide no transfers to their children because the marginal returns to education (r_j) are above the returns on financial assets (i) even if all resources are invested in child 2 as at E_2^* (i.e., Y_2^* in the figure). In this case, the trade-off is between E_2 and E_1, and the wealth

---

7. The first equality occurs if E_1^* equals E_2^*, a razor's edge possibility. The last equality holds if $Y_1^* = Y_2^*$, also a razor's edge possibility.

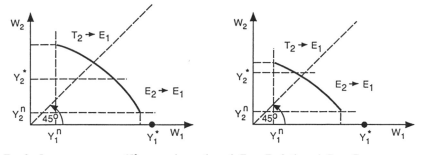

FIG. 3   Low resource case, 45° ray passing a, through $T_2 \to E_1$; b, through $E_2 \to E_1$

model reduces to the SET model of Behrman, Pollak, and Taubman (1982, in this volume). Since educational expenditures are subject to diminishing returns, the wealth possibility set is strictly convex.[8]

The implications of the *low resource case* (figs. 3a and 3b) are similar except that, if all resources are devoted to child 2, E_2^* is invested in education and $R - E_2^*$ is given as transfers. Although the resource constraint permits a family concerned only with child 2 to invest enough in that child's education to reduce r_2 to i, the resource constraint does not permit a family concerned only with child 1 to invest enough in E_1 to equate r_1 to i.

Parents whose preferences favor the more educable child allocate more resources to child 1 and less to child 2. Scanning a sequence of such families, we would observe a reallocation of resources from child 2 toward child 1, with parents reducing T_2 (whose return is i) and increasing E_1 until T_2 reaches zero. Further increases in the education of child 1 must reduce the education of child 2. These reallocations can continue until the resources devoted to child 2 reach zero; even here the educational level of child 1 is less than E_1^*. Within the low resource case, we thus can identify two regions: $T_2 \to E_1$ and $E_2 \to E_1$. Since educational expenditures are subject to diminishing returns, the wealth possibility set is strictly convex.

In the *moderate resource case* (figs. 4a, 4b, and 4c), parents still cannot simultaneously provide both children with the wealth-maximizing levels of education. The frontier consists of three regions between $Y^n{}_1$ and $Y^n{}_2$: $(T_2 \to E_1)$, $(E_2 \to E_1)$, and $(E_2 \to T_1)$. The first two regions are the same as in the low resource case, but now there is a third region that begins at the point at which $E_1 = E_1^*$ (i.e., $Y_1 = Y_1^*$ in the figure). Further reallocations away from child 2 reduce the education of child 2 and increase transfers to child 1. Because edu-

8. If children with no education receive positive earnings, Y_1^n and Y_2^n, then there are two additional regions starting at the axes. Since these regions are of secondary importance for our analysis, we do not discuss them further. Here and throughout the text, our assertion that the wealth possibility set is strictly convex applies only to the region between Y_1^n and Y_2^n.

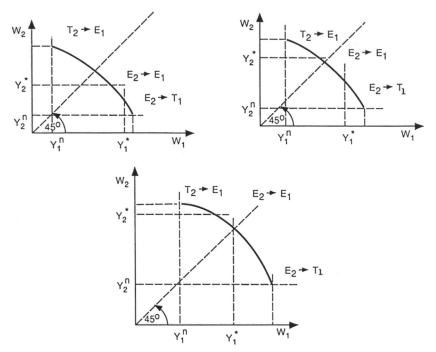

FIG. 4   Moderate resource case, 45° ray passing a, through $T_2 \rightarrow E_1$; b, through $E_2 \rightarrow E_1$; c, through $E_2 \rightarrow T_2$ with $Y_2^* > Y_1^*$.

cational expenditures are made in each region, the wealth possibility set is strictly convex. If the more educable child has greater earnings, the 45° ray, which is the locus of points at which the children have equal wealth, must pass through one of the first two of these regions (figs. 4a and 4b). If the more educable child has lesser earnings, the 45° ray might pass through $E_2 \rightarrow T_1$, as in figure 4c.

In the *high resource case* (figs. 5a and 5b), parents devote enough resources to children that it is feasible to provide each child with the wealth-maximizing level of education. The high resource case is compatible with both children receiving transfers and both receiving the wealth-maximizing levels of education—this corresponds to the linear segment of the frontier—or with only one child receiving transfers and wealth-maximizing education while the other child receives wealth-maximizing education but no transfers. It is not, however, compatible with both children receiving only education because that would imply that at least one of them was receiving more than the wealth-maximizing level. If all resources are allocated initially to child 2, any reallocation involves reducing T_2 and increasing E_1. This region ends when child 1's education

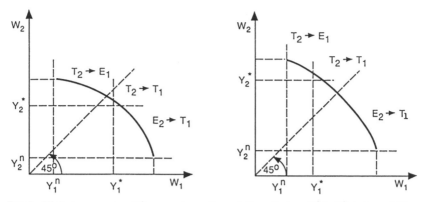

FIG. 5   High resource case, 45° ray passing a, through $T_2 \rightarrow E_1$ since $Y_1^* > Y_2^*$; b, through $T_2 \rightarrow$ E_1 since $Y_2^* > Y_1^*$.

reaches E_1^* with T_2 still positive. Since further reallocation to child 1 involves reducing T_2 and increasing T_1, the next portion of the frontier is linear with a slope of minus one. The region corresponding to these dollar-for-dollar reallocations ends when transfers to child 2 are exhausted; beyond this point, further transfers require reducing the education of child 2. The frontier thus consists of three regions between Y_1^n and Y_2^n: $(T_2 \rightarrow E_1)$, $(T_2 \rightarrow T_1)$, and $(E_2 \rightarrow T_1)$. The wealth possibility set is convex but, unlike the wealth possibility sets in the three previous cases, it is not strictly convex since the frontier contains a linear segment. This linear segment is not intersected by the 45° ray from the origin. If the more educable child has the greater earnings, the 45° ray must pass through the $T_2 \rightarrow E_1$ region, as in figure 5a. But if the more educable child has lesser earnings, the 45° ray must pass through the $E_2 \rightarrow T_1$ region, as in figure 5b.

In the *very high resource case* (figs. 6a and 6b), the three regions are the same as in the high resource case. The difference between the very high and the high resource cases is that in the very high resource case the linear segment in which both children receive transfers and along which both children receive the wealth-maximizing level of education (i.e., the $T_2 \rightarrow T_1$ segment) is intersected by the 45° ray. The intersection of the linear segment of the frontier with the 45° ray is significant if parents' preferences exhibit "equal concern" (i.e., if the parental welfare function is symmetric around the 45° ray).[9] Equal concern—the assumption made in Becker and Tomes (1976)—implies that in the very high resource case parents provide each child with the wealth-maximizing

---

9. Becker and Tomes describe the symmetric welfare function as "neutral," but we find "equal concern" more descriptive.

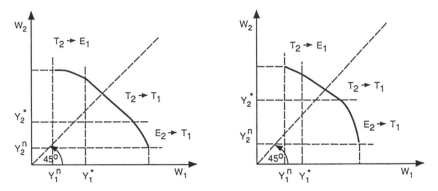

FIG. 6   Very high resource case, 45° ray passing a, through $T_2 \rightarrow T_1$, with more transfers to child 2 since $Y_1^* > Y_2^*$; b, through $T_2 > T_1$, with more transfers to child 1 since $Y_2^* > Y_1^*$.

level of education and then use transfers to offset fully any differences in earnings (i.e., to equalize the children's wealth).[10]

The relationships among these five cases are further clarified under the assumption of equal concern by considering a sequence of otherwise identical families that devote successively lower levels of resources to their children. In the very high resource case, the linear segment of the frontier $(T_2 \rightarrow T_1)$ is the segment on which both children receive the wealth-maximizing level of education and both children receive transfers. Initially, reductions in R reduce transfers to both children equally, maintaining equal wealth; this process continues until transfers to one child reach zero; at this critical value (R^+) the allocation that maximizes the parental welfare function is at an endpoint of the linear segment. Further reductions in R move us into the high resource case: the length of the linear segment $(T_2 \rightarrow T_1)$ is reduced, the allocation that maximizes the parental welfare function no longer lies on the linear segment, and at that welfare maximizing allocation only one child receives the wealth-maximizing level of education. If resources are reduced all the way to R^*, the linear segment vanishes, and there are only two regions, $(T_2 \rightarrow E_1)$ and $(E_2 \rightarrow T_1)$, separated by the point, (Y_1^*, Y_2^*). Further reductions in R move us into the moderate resource case, which contains three regions; the middle region in this case is one in which $(E_2 \rightarrow E_1)$, and the tangency between the indifference curve and the frontier is at the point (Y_1^*, Y_2^*). Thus, the point (Y_1^*, Y_2^*) is a

10. This implication follows from the mathematically much weaker assumption that the welfare function is "locally symmetric" around the 45° ray from the origin. It is easy to draw indifference maps corresponding to welfare functions that exhibit local symmetry but not global symmetry; however, we see no plausible economic assumption that implies local symmetry other than equal concern, which, of course, implies global symmetry.

pivotal one in defining the middle region in both the moderate resource case and the high resource case.[11]

The disinheritance of one sib for resources at R^+ is inconsistent with common experience—our parents did not treat us this way, and we will not treat our children this way. It might be objected, however, that the case in which the resources devoted to children are exactly equal to R^+ is a razor's edge case, so we would not expect to observe it. This objection misses the point. The unlikely behavior associated with the razor's edge case does not disappear if R is less than R^+. Furthermore, even without equal concern, there still is a critical resource level below which one sib is disinherited.[12]

Some of these points can be illustrated with a parametric example using a generalized CES parental welfare function:

$$V(W_1, \ldots, W_n) = \sum_{k=1}^{n} a_k (W_k - b_k)^c, \quad -\infty < c \leq 1. \qquad (2)$$

The b_k are "translation parameters" that can be interpreted as minimum levels of wealth parents require for each child before they are willing to trade off the wealth of one child against that of another. The elasticity of substitution parameter, c, reflects parents' aversion to inequality in their children's wealth above these minimum levels. For our illustration, we restrict our attention to the special case of the generalized CES that exhibits equal concern, the case in which $a_k = a$ and $b_k = b$ for all k.

With this equal concern welfare function there are two polar cases and a set of intermediate cases. First, if $c = 1$, the indifference curves are linear, and parents allocate resources to maximize the sum of their children's wealth with no concern about distribution among children:

$$V(W_1, \ldots, W_n) = W_1 + W_2 + \ldots + W_n. \qquad (3)$$

In this case, each child receives the wealth-maximizing level of education, provided the parents devote enough resources to the children, but the distribution of transfers among the children is indeterminate.[13] Second, if c approaches mi-

---

11. If child 1 has higher average and higher marginal returns to education than child 2, the point (Y_1^*, Y_2^*) lies to the right of the 45° ray.

12. This critical resource level depends on parental preferences and may be below or above R^+.

13. Lexicographic preferences can mitigate this defect of the linear parental welfare function. With lexicographic preferences, if an allocation that maximizes the sum of the children's wealth is not unique, parents turn to a second-level (tie-breaking) criterion to choose from among allocations providing maximal total wealth. In the high and very high resource cases, lexicographic preferences that give first priority to maximizing the sum of the children's wealth imply that parents provide each child with the wealth-maximizing level of education. If the second criterion can be represented by a utility function exhibiting equal concern, then, in the very high resource case, the

nus infinity, the generalized CES with equal concern reduces to the Rawlsian utility function

$$V(W_1, \ldots, W_n) = \min\{W_k\}. \tag{4}$$

In this case, parents either equalize their children's wealth or devote all resources to the child with lowest wealth. Third, for the intermediate cases in which c is less than one and greater than minus infinity, the children receive equal wealth only in the very high resource case (i.e., if and only if the wealth possibility frontier has a slope of minus one at the point where it intersects the 45° ray). Thus, even with equal concern, wealth equalization occurs only in the very high resource case and in the Rawlsian case, and all children receive wealth-maximizing level of education only in the very high resource case.

Because equal concern and very high levels of resources devoted to children imply equal wealth for all siblings, one might conjecture that inequality in sibs' wealth must decrease monotonically as R increases. But consider the following counterexample: for wealth vectors satisfying the regularity conditions ($W_k - b$) greater than zero for all k, the parental welfare function is given by the symmetric Klein-Rubin linear expenditure system

$$V(W_1, \ldots, W_n) = \sum_{k=1}^{n} \log (W_k - b), \tag{5}$$

and for all other wealth vectors, it is given by the fixed coefficient preference ordering, (4).[14] This preference ordering is well behaved for all nonnegative wealth vectors. Sufficiently high levels of R imply equal wealth for all children. Because this utility function is Rawlsian for W_k less than b, low levels of R also imply equal wealth for all children. With an asymmetric opportunity set (reflecting unequal endowments), intermediate resource levels imply unequal wealth.

Does the wealth model imply that parents reinforce endowment differentials by investing more in children with greater endowments, as Becker and Tomes (1976) suggest they do if parental preferences exhibit equal concern?

a) In the very high resource case with equal concern, Becker and Tomes's conclusion that parents reinforce endowment differentials depends on the additional assumption that the child with the greater endowment has both higher marginal and higher average returns to education. In the *Treatise* (1981,

---

implications of this lexicographic model coincide with those of the wealth model with equal concern. This lexicographic model does not eliminate the basic defect of the linear parental welfare function with equal concern: in a wide range of resource levels, parents with these preferences behave as if they are concerned only with maximizing the sum of their children's wealth.

14. We assume that b is greater than zero, so (5) does not by itself define a preference ordering over all nonnegative wealth vectors.

p. 123), Becker asserts: "Rates of return on human capital are likely to be higher for abler children because they benefit more from additional human capital," but he offers no supporting evidence. As is illustrated in figure 1*b*, this need not be the case.

b) With equal concern, outside the very high resource case, whether parents reinforce or compensate depends on both parental preferences and the form of the earnings production function. For example, in the very low resource case, transfers must be zero, and the wealth model reduces to the Behrman, Pollak, and Taubman (1982, in this volume) SET model. In the SET model, if the parental welfare function is CES and the earnings production function is Cobb-Douglas, parents reinforce if and only if the elasticity of substitution parameter is greater than zero.[15] Also for the three intermediate resource cases with equal concern, the location of the point of tangency of the wealth frontier and an indifference curve depends on the shape of the two curves, unless one or the other is at the fixed coefficient extreme.

c) In the very high resource case without equal concern, parental preferences may favor or disfavor a particular child strongly enough to upset Becker and Tomes's conclusion about reinforcement even if the child with greater endowments has both higher marginal and average returns to education.

To summarize: at sufficiently high resource levels, parents make positive transfers to both children and, hence, provide both children with the wealth-maximizing level of education. If parents who devote sufficiently high resources to their children also have equal concern, they also equalize wealth among their children. If, in addition to sufficiently high resources and equal concern, the earnings production function implies higher marginal and higher average returns to education for the child with greater endowments, the parents reinforce endowment differentials by investing more in the child with greater endowment. Thus the full Becker-Tomes conclusion that parents reinforce endowment differentials, invest in the education of all of their children at the wealth-maximizing levels, and use transfers to equalize wealth among their children requires (*a*) sufficiently high resources devoted to the children, (*b*) equal concern, and (*c*) higher marginal and average returns to the child with greater endowments.

With successively lower levels of parental resources devoted to children, transfers to the children are reduced. At some critical resource level (R^+ in the case of equal concern), transfers to one child reach zero. At that crucial resource level, one of the sibs is disinherited; that sib receives neither gifts nor bequests. At and below that resource level, at least one sib receives less than

15. If the earnings production function also is CES, the critical question is whether the product of the elasticity of substitution in the parental welfare function and that in the earnings production function is greater than, equal to, or less than unity.

the wealth-maximizing education, and whether there is reinforcing or compensating investment depends on the characteristics of both the earnings production function and the parental welfare function. The Becker-Tomes conclusion regarding the triad of reinforcement, wealth-maximizing investments, and wealth equalization does not hold below that critical resource level. In fact, though reinforcement and wealth equalization may be the outcomes in some particular cases, wealth-maximizing investments in the education of all children does not occur below that critical resource level.

II. Empirical Evidence

We focus on two empirical implications of the wealth model for investments in education and patterns of transfers. We state these for two-child families:

1. If parents are sufficiently wealthy and altruistic, they provide both children with wealth-maximizing levels of education and use transfers to achieve their distributional objectives. For the special case of equal concern, parents use transfers to offset fully differences in their children's earnings and, hence, to equalize their wealth.

2. If parents are not sufficiently wealthy and altruistic that they provide both children with the wealth-maximizing levels of education, then they provide one child with less than the wealth-maximizing level of education and with zero transfers; the other child may receive the wealth-maximizing level of education and positive transfers or may receive less than the wealth-maximizing level of education and zero transfers. For the special case of equal concern, the higher-earnings child must receive less than the wealth-maximizing level of education and zero transfers.

These implications of the wealth model cannot be tested directly because no data set contains all of the necessary information on transfers, education, and earnings for siblings. Indeed, it is difficult to assign families to the five resource cases because no data set reports the lifetime transfers parents make to their children and the lifetime earnings of the children; most data sets that report transfers and earnings for siblings report them for a specified time interval, usually a single year.

Two additional implications of the wealth model are even more difficult to test empirically, and we shall not attempt to do so:

3. In the very low resource case, parents allocate additional resources to education, not to transfers; at the other extreme, if parents are sufficiently wealthy and altruistic that they provide both children with the wealth-maximizing education, they allocate additional resources to transfers. In intermediate cases, parents allocate additional resources in part to education for one child and in part to transfers for the other. In all cases, both children benefit from additional parental resources. This implication and, more generally, the

proposition that, as total resources devoted to children increase, a declining fraction of those resources is allocated to education are difficult to assess empirically because of the need to control for unobserved endowments that are likely to be correlated across generations. Theoretical assertions (e.g., about the effect of an increase in resources on education or transfers) usually assume that endowments are held constant, but holding them constant in empirical work is difficult because of the paucity of data on endowments.[16]

4. Unless parents are sufficiently wealthy and altruistic that they provide both children with the wealth-maximizing levels of education, the marginal rate of return to education exceeds the rate of return on financial assets for at least one child. In the very low resource case, the marginal rates of return to education exceed the rate of return on financial assets for both children. This implication is difficult to assess empirically because marginal rates of return to education are not observed, and we do not see how to estimate them with available data.[17]

Although data limitations preclude rigorous testing of the wealth model, we can gain some insight into the empirical validity of its first two implications by piecemeal examination of U.S. data. In this section we review previous studies and present some new evidence. We consider patterns of sibling differences in earnings and differences in the two components of transfers, bequests and inter vivos gifts.

Earnings Differentials

The Panel Study of Income Dynamics (PSID) began in 1969 with a stratified random sample of about 5,000 people, oversampling the poor. The sample has been followed annually with some changes in the questions and some attri-

16. The thought experiment here involves increasing parental resources devoted to children while holding fixed child endowments. Some empirical estimates suggest strong intergenerational correlations in endowments (e.g., Behrman and Taubman 1989, in this volume) and that endowments affect earnings strongly (e.g., Behrman, Hrubec, Taubman, and Wales 1980; Behrman, Rosenzweig, and Taubman 1994). Hence, there is likely to be a positive association between parental income (and the resources that parents devote to their children) and the wealth-maximizing levels of investments in their children (if the marginal rate of return to a given level of educational investments is positively affected by endowments) through the intergenerational correlation in endowments. Few data sets contain variables that can be used to control for endowments.

17. If we could assign families to the appropriate parental resource cases, we could estimate for each case the Mincerian (1974) semilog earnings-schooling relation in which the coefficient of schooling is the rate of return to the opportunity cost of time spent in school; we could then test whether the rate of return tended to decline for children in the higher parental resource cases. A difficulty, beyond the initial difficulty of assigning families to resource cases, is that the Mincerian rationale for the semilog form assumes that the earnings production function is not subject to diminishing returns; hence, there are an infinite number of levels of wealth-maximizing education, a specification that is inconsistent with the wealth model.

tion.[18] An unusual feature of the PSID is that individuals who split off from the households of those in the original sample were added to the sample. In this study we link children with the original household head.[19] We use the reporting period 1982–87 for earnings of and gifts to sibling offspring from the original PSID households (although we use fewer years when data are missing).[20] All data are in 1987 dollars. Our choice of this 6-year time period represents a compromise between the advantage of having more years to average out transitory fluctuations and the disadvantage of having more missing observations.[21] By focusing on differences in earnings and in gifts within sibling pairs, we eliminate error components that are common to both sibs, including macroeconomic effects. We consider same-sex sibling pairs to control for gender differences.

To classify sibling pairs into the five resource cases, we require data on the wealth-maximizing level of education, actual education, lifetime earnings, and lifetime transfers, including all inter vivos gifts and bequests. Such data are not available. We can, however, draw some inferences from the patterns of transfers reported in the 1982–87 surveys. The wealth model implies that families in which all siblings received transfers in 1981–86 *must* be in a sufficiently high resource case that all children received the wealth-maximizing education (e.g., with equal concern, in the very high resource case). Those families in which at least one sibling received transfers cannot be in the very low resource case and, hence, must either be in the very high resource case or else in one of the three intermediate cases. Only those families in which no sibling received transfers during the period 1981–86 *might* be in the very low resource case.

In table 1 we present means, standard deviations, and coefficients of variation in the absolute difference in earnings between same-sex sibling pairs for

18. Becketti, Gould, Lillard, and Welch (1988, p. 49) conclude that neither attrition nor entry "has any effect on estimates of the parameters of . . . earnings equations."

19. More precisely, we do this for children who were living in a parental household in 1969 and who were less than 18 years old then and not full-time students, not coresident with their parents in 1982–87, and at least 24 years old in 1982 or in the year in which they subsequently were added to the data set.

20. For each year of the panel the respondents report earnings and gifts for the previous year, so the reporting period 1982–87 corresponds to earnings and transfers for 1981–86.

21. A longer time period implies more missing observations because as we go back in time more children were still in school or still coresident with their parents. We do not use the 1988 PSID, although it placed more emphasis on the sources of transfers than earlier rounds, because the 1988 PSID does not distinguish between gifts and loans. Behrman and Taubman (1990, in this volume) and Solon (1992) emphasize the importance of transitory fluctuations in estimating the magnitude of intergenerational correlations in these data. We have calculated that the mean absolute difference in earnings is 31% greater for 1 year than for the 1981–86 period for male sibling pairs and 24% greater for female sibling pairs due to such transitory factors. (Only those with positive earnings are included in these calculations.)

Table 1 Mean Absolute Differences in Nominal and Full Earnings in 1987 Dollars, 1981–86, Brother and Sister Pairs, with Categorization by Whether Neither, One or Both Received Transfers

Same-Sex Sibling Pairs	Cash Help from Relatives			Cash Help plus Housing		
	Mean Absolute Difference in Earnings	Standard Deviation of Absolute Differences in Earnings	Coefficient of Variation of Absolute Differences in Earnings	Mean Absolute Difference in Earnings	Standard Deviation of Absolute Differences in Earnings	Coefficient of Variation of Absolute Differences in Earnings
Sons:						
Nominal earnings:						
Neither	8,794	8,492	.97	9,200	8,726	.95
One	10,541	16,492	1.56	10,922	16,281	1.49
Both	6,167	6,330	1.03	5,254	5,820	1.11
Full earnings						
Neither	10,964	12,240	1.12	11,575	12,668	1.09
One	12,800	23,018	1.80	14,211	21,429	1.51
Both	8,276	10,040	1.21	4,232	13,678	3.23
Daughters:						
Nominal earnings:						
Neither	6,680	5,742	.86	7,223	5,758	.80
One	7,253	6,536	.90	7,167	6,553	.91
Both	6,174	6,162	1.00	5,103	5,371	1.05
Full earnings:						
Neither	9,748	11,204	1.15	10,761	11,537	1.07
One	10,745	12,061	1.12	10,381	12,027	1.16
Both	10,193	11,342	1.12	8,250	10,102	1.22

NOTE—Siblings were found by examining "Relationship to Head" in 1968. Siblings were separated into males and females, sorted by year of birth, then paired, oldest to second oldest, third with the fourth, and so on. All offspring used were at least 24 years old. All earning figures come from the earnings of the head of household or his wife. Therefore, if the sibling was not a household head or wife in any year in the 1981–86 period, he or she was dropped for that year. All data are in 1987 dollars.

the three categories that we can distinguish in the data: both sibs received gifts; one sib received gifts and one did not; and no sib received gifts.[22] We use two alternative definitions of receiving gifts: (1) receiving "cash help from relatives" and (2) receiving "cash help from relatives" and/or receiving their first house as a gift.[23] We present means for both actual earnings and full earnings.[24]

These data suggest that, in same-sex sibling pairs, if resources are sufficiently high that both sibs receive the wealth-maximizing education, mean nominal absolute earnings differentials are in the $4,000–$8,000 range for males and in the $5,000–$10,000 range for females.[25] Such values imply that, if parents were to equalize their children's wealth and if all transfers took the form of annual inter vivos gifts (i.e., zero bequests), then the within-family *difference* in these annual gifts to the siblings would have to average more than $5,000 per year. Alternatively, if all transfers took the form of bequests (i.e., zero inter vivos gifts), then the within-family *difference* in bequests to the siblings would have to average on the order of magnitude of hundreds of thousands of dollars, depending on the interest rate, on the children's ages when

22. If the PSID reports earnings for three same-sex siblings from the same family, we select one same-sex sibling pair. We also have made similar calculations for identical twins, fraternal twins, and the twins' offspring from the NAS-NRC Twin and Offspring samples using one year of data. (For descriptions of the National Academy of Science-National Research Council [NAS-NRC] Twin sample, see Behrman, Hrubec, Taubman, and Wales 1980; for the NAS-NRC Twin Offspring sample, see Behrman and Taubman 1985). The mean absolute differences between earnings for same-sex sibling pairs in these other data sets are similar in magnitude to those for one year (1987) for all siblings in same-sex pairs in the PSID. With these other data sets, however, we cannot average over several years to lessen the effect of transitory fluctuations, nor can we classify the data as in table 1 because of the paucity of information on transfers.

23. The imputed rent variable may be deficient for two reasons. First, if parents buy a child's first house and the child sells it and buys another, the second house would not be reported as a gift. Second, we calculate imputed rent as if the entire value of the house were provided by relatives, while in many cases relatives probably provided much less than the total value of the house (e.g., by providing some or all of the downpayment). These two errors work in opposite directions, but there is no reason to think that they cancel out.

24. We calculated full earnings by assuming full-time employment at the individual's wage rate, which we inferred from the data by dividing reported earnings by reported hours worked.

25. The ranges reflect alternative definitions of earnings and transfers. After-tax differences in earnings are somewhat smaller, and their calculation is complicated with progressive taxes based on family income. Some sibling pairs in the other two groups also may be cases in which both siblings received the wealth-maximizing education levels and transfers over their lifetimes but for which at least one sibling did not receive transfers in the 1981–86 period. The mean absolute differences are somewhat larger for those pairs in which at least one sibling did not receive transfers in the 1981–86 period (with the single exception of full earnings for daughters in which neither sib received transfers during 1981–86 and the narrower definition of transfers is used) but are of approximately the same magnitude.

they inherit, and on the number of years worked.[26] Without equal concern, the required mean absolute differences in gifts and bequests are of these magnitudes if the "bias" in the parental welfare function is uncorrelated with the wealth-maximizing earnings levels of the children and is distributed symmetrically around the equal concern case.

Bequest Patterns

Are bequest patterns consistent with the wealth model's implications that at sufficiently high resource levels parents use transfers to achieve the wealth distribution they desire and that at lower resource levels at least one sibling receives zero transfers? Pechman (1987, p. 350) reports that, in the late 1970s, about 8% of U.S. decedents had estates of at least $60,000, the threshold level requiring filing of a federal estate tax return; in the mid-1980s, the filing limit was raised to $300,000 and filings fell to 1.5 percent of decedents. These figures suggest that for most families bequests alone are too small to offset fully average earnings differentials among their children.

Menchik (1980) studied the division of large estates among siblings using data from Connecticut for the period 1930–45. He found equal sharing predominated, and estate shares were independent of estate size.[27] Tomes (1981) studied estate shares using a sample of beneficiaries drawn from Cleveland probate records of 1964–65 covering all estate sizes. In 1970 he collected data on bequests from the recipients in his sample by mail questionnaires and interviews, and found less than half of the sibs reported receiving equal amounts. Menchik (1988) studied a random sample of wills from the Cleveland probate records for the same time period as Tomes. He found about 80 percent of sibships shared the estate equally. Tomes's results may reflect measurement error, perhaps arising from the 5 to 6 years that elapsed between the bequest and the survey. Furthermore, Menchik (1988) points out that, when unequal divisions occur, the wills themselves often offer an explanation, for example, referring to the favored child's role in taking care of the parent. This suggests that the

---

26. If bequests are received at the beginning of a 40-year work life, then to offset a $1.00 difference in annual earnings requires a $16.30 difference in bequests if the real interest rate is 5% and a $26.54 difference in bequests if the real interest rate is 1%. If bequests are received at the end of a 40-year work life, then to offset a $1.00 difference in annual earnings requires a $126.75 difference in bequests if the real interest rate is 5% and a $48.17 difference if the real interest rate is 1%. To offset a $5,000 difference in annual earnings, the smallest of these numbers implies a bequest difference of over $80,000, and the largest a bequest difference of over $630,000.

27. This conclusion holds even if he included reported inter-vivos gifts and imputed grandparents' bequests to grandchildren to their parents.

decedents recognized social norms favoring equal sharing in the absence of a socially acceptable reason for deviating from equal shares.

Wilhelm (1991) has used the federal estate tax files for 1982 for estates of at least $300,000, which at that time was the minimum federal taxable estate. The Internal Revenue Service has matched these files with inheritors' federal income taxes returns for 1981 when they can be found for all inheritors; the resulting matched sample contains 5,777 decedents. Wilhelm finds equal sharing among sibs in about two-thirds of the cases and shares within 5 percent of equal sharing in 90% of the cases. Moreover, for children receiving unequal bequests, the difference in transfers is *not* related to the difference in earnings. Hence, these data suggest that very few parents use bequests to offset unequal earnings among their children.[28]

In the United States, the limited empirical evidence thus suggests that, regardless of estate size, the typical pattern is equal bequests. If all transfers to children took the form of bequests or, more generally, if the patterns in the division of total transfers were highly correlated with the patterns in the division of bequests, then this bequest evidence would be inconsistent with two implications of the wealth model: (1) that at sufficiently high resource levels parents use transfers to obtained desired wealth distributions among children, and (2) that over a range of lower resource levels one sibling receives zero transfers while the other receives positive transfers.

Inter Vivos Gifts

Even if bequests are divided equally, inter vivos gifts may enable parents to attain the wealth distribution they desire. Unfortunately, little is known about the magnitude and distribution of inter vivos gifts.

Hurd and Mundaca (1987) have examined the relative importance of bequests and gifts among the affluent in 1964. They find that their total contribution to wealth is small and that bequests are about twice as important as gifts.[29]

28. The 1988 wave of the PSID reports inheritances received in the previous year. For the offspring sample defined using a definition parallel to the one we used above (the age range of which was 24–39 with a central tendency of about 30), 1% received inheritances in the previous year, and these averaged about $17,000. This sample is too small to permit examination of inheritances.

29. Kurz (1984), Chiswick and Cox (1987), Cox (1987), and Cox and Raines (1985) used the President's Commission on Pension Policy Sample, which has data on gifts paid and received by individuals. Unfortunately, the data on sibs are very limited, and the sample reports the income of both parent and child only if they live in the same household. To assess the relative importance of gifts and bequests, one would have to think about (*a*) the age of the child when gifts are received, (*b*) the age of the child when the parent(s) die(s), and (*c*) the interest rate. Unfortunately, Hurd and Mundaca do not present any information on these issues.

Cox and Rank (1992) use the National Survey of Families and Households (NSFH) to study private gifts received (net of those given) by individuals.[30] They find that an increase in own earnings decreases the probability of receipt but increases the amount received. They claim that this pattern is consistent with an "exchange model" but inconsistent with an altruistic model of transfers, by which they mean the wealth model. We are not persuaded that exchange models predict this pattern of gifts or that this pattern contradicts the wealth model; Behrman (1995) provides further discussion of their approach.

Eggebeen and Hogan (1990) also use the NSFH and limit their analysis to gifts between adults and non-co-residential parents. Over half of the adults received no support. They characterize the support that was received as being primarily episodic when the adult children were young and getting started, sick, or had young children.

Some crude inferences about the role of inter vivos gifts can be drawn from the PSID data on "help from relatives." The wealth model predicts that, if resources devoted to the children are large enough that all children receive the wealth-maximizing education, then the difference in transfers received by the children should achieve the wealth distribution the parents desire despite differences in the children's earnings. The wealth model predicts that, for a range of intermediate resource levels, although not in the very low resource case, only one child receives transfers. Because siblings generally receive equal bequests, the wealth model implies that inter vivos gifts must play a crucial role.

Is the magnitude of help from relatives large enough to offset most or all of the earnings differentials reported in table 1? Table 2 provides a partial answer, presenting summary statistics for gifts received by the higher-earning sib minus those received by the lower-earning sib. We use the two definitions of gifts discussed above: cash help received from relatives and the sum of cash help and imputed rent from houses that were gifts. For son pairs and for daughter pairs in which only one daughter (but not both) received gifts, the lower-earning sib on the average received more gifts. The average differences in gifts received, however, are small relative to the average earnings differentials reported in table 1. For son pairs in which both received gifts, for example, the gift differential including imputed rent offsets only 4.9% of the average actual earnings differential and only 6.0% of the average full earnings differential. For daughter pairs in which both received gifts, as noted above, the gift differentials reinforce rather than offset the earnings differentials by 2.2% and 1.4%, respectively, for the average actual and full earnings differentials. For pairs in which only one sib receives gifts, the mean gift differential (again, including imputed rent) offsets only 3.5% of mean nominal earnings differentials for sons

30. The NSFH does not permit comparisons of gifts received by siblings. It is not clear whether these gifts include those for education.

Table 2 Transfers Received By Higher-Earnings Sib Minus Those Received by Lower-Earnings Sib in 1987 Dollars, 1981–86, Brother and Sister Pairs, with Categorization by Whether Both or One Received Transfers

SAME-SEX SIBLING PAIRS	CASH HELP FROM RELATIVES			CASH HELP PLUS HOUSING		
	Mean Difference in Transfers	Standard Deviation of Differences in Transfers	Coefficient of Variation of Differences in Transfers	Mean Difference in Transfers	Standard Deviation of Differences in Transfers	Coefficient of Variation of Differences in Transfers
Sons:						
One	−160	645	4.03	−383	897	2.35
Both	−211	576	2.72	−256	938	3.66
Daughters:						
One	−76	419	5.53	−146	787	5.38
Both	62	548	8.88	114	776	6.78

Table 3   Sibling Difference in Help from Relatives:
Ordinary Least Squares Estimates, Using Sons from the Panel Study
of Income Dynamics, 1981–86 ($N = 325$)

Sibling Difference Variable	Sibling Difference in Mean Cash		Sibling Difference in Mean (Cash + Imputed Rent if House Gift) Help	
	(1)	(2)	(3)	(4)
Constant	−56.73	−57.64	−21.45	−28.73
	(1.4)	(1.4)	(.3)	(.4)
Labor income	−.0042		−.010	
	(2.5)		(3.7)	
Income excluding help from relatives		−.0025		−.0086
		(1.8)		(3.8)
Age	6.39	5.05	−3.08	−2.04
	(.6)	(.5)	(.2)	(.1)
$\bar{R}^2$	.0123	.0039	.0366	.0403

NOTE—Absolute values of t-statistics are in parentheses beneath the point estimates.

and 2.0% for daughters (and only 2.7% and 1.4%, respectively, of mean full earnings differentials). Thus these data suggest that inter vivos gift differentials do not substantially alter the wealth differentials that emanate from labor earnings.

The data in table 2 do not control for age differences. Given standard life-cycle earnings patterns, two siblings with identical life-cycle earnings paths may have different earnings in a particular time period because the older sib is further along on the age-earnings profile. Therefore in tables 3 and 4 we describe the gift differences within sibling pairs relative to alternative measures of earnings or income differences that control for age differences.[31] The results are presented for both alternatives for gifts (i.e., excluding and including imputed rent from houses that were gifts). We consider the difference in total household income (net of gifts received from relatives) as an alternative since the income received of a spouse or gifts from in-laws may affect the parents' willingness to provide gifts.

What do these estimates suggest? First, the control for age differences does not seem important; the signs vary and the point estimates are not significantly different from zero even at the 25% level. Second, the signs of the earnings or

31. We use ordinary least squares within-sibling regressions of earnings or income on age for sons and daughters separately.

Table 4 Sibling Difference in Help from Relatives: Ordinary Least Squares Estimates, Using Daughters from the Panel Study of Income Dynamics, 1981–86 ($N = 434$)

Sibling Difference Variable	Sibling Difference in Mean Cash			Sibling Difference in Mean (Cash + Imputed Rent if House Gift) Help		
	(1)	(2)	(3)	(4)	(5)	(6)
Constant	−27.74 (1.0)	−23.72 (.9)	−7.70 (.2)	−15.02 (.3)	26.68 (.5)	14.53 (.2)
Labor income	−.0023 (1.4)			−.0048 (1.5)		
Head's labor income			−.0032 (1.4)			−.0082 (1.6)
Income excluding help from relatives		−.0019 (2.1)			−.0085 (5.1)	
Age	2.71 (.4)	2.95 (.4)	−10.05 (1.1)	−10.91 (.8)	−7.66 (.6)	−16.07 (.8)
$\bar{R}^2$	−.0001	.0060	.0076	.0024	.0550	.0077

NOTE.—Absolute values of t-statistics are in parentheses beneath the point estimates.

income differentials are uniformly negative, as implied by the wealth model with equal concern. Third, for son pairs the difference in own earnings has a significant effect, but for daughter pairs only total income differences (excluding help from relatives) are significant, suggesting that spousal earnings differentials are more important for daughters than for sons. Fourth, the magnitudes of the coefficient estimates for the earnings or income differentials are small (and the precision of the point estimates quite limited), suggesting that 1% or less of the earnings or income differential is offset by gift differentials.[32]

Thus, the data on inter vivos gifts provide little support for the wealth model. On average, differences in such gifts between siblings do tend to offset differences in earnings, but these differences are insufficient to offset more than a small fraction of the difference in earnings.

III. Conclusion

The wealth model implies that, at sufficiently high resource levels, parents make positive transfers to all of their children and, hence, provide all of their children with the wealth-maximizing level of education. If parents who devote sufficiently high resources to their children also have equal concern, then they also equalize wealth among their children. If, in addition to sufficiently high resources and equal concern, the earnings production function implies higher marginal and higher average returns to education for the child with greater endowments, then the parents reinforce endowment differentials by investing more in children with greater endowments.

The evidence appears inconsistent with the implications of the very high resource case of the wealth model. Information on bequests suggests that estates are typically small and equally shared. Therefore, the very high resource case is likely to be relevant only for parents who are able to provide their children with large inter vivos gifts and willing to distribute such gifts unequally among their children. Examining data on "help received from relatives," we find some support for the implications of the wealth model that the lower-earning sib tends to receive more transfers. But the magnitudes of the transfer differences are so small that, even for families that apparently are in the very high resource case, on average very little of the observed earnings difference is offset by transfer differences.

32. As is well known, random measurement error may bias such coefficients toward zero. The use of earnings averaged over 6 years apparently eliminates much of such measurement error (see Behrman and Taubman 1990, in this volume; Solon 1992; and Zimmermann 1992). It would require very large measurement error indeed for the true effects to be substantial in the sense of accounting for, say, a quarter or a third of the earnings gap and to be consistent with the estimates in tables 3 and 4.

As parental resources devoted to children fall from sufficiently high levels for the very high resource case of the wealth model, transfers fall until, at some critical resource level, transfers to one child reach zero. At that crucial resource level, one of the sibs is disinherited; that sib receives neither inter vivos gifts nor postmortem bequests. In the intermediate resources cases below that resource level at least one sib receives less than the wealth-maximizing education, and whether investments are reinforcing or compensating depends on the characteristics of both the earnings production function and the parental welfare function. The Becker-Tomes triad of conclusions (wealth-maximizing investments in education, wealth equalization, and reinforcement) do not hold below that critical resource level.

The plausibility of the wealth model, and hence this triad of conclusions, is challenged by the implausibility of the distributional implications in a range of intermediate resource cases. The wealth model implies that over a range of intermediate resource levels parents make zero transfers to some children while making positive transfers to others. We do not often observe one child receiving bequests and inter vivos gifts while another child receives neither.

6

A Transaction Cost Approach to Families and Households

ROBERT A. POLLAK

Families are fashionable. Within the last decade, social scientists have redis-covered families and households as fit subjects for serious analysis. Demogra-phers and historians, anthropologists and sociologists have played the major roles; economists, traditionally preoccupied with markets, have been less involved.[1]

The traditional economic theory of the household focuses exclusively on observable market behavior (i.e., demand for goods, supply of labor) treating the household as a "black box" identified only by its preference ordering.[2] The "new home economics" takes a broader view, including not only market be-havior but also such nonmarket phenomena as fertility, the education of chil-dren, and the allocation of time. The major analytic tool of the new home eco-nomics is Becker's household production model, which depicts the household as combining the time of household members with market goods to produce the outputs or "commodities" it ultimately desires.[3]

Reprinted from *Journal of Economic Literature* 23 no. 2 (June 1985): 581–608.

This research was supported in part by the National Science Foundation, the National Institutes of Health, and the Population Council. My intellectual debts to Oliver E. Williamson are even greater than the references to his work suggest. I am grateful to Judith Goff, Claudia Goldin, Vivian Pollak, Samuel H. Preston, and Susan Watkins for helpful comments and conversations during this paper's prolonged gestation. I am also grateful to Gary S. Becker, Peter Davis, Stefano Fenoaltea, Janet T. Landa, Marilyn Manser, and Ann D. Witte for helpful comments. The views expressed are my own and the usual disclaimer applies.

1. Peter Laslett (1972), Tamara K. Hareven (1977b), and John Demos and Sarane Spence Boo-cock (1978) are collections exemplifying the work outside economics. Gary S. Becker's work over the last fifteen years, culminating in his *Treatise on the Family* (1981), is the leading example within economics. For a legal scholar's enthusiastic endorsement of the power of economic analy-sis in this area, see Richard A. Posner (1980). Victor R. Fuchs (1983), writing for a less specialized audience than Becker, provides an empirical analysis of "how we live" from an economic per-spective and discusses its implications for public policy.

2. On the theoretical side, see Gerard Debreu (1959) or Kenneth J. Arrow and Frank H. Hahn (1971); on the empirical side, Laurits R. Christensen, Dale W. Jorgenson, and Lawrence J. Lau (1975) or Robert A. Pollak and Terence J. Wales (1978, 1980).

3. The *locus classicus* of the household production literature is Becker (1965). Robert T. Mi-chael and Becker (1973) provide a sympathetic restatement; Marc Nerlove (1974) and Zvi Gril-

The new home economics ignores the internal organization and structure of families and households. Although this may surprise noneconomists who tend to believe that the internal organization and structure of an institution are likely to affect its behavior, economists find it natural. For the economist the most economical way to exploit the fundamental insight that production takes place within the household is to apply to households techniques developed for studying firms. Since neoclassical economics identifies firms with their technologies and assumes that firms operate efficiently and frictionlessly, it precludes any serious interest in the economizing properties of the internal structure and organization of firms. The new home economics, by carrying over this narrow neoclassical view from firms to households, thus fails to exploit fully the insight of the household production approach. In this essay I argue that the transaction cost approach which recognizes the significance of internal structure provides a broader and more useful view of the economic activity and behavior of the family.

The transaction cost approach has been primarily concerned with firms and the organization of production.[4] The treatment of vertical integration is paradigmatic. Neoclassical economics explains vertical integration as a response to technological inseparabilities; transaction cost economics explains vertical integration as a response to the difficulties of regulating ongoing relationships by means of contracts.[5] Transaction cost analysis of vertical integration posits a situation in which efficiency requires the use of physical or human capital that is specific to the relationship between a particular supplier and a particular customer; since the value of such "idiosyncratic" capital depends on establishing and maintaining the supplier-customer relationship, the willingness of either party to invest in idiosyncratic capital depends on assuring the stability of the relationship. Firms often avoid using contracts to structure complex, ongoing relationships because doing so is hazardous. Short-term contracting is hazardous because, even when contract renewal is mutually beneficial, one party or the other may have advantages that can be exploited in bilateral negotiations over renewal terms; hence, short-term contracts make it risky to accu-

---

iches (1974) express some reservations; Pollak and Michael L. Wachter (1975) emphasize its limitations. Richard A. Easterlin, Pollak, and Wachter (1980) discuss applications to fertility and provide references to the recent literature.

4. Oliver E. Williamson (1975, 1979, 1981), building on the older institutionalist tradition, on the work of Ronald H. Coase (1937), and on the "Carnegie tradition" (e.g., Herbert A. Simon 1957), has been primarily responsible for developing the transaction cost approach. Other important transaction cost papers are Victor P. Goldberg (1976), and Benjamin Klein, Robert G. Crawford, and Armen A. Alchian (1978).

5. Time thus plays a crucial role in transaction cost analysis, a point emphasized by Gordon C. Winston (1982, Ch. 12).

mulate capital whose value is contingent on the relationship continuing and thus discourage investment in such specific capital. The problems of contract renewal can be avoided or at least postponed by long-term contracts, but only if such contracts are "complete" in the sense that they specify the obligations of the parties under every possible contingency. Complete long-term contracts are costly or impossible to write and enforce, however, a reflection of bounded rationality and asymmetric information; and incomplete long-term contracts which fail to deal with every contingency expose the parties to the hazards of bilateral bargaining. To avoid these contracting hazards firms often rely on some more complete form of integration such as merger. Thus, contracting difficulties—the problems of negotiating, writing, monitoring, and enforcing agreements—are central instances of transaction costs, and transaction cost economics asserts that they are significant determinants of the organization of production. Since bureaucratic structures have their own characteristic disabilities, internal governance does not eliminate all difficulties associated with a transaction or exchange. Nevertheless, replacing a market relationship by an organization with an appropriate governance structure often safeguards the interests of both parties.

The transaction cost approach focuses on the role of institutions in structuring complex, long-term relationships. Applied to the firm, transaction cost economics studies the boundaries, structure, and internal organization of producing units. To do so, it relaxes the assumption of frictionless efficiency and views the firm as a hierarchical governance structure within which production takes place. By focusing on structure the transaction cost approach provides an alternative explanation of market behavior that traditional economics ascribes to technology, and it illuminates aspects of nonmarket behavior that traditional economics ignores. In many respects the neoclassical and transaction cost approaches are complements rather than substitutes, addressing somewhat different issues and offering somewhat different ranges of admissible explanations.

The transaction cost approach analyzes the "economizing properties of alternative institutional modes for organizing transactions" (Williamson 1979, p. 234). The presumption is that the costs to be minimized include transaction costs, that these costs vary systematically from one institutional mode to another, and that each activity is carried out by the institution that can perform it most efficiently. The transaction cost literature has thus far emphasized production activities and, more particularly, intermediate-product transactions; the central issue has been whether technologically separable activities will be carried out by a single vertically-integrated firm rather than by separate firms dealing with each other through markets. Addressing the fundamental problems of institutional choice—whether particular activities will be mediated by markets or carried out within families, firms, governments, or nonprofit institutions—

requires extending the transaction cost analysis from firms to families and to other institutional modes.[6]

The transaction cost literature has virtually ignored families and households.[7] The neglect of families in Williamson's *Markets and Hierarchies* (1975) probably flows from his assumption that "in the beginning, there were markets" (p. 20). While this assumption is clearly intended to provide an analytical rather than an anthropological origin, it is probably responsible for his neglect of family organization as a theoretical or an actual solution to the incentive and monitoring problems encountered by peer groups and simple hierarchies. The neglect of families and households represents a missed opportunity.

Applied to the family, the transaction cost approach generalizes the new home economics by recognizing that internal structure and organization matter. It treats the family as a governance structure rather than a preference ordering or a preference ordering augmented by a production technology. This has two consequences for the analysis of the family. First, by focusing on the family's

6. Henry B. Hansmann (1980) provides an excellent transaction cost analysis of nonprofit enterprise. There does not appear to be a corresponding transaction cost analysis of the state, although Goldberg (1976) and Williamson (1976) hint at such a theory in their discussions of regulation. The "Chicago School" theory of economic regulation fails to offer such an analysis of the state. On the contrary, it assumes that such an analysis is unnecessary because the state does not differ significantly from other organizations. Posner (1974), for example, asserts: ". . . no persuasive theory has yet been proposed as to why (government) agencies should be expected to be less efficient than other organizations. The motivation of the agency employee to work diligently and honestly is similar to that of the employee of a business firm" (p. 338).

7. Transaction cost papers often mention in passing that the analysis applies to marriage or the family. Goldberg (1976, p. 428, fn. 9) does so in a sentence in a footnote; Klein, Crawford, and Alchian (1978, p. 323) devote a paragraph to it; and Williamson (1979, p. 258), two paragraphs. Yoram Ben-Porath (1980) is the only sustained transaction cost analysis of issues related to marriage or the family and in some respects my discussion parallels his. He begins by noting that neoclassical economic theory assumes that economic agents—individuals and firms—transact with "the market" rather than directly with other agents; in this sense, neoclassical theory postulates "anonymous" agents and "impersonal" transactions. Ben-Porath's analysis of the family flows from his more general concern with relaxing this assumption and recognizing that the "identity" of economic agents—their ability to recognize and be recognized by one another—is crucial to many types of economic interactions. His title, "The F-Connection: Families, Friends, and Firms and the Organization of Exchange," is indicative of these broader concerns. Ben-Porath emphasizes the changing role of the family in various stages of economic development and the effect of development on the family. In a review of Becker's *Treatise* (Ben-Porath 1982), he summarizes his own views:

> The traditional family is the epitome of specialization by identity, based on own use of productive services and on mutual insurance and support . . . Modern economic organization is associated with a market structure based on specialization along the impersonal dimensions of transactions . . . Thus, in a modern economy, the family sheds much of its productive activities and specializes more in affective relationships and joint consumption [p. 61].

ability to provide incentives and monitor performance and on how its ability to do so differs among activities and societies, it clarifies which activities are carried out by the family. Second, by emphasizing the role of institutions in structuring complex, long-term relationships, the contracting perspective of the transaction cost approach elucidates allocation and distribution within the family.

Because of the central role of unobservable variables (e.g., preferences, household technology, genetic endowments), the new home economics view of the family does not lead simply or directly to a model capable of empirical implementation.[8] Unobservable variables also play a key role in the transaction cost approach; and, even in the context of the firm and vertical integration, the transaction cost approach is often charged with failing to provide a framework for empirical research. Not surprisingly, the offspring of the marriage of the subject matter of the new home economics with the analytical orientation of the transaction cost approach is not a system of equations that an econometrician could estimate. Nevertheless, because the ability of the transaction cost approach to provide a framework for empirical analysis is a crucial issue, throughout this essay I identify topics and areas of research suggested by the transaction cost approach.

My primary purpose, however, is to describe an *approach,* not to specify a *model.* This paper is an essay, not a research program or agenda. The methodological justification for such an enterprise is that an occasional exploratory essay is useful because formal models are self-contained constructs and cannot tell us what phenomena are worth modeling.[9]

The paper is organized as follows. In the first section I examine the advan-

8. Michael T. Hannan (1982), in a review of Becker's *Treatise,* points out that Becker fails "to make clear exactly what kinds of evidence would be inconsistent with the theory." He emphasizes the crucial role of unobserved variables, wonders "whether *any* data could be shown convincingly to be inconsistent with the theory," and hence is "not prepared to agree that the theory has already gained a high degree of empirical verification" (p. 71, emphasis in original).

9. Critics of the transaction cost approach often object that it is difficult or impossible to test, refute or falsify, claiming that it explains everything and, therefore, explains nothing. Williamson (1979, p. 233) discusses this criticism and argues that carefully formulated versions of the transaction cost approach are not vulnerable to it. We have already seen that this objection is sometimes raised against the new home economics (Hannan 1982, p. 71). The objection is often expressed in the positivistic language that Paul A. Samuelson's *Foundations of Economic Analysis* (1947) has made familiar to economists. Twenty years after Thomas S. Kuhn's *The Structure of Scientific Revolutions* (1962), many philosophers of science are pessimistic about the possibility of "testing" competing theories or paradigms, even in the physical sciences. Closer to home, it is not clear what set of observations would cause economists to abandon the neoclassical theory of consumer behavior, or even to reject the version of it which assumes that preferences (for unobservable "commodities") are exogenous and identical over time and space (George J. Stigler and Becker 1977). Similarly, it is not clear what set of observations would convince sociologists that tastes are exogenous.

tages and disadvantages of family governance and apply the analysis to two types of economic activity: production for home consumption and production for a market. In the second section I turn to the internal organization of families and households, focusing on allocation and distribution within the family. I begin by analyzing marriage as a "contracting problem." I then argue that the transaction cost approach is broadly consistent with bargaining models of marriage, and examine the roles of marriage-specific capital from a bargaining perspective. Finally, I discuss social exchange theory and its relationship to the transaction cost approach. Section III is a brief conclusion.

I. The Family as a Governance Structure for Economic Activity

The advantages of the family as a governance structure for organizing particular activities flow from its ability to integrate those activities with preexisting, ongoing, significant personal relationships.[10] I examine the advantages of family governance and its corresponding disadvantages in Section A. In Section B I discuss the role of transaction cost considerations in the family's production for its own consumption, focusing on the family's role as a provider of insurance, that is, protection against the economic consequences of uncertain, adverse events. The family has been the traditional source of such protection throughout history; even in advanced industrial societies some types of insurance continue to be provided by the family, while others are provided by the market, and still others by the state. In Section C I examine the role of transaction cost considerations in family governance of market-oriented work by discussing family farms and family-managed firms, that is, firms in which several family members play active managerial roles. Finally, in Section D, I compare the characteristic advantages and disadvantages of family governance with those of market governance and argue that certain identifiable types of activities are more efficiently organized through markets while others are more efficiently carried out by families.

A. Advantages and Disadvantages

The advantages of family governance can be grouped into four categories: incentives, monitoring, altruism, and loyalty. All of the family's incentive advantages arise because its members have claims on family resources; some of these advantages can be analyzed in a single period setting, while others depend on the anticipated continuity of family membership. Even in a one-period setting family members have reason to take account of the effects of their actions on family wealth. The strength of this incentive effect depends on the size

---

10. Burton Benedict (1968, p. 2) refers to such relationships as "affectively charged."

of the family and on its sharing rule: It is weakest in large families with equal sharing, and strongest in small ones with sharing rules conditioned on individual behavior. Those incentive advantages that arise only in a multiperiod setting and that depend on expectations of lifelong family membership make individuals reluctant to sacrifice long-run benefits for short-run gains. Without such expectations individuals would be less certain that their claims would be honored in the future and, hence, would act to move family consumption or income toward the present. Furthermore, individuals may value family consumption and income beyond their own lifetimes because of their concern for the welfare of their own children or grandchildren. Thus, prudential and dynastic considerations combine to give family members direct, long-term interests in the family's well-being.

Because economic relationships are entwined with significant personal ones, the family commands rewards and sanctions not open to other institutions. Severe misconduct involves not simply the risk of dismissal from a job but also the risk of ostracism or expulsion from the family, a penalty drastic enough that it is likely to be an effective deterrent to serious malfeasance.

The monitoring advantages of the family also flow from the entwining of economic and personal relationships. Diligence and work habits, consumption patterns and lifestyles are more likely to be observable because the network of relationships involving "economic activity" and "family" are integrated. The family's informational advantages are greatest when its members live together as a joint or extended family household—a common arrangement in many developing countries. But monitoring advantages, although facilitated by communal living arrangements, do not depend exclusively on them: Social contacts within the family provide information unavailable to outsiders.

"Altruism," based on "love," "affection," and "caring," serves to limit opportunistic behavior within the family.[11] The affectional relationships among family members, whatever their basis, may provide a relatively secure and stable foundation for a wide range of activities.

"Family loyalty" provides a convenient rubric for discussing dimensions of incentives and monitoring that economists are trained to ignore. Although what we call family loyalty may be a consequence of altruism or of the particular incentive, monitoring, and altruism attributes of the family, it is useful to treat loyalty as a separate category and to examine its social and psychological basis.

The social basis of family loyalty rests on generally accepted norms or standards of conduct regarding the treatment of family members which are en-

11. Becker uses the term "altruism" to refer to a very special type of interdependent preferences. I discuss Becker's notion of altruism and his theory of allocation within the family in Section IIB.

forced through reputation. Individuals perceived as fulfilling family obligations are rewarded with respect and esteem and those perceived as violating them are punished by loss of reputation. The value and importance of reputation varies from one society to another: In traditional societies with little geographical mobility, reputation may be an important factor in personal and business success, and loss of reputation a significant penalty.

The psychological basis of family loyalty depends on individuals' internalizing society's values, standards, and expectations. Fulfilling family obligations becomes a source of pleasure, pride, and satisfaction, and violating them a source of guilt. The rewards and sanctions are thus internalized, incorporated into individuals' preferences and values.

The value of loyalty is not confined to families. Nations, clubs, and firms attempt to instill and foster loyalty in their citizens, members, employees, and managers. Indeed, the language of loyalty itself relies heavily on family metaphors. Citizens are urged to support "Mother Russia" or the "Fatherland"; college students join "fraternities" or "sororities"; workers join labor unions whose names often include the word "brotherhood"; firms like "Ma Bell" have encouraged employees to view them as a family and in doing so claim their allegiance, support, and love. These attempts to encourage loyalty reflect its instrumental value to organizations, as Albert O. Hirschman (1970) and Armen Alchian and Harold Demsetz (1972, pp. 790–91) have argued. Almost unconscious reliance on family metaphors to describe or foster loyalty suggests that family ties are recognized as ties that bind.[12]

Notwithstanding its advantages, family governance has four characteristic disadvantages. First, conflict may spill over from one sphere into the other. Although the family may function harmoniously, bound together by ties of affection and interest, even the most casual empiricist must recognize the possibility of discord. The largely anecdotal literature on family firms emphasizes conflicts between parents and children and conflicts among siblings.[13] Conflicts

12. Janet T. Landa (1981) analyzes the role of ethnic ties as well as kinship ties and the importance of gradations in these relationships in establishing the reliability of trading partners. Landa and Janet W. Salaff (1982) examine the rise and fall of the Tan Kah Kee Company, a Singapore-based family firm which they describe as the largest Chinese-owned rubber manufacturing and exporting firm in Southeast Asia in the 1920s (p. 21). Drawing on Landa's analysis, they show that kinship and ethnic ties played an important role in the growth of the firm. They attribute the fall of the Tan Kah Kee Company to the collapse in rubber prices during the Depression and the consequent necessity of ceding control of the firm to "outsiders" (i.e., British bankers and their agents). Landa and Salaff provide extensive references to the literature on family firms in sociology, anthropology, and development economics.

13. Peter Davis (1983) summarizes this literature and presents an analytical framework that is broadly consistent with the transaction cost analysis developed here. An article in *Fortune*, "Family Business is a Passion Play," (Gwen Kinkead 1980) gives the flavor of the popular literature.

between parents and children centering on the desire of children for independence and of parents to retain control may be continual sources of friction and may pose particularly difficult problems of leadership succession for family firms. Sibling tensions and rivalries whose roots lie buried in early childhood can influence the behavior and relationships of middle-aged men and women as their generation assumes control of the family firm. By linking the firm and the family, the family's stability becomes a source of strength for the firm, but the family's instability becomes a source of weakness.

Second, inefficient behavior or slack performance may be tolerated because of the difficulty of evaluating and disciplining family members. Objective and dispassionate evaluations of the ability and performance of family members are difficult to make. Furthermore, acting on adverse evaluations may provoke deep-seated resentment persisting through generations. The threat of ostracism gives family firms an advantage in controlling gross malfeasance; but because of its severity and because its use imposes significant costs on others in the family, ostracism is not a credible threat against shirking, slack performance, or minor infractions. The family has available a wide range of social rewards and sanctions that it could in principle use to express its approval or disapproval of an individual's actions or behavior; in practice, however, the family may not be able to calibrate and utilize these rewards and sanctions effectively. It is unclear whether family governance is more or less effective than nonfamily governance in discouraging minor infractions and slack performance. Furthermore, nepotism may prove a serious problem for the family firm.[14]

Third, the capacities, aptitudes, and talents of family members may fail to mesh with the needs of the family's economic activities. The problem is not that certain activities require training; traditionally families have assumed responsibility for children's education and for vocational training. The problem is that certain activities require special talents. Whether the talent mix available within the family in a particular generation meshes well with the requirements of the family's activities depends in part on genetics and in part on luck. When no available family members manifest the required aptitudes, then such activities, if they are to remain within the family, must be carried on without suitable personnel. Whether family governance entails substantial inefficiencies depends on the ability of alternative governance structures to achieve better

14. Nepotism may be an even more serious problem in other governance structures, and it is likely to be most serious in those that delegate substantial discretionary authority to individuals who lack commitment to the organization's objectives. It is no coincidence that the term "nepotism," from the Italian *nepotismo,* "favoring of 'nephews,' " was first used to describe practices of the pre-Reformation Catholic Church: "A euphemistic use of 'nephew' is that of the natural son of a pope, cardinal or other ecclesiastic; and from the practice of granting preferments to such children the word 'nepotism' is used of any favouritism shown in finding positions for a man's family" ("Nephew," *Encyclopaedia Britannica,* 11th ed. 1911).

matches between individuals and activities. Thus, family governance is most efficient in activities requiring talents that are difficult for nonfamily institutions to evaluate and in those not requiring rare or unusual aptitudes.

Fourth, size limitations implied by family governance may prevent the realization of technologically achievable economies of scale. The boundaries of the family or kin group relevant for organizing economic activity are influenced by economic considerations, not rigidly determined by biology. Nevertheless, because expansion weakens the incentive and monitoring advantages of family governance, the family is ill-equipped to exploit scale economies.[15] Insurance, an activity in which limited scale implies limited risk-spreading, provides a range of illustrations, including some in which the balance of advantages and disadvantages favors family governance.

B. Family Governance of Production for Home Consumption: Insurance

Home is the place where, when you have to go there,
They have to take you in.

Robert Frost
"The Death of the Hired Man"

The household production approach, with its emphasis on prices and technology, has dominated the analysis of activities in which households or families produce goods for their own consumption. This analysis captures the essence of some household "make-or-buy" decisions, but other household production activities—such as the provision of education, health care, and insurance—are better analyzed from a transaction cost perspective.

Protection against the adverse economic consequences of old age, separation and divorce, unemployment, or the illness or death of an earner can be provided in many ways. In many societies the family is the principal provider of such protection. In advanced industrial societies the family, the market, and the state provide varying degrees of protection against these and other adversities. Market insurance typically provides monetary benefits according to an explicit schedule (e.g., aid to dependent children) and sometimes benefits in kind (e.g., direct provision of care for the sick, handicapped, or disabled); such benefits, whether in cash or in kind, are not always characterized as insurance. The family, in contrast, typically provides benefits in kind rather than in cash and according to an implicit rather than an explicit schedule.

15. Family firms, if they are to grow in size and complexity to exploit economies of scale, face the problem of integrating professional nonfamily managers with family managers. The growth possibilities of a family firm are severely constrained if it is unable or unwilling to attract and accept nonfamily managers, yet success in introducing nonfamily managers may undermine its character as a family firm.

Family provision of benefits often entails restructuring domestic arrangements so that family members who had previously lived in separate households form a single residential unit. Unemployed young adults and recently separated or divorced individuals and their children often move in with parents; orphans are taken in by relatives; elderly parents often move in with their children. Because the household and the nuclear family tend to coincide, the terms "household" and "family" are often used interchangeably.[16] This usage is misleading even for advanced industrial societies and it is seriously misleading for developing countries. Analysis of household formation—the establishment of separate households by the young and the elderly, or as a consequence of separation or divorce—and, more generally, analysis of the role of kin ties in economic relationships requires maintaining the distinction between households and families.[17] Although the phrase "household production" is too well-established to be displaced by "family production," in the provision of insurance and in many other activities, the fundamental unit is not the household but the family.

The insurance literature identifies two reasons why market insurance may be inefficient: "adverse selection" and "moral hazard."[18] Adverse selection arises when each individual knows his probability of loss better than potential insurers (asymmetric information) and when individuals can opportunistically misrepresent their loss probabilities to potential insurers.[19] This conjunction of asymmetric information and opportunism leaves individuals without credible ways of communicating to a potential insurer their true risk characteristics. Under these circumstances potential insurers find it costly or impossible to distinguish between high-risk and low-risk individuals and, hence, the market must charge everyone the same premium. Low-risk individuals may find this premium excessive and choose to self-insure (i.e., to cover their own losses

16. For example, Laslett (1972) uses the term "family" to refer to a household—a co-resident domestic group—and much of his work has been devoted to documenting the predominance of nuclear households in Europe during the last three centuries.

17. Fuchs (1983) provides an overview and references to the literature on many of these issues. On separation and divorce, see Becker, Elisabeth M. Landes and Michael (1977). On the establishment of separate households by the young and the elderly, see Marjorie B. McElroy (1985) and Michael, Fuchs and Sharon R. Scott (1980), respectively. For work emphasizing the strength and importance of kin ties and challenging the myth that the predominance of nuclear households implies the irrelevance of other family relationships, see, for example, Philip J. Greven, Jr. (1970), Michael Anderson (1971) and Hareven (1977a, 1978).

18. Mark V. Pauly (1974), Michael Rothschild and Joseph E. Stiglitz (1976), and Charles Wilson (1977). Two important and widely cited papers going well beyond the insurance issues are Arrow (1963) and George A. Akerlof (1970). Isaac Ehrlich and Becker (1972) discuss the role of "self-protection" as a substitute for market insurance.

19. Williamson (1975, p. 31–33) terms this conjunction of asymmetric information and opportunism "information impactedness."

instead of purchasing market insurance). With a continuum of risk-classes, it may be impossible for market insurance to operate at all: there may be no premium level that would induce purchases by a group of individuals whose total expected losses would be covered by their total premium payments.[20] Moral hazard arises because individuals can undertake activities that alter the probabilities they will suffer losses or that mitigate the magnitudes of losses that do occur. Because insurers cannot easily monitor whether individuals have undertaken such activities and because individuals can opportunistically misrepresent whether they have done so, market insurance arrangements may provide protection against the economic consequences of uncertain, adverse events only at the cost of substantial inefficiency.

The state has certain advantages over market insurers in dealing with adverse selection and moral hazard. Compulsory insurance—whether provided by the market, as with automobile liability insurance, or by the state, as with social security—avoids adverse selection by preventing low-risk individuals from opting out. State-imposed standards of conduct can reduce moral hazard, but asymmetric information and opportunism pose problems for the state as well as for market insurers. While state enforcement may be more effective than private enforcement, it is hardly a panacea: Requiring recipients of unemployment compensation to seek work has proved difficult to enforce.

As a provider of insurance, the family has three important transactional advantages over the market and the state. First, adverse selection is limited because outsiders cannot easily join the family nor insiders easily withdraw. Second, information disparities between individuals and their families are generally smaller than those between individuals and nonfamily insurers. Proximity yields substantial monitoring advantages, permitting the family to assess health or intensity of job search more easily, economically, and accurately than the market or the state. Third, both family loyalty and cultural norms limit opportunistic behavior. Virtually every society condemns cheating one's family far more strongly than cheating strangers—blood is thicker than water.

As a provider of insurance the family also has characteristic disabilities. First, conflicts originating in personal relationships can impinge on the insur-

---

20. In the "lemons" paper (Akerlof 1970) the used-car market serves to illustrate this phenomenon. Sellers know the quality of the cars they are offering for sale, but potential buyers know only the average quality of used cars sold in the market. These circumstances can give rise to two distinct problems. First, as Akerlof points out, "it is quite possible to have the bad driving out the not-so-bad driving out the medium driving out the not-so-good driving out the good in such a sequence of events that" no transactions take place (p. 239)—that is, the only equilibrium may be one in which there is no trade. Second, as Rothschild and Stiglitz (1976) point out, equilibrium may fail to exist. Wilson (1980) shows that price-setting conventions can play a crucial role in markets with adverse selection.

ance arrangement. Such conflicts may make those obligated to provide benefits unwilling to do so, especially when the benefits call for restructuring living arrangements by combining households. Additionally, disputes growing out of the insurance arrangement itself are potential sources of family conflict.

Second, it is difficult to make objective and dispassionate evaluations of risk and of the extent to which individuals undertake to alter these probabilities or mitigate the magnitude of losses. Furthermore, once such evaluations of family members are made, they may be difficult to act on: Poor risks, once identified, cannot easily be excluded from participation in family insurance arrangements.

Third, because the family or kin group is relatively small, risks cannot be spread widely enough to realize fully the advantages of insurance. This problem is most serious in situations involving small probabilities of large losses. Furthermore, when family members face risks that are positively correlated, the family's ability to protect itself through self-insurance is even more limited than its size would suggest. For example, family members working in the same industry or growing the same crops in the same region are poorly positioned to provide each other with unemployment insurance or crop insurance. Thus, since the effectiveness of insurance depends on both the size of the insured group and on the independence of the risks to which its members are exposed, the transaction cost advantages of family insurance are balanced by technical disadvantages.

Insurance is typical of a substantial class of economic activities for which the transaction cost advantages of family governance often outweigh the technical advantages of nonfamily governance. The balance between these advantages and disadvantages is not immutable, as demonstrated by the shifting of some, but by no means all, insurance functions from the family to the market, to nonprofit institutions, and to the state. With insurance, as with the provision of education and health care, market governance entails substantial transaction cost difficulties. Hence, in societies in which these functions are not carried out by the family, they tend to be assumed by nonprofit institutions and the state rather than by profit-oriented firms.

C. Family Governance of Market-Oriented Work: Family Farms and Family-Managed Firms

The family-managed firm and the family farm solve different organizational problems: The family-managed firm is a response to the difficulty of supervising managers, the family farm a response to the difficulty of supervising workers.[21] Despite the differences between supervising managers and super-

---

21. I distinguish family-managed firms both from firms that are merely family-owned and from those in which only a single family member participates in management.

vising workers, the advantages and disadvantages of family-managed firms and family farms are similar, and both illustrate the role of family governance of market-oriented work.[22]

The family farm—typically worked jointly by a married couple and their children or, in many societies, by members of an extended family who live together in a single household—is the dominant form of agricultural organization in the United States and in most developed and developing countries.[23] The family farm can be regarded as an organizational solution to the difficulty of monitoring and supervising workers who, for technological reasons, cannot be gathered together in a single location.

When agricultural tasks can be monitored easily in terms of inputs or outputs, family farms are often overshadowed by other forms of agricultural organization. For some crops and some tasks hired labor can be concentrated into work gangs and supervised directly, so plantation agriculture is possible.[24] For other crops and tasks (e.g., harvesting) output can be measured directly and workers paid on a piece-rate basis. Thus, agricultural wage labor, hired on a daily or a seasonal basis, is important in both developed and developing countries. Nevertheless, since most farm tasks are not susceptible to either of these

22. In both cases the focus on the incentive properties of family governance of market-oriented activity suggests a comparison with consumer or producer cooperatives or labor-managed firms. Jaroslav Vanek (1969) makes strong claims for the advantages of the latter:

> Without any doubt, labor-management is among all the existing forms of enterprise organizations the optimal arrangement when it comes to the finding of the utility-maximizing effort, i.e., the proper quality, duration and intensity of work, by the working collective. Not only is there no situation of conflict between management and the workers that might hinder the finding of the optimum, but the process of self-management itself can be viewed as a highly efficient device for communication, collusion control and enforcement among the participants [p. 1011].

Whether labor-managed firms actually realize these advantages is an open question; Williamson's analysis of the disabilities of peer group organization of production suggests that they may not. Furthermore, the ability of a family to realize these alleged advantages must depend on its internal organization and structure: A hierarchical family (e.g., patriarchal) would not operate in the manner Vanek suggests, although it might offer other advantages for organizing production.

23. Family farms accounted for 67.6 percent of the value of farm products sold in the U.S. in 1974, the most recent year for which these data were reported in the *Statistical Abstract of the United States* (10th ed., 1984, p. 653, Table 1143).

24. Plantation agriculture is sometimes compatible with slavery. Stefano Fenoaltea (1984), in a rich and fascinating paper, argues that the "pain incentives" to which slaves can be subjected make slave labor more suitable for "effort-intensive" than "care-intensive" activities, and that the threat of sabotage makes slave labor more suitable for land-intensive than capital-intensive activities. Thus slave gangs were better suited to the cotton and corn agriculture of the American South than to the vine and olive arboriculture of the Mediterranean.

forms of supervision or monitoring, the family farm is the dominant form of agricultural organization.[25]

Empirical work on agricultural organization has seldom distinguished between family and nonfamily labor, although recent research suggests the importance of doing so.[26] The transaction cost approach draws attention to this distinction by offering two reasons why family and nonfamily labor might be imperfect substitutes: the incentive and monitoring advantages of family organization which I have emphasized in this essay and the idiosyncratic information and knowledge of local conditions that family members are likely to possess.[27] The transaction cost approach generates interesting empirical research projects in this field because it helps to analyze the degree to which family and nonfamily labor are imperfect substitutes in various types of agricultural production and it helps to sort out the roles of incentives and asymmetric information.[28]

Managers in family-managed firms have expectations of a continuing relationship with the firm and claims on its profits and, therefore, are subject to different and perhaps more effective rewards and sanctions than managers in

25. Discussions of agricultural organization in economics have focused almost exclusively on other issues. The principal focus has been on sharecropping, and while incentive and monitoring issues are sometimes mentioned (along with risk aversion and imperfections in capital and other markets) family aspects of agricultural organization are ignored. In particular, most discussions assume that the sharecropper is an individual worker. Similarly, discussions of rural labor markets often treat labor as homogeneous, failing to distinguish among men, women, and children and seldom offering integrated models of family labor supply. See Howard N. Barnum and Lyn Squire (1979) and Hans P. Binswanger and Mark R. Rosenzweig (1984). Peter Murrell (1983) offers a transaction cost analysis of sharecropping, although he does not discuss the role of the family.

26. Anil B. Deolalikar and Wim P. M. Vijverberg (1983) provide references to the literature and report evidence on the heterogeneity of family and nonfamily labor using district-level data from India. Deolalikar and Vijverberg (1987) report similar findings using farm-level data from India and Malaysia.

27. Rosenzweig and Kenneth I. Wolpin (1985), for example, build a model of intergenerational transfers around the "specific experience" hypothesis.

28. Binswanger and Rosenzweig (1982) view agricultural organization as a consequence of the interplay between asymmetric information and what they term the "material conditions of agriculture" (p. 58). Thus, they argue, differences in the characteristics of the technology from one crop to another have predictable effects on the organization of production. For example, with trees whose continued value depends on pruning and maintenance (e.g., coffee, cocoa, apples) "an owner is unlikely to rent out his trees to a tenant-operator in a contract whose duration is less than the productive life of the tree, given the difficulty of assessing maintenance intensity in the short-run" (p. 47). On the other hand, "coconuts do not require pruning" and "tenancy in coconut trees is quite frequent in India" (p. 49). Although they recognize that family labor has both informational and incentive advantages over nonfamily labor (pp. 31–35), they do not systematically examine the asymmetric information in the context of particular agricultural technologies.

other firms. Both types of firms can reward successful managers with salary increases and promotions, but performance is often difficult to assess and managers may be able to manipulate short-run indicators of performance at the expense of the long-run objectives of the firm. Because family managers expect a continuing relationship with the firm, they are less tempted to sacrifice long-run advantages for short-run gains.[29]

The behavior of family managers can usually be monitored more easily than that of nonfamily managers. The general principle requires no further elaboration, but it must be qualified by the observation that family members living three thousand miles apart may monitor each other less effectively than managers in nonfamily firms located in a small city. Family relationships are not the sole determinant of monitoring costs.

Sally Griffen and Clyde Griffen (1977) emphasize the role of family loyalty and trust in business in nineteenth-century America. Discussing families' use of bankruptcy laws, they write:

> In the Darwinian jungle of small business in the United States, survival frequently involved use of family relationships, founded in trust, to take advantage of loopholes in the law [p. 154].
>
> The family proved most useful in all of these legal maneuverings because of trust between its members. Family members could betray that trust—wives could leave their husbands and parents could let their children remain stranded—but the assumption apparently was that they would not or, at least, that relationships outside the family would be even less trustworthy. The same need for trust and loyalty in a mobile society undoubtedly accounts for the frequency of family members in business partnerships in the city. No less than 48% of the firms ever run as partnerships in Poughkeepsie brought together relatives at one time or another [p. 156].

Neoclassical theory obviates the need for distinguishing between family and nonfamily governance by assuming that all firms are frictionless profit-maximizers. Because of this theoretical presumption and the paucity of statistical data, economists have virtually ignored family firms. The major exceptions fall into two subfields—development economics and economic history—but as a consequence of the limitations of theory and data, the treatment of family firms is largely anecdotal.

The transaction cost approach cannot provide the data, but it does provide a

29. Nonfamily firms can and do attempt to provide incentives that bind managers to the firm and induce them to take a long view. Profit-sharing, for example, gives managers an interest in the short-run performance of the firm, while pension plans and stock options represent (among other things) attempts to tie managers' rewards to the long-run performance of the firm as a whole and their interests to the long-run interests of the firm.

theoretical rationale for distinguishing between family and nonfamily firms and it suggests that their behavior might differ systematically. Two behavioral dimensions in which comparison seems especially promising are efficiency and innovation. Recently developed techniques for measuring the efficiency of firms (Finn R. Førsund, C. A. Knox Lovell, and Peter Schmidt 1980) could be used to compare the efficiency of family and nonfamily firms in particular industries. It is often asserted that family firms are technologically conservative and slow to exploit newly emerging profit opportunities; on the other hand, it is also often asserted that owner-entrepreneurs are more likely than professional managers to be innovators. It would be interesting to know whether, controlling for firm size and for industry, family firms are more or less likely to innovate than nonfamily firms. Although the transaction cost approach offers a set of reasons why the efficiency and innovativeness of family and nonfamily firms might differ, it does not offer unambiguous predictions about which will be more efficient or more innovative. Hence, a finding that family and nonfamily governance differ systematically in efficiency, innovativeness, or other behavioral dimensions would not constitute a "test" of the transaction cost approach.[30] It would demonstrate, however, its fruitfulness in suggesting interesting topics for investigation.

D. Assessment: Family vs. Nonfamily Governance

Family governance of economic activities is likely to assure loyal and trustworthy performance; nonfamily governance is likely to assure technical competence and skill. The relative importance of these sets of attributes varies from society to society and from sector to sector. The possible combinations are exhibited in Table 1. One would expect family governance to predominate in low-trust environments (that is, in societies in which nonfamily members are not expected to perform honestly or reliably) and in sectors utilizing relatively simple technologies (that is, in sectors using technologies which a high proportion of adults in the society are capable of mastering quickly).[31] Conversely, nonfamily governance would predominate in high-trust environments and in sectors using complex technologies. In the case of high trust and simple tech-

30. The analysis proposed here is relevant for both family firms and family farms.

31. Edward C. Banfield's *The Moral Basis of a Backward Society* (1958) explains the economic and political backwardness of southern Italy by "the inability of the villagers to act together for their common good or, indeed, for any end transcending the immediate material interest of the nuclear family" (p. 10). Banfield argues that this cultural ethos, which he terms "amoral familism," with its emphasis on the nuclear family rather than some larger group (e.g., the extended family or nonfamily political, religious or social groups) is pathological (p. 163). He does not, however, discuss the forces that bind the nuclear family together, nor does he offer a convincing analysis of the origins of amoral familism (pp. 153–54).

Table 1   Environment, Technology, and Organizational Form

	Simple technology	Complex technology
Low-trust environment	family governance	?
High-trust environment	both family and nonfamily governance	nonfamily governance

nology, family and nonfamily governance may coexist. In the final case, low trust and complex technology, both family and nonfamily governance encounter serious difficulties, and neither form may be viable. The relative decline of family-based economic activities in advanced industrial societies may reflect a shifting balance between the importance of their characteristic advantages and disabilities—a secular movement from low-trust and simple technology environments favoring family governance to high-trust and complex technology environments favoring nonfamily governance.

This discussion and the corresponding table have focused on only one feature of the technology, its complexity, and only one feature of the environment, the reliability and trustworthiness of nonfamily members, implicitly holding fixed other features of the technology and the environment. Another feature of the technology, the minimum efficient scale of production, and another feature of the environment, the trustworthiness of family members and the stability of family ties, deserve further attention.

Like increases in complexity, increases in minimum efficient scale favor market governance over family governance. Such increases may reflect technological innovations or, as Williamson (1975, Chs. 8, 9; 1981, Section 4) has stressed, organizational innovations such as the multidivisional or M-form firm, the conglomerate, and the multinational corporation. Technological innovations over the last two-hundred years have increased minimum efficient scale and thus favored nonfamily over family governance. Organizational innovations have also favored larger units by making it administratively feasible to take advantage of technically feasible economies of scale and scope.

Decreases in the trustworthiness and reliability of family ties also favor nonfamily over family governance. Economists have tended to view the family as a harmonious unit and to regard conflict and discord as aberrations of little relevance for economic analysis. In the next section I consider issues related to the causes and consequences of such conflicts.

II. Internal Organization of Families

The family's internal organization is a determinant of its effectiveness as a governance structure for economic activities and for distribution within the family.

I begin in Section A by examining marriage from a contracting perspective, emphasizing the difficulties of using contracts to structure complex, ongoing relationships. In Section B I turn to allocation and distribution within the family, bargaining models of marriage, and the roles of marriage- or family-specific capital. In Section C I discuss social exchange theory, arguing that it is broadly consistent with approaches emphasizing bargaining. Section D summarizes the case for bargaining models.

A. Marriage and Contract

Individuals desire secure long-term family relationships to provide a stable environment in which to live and to rear children and, in Becker's terminology, to reduce the risks associated with accumulating marital-specific or marriage-specific capital.[32] This requires an institutional structure that is both flexible enough to allow adaptive, sequential decisionmaking in the face of unfolding events and rigid enough to safeguard each spouse against opportunistic exploitation by the other. Marriage is a governance structure which, more or less satisfactorily, accommodates these requirements.

In *Ancient Law* (1861) Sir Henry Sumner Maine identified the progress of civilization with a movement *"from Status to Contract."* He argued that modern society is founded on obligations that individuals create for themselves by voluntary agreements and promises rather than on obligations involuntarily and automatically imposed on them because of their status within the family. Maine's thesis provides a starting point for several recent discussions of marriage. Tony Tanner (1979), for example, begins by quoting several long passages from Maine and views adultery against this background: ". . . adultery can be seen as an attempt to establish an extracontractual contract, or indeed an anticontract . . ." (p. 6) that threatens the fabric of society. "For bourgeois society marriage is the all-subsuming, all-organizing, all-containing contract. It is the structure that maintains the Structure . . ." (p. 15). For this reason ". . . the problem of transgressing the marriage contract . . . is at the center . . ." of the late eighteenth- and early nineteenth-century novel (p. 12).

Like Tanner, Lenore J. Weitzman (1981) begins with Maine but she denies that his thesis applies to family law: ". . . marriage has not moved from status to contract" (p. xix). The tension between the status and the contract views of

32. Becker uses the phrase "marital-specific capital" to refer to capital that would be "much less valuable" if the particular marriage dissolved (Becker, Landes and Michael 1977, p. 338). "Children are the prime example, especially young children, although learning about the idiosyncrasies of one's spouse is also important . . ." (Becker 1981, p. 224). Becker, Landes and Michael also include "working exclusively in the nonmarket sector" (pp. 1142, 1152), as marriage-specific capital. I return to marriage-specific capital in Section B.

marriage is summarized in a recent family law case book by Walter O. Weyrauch and Sanford N. Katz (1983):

> *Maynard, Ponder,* and *Ryan* relate to the nature of marriage as seen
> in the light of Sir Henry Sumner Maine's famous statement, "that the
> movement of the progressive societies has been a movement *from
> Status to Contract.*" In legal practice this statement has never had the
> same significance it has had for scholarship, but relational and con-
> tractual aspects of marriage have lived side by side relatively undis-
> turbed. These cases illustrate that legal practice can live with and ac-
> commodate apparent contradictions with ease. *Maynard* stands today
> for the proposition that marriage is something more than a mere con-
> tract, that it is a status or a relationship and, as such, subject to regu-
> lation by the government.
> *Ponder,* on the other hand, . . . , continues to be relied on for the
> seemingly opposite proposition that marriage is contract rather than a
> mere relationship, and that legislation regulating marriage could con-
> ceivably impair the obligation of contract if it affects vested rights. . . .
> *Maynard* can be cited whenever an argument in support of the police
> power of the state to regulate marriage is made, while *Ponder* can be
> cited in support of the contractual autonomy of marital parties to regu-
> late their own affairs. In an extreme case this may be done within the
> same case, and *Ryan* demonstrates this capacity to draw from contra-
> dictory sources for support [p. 59].

Firms do not marry, but transaction cost analysis argues that they often resort
to merger or vertical integration to avoid using contracts to structure complex,
ongoing relationships. Short-term contracts require frequent renegotiation,
making it risky to accumulate capital whose value is contingent on the relationship continuing and discouraging investment in such specific capital. Complete
long-term contracts which specify every possible contingency are costly or impossible to write, a reflection of bounded rationality and asymmetric information. Incomplete long-term contracts which fail to specify every possible contingency are perilous because uncovered contingencies must be dealt with
through bilateral negotiations under circumstances that may give one party or
the other a strategic advantage. While the parties have some control over how
complete their contract is to be, more complete contracts are relatively expensive to write and relatively rigid to apply. To avoid these contracting hazards
firms often rely on some more complete form of integration such as merger.
Since bureaucratic structures have their own characteristic disabilities, internal
governance does not eliminate all difficulties associated with a transaction or
exchange. Nevertheless, replacing a market relationship by an organization
with an appropriate governance structure often safeguards the interests of both
parties.

Comparing marriage and merger calls attention to the difference between individuals and firms. When two firms merge, at least one of them loses its legal identity and disappears. When two individuals marry, this is not the case, or, more precisely, this is no longer the case. Sir William Blackstone (1765), describing marriage under eighteenth-century common law, wrote:

> By marriage, the husband and wife are one person in law . . . [T]he very being or legal existence of the woman is suspended during marriage, or at least is incorporated and consolidated into that of the husband, under whose wing, protection, and cover she performs everything; and is therefore called . . . a femme-covert; and her condition during her marriage is called her coverture.[33]

Thus under the eighteenth-century English common law the parallel between marriage and merger was striking: the wife's legal personality was merged with and submerged in her husband's.

Recent legal scholarship that emphasizes the diversity of contracting modes provides a closely related analysis of these issues. Ian R. Macneil (1978) distinguishes among "classical," "neoclassical," and "relational" contracting.[34] The classical paradigm ignores any relationship between the parties other than that established by the contract itself: The parties' identities are irrelevant, since they may be viewed as trading with the market rather than with each other. The classical paradigm thus adopts a discrete transactions view that is very close to the economist's stereotype of contract law. Neoclassical and relational contracting arose in response to the difficulties of using contracts to structure complex, long-term relationships. Neoclassical contracting introduces a governance structure, often involving third-party arbitration, to reduce these hazards. Relational contracting goes a step further in this direction by treating the ongoing relationship between the parties rather than the contract as central. Collective bargaining is the leading example. Thus, the disabilities of contracts for structuring complex, long-term relationships apply to both commercial and personal contracts.

In Macneil's terminology marriage is a relational contract. The feature that makes classical and neoclassical contracting inappropriate for structuring labor relations agreements—their inability to view specific disputes in the context of a continuing relationship requiring adaptive, sequential decisionmaking— makes them at least equally inappropriate for structuring marriage. Relational contracting provides a more instructive model.

33. After quoting this passage Weitzman (1981) goes on to quote Justice Black: "this rule has worked out in reality to mean that though the husband and wife are one, the one is the husband" (p. 1). U.S. v. Yazell, 382 U.S. 341, 359 (1966).

34. Williamson (1979) develops the implications of Macneil's analysis for the transaction cost approach. See also Macneil (1974, 1980).

Weitzman (1981) and others have recently urged that privately negotiated marriage contracts be treated like other contracts, enforceable through the courts, but not accorded special treatment.[35] The contracting analysis of Williamson and Macneil draws attention to the range of contracting modes and implies that relational contracts, because they are likely to be less complete than other contracts, are more dependent on legal rules and on institutions for their interpretation and articulation. This dependence on rules and institutions signals a larger role for the state, organized religion, or custom, and a correspondingly smaller role for the contracting parties than is typical in classical and neoclassical contracting.[36] This is evident in labor law, where relational contracting is most fully developed: Special rules and institutions have been created to circumvent the perceived defects of classical and neoclassical contracting.[37] Treating marriage contracts "like any other contract" is to treat them as classical contracts. But marriage contracts, because they are relational contracts, do require "special treatment": Dispute resolution would require special

35. Weitzman describes marriage as a contract whose terms are imposed by the state rather than negotiated privately by the parties and examines the terms of that state-imposed contract. She then offers examples of privately negotiated marriage contracts and argues that such "intimate" contracts provide a means of redressing the sexual imbalance which she believes remains present in family law and of providing the certainty, clarity, and assurance that are often absent in family courts. Her argument relies heavily on an analogy between personal relationships and business or commercial ones: Our legal system recognizes the advantages of allowing individuals and firms considerable latitude in structuring business relationships by privately negotiated contracts; why not allow individuals similar latitude in structuring their personal, intimate relationships? This analogy provides some support for the use of contracts to structure personal relationships, but it also draws attention to the difficulties of doing so. Privately negotiated contracts can increase individuals' abilities to determine the duties and obligations of their personal relationships. Using contracts to structure complex, long-term relationships, whether commercial or personal, is intrinsically hazardous, however, and certainty, clarity, and assurance are not to be found in relational contracts.

36. Because all contracts are subject to certain general rules of law, this distinction is one of degree. Although economists sometimes assume that contracting parties are free to strike any mutually advantageous bargain, this assumption is unwarranted: In the United States some contract provisions are unenforceable because they have been prohibited by statute; others are unenforceable because the courts have held them "contrary to public policy."

37. These rules affect not only dispute resolution under existing collective bargaining agreements but also the conditions under which collective bargaining takes place in the absence of a prior contract or after the expiration of an existing agreement. Recently some U.S. courts have held that, even absent a collective bargaining agreement or an individual contract, "employers cannot dismiss employees arbitrarily or in bad faith." In Europe protection against dismissal without cause is provided through legislation (William B. Gould 1982, p. 7). Clyde W. Summers (1983) provides a brief overview in his introduction to a recent symposium on "employment at will." Mark R. Kramer (1984, pp. 243–47) summarizes recent developments in this rapidly changing area of the law.

rules and perhaps special institutions.[38] Privately negotiated marriage contracts articulated through public rules and institutions that reflect society's values and mores might yield results not very different from those obtained through a system of family courts.[39]

B. Allocation and Distribution within Families

Economists have considered three models of allocation and distribution within families: Samuelson's family consensus model, Becker's altruist model, and recent bargaining models. Although these models usually focus on husbands and wives, they also provide a framework for examining relationships between parents and children. Samuelson's consensus model, explictly articulated in Samuelson (1956), resolves the problem of intrafamily allocation and distribution by postulating a family social welfare function. Samuelson begins by noting that "the fundamental unit on the demand side is clearly the 'family' " (p. 9), and goes on to pose what he terms the "Mr. Jekyll and Mrs. Jekyll" problem: How can we expect family demand functions to obey any consistency conditions? This question, a crucial one from the standpoint of revealed preference theory, provided the motivation for Samuelson's theory of intrafamily allocation:

> Of course, we might try to save the conventional theory by claiming that one titular head has sovereign power within the family and all of its demands reflect his (or her) consistent indifference curves. But as casual anthropologists we all know how unlikely it is in modern Western culture for one person to "wear the pants." It is perhaps less unrealistic to adopt the hypothesis of a consistent "family consensus"

38. This would be true even absent children and the third-party effects associated with them. The presence of children provides a further rationale for state regulation of marriage and the family.

39. As Becker (1981, p. 27, fn. 6) notes, Chinese, Japanese, and Christians have generally relied on oral and customary rather than written marriage contracts. In Christian Europe marriage was historically governed not by the state but by the Church through canon law and ecclesiastical courts. The Jewish marriage contract, the Ketuba, is traditionally written. In Islamic law marriage is a civil contract (John L. Esposito 1982, p. 16) but the parties' latitude to specify its terms is circumscribed (N. J. Coulson 1964, pp. 189–91; Esposito 1982, pp. 23–24).

The special legal rules and institutions governing marriage and the family in the U.S. may be viewed as society's response to the difficulties inherent in structuring such relationships. Four features deserve attention. A standard form marriage "contract" is imposed on the parties to avoid problems of overreaching and unconscionability; specialized courts are responsible for administering family law; courts generally refuse to intervene in ongoing marriages; and the legal system provides a complex and unsatisfactory set of rules in the one area in which they cannot escape involvement: marital dissolution.

that represents a meeting of the minds or a compromise between them. (Perhaps Arrow will produce a proof that such a consensus is impossible.) [p. 9].

Samuelson goes on to consider what he characterizes as "one extreme polar case of family organization":

> This family consists of two or more persons: each person consumes his own goods and has indifference curves ordering those goods, and his preferences among his own goods have the special property of being independent of the other members' consumption. But since blood is thicker than water, the preferences of the different members are interrelated by what might be called a "consensus" or "social welfare function" which takes into account the deservingness or ethical worths of the consumption levels of each of the members. The family acts *as if* it were maximizing their joint welfare function [p. 10].

While Samuelson's approach determines allocation and distribution within the family, this is not his principal concern even in the section of "Social Indifference Curves" entitled "The Problem of Family Preference." His primary point is the logical parallel between distribution in the family and distribution in society. His secondary point, crucial for demand analysis, is that the Mr. Jekyll and Mrs. Jekyll problem can be finessed: The consensus or family social welfare function approach provides a rationale for treating family demand functions as if they were individual demand functions. But because Samuelson's "consensus" is postulated, not derived, his family is simply a preference ordering. Samuelson's concern is to keep the lid on the "black box," not to look inside.

The second model of allocation and distribution within the family is the altruist model articulated in Becker (1974a, 1981).[40] Becker, unlike Samuelson, is primarily concerned with intrafamily allocation. He begins by postulating that the family contains one "altruistic" member whose preferences reflect concern with the welfare of the others.[41] Becker then argues that the presence of one altruist in the family induces purely selfish but rational family members to behave altruistically and that the resulting intrafamily allocation is the one that maximizes the altruist's utility function subject to the family's resource constraint. He concludes that individual differences can be submerged and the

40. Becker (1973) proposes an alternative model of allocation and distribution within the family in which outcomes are essentially determined by the market.

41. Becker's use of the term "altruism" differs from its meaning in sociobiology, although Becker (1976) claims they are closely related.

family treated as a single harmonious unit with consistent preferences, those of the altruist, without arbitrarily postulating Samuelson's family social welfare function: "In my approach the 'optimal reallocation' results from altruism and voluntary contributions, and the 'group preference function' is identical to that of the altruistic head, even when he does not have sovereign power" (1981, p. 192, footnote omitted).

Becker's claims have been challenged. Marilyn Manser and Murray Brown (1980, p. 32) argue that Becker's conclusion depends not merely on the presence of an altruist but also on implicitly introducing a particular bargaining rule, the rule that the household maximizes the altruist's utility function. Manser and Brown are correct that Becker's analysis is seriously flawed, although Becker is correct that his result does not depend on the altruist having sovereign power. Neither Becker nor Manser and Brown have analyzed the conditions under which Becker's results hold. In addition to the dictatorial case, it also holds when the altruist is a player in an asymmetric bargaining game in which he can offer the others all-or-nothing choices.[42, 43]

Bargaining models of allocation and distribution within families, developed independently by Manser and Brown (1980) and by McElroy and Mary J. Horney (1981), treat marriage as a cooperative game.[44, 45] These models do not require that either spouse be altruistic, although one or both may be. Spouses are assumed to have conflicting preferences and to resolve their differ-

42. And in which the others are not allowed to form coalitions.

43. Becker mentions that his result need not hold in the case of "corner solutions" (1981, pp. 191–92). Under my interpretation, corner solutions are relevant when the altruist does not have enough resources to move the others to his preferred allocation by offering them an all-or-nothing choice. To see that Becker's solution does not follow from altruism alone, consider a family with two altruists. Alternatively, consider a family with one altruist and one egoist, but suppose that the egoist has dictatorial power or that the egoist can offer the altruist an all-or-nothing choice. Becker's result depends not on altruism, but on implicit assumptions about power or, equivalently, about the structure of the bargaining game.

44. A cooperative game is one in which "the players have complete freedom of preplay communication to make joint *binding* agreements"; a non-cooperative game is one in which "absolutely no preplay communication is permitted . . ." (R. Duncan Luce and Howard Raiffa 1957, p. 89; emphasis in original). Simone Clemhout and Henry Y. Wan, Jr. (1977) is the only paper I know that models marriage as a non-cooperative game.

45. Manser and Brown and McElroy and Horney are specifically concerned with marriage rather than the family, but the analytical issues are similar. The differences between models of allocation between husbands and wives and between parents and children are twofold. First, marriage can be treated as a two-person game, while allocation between parents and children may involve more than two players and, hence, raises the possibility of coalition formation. Second, timing issues, which deserve more attention than they have thus far received in models of marriage, become crucial in models involving parents and children.

ences in the manner prescribed by some explicit bargaining model.[46] The utility payoffs to the spouses if they fail to reach agreement—called "threat points" in cooperative game theory—play a dual role in bargaining models. They are essential both to determining the negotiation set—the set of utility payoffs which are Pareto optimal and individually rational (i.e., better for both parties than failing to reach agreements)—and to determining a particular solution, often a unique solution, within the negotiation set. In some bargaining models the threat point corresponds to the payoffs associated with clearly defined "next best" alternatives for each party; in a bargaining model of marriage, for example, the next best alternative for one or both spouses to remaining in a particular marriage might be becoming and remaining single. Usually, however, the threat point corresponds to the expected utility taken over some set of alternatives, for example, the expected utility associated with leaving the present marriage and searching for another spouse.[47]

Bargaining models of intrafamily allocation, in contrast to Becker's model, emphasize the role played by threat points or alternatives in determining allocation and distribution within the family. Thus, investigating whether threat points or alternatives affect intrafamily allocation and distribution may permit us to distinguish empirically between bargaining models and Becker's model.[48]

Bargaining models explicitly embed the problem of intrafamily allocation and distribution in a game-theoretic context, and therefore they provide an in-

46. Alvin E. Roth (1979) provides a survey of alternative bargaining models. Manser and Brown and McElroy and Horney consider the Nash solution (John F. Nash 1950) to the bargaining problem, and Manser and Brown also consider the Kalai and Smorodinsky solution (Ehud Kalai and Meir Smorodinsky 1975). Sharon C. Rochford (1984) analyzes the implications for assignment or matching in the marriage market of a model in which allocations within marriages are determined by Nash bargaining with transferable utility.

47. In bargaining models the threat point almost never involves the threat of physical violence. Economists' models of conflict, whether between husbands and wives or between workers and firms, seldom recognize even the possibility of violence. Helen V. Tauchen, Ann D. Witte, and Sharon K. Long (1991) summarize the sociological literature on family violence, which distinguishes between "expressive" violence (i.e., violence as an end in itself) and "instrumental" violence (i.e., violence as a means of coercion). They then propose a game-theoretic model in which violence and credible threats of violence can be instruments of social control and can affect allocation within the family.

48. This is too simple. In the market-determined model of Becker (1973) alternatives outside the marriage completely determine allocation within marriage. That model, however, implies a negotiation set which reduces to a single point and, not surprisingly, all models give identical predictions in this case. In Becker (1974a, 1981) the negotiation set is determined by the alternatives available to each spouse, but the altruist chooses the point in the negotiation set he prefers. Thus, unless the altruist chooses a "corner solution," changes in alternatives which do not eliminate the allocation chosen by the altruist from the negotiation set cannot force him to a less preferred allocation. Finally, there remains the empirical problem of identifying threat points or alternatives.

tellectually satisfying framework for addressing these issues. Game-theoretic models serve a similar function in industrial organization: Posing the duopoly or bilateral monopoly problem in game-theoretic terms does not resolve the difficulties inherent in modeling the interaction of two firms that recognize their mutual interdependence. For both families and firms, however, the game-theoretic formulation exposes the fundamental nature of the analytical problem.

The transaction cost approach, although broadly consistent with the spirit of the bargaining models, implies that one-period bargaining models are seriously deficient. Neither adaptive sequential decisionmaking, required to deal with new information and unfolding events, nor a governance structure, required to protect each spouse against changes in threat points that strengthen the bargaining position of the other and leave the disadvantaged spouse vulnerable to opportunistic exploitation, has any place in one-period models. Formulation of multiperiod bargaining models depends, however, on developments in the theory of cooperative games.[49]

Focusing on opportunism and the need for a governance structure that limits its scope allows us to understand better the dual role of family- or marriage-specific capital. Marriage-specific capital is defined by two characteristics: It increases productivity in the household and it is worthless if the particular marriage dissolves.[50] Thus, other things being equal, an increase in marriage-specific capital widens the gap between remaining in a particular marriage and leaving it, either to become and remain single or to search for a better marriage. By widening this gap the accumulation of marriage-specific capital stabilizes the marriage and reduces the risk of further investment in productive marriage-specific capital.[51]

Becker, Landes and Michael (1977, p. 1142) characterize "working exclusively in the nonmarket sector" as a form of marriage-specific investment. This characterization fails to recognize the two distinct channels through which working exclusively in the nonmarket sector affects both marital stability and intrafamily allocation. Working in the home creates nontransferable skills that increase productivity in the marriage; these skills represent marriage-specific capital which increases the payoff associated with remaining in a particular

---

49. If marriage is modeled as a non-cooperative game, then the multiperiod formulation is a super-game in which the constituent game changes from one period to another.

50. In some respects a spouse acquiring marriage-specific capital is analogous to a worker acquiring firm-specific human capital. A major difference is that in labor markets workers are protected by the firm's need to maintain its reputation so it can hire workers in the future, while in marriage markets this protection is attenuated.

51. Becker is well aware that marriage-specific capital plays both of these roles (Becker, Landes and Michael 1977, p. 1152; Becker 1981, p. 224).

marriage. But a decision to work exclusively in the nonmarket sector is also a decision not to acquire market human capital. Thus the effects of such a decision on the payoffs are twofold: Because marriage-specific capital has been accumulated, it increases the "married payoff"—the payoff associated with remaining in the marriage; and, because market human capital has not been accumulated, it decreases the "divorced payoff"—the payoff associated with leaving the marriage and starting work in the market sector.[52]

The relative importance of the married payoff and divorced payoff depends on the rates at which marriage-specific and market human capital accumulate. There are two polar cases. In the first, productivity in the home depends on the accumulation of marriage-specific human capital while wages are independent of experience in the market sector: In this case, working exclusively in the nonmarket sector affects marital stability and intrafamily allocation only by increasing the married payoff; the divorced payoff at a given future date will be the same regardless of whether the intervening period has been spent exclusively in the nonmarket sector. In the second polar case, productivity in the home is independent of experience in the nonmarket sector while wages depend on accumulated experience in the market sector: In this case working exclusively in the nonmarket sector affects marital stability and intrafamily allocation solely by decreasing the divorced payoff; the married payoff will be the same regardless of whether the intervening period has been spent exclusively in the nonmarket sector. In this second case working exclusively in the nonmarket sector involves no accumulation of marriage-specific human capital. Between these poles lies a continuum of cases in which marriage-specific capital and market capital both accumulate at nonzero rates. It is an unresolved and virtually unexplored empirical issue whether working exclusively in the nonmarket sector increases marital stability primarily by increasing marriage-specific capital, thus increasing the married payoff, or primarily by failing to increase market capital, thus decreasing the divorced payoff.[53]

Becker, Landes and Michael (1977, p. 1152) also characterize children as marriage-specific capital "since one parent usually has much less contact with

52. The bases for these comparisons are the payoffs that would be realized at a particular future date in each of the two states—remaining in the marriage and leaving it—if the individual had not worked exclusively in the nonmarket sector. The married payoff refers to the total to be divided between the spouses; in a bargaining model the division of this total depends on the threat point (i.e., the divorced payoff). The "total to be divided between the spouses" is a problematic notion without special assumptions such as transferable utility.

53. Marriage-specific capital is, by definition, idiosyncratic to a particular marriage. The discussion could be generalized, however, to consider the role of human capital which is specific to the household sector but not to a particular marriage. This distinction is analogous to that in the labor market literature between firm-specific and industry-specific human capital.

the children after dissolution."[54] This characterization is misleading for two reasons. First, unlike marriage-specific capital, children do not disappear when a marriage dissolves; typically one parent or the other is granted custody of the children. The observation that one parent usually has much less contact with the children after dissolution suggests that children are like public goods within the marriage, not that they are marriage-specific capital. Second, like working exclusively in the nonmarket sector, children increase the payoff associated with remaining in a marriage and reduce the payoff associated with leaving it.[55, 56] Hence, the presence of children affects both marital stability and intra-family allocation through two distinct channels. The increased payoff associated with remaining in the marriage reflects the "productivity" of children as sources of satisfaction in the intact marriage. The reduced payoff associated with leaving reflects the role of children as "hostages."[57, 58]

The transaction cost approach suggests a number of empirically implement-able research projects on allocation within the family—between husbands and wives, between parents and children, and among children. Allocation between husbands and wives is difficult to investigate empirically because of the per-vasiveness of public goods within the household. Neglecting corner solutions, Becker's altruism model implies that the allocation between spouses depends on the sum of their resources, but not on each spouse's individual wealth, in-come, and earning power except as they affect this total: The altruist's utility

54. Becker (1974a, p. S23, fn. 36) notes that children "would be a specific investment if the pleasure received by a parent were smaller when the parent was (permanently) separated from the children."

55. Pollak and Wachter (1975, pp. 273–76) criticize the new home economics literature for failing to distinguish between "household production processes" that produce observable and measurable commodities and those that produce "satisfaction" or unmeasurable commodities such as "child services."

56. Utility payoffs to each spouse in the event of dissolution are conceptually unambiguous. Utility payoffs to each spouse when the marriage remains intact presuppose a particular solution to the problem of distribution within marriage.

57. Williamson (1983) discusses the use of hostages to lend stability to bilateral governance structures. He argues that reciprocal selling arrangements and product exchanges among rival firms, practices usually condemned as anticompetitive, under certain conditions may represent exchanges of hostages that facilitate socially beneficial trading.

58. The hostage effect has two components. The first is psychological: Even if leaving a marriage with children entailed no financial obligations, leaving such a marriage would be different from leaving a childless marriage. The second is financial: To the extent that parents retain child support obligations after leaving a marriage, the payoff to leaving a marriage with children is less than the payoff to leaving a childless marriage. These costs may be magnified if there are "econo-mies of scale in consumption" that are lost with dissolution. The financial effect on the payoffs of the parents depends on the extent to which child support is borne by the state and how the portion of it not borne by the state is divided between the parents.

function is maximized subject to the family's resource constraint. The transaction cost approach, like the bargaining models, suggests that the allocation between spouses depends systematically on the individual wealth, income, and earning power of the spouses as well as on their sum. Although the transaction cost approach does not imply a specific bargaining model, by viewing marriage as a governance structure which permits some flexibility while protecting the parties against the hazards of unconstrained bilateral bargaining, it does suggest that alternatives and threat points affect allocation within marriage.

Direct econometric implementation of any model of allocation within marriage depends on identifying and measuring goods, commodities, or activities desired by one spouse but not the other.[59] For example, contributions of husbands and wives to their respective undergraduate colleges are likely to fall into this category. Or, if either or both spouses have children by previous marriages, then the consumption of these children or expenditures on their education are likely to be of more interest to the children's parent than to the other spouse: An uncluttered case would be one in which a widow with children married a widower with children. Using data from a developing country, one might investigate whether the nutrition of a child in such a family depended only on the family's total resources or whether those of the child's parent had an independent effect on the child's consumption. Using contemporary U.S. data, one might investigate whether the educational attainment of a child depended only on the new family's total resources, or whether the resources of the child's parent had a systematic, independent effect. Although the data needed to estimate models based on the transaction cost approach are difficult to obtain, in the long run data availability is endogenous. Data collection by government agencies or by individual researchers—a practice less common in economics than in other disciplines—depends in large part on the apparent demand for such data by the research community.

C. Social Exchange Theory

Social exchange theory, a framework developed by sociologists and social historians which draws heavily on economics, has been used to analyze a wide range of social phenomena, including intrafamily allocation.

---

59. Empirical implementation need not be either direct or econometric. At least two other strategies are available. The first, which I have already discussed, is indirect and focuses on the implications of the transaction cost approach for marital stability, labor force participation, or other variables for which data are widely available. The second is direct but non-econometric and uses qualititative rather than quantitive evidence. Appealing to narrative case studies does not solve the problem of econometric implementation, but challenges the importance of doing so by implicitly raising the question of what types of evidence are admissible in economics.

Greven's *Four Generations* (1970), a study of colonial Andover, explains the changing relationships between successive generations in terms of changing economic opportunities and alternatives:

> With abundant land for themselves and their off-spring, the first generation established extended patriarchal families, in which fathers maintained their authority over their mature sons, mainly by withholding control over the land from them until late in their lives. The delayed marriages of sons testified to their prolonged attachment to paternal families . . . [p. 268].

Greven argues that age at marriage is a sensitive indicator of the assumption of adult status and responsibility (pp. 31–32), that marriage required parental support (p. 75), and that the first-generation fathers retained legal control of their lands until their deaths (p. 78). In the middle decades of the eighteenth century, the fourth generation, "married younger, established their independence more effectively and earlier in life, and departed from the community with even greater frequency than in earlier generations" (p. 272). Many sons in the fourth generation acquired land from their fathers by deeds of gift or sale during the father's lifetime, rather than by bequest at the father's death (p. 241).

Greven explains these changes in terms generally consistent with a bargaining framework in which threat points (i.e., alternatives or opportunities) play a significant role:

> A combination of circumstances probably fostered the relatively early autonomy of many fourth-generation sons and encouraged their fathers to assume that their sons ought to be on their own as soon as possible. The rapid expansion of settlements and the emigration of many third-generation Andover men had amply demonstrated the opportunities which existed outside Andover for those willing and able to leave their families and begin life for themselves elsewhere. The diminished landholdings of many families and the constantly rising prices of land in Andover during the first half of the century also put great pressure upon sons who wished to remain as farmers in Andover and made it imperative that many sons take up trades instead or move elsewhere for the land they needed [p. 222].
>
> If partriarchalism was not yet gone, it had been made less viable by the changing circumstances. The earlier economic basis which had sustained the attempts by fathers to establish and to maintain their control and influence over the lives of their sons no longer was to be found among the majority of families living in Andover. Only the wealthy and only those with sons who were willing to accede to their fathers' wishes regarding the possession and ownership of the land could still consider themselves to be patriarchs [p. 273].

Anderson (1971) utilizes an explicit conceptual framework for analyzing the impact of urbanization and industrialization on family structure in nineteenth-century Lancashire. His framework is an elaboration of "social exchange theory," which postulates that individuals engage in exchange to maximize "psychic profit." [60] Anderson, however, stresses two considerations that exchange theory neglects: whether reciprocation is immediate or in the distant future, and whether reciprocation is certain or uncertain (p. 9). The exchange theory foundation of Anderson's analysis is consonant with a bargaining approach, and the two additional considerations he introduces, timing and uncertainty, suggest modifying social exchange theory in the same general directions as transaction cost analysis suggests modifying bargaining models.

Anderson documents the effect of children's employment opportunities on their relationships with their parents:

> . . . children's high individual wages allowed them to enter into relational bargains with their parents on terms of more or less precise equality. If, as was usually the case, a bargain could be struck which was immediately favourable to both parties, then all was well, and the relationship continued, though the degree of commitment to such a relationship must often have been low. If a better alternative was obtainable elsewhere the child could take it. The contrast between the choice element in these relationships between urban children and their parents, and the situation in rural areas . . . is very marked. In the rural areas even in the short run, child and father entered a bargaining situation with the child at a very considerable disadvantage, because the father had complete control over the only really viable source of income [pp. 131–32].

Summarizing his findings, Anderson writes:

> . . . one crucial way in which urban-industrial life in the nineteenth century affected family cohesion was by offering to teenage children wages at such a level that they were able to free themselves from total economic dependence on the nuclear family. Because normative controls were weak and because housing, food, and other day to day necessities could be obtained on the open market, many could . . . live as well or better than they could with kin or parents. Some children did desert their families and I have presented some evidence which suggested that even where they did not do so many children were conscious of the existence of this possibility and the alternatives it

---

60. The basic social exchange theory framework is borrowed from social psychology. The seminal works are George C. Homans (1961) and Peter M. Blau (1964); for an analytical survey and references to the literature see Anthony F. Heath (1976).

offered, and used it as a way of bargaining a highly independent relationship with their families [p. 134].

Social exchange theory provides an analytical framework for sociology and social history which appeals strongly to economists; its appeal to sociologists and social historians is somewhat less powerful. For example, Michael Katz (1975), a social historian, contrasts Anderson's work on nineteenth-century Preston with his own analysis of nineteenth-century Hamilton, emphasizing the narrowness of Anderson's exchange theory approach. He argues that it "constricts the range of human motivation," and "it assumes a greater degree of rationality than probably underlies ordinary behavior" (p. 302).[61]

D. The Case for Bargaining Models

Even without the contracting problems emphasized by the transaction cost approach, bargaining models would often be required to analyze intrafamily allocation. There are three exceptions: (1) there is a family consensus on resource allocation, (2) some "altruistic" family member has the power to choose an allocation from the negotiation set and impose his choice on the others, and (3) the negotiation set is a single point, so there is no surplus over which to bargain. Virtually any other circumstances require a bargaining analysis to determine an equilibrium allocation within the negotiation set.

The negotiation set corresponding to a particular marriage depends on the next-best alternative of each spouse. When the negotiation set is small, determining an equilibrium allocation within it becomes uninteresting. The well-being of each spouse is essentially determined by the negotiation set, not by bargaining within the marriage to determine an allocation within the negotiation set. In the limit, when the negotiation set shrinks to a single point, the well-being of each spouse is uniquely determined by his or her alternatives outside the marriage.[62]

A bargaining approach to intrafamily allocation is required because negotiation sets in ongoing marriages are often large and because intrafamily allocation cannot be resolved at the outset. The emergence of a surplus in ongoing marriages can be ascribed to the accumulation of idiosyncratic or marriage-specific capital or, more simply, to a random process in which marriages with empty negotiation sets dissolve while those with nonempty negotiation sets continue. Because bounded rationality precludes complete long-term contracts which specify intrafamily allocations under every possible contingency, intra-

61. Katz also argues that Anderson's theory "is not supported by the data in his book" (p. 302).
62. The limit is a limit for the marriage to continue. If the bargaining set is empty, the marriage will presumably dissolve.

family allocation must be dealt with in an adaptive, sequential way—in short, through bargaining.

III. Conclusion

Although the metaphor of household production can usefully be applied to a wide range of activities, the formal framework of the household production model is best suited to analyzing processes that combine household time and purchased inputs to produce well-defined and measurable outputs. The family's role in many economic activities, however, is explicable not in terms of technology but of governance.

The transaction cost approach provides a new perspective on families and households. Unlike the new home economics, which focuses exclusively on household production, it recognizes the importance of household organization and family structure. The transaction cost approach views marriage as a "governance structure," emphasizes the role of "bargaining" within families, and draws attention to the advantages and disadvantages of family organization in terms of incentives and monitoring, and to the special roles of "altruism" and "family loyalty." It also recognizes the disadvantages of family governance: conflict spillover, the toleration of inefficient personnel, inappropriate ability match, and inability to realize economies of scale. If activities are assigned to institutions in an efficient or cost-minimizing fashion, the balance of these advantages and disadvantages plays a major role in determining which activities are carried out within families and which are performed by firms, nonprofit institutions, or the state.

A principal defect of the transaction cost approach is its failure to provide a structure for rigorous econometric investigations. Developing such a framework requires incorporating the insights of the transaction cost approach into formal models and specifying such models in sufficient detail to permit estimation. The present essay represents a first step toward that goal.

7
Tied Transfers and Paternalistic Preferences

ROBERT A. POLLAK

Why do parents make inter vivos transfers to their children and leave them postmortem bequests?[1] Gary Becker's notion of "altruism" (1981, ch. 8)—by which he means that children's utilities are arguments of their parents' utility function—provides one explanation. Denoting the children's utility functions by $U^i(c_i)$, where c_i denotes consumption by child i, the preferences of parents with two children can be represented by a utility function of the form $W[c_p, U^1(c_1), U^2(c_2)]$ where c_p is the parents' own consumption.[2] In the altruistic model, parents' sole motive for intergenerational transfers is to increase their children's utility. In other models, however, parents may have nonaltruistic as well as altruistic motives for transferring resources to their children.

The literature on economic development emphasizes old-age support as a motive for fertility and, to a lesser degree, as a motive for providing children with human capital as part of an explicit or implicit intergenerational contract. When human capital formation is the primary focus of the analysis, as in discussions of education and earnings, it is useful to decompose inter vivos transfers into "human capital formation" and "other inter vivos transfers." Such a decomposition can mislead in discussing intergenerational transfers, however, because it obscures the fact that the provision of human capital by parents constitutes an intergenerational transfer.

Laurence Kotlikoff and Avia Spivak (1981) analyze another old-age support model, one in which the family operates as an "incomplete annuities market." In their model, children make regular transfers to their aging parents, and the share that each child contributes to the parents determines his or her share of the parental estate. Although the prospect of old-age support may be an impor-

Reprinted from *American Economic Review* 78, no. 2 (May 1988): 240–44.

I am grateful to the National Science Foundation and the National Institutes of Health for financial support, to Gary Becker, Samuel Preston, David Stapleton, and Paul Taubman for helpful comments, and to Judith Goff for editorial assistance.

1. Even if bequests are unplanned, as some versions of the life cycle savings model assume, inter vivos transfers must be intentional.

2. I ignore the possible dependence of the children's utility on their own children's utility, etc., because it is not relevant to the issues discussed in this paper.

tant motive for "downstream" intergenerational transfers (i.e., from parents to children) in some societies, in the United States today "upstream" transfers appear too small and too uncertain to make this motive credible.

To explain downstream transfers in the United States today, economists have investigated other models in which parents have selfish as well as selfless motives. For example, B. Douglas Bernheim, Andrei Shleifer, and Lawrence Summers propose a model in which parents use the prospect of bequests to exact services from their children: "we envision a testator who, though altruistic, is also affected by actions taken individually by a number of potential beneficiaries (he may, e.g., enjoy receiving attention from his children)" (1985, p. 1046). Bernheim et al. assume that such actions increase parents' utility and decrease children's utilities. In their model the children's utility functions become $U^i(a_i, c_i)$, where a_i denotes services the ith child provides the parents, and the parents' utility function becomes $W[c_p, a_1, a_2, U^1(a_1, c_1), U^2(a_2, c_2)]$. To measure these services, Bernheim et al. use frequency of contact (i.e., visits plus telephone calls) between parents and children.

This approach expands the concept of child services to include those provided by adult children who live outside the parents' household in an attempt to explain bequests and inter vivos transfers. "Child services" originally appeared in discussions of fertility and the allocation of resources to young children living with their parents, and thus tends to evoke the joys of young parenthood (the pitter-patter of little feet). In that context there are two versions of the child services or "child quality" model. The first focuses on a number of narrowly defined child-related commodities produced by the household's technology (for example, musical skills, mathematics grades, the negative of the number of ear aches). The second focuses on a single broadly defined "commodity" that is best interpreted as the value of a separable component of the parental utility function defined over the vector of narrowly defined child commodities. The boundary separating the young children to whom the child quality model applies from the adult children to whom the altruism model or the adult version of the child services model applies is a broad band rather than a narrow line; college students, for example, are an ambiguous case. As in the story of the six blind men each describing a different part of the elephant, one might believe that the child quality model and the other models each capture an important part of the situation without believing that any one of them captures it all.

In this paper I propose the "paternalistic preferences" model, which accounts for aspects of downstream transfers, whether inter vivos or bequests, that neither Becker's pure altruism model nor the child services model can explain. The most crucial of these aspects is the prevalence of conditional or "tied" transfers. In the paternalistic preferences model, parents' utility depends directly on their children's consumption patterns as well as on their children's utilities, so that the parents' utility function is of the form $W[c_p, c_1, c_2, U^1(c_1), U^2(c_2)]$, where the c's must now be interpreted as consumption vectors.[3] The fundamental insight of the paternalistic preferences model is that parents care about their children's consumption patterns even after the children are grown and have left home. The model thus occupies the middle ground between the child quality models and the other models.

Intergenerational transfers are often tied to the child's consumption of particular goods and services. Three examples illustrate the point. (i) Many parents spend substantial resources on their children's college educations. Suppose your college-age daughter announces that she would rather use the money for something else, for example, to contribute to Greenpeace or to buy a Mercedes. As a parent I would find such an announcement distressing, and I suspect most parents would; my guess is that in most families the daughter would not get the money for Greenpeace or for the Mercedes. Why? (ii) Anecdotal evidence suggests the importance of financial help from parents in providing down payments for home purchases; some confirmation—it has been suggested that "data" is the plural of anecdote—is provided by statistics from the National Association of Realtors (1986, p. 25) showing that gifts are the source of 19 percent of the funds used for down payments on first houses. Suppose you were planning to give your son the money for the down payment on his first house, but that he would rather use the money for something else, for example, to contribute to Greenpeace or to buy a Mercedes. I suspect that few of the parents who were willing to give their son the money for the down payment would give him the money for Greenpeace or for the Mercedes. Why? (iii) Anecdotal evidence suggests that parents with substantial wealth are sometimes concerned that their children will misuse, squander, or waste resources that are transferred to them. To mitigate these concerns, parents sometimes establish trust funds that limit children's control over resources and thus their opportunities to misuse them. What lawyers call "spendthrift trusts" are specifically designed to restrict children's control over resources, often well beyond the children's minorities and the parents' lifetimes. Why?

The altruistic model and the child services model find tied transfers anomalous.[4] In the altruistic model, parents want each child to choose the consump-

3. Formally, paternalistic preferences generalize the child services model by including actions that have positive as well as negative effects on the children's utilities. For expositional ease, I focus on actions with positive effects.

4. This is overstated. At least for education, tied transfers are compatible with a multiperiod version of the altruistic model in which parents implicitly insure their children against income shortfalls and, hence, have an interest in their children's self-sufficiency. Insurance and inalienability do not, however, provide a satisfactory account for houses and other tied transfers. Later in the paper, I discuss anecdotal evidence suggesting that these motives do not provide a complete account of the transfers associated with education.

tion pattern that maximizes his or her utility, subject to the appropriate resource constraints. In the child services model, parents want to exact services from their children, but once the vector of services provided to the parents is fixed, parents want each child to choose the consumption pattern that maximizes his or her utility, subject to the appropriate resource constraints. Thus, these models cannot explain why parents are willing to transfer resources to their children only when those resources are committed to particular uses. In the paternalistic model, parents want the child to choose a consumption pattern that reflects not only the child's utility, but also the parents' desire that the child consume certain goods and eschew others. Thus, the paternalistic model explains tied transfers.

What motives might underlie paternalistic preferences? First, parents might want their children to attend college or own a house because it gives the parents pleasure or satisfaction, independent of their children's preferences. This might reflect the parents' own values and aspirations, or their concern with status ("my daughter the doctor"). Second, parents might believe that attending college or owning a house is in the child's true, long-run interest ("when you're older, you'll thank me for this"). In this case the parents' motives are "altruistic" in the ordinary language sense (i.e., concerned with the welfare of others), although not in the Beckerian sense of respecting their children's preferences.

Parents attempt to influence their children's consumption patterns in two ways: by altering the preferences of children and by altering the opportunities of children. Although economists rely heavily on the assumption that preferences are fixed and immutable, many would concede that preferences can be influenced by example and persuasion, and that families play a crucial role in preference formation. Parents may alter opportunities in two ways. In the household production framework, the technology by which market goods are transformed into commodities is a determinant of a child's opportunities. Any analysis based on the acquisition of tastes can be reformulated in terms of the acquisition of technology. Second, parents may alter opportunities by subsidizing the consumption of certain goods—that is, by offering tied transfers.

The phrase "paternalistic preferences" is familiar from public economics, where it appears in the analysis of "merit wants" and "merit goods." Parallels between the family and society are commonly drawn in both economics and political theory. Paul Samuelson's classic paper on social indifference curves (1956), which used the Bergson-Samuelson social welfare function in the context of intrafamily allocation, was the first to identify a precise analytic correspondence. In the light of these parallels, it is not surprising that the reason we, as a society, provide the poor with access to certain goods (for example, through food stamps and medicaid) rather than with the resources to purchase goods corresponds to the reason we, as parents, provide our children with tied transfers. To the extent that social policy reflects concern for the children of the poor rather than for the adult poor, the two meanings of "paternalistic" intertwine and reinforce each other. Nevertheless, the word paternalistic has unfortunate connotations because of its not entirely coincidental gender coding.

To construct an intergenerational allocation model, we must combine assumptions about preferences with assumptions about constraints (which I shall not discuss) and assumptions about equilibrium or solution concepts (to which I now turn). In my paper (1985, in this volume), I argue that Becker completes his altruistic model by implicitly assuming that the altruist (the husband-father-patriarch-dictator) has the power to impose his preferred allocation on the other family members, subject only to the constraint that none of them can be made worse off than they would be if they withdrew from the family. This solution depends crucially on the implicit assumption that it is the altruist rather than the rotten kid who, by the rules of the game, can face the other players with a take-it-or-leave-it choice. If the altruist can make the final offer, then he gets the entire utility surplus; if the rotten kid can make the final offer, he grabs it all. Donald Cox (1987) uses this approach to analyze inter vivos transfers in a child services model, treating the problem as one in which parents maximize utility subject to the constraint that no child can be made worse off than he or she would be by withdrawing from the family.

Bernheim et al. formulate the intergenerational allocation problem as a noncooperative game involving parents and two or more children. They assume parents want to leave their estate to their children (so that leaving everything to other relatives, to friends, or to charity is not a credible threat), but that parents are indifferent among alternative divisions of their estate among their children (so that leaving everything to one child and disinheriting the others is a credible threat). Bernheim et al. also assume the children compete with one another for parental favor (so the children do not form a coalition). Under these assumptions, they show that the solution is one in which the parents get the entire utility surplus. The principal contribution of Bernheim et al. is their formulation of the intergenerational allocation problem as a noncooperative game rather than the particular formulation they propose. Indeed, the appeal of the particular Bernheim et al.–Bertrand formulation will be greatest to those who expect duopoly to yield competitive prices. The analogy with game-theoretic models of duopoly suggests two lessons: the vastness of the range of alternative modeling assumptions and the sensitivity of solutions to these assumptions. Thus, the Bernheim et al. analysis is unlikely to be the last word on the subject.

The paternalistic preferences model presents similar modeling choices. The simplest formulation is one in which parents maximize their own utility, subject to the constraint that no child can be made worse off than he or she would be outside the family. More complex formulations would use cooperative or noncooperative game theory.

How do the implications for investment in human capital differ between the altruistic model and the parental preferences model? The maximizing version of the altruistic model yields sharp results, at least in special cases. Suppose children value education only for its economic returns (so that they derive neither utility nor disutility from attending school or from the prospect of being an educated man or woman). Assuming positive inter vivos transfers or bequests to all children, Becker and Nigel Tomes (1976) show that the altruistic model implies a two-stage allocation process. First, parents invest in each child's schooling until the marginal return equals the return on financial assets; then they make transfers and bequests among their children to obtain the desired income distribution.[5]

When parents value their children's educational attainments, the maximizing version of the paternalistic preferences model implies that under the assumptions of the previous paragraph (i.e., children value education only for its economic returns; parents make positive transfers or bequests to all children), the marginal return on education should be less than the return on financial assets. Some anecdotal evidence supports this conclusion, although there is little systematic evidence. The anecdotal evidence I have in mind involves the education of children from upper-income families. Instead of focusing on years of schooling, consider expenditure on schooling. Private colleges are expensive: tuition at the University of Pennsylvania, an Ivy League school, is $11,976; at Pennsylvania State University, a public institution, tuition for an in-state student is $3,292. If children from upper-income families are more likely to attend private colleges and universities than children of equal ability from less wealthy families, then we must conclude that either (a) wealthier families "overinvest" in education (i.e., invest beyond the point at which the marginal returns are equal to the return on financial assets), or (b) less wealthy families "underinvest" in education.[6] Private secondary school education poses the same issue: if children from wealthy families are more likely to attend such schools than children of equal ability from less wealthy families, this indicates either that the returns to such education are greater than the returns on financial assets or that some of the benefit from such education accrues to the parents

5. Hence, if parents place any value on equality in the distribution of income among their children, they will compensate children with lower earnings by providing them with greater transfers and/or bequests. Furthermore, assuming parental preferences exhibit "equal concern" for all their children, the parents will use transfers and bequests to offset fully differences in earnings.

6. By equal ability I mean identical "earnings production functions"—i.e., the same equation determines each child's earnings as a function of his or her education.

rather than to the children—in short, that such education can only be understood in terms of paternalistic preferences.[7]

Tied transfers are important, yet the desire of parents to prevent their children from squandering, misusing, or wasting resources is unintelligible in the altruistic model in which parents passively accept their children's preferences. It is also unintelligible in the child services model, in which parents accept their children's preferences but also want their children to provide services. It is fully comprehensible in a model in which parents evaluate their children's consumption patterns according to their own paternalistic preferences.

7. Throughout this paper I have avoided the term "gifts," which sociologists and anthropologists use, in favor of the more neutral "transfers." The basic work on gifts and "gift economies" (Marcel Mauss, 1925) emphasizes that "gift exchanges" (a telling phrase) are governed by rules and obligations: to make the gift, to receive the gift, and to reciprocate. Even in the gift economy, there is no free lunch. The relationship between practices in "primitive" gift economies (for example, the potlatch of the Kwakiutl and other Northwest Coast Indians and the Kula ring of the Trobriand Islanders) and intrafamily transfers in advanced industrial societies is unclear. Whether donors and recipients characterize a particular transfer as a gift may signal whether they believe it carries with it reciprocal obligations. For example, if a parent provides $10,000 for a child's down payment on a house, it is called a gift. If a parent provides $70,000 to send a child to college, it is not called a gift.

Part Three
Intrahousehold Allocations and Interpretation of Schooling Effects

8

Is Child Schooling a Poor Proxy for Child Quality?

Jere R. Behrman

Child quality has a critical role in family fertility and child investment in the dominant economic model of fertility, as developed by Becker and Lewis (1973), Willis (1973), and others. Child quality is also of considerable interest in itself because of its relation to well-being and to productivity in various activities. Indeed, in the recent demographic literature, there is an increasing interest in the quality of the population per se in addition to the longer-standing interest in quality that is associated with the relation between quality and quantity.

In the theoretical literature, child quality is often a fairly vague concept, perhaps a vector of desirable characteristics, though recently child quality has at times been equated with expected adult earnings or income (e.g., Becker, 1981). In empirical explorations in this tradition, child quality is not directly observed but is usually represented by child schooling, though occasionally by variables related to other child characteristics (e.g., health).[1] In her Population Association of America presidential address, for example, Blake (1981) explicitly equated child schooling with child quality. This widespread empirical practice raises the question posed in the title: How good a proxy for child quality is child schooling? The answer to this question bears importantly on empirical explorations by demographers of population quality and of quality–quantity trade-offs.

Schooling is widely, perhaps universally, thought to be a critical *input* into the production of child quality, meaning that schooling is likely to be highly associated with child quality, *all else being equal*. But all else is not equal across children in the real world. Children differ significantly—both within and among families—in the endowments, genetic and otherwise, embodied in them when they come to school.[2] If schooling investments are allocated, im-

---

Reprinted from *Demography* 24, no. 3 (August 1987): 341–59.

1. For example, see Barechello (1979), Blake (1981), Castañeda (1979), DeTray (1973, 1978), Gomez (1980), Leibowitz (1977), Makhya (1978), Rosenzweig (1982), Rosenzweig and Wolpin (1980), and Singh, Schuh, and Kehrberg (1978).

2. For review of evidence that such endowments are important in determining schooling and adult socioeconomic success, see Leibowitz (1977), Behrman et al. (1980), Behrman and Wolfe (1984), Birdsall (1985), and Olneck (1977).

plicitly or explicitly, to compensate partially for the distribution of such endowments, schooling may not be a very good proxy for child quality. Families in different regions of a country or in different countries, moreover, may face different relative prices for schooling versus nonschooling investments (e.g., nutrients and other health-related inputs). If so, the optimal composition (i.e., how much schooling, how much other investment) of investments in such children differs, which again weakens the schooling–quality association.

The absence of satisfactory direct observations on child quality and on child endowments precludes directly testing the empirical association between child quality and schooling. (Of course if better observations existed on child quality, they could be used directly in empirical tests rather than using schooling to represent child quality.) Some important insights can be obtained, however, by considering the implications of preference models of parental investments in schooling of their children developed by Becker (1981), Becker and Tomes (1976), and Behrman, Pollak, and Taubman (1982, in this volume). Such models provide an interesting framework for considering the association between child schooling and quality both because they are being used increasingly to explore demographic phenomena by economic demographers and because they are in the same general intellectual tradition as the quantity–quality fertility model.

In these models, parents are posited to have preferences regarding the distribution of expected quality outcomes among their children. These preferences relate to the trade-off between equity and productivity, or to what extent parents are willing that their children have lower aggregate expected quality in order to assure more equal distribution of expected qualities among their children. Propositions about behavior are derived by assuming that parents maximize such preferences subject to constraints imposed by the total resources available for investment in or distribution to the children and the production functions that convert investments in individual children into the outcomes of interest. The patterns of investments in schooling and in other human capital and of parental gifts and bequests among their children are the major means by which the parents attempt to maximize their satisfaction associated with the quality of their children. Thus the pattern of schooling investments among a family's children is integral to both the maximization of parental preferences and the determination of the distribution of quality among these children.

I use this framework to explore the question: How good a proxy is child schooling for child quality? The answer is shown to depend on the definition of quality, the nature of intrafamilial allocation processes, interfamilial differences in the determinants of schooling investments, and the extent of imperfect information at the time of schooling investments.

If quality is defined to be embodied in the children (e.g., as measured by labor market earning capacities), then within households there may be a negative, zero, or positive association between schooling and child quality. The sign and magnitude of this association depends on (1) how easily schooling can be substituted for endowments in the production of quality, (2) the extent of productivity–equity trade-off in parental preferences concerning the distribution of quality among their children, and (3) whether schooling prices for individual children depend on the endowments of the individual children. The less the substitution between schooling and endowments in the quality production process, the less the parental concern about equity in the distribution of quality among their children; and the more schooling prices for individual children are inversely associated with endowments, the higher the schooling–quality association. Existing estimates of the first two of these factors, under the assumption that all children in a household face the same prices for schooling, suggest that the intrahousehold association between schooling and quality is about zero or even negative.

If quality is defined by a broader measure than what is embodied directly in the children to include items that the children are expected to own (e.g., their expected total wealth or income as adults, including returns from financial and physical assets in addition to own earning capacities) and the transfer of assets from parents to all children is positive, the model predicts that the intrahousehold association between schooling and quality is zero.

Interfamilial variations in child endowments, schooling prices, prices of other human capital investments, and resources devoted to children are likely to be greater than intrafamilial variations. To the extent that these interfamilial variations are random, they are likely to make the interfamilial association between schooling and quality weaker than the intrafamilial association. On the other hand, if there are some systematic associations among these variables across families, they may increase observed schooling–quality correlations. If quality is embodied in the children, schooling prices are inversely associated with endowments and child endowments vary systematically across households, for example, the interfamilial association between schooling and quality tends to be greater than the intrafamilial associations. If quality is also defined to include the physical and financial assets expected to be owned by the child and if child endowments and parental wealth are positively correlated, the interfamilial association between schooling and quality tends to be greater than the intrafamilial association.

Finally, imperfect information may affect the schooling–quality association. If marginal schooling decisions are made with imperfect information about endowments and are not reversible and if actual quality depends on actual endowments, the schooling–actual quality association is weakened.

This review of the implications of parental preference models for intrahousehold investments in children clarifies what determines the schooling–quality association if parents make constrained maximizing investments in the

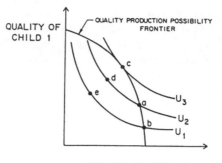

FIG. 1   Constrained maximization of parental preferences over distribution of quality between child 1 and child 2.

schooling of their children. It also leads to considerable doubt about whether schooling–quality associations are likely to be very strong, or even necessarily positive. The answer to the question posed in the title is likely to be affirmative: child schooling probably often is a poor proxy for child quality. Therefore, its use as such a proxy should be interpreted with great care; there would be substantial gain in clarity if schooling simply is called "schooling" and not "quality"; and in terms of understanding, there may be substantial payoff to efforts to develop better representations of quality.

Parental Preference Model Framework for Intrafamilial Child Schooling–Child Quality Associations

A modified general preference model for analyzing parental allocations of resources among their progeny provides a basic framework for analysis. This section describes the essence of this model in geometrical and verbal terms so that it is easily understood by a broad audience. The Appendix presents the model and related insights in more formal terms for those interested.

Figure 1 illustrates the essence of this model for the two-child case, which is used with no loss of generality to keep the geometry as simple as possible. Parents are assumed to have preferences over the expected qualities of their children.[3] Such preferences imply that the parents are generally better off if the expected qualities of their children are greater, but that there is a diminishing positive marginal impact on the parents' satisfaction if the expected quality of one child is increased and the expected quality of the other is held constant.

---

3. Parental preferences are also affected by other factors, such as their own consumption of goods, services, and leisure time and their number of children. To simplify the presentation, however, I focus only on the impact of the distribution of the expected quality of their children. (Also see note 6.)

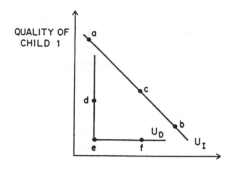

FIG. 2   Extreme curvatures for parental preferences: pure investment case (U_I) and only distributional concerns (U_D).

The preference or utility curves (U_1, U_2, U_3) in figure 1 display these properties. Each curve indicated by U_i gives combinations of expected qualities for the two children that generate the same level of parental satisfaction; generally, a reduction in the expected quality for child 1 can be offset by an increase in the quality of child 2, leaving the parents exactly as well off (though there is an exception discussed later). The curves are numbered in order of increasing parental satisfaction, so more expected quality for one or the other or both children implies greater parental satisfaction (i.e., $U_3 > U_2 > U_1$).

The shape of the parental preference curves indicates the nature of the parental preference trade-off between productivity and equity regarding expected child qualities for the two children.[4] Figure 2 illustrates two extreme possible shapes of the parental preference curves. The linear preference curve (U_I) represents the pure productivity or investment case in which the parents are concerned only with the aggregate or total quality of their children, and *not* with how that quality is distributed among the children. Therefore parental satisfaction is the same at points *a, b,* and *c,* since the total expected quality is the same, even though the distribution of that quality differs greatly among these three points (with most going to child 1 at *a,* most going to child 2 at *b,* and

4. Whether or not the curves are symmetrical around a 45° ray from the origin reflects whether or not parents weight in their preferences equally identical levels of expected qualities for the two children. For example, do parents weight equally identical expected quality outcomes for boys and girls or for first-born and higher birth orders? If not, the preference curves are not symmetrical around the 45° ray from the origin. For evidence that such asymmetries favor earlier-born children in the United States and India, boys in India, and girls in the United States, see Behrman (1988*a,* 1988*b*), Behrman, Pollak, and Taubman (1986, in this volume), and Behrman and Taubman (1986, in this volume). For this paper the parental preference curves are assumed to be symmetrical around the 45° ray from the origin, since asymmetries in preferences only complicate, but do not change, the basic point as long as they do not depend on endowments.

equality at c). The right-angled preference curve (U_D), in contrast, reflects extreme parental concern with the distribution of expected qualities among the children. Parental satisfaction does not increase if the expected qualities change from the combination at e to that at d or at f, even though the expected quality of one or the other child improves with both of these changes. Parental preferences are determined only by the expected child quality for the worst-off child, for which reason such a preference curve is sometimes referred to as Rawlsian.

The preference curves in figure 1 represent an intermediate case between the two extremes of figure 2. In such intermediate cases there are trade-offs between productivity and equity, with productivity being weighted more heavily in parental preferences the flatter the curves are (and thus the closer in shape to U_I in fig. 2) and with equity being weighted more heavily in parental preferences the sharper the curves are (and thus the closer in shape to U_D in fig. 2). The more productivity is emphasized in parental preferences, the more parents maximize their preferences by following *reinforcing behavior* and investing more in the child with better endowments, if greater endowments increase the returns to such investments (e.g., by investing more in the schooling of the innately more intelligent child). On the other hand, the more equity is emphasized in parental preferences, the more parents maximize their preferences by *compensating behavior* and invest more in the child with lesser endowments to offset (partially or completely) the lesser endowments. There is an intermediate case in which parents maximize their preferences by neither compensating nor reinforcing endowment differentials among their children that is characterized as *neutral behavior.*[5]

Before proceeding to discuss how the curvature in the parental preferences may affect the schooling–quality association, it is necessary to distinguish whether or not child quality is embodied in the child. One possibility is that child quality is embodied, for instance, by investing in the education or health of the child. This seems consistent with the use of the term "child quality" by most observers. If such quality is valued alone for its potential returns in the labor market, child quality is equated with the child's expected adult earning capacity.

An alternative possibility is that quality also includes the child's expected adult control over resources from physical or financial assets. In this case quality might be equated with the child's expected wealth or income as an adult, with no concern about whether that income comes from own earnings or from ownership of physical or financial assets. This broader definition is consistent with the modeling of Becker and Tomes (1976) and Becker (1981) in which

5. These definitions are consistent with those used by Arrow (1971), Becker and Tomes (1976), and Behrman, Pollak, and Taubman (1982, in this volume).

parental preferences are defined over the distribution of expected wealth among their children, with no concern about whether the wealth is from the child's own human capital (and therefore embodied in his or her earning capacity) or from physical or financial capital.

If child quality is embodied in the human capital of children and a major form of parental investment in children is in their schooling, one critical determinant of how good a proxy schooling is for expected child quality is the curvature in parental preferences over the distribution of qualities among their children. The sharper this curvature is, the more maximizing parents tend to compensate for endowment differentials by investing more in the schooling of the less endowed child. If such compensation is less than complete, as is the case for all but the extreme right-angled case (U_D in fig. 2), the child in whose schooling the parents invest more may be the child with the lesser expected quality (including the effect of the greater schooling investment than would be made if the parents had no concern about the distribution of qualities among their children). Among children within a family, if parental preferences are sufficiently sharply curved because of heavy weight on equity, therefore, schooling is inversely associated with expected child quality.

But parental preferences are only part of the parental preference model for investment in children with quality embodied in children. The other part of the model pertains to the constraints under which such preferences are maximized. These constraints include the total resources that the parents invest in their children[6] and the expected quality production function that translates the endowments, schooling investments, and other investments in the child into expected child quality. All of these factors translate into an expected child quality production frontier, which constrains the expected child quality options of the parents. If parents maximize their preferences, they choose a point on this frontier.[7] Figure 1 illustrates a quality production possibility frontier (still for quality embodied in a child) that reflects that child 1 has greater endowments than does child 2, thus it is elongated in the direction of the expected quality

6. The overall resource constraint of the parents depends on their total wealth or income from all sources (including any transfers). Part of these resources are allocated directly to parental consumption of goods, services, and leisure. The allocation of resources between the parents own direct use of these resources and investment in their children can be considered to be the outcome of the maximization of parental preferences defined over their own consumption, their number of children, and the distribution of expected qualities among their children. For simplicity, but without affecting the basic point of this paper, I am assuming that this larger maximization process can be decomposed into steps in which first the total resources devoted to the children are determined and then the pattern of investment among those children is determined. In the text attention is focused only on this second step.

7. Options of points inside the frontier exist, but preferences are maximized by choosing the right point on the frontier.

of child 1.[8] Parental preferences are maximized, subject to the constraint of the expected child quality production possibility frontier, at the tangency at point c. Other points on the frontier (e.g., a or b) or inside of the frontier (e.g., d or e) result in less than the possible constrained maximization of parental preferences.

At the point at which parent preferences are maximized, the expected quality of child 1 is higher than that of child 2 unless the parental preference curves are right-angled (in which case the expected child qualities are the same for the two children). But the schooling and other investments in child 1 *may* or *may not* be greater than those in child 2. In general, in which child the schooling investment is greater depends on three factors.[9] The first factor (as discussed previously) is the curvature (or the equity–productivity trade-off) in the parental preference curve. The sharper the curve (i.e., the greater the relative concern about equity), the more likely that the lesser endowed child receives greater schooling investments. The second and third factors relate to the curvature of the expected child quality production possibility frontier. If in the underlying expected quality production process substitution is easy among schooling investment, child endowments, and nonschooling forms of child investment, the frontier is less elongated for given endowment differentials, and optimizing combinations of schooling and expected quality are less associated.[10] If schooling prices depend on quality, the shape of the expected quality production possibility frontier is also affected. For instance, if merit scholarships are awarded, schooling prices are inversely associated with endowments; then the quality production possibility frontier is more elongated than it would be with prices

8. The shape of this frontier also reflects the assumption that eventually equally sized added increments of schooling or other investment in a child have diminishing impact on expected child quality due to the fixed initial child endowment. If equal additional schooling increments were always to cause additional equal expected quality increments, the frontier would be linear.

9. I assume that nonschooling prices (e.g., prices of nutrients) are the same for all children in the family. If such prices differed, exactly how they differed would also make a difference. It seems plausible, however, to assume that the price of rice, for example, is the same for a family independent of which child consumes the rice.

10. The frontier is less elongated because schooling can easily offset (at least partially) endowment differentials if substitution in quality production is high. In this case schooling-to-quality ratios may vary greatly with initial endowments, so the schooling–quality association is not strong. In contrast, if there is little possibility of technical substitution between schooling and endowments in producing quality, the schooling–quality association is high for the technical reason that schooling must be used in approximately fixed proportions with endowments to produce quality. Parallel considerations hold for the substitution between schooling and other nonschooling investments in children (e.g., food, health care); the greater is this substitutability, the less may be the schooling–quality association (and, the model predicts, the less the association will be if relative prices for schooling versus other investments differ across children in a way that is not systematically inversely associated with endowments).

that are independent of endowments, which implies a greater schooling–quality association than would occur if schooling prices do not depend on endowments. On the other hand, special education programs that reduce the schooling prices for children with lesser endowments reduce the schooling–quality association.

What do such considerations imply for the empirical association between schooling and expected quality? Conditional on explicit, fairly flexible, commonly used functional forms for the parental preference function and for the quality production function and schooling prices being independent of endowments, the critical question is, What is the value of the product of a parameter referring to the curvature in the parental preference function and a parameter referring to substitution among schooling, endowments, and nonschooling investments in the quality production function?[11] A value of this product equal to zero indicates no association between schooling and expected quality. A value greater than zero indicates positive association, with a value of one implying a perfect association. A value less than zero implies a negative association.

Under the assumptions that different members of the same household face the same prices and that realized quality is well represented (except for a random factor) by adult earnings (since elements of individual quality can be thought to have a value determined by the market), estimates of this critical product have been obtained for two generations in the U.S. (Behrman, Pollak, and Taubman, 1982, 1986, both in this volume). Adult sibling data are useful because they permit the estimation of the tangency condition at point c in figure 1 without usually unobservable data on child endowments, the Lagrangian for the household budget constraint, and prices that differ across households. These studies all obtain an estimated value of the critical product that is between 0.0 and 0.1 and is significantly greater than zero and significantly less than one. This suggests that schooling and quality are positively associated, but weakly so. Moreover, due to simultaneity, these estimates are upward biased, so the true value of the critical product probably is negative (see Behrman and Taubman, 1986, in this volume). Therefore, such results suggest that if quality is embodied in the children, schooling is a poor proxy for quality within the family, with at best a small positive association and more likely an inverse association.

If expected child quality is equated with expected wealth or income and for each child part of that expected income comes from assets transferred from the

11. Both functions are of a constant elasticity of substitution form, which includes the range from the right-angled preference curve (U_E) to the straight-line preference curve (U_I) and the range between zero and perfect substitution among schooling, endowments, and nonschooling investments in the production of child quality. See the Appendix to this chapter for details.

parents via gifts or bequests, then it is efficient for parents to allocate their schooling and other investments in their children in the most productive way (i.e., to follow a reinforcing investment strategy and maximize the children's total expected earnings) and then compensate for differential expected earnings capacities among the children by differential asset distribution among the children. In this case, the initial endowment disparities in the children are offset exactly by asset transfer disparities, so the effective quality production possibility frontier in figure 1 has a 45° slope at the point at which it crosses the 45° ray from the origin, at which point parental preferences are maximized.[12] In such a case, among siblings the part of income due in part to schooling investment is highly positively associated with schooling across children, the part that is independent of schooling investment is highly negatively associated with schooling, and the total expected income (equivalent to expected quality) is unassociated with the schooling across children.[13]

Interfamilial Associations between Schooling and Child Quality Implied by the Parental Preference Intrahousehold Allocation Model

Of course, most empirical studies that use schooling to represent quality utilize data on individuals who are generally not from the same family. The covariance of schooling and quality across individuals (including those from the same and those from different families) can be decomposed into that within a family and that between families, so consideration of individuals at least implicitly requires consideration of interfamilial differences in addition to intrafamilial differences. What does the parental preference model of intrahousehold investment in children imply about the interhousehold schooling–quality association?

To think about this question, it is useful to return to the considerations of the previous section. The schooling investment in each child is determined by the maximizing process in some household. Through the parental preference maximizing decisions, schooling investment, other investments, and expected quality of each child are determined. If quality is embodied in individuals, schooling investment and quality of each child can be expressed as a function of the child's endowment, the prices that the household faces for schooling and other

---

12. The symmetry in parental preferences assures that the preference curve has a 45° slope at this point. (See note 4.)

13. The implications of this second definition of quality may not be important, however, since empirically parents do not seem to allocate sufficiently different physical and financial assets among their children to compensate for endowment differentials, at least for recent generations in the U.S. See Menchik (1980, 1982) and Behrman, Pollak, and Taubman (1988).

investments in the child, the relative weight in the parental preference function for the expected quality of that child, and the marginal parental welfare value for resources devoted to children in that family. For comparisons across children *within* a family, most prices and the marginal parental welfare value for resources devoted to children effectively drop out because they are the same for all children within a household. The weights in the parental preference function also drop out if the parental welfare function is symmetrical around a 45° ray from the origin (see note 4). Under this latter assumption, therefore, the schooling–quality association across children within a family depends on their relative endowments (including the possible dependence of schooling prices on such endowments) and the previously emphasized characteristics of the parental preferences (i.e., the equity–productivity trade-off or curvature) and of the quality production function (i.e., the technical substitutibility among schooling, endowments, and other nonschooling investments in producing quality). It is easy to see that the relative endowments are important because if they are the same for two children (e.g., identical twins), the optimal schooling, other investments, and quality for those two children are identical, and schooling and quality across the two children are perfectly associated for all parental preference curvatures and for all degrees of substitution among schooling and endowments in the production process. That is, not surprisingly, identical children are treated identically in the maximization of parental preferences.

The implications of this review of the intrafamilial allocation process for interfamilial associations of schooling and embodied child quality are three. First, interhousehold variations in endowments probably are greater than intrahousehold variations (e.g., see Behrman et al., 1980; Behrman and Wolfe, 1984; Olneck, 1977). If endowment variations do not affect schooling prices much or at all, the interfamilial association between schooling and quality may well be less than the intrahousehold association due to the greater interfamilial endowment variations. Second, the factors that drop out in the intrahousehold allocation are much less likely to drop out in interfamilial comparisons. Different households may face different prices, have different marginal parental welfare values for resources devoted to children, and have different preference weights on the expected child qualities. For example, the relative schooling-to-nutrient price may vary substantially with the degree of urbanization, with rural areas having higher effective schooling prices due to transportation costs and the opportunity costs of using children in farm activities and lower food prices. Such differences are likely to make the schooling–child quality association weaker, if anything, across families than within families. Third, the parameters in the underlying parental preference and child quality production functions may vary across families. If so the interfamilial schooling–quality association once again is likely to be weaker among than within families.

For the broader definition of quality that includes all income or wealth, random interfamilial differences in prices, marginal parental welfare values, preference weights, and endowments are also likely to make the interfamilial schooling–quality association at least as weak as the intrafamilial one. If there is not a systematic positive association between wealth and child endowments or a systematic negative association between wealth and marginal interest rates, moreover, within this framework families with greater wealth do *not* invest more in their children's schooling, even if child quality is a normal good for which the wealth (or income) elasticity is positive, as is generally assumed to be the case. Instead, wealthier parents simply assure higher child quality broadly defined by giving their children more assets, since the marginal return on such assets is at least as great as that in schooling. If there is a systematic positive association between child endowments and total resources devoted to children, however, the interfamilial schooling–quality association may be greater than the intrafamilial one if wealthier parents tend to have children with greater endowments (and therefore higher returns on given schooling investments and thus greater schooling investments[14]) and larger total expected income (and therefore greater quality broadly defined). Likewise, if there is a systematic inverse association between parental wealth and the marginal cost of funds (e.g., due to greater collateral), wealthier parents tend to invest more in the schooling of their children until the marginal returns equal the lower marginal cost of funds even if their concern is quality broadly defined.

Imperfect Information about Child Endowments at the Time of Marginal Schooling Decisions

To this point I have assumed that the endowments of the children are fully known at the time of the marginal schooling decision within a one-period model. A more realistic assumption may be that child endowments are known imperfectly, particularly in cases in which marginal schooling decisions are made when children are fairly young (e.g., for some empirical evidence for Brazilian males, see Behrman and Birdsall, 1986). But child quality depends on the actual endowments that may only be revealed later, not those perceived at the time of marginal schooling decisions. If the original schooling decisions cannot be adjusted without cost, the imperfect knowledge about endowments at the time of marginal schooling decisions weakens the schooling–actual quality association. This should be intuitively clear by considering the situation in which the noise in perceived endowments is so large that parents invest equally

14. Schooling prices that are directly (inversely) related to endowments oppose (reinforce) this tendency.

in all of their children's schooling; but subsequent actual embodied qualities depend on actual endowments, so they vary among children, leading to an intrafamilial association between schooling and realized embodied qualities of zero.

Concluding Remarks

The quality of children is a construct that is of interest in its own right given demographers' growing concern about not only the quantity but also the quality of the population. It is also of interest because of its relation to fertility and mortality within the framework of quality–quantity demographic models.

But child quality is not well defined in a way that leads easily to direct empirical representation. The most commonly used empirical proxy is schooling. Logically, however, schooling is an input into the production of quality, together with endowments and nonschooling investments in the children. Inputs may be good proxies for outputs if there is a fixed-coefficient technical relation (or near to such a relation) between the input and the output or if despite the possibilities of technological substitution between the input of interest and others, the nature of behavior (given constraints, prices, and resources) assures approximately fixed ratios between the input and the output. But if technological substitution in the production of the quality output is possible, it is *not* sufficient merely that a particular input like schooling have a positive marginal product for that input to be a good proxy for the output. To the contrary it is possible that if the particular input is allocated to compensate for the availability of other inputs, it may be associated inversely with the quality output. Such a pattern is not likely to be observed if everyone faces similar prices and has similar fixed resources. For the production of child quality, however, different people even within a given society face different prices and have different resources. Perhaps most notably, different children have different initial endowments, genetic and otherwise. In addition, different families in different localities are likely to face different relative prices for schooling versus other investments in their children. Therefore, it is at least conceptually possible that schooling is used to compensate partially for such endowment and price differentials, with the result that schooling is a poor proxy for child quality.

Some insight into such a possibility could be gained in principle by direct estimation of the quality production function to see whether substantial substitution is possible among schooling, endowments, and nonschooling investments. Such an approach, however, has several problems. First, there is the question of how to represent quality empirically. Second, endowments are not directly observable. Third, such an estimate could establish a sufficient condition for schooling to be a good proxy (i.e., the technical substitution possibilities are very low), but not a necessary one (since schooling may be a good proxy even if substitution is possible, as noted earlier).

An alternative approach taken in this paper is to consider possible behavior that leads to the allocation of investment in schooling given child endowments. It demonstrates, within a parental-preference intrahousehold allocation model, what conditions determine how good a proxy for quality schooling is both within and across families. These considerations lead to considerable doubt about how good a proxy it is. The intrahousehold model suggests that schooling and quality are not associated within the family if quality is not completely embodied in individuals and all children receive physical or financial transfers from their parents. If quality is completely embodied, this model allows a wide range of intrafamilial associations between schooling and quality, but empirical estimates suggest that parents are sufficiently concerned about inequality and that there is sufficient substitution among schooling, other investments in children, and endowments in producing quality that the actual schooling–quality association is small and probably inverse. Interfamilial considerations probably lead to algebraically smaller schooling–quality associations than do the intrafamilial considerations; with the preferred embodied-quality definition, it would require a fairly large inverse association between schooling prices and endowments to offset the greater interfamilial variation in other factors for the interfamilial schooling–quality association to exceed the intrafamilial one.

Therefore, empirical economic and demographic studies that claim to study the determinants of or the effects of child quality by using child schooling to represent quality should be interpreted with care, and further efforts to devise better measures of quality may well be worthwhile.

Acknowledgments

I thank, but do not implicate, anonymous referees for comments, my colleagues Robert A. Pollak and Paul Taubman for useful discussions and extremely valuable collaboration on related topics, and the National Institutes of Health for research support.

Appendix

This is a presentation in more formal terms of the argument in the text. The first part presents the parental preference model of intrafamilial investment in the schooling of children and its implications for the association between schooling and child quality. The second part illustrates intrafamilial allocation with specific functional forms for embodied quality. The third section considers interfamilial associations between schooling and child quality, and the final section discusses the implications of imperfect information about endowments at the time of the marginal schooling decision.

Parental Preference Model of Intrafamilial Investment in the Schooling of Children and Implications for the Association between Schooling and Child Quality

Parental preferences are assumed to be given by a one-period utility function $U(C, L, E_1, \ldots, E_n, B_1, \ldots, B_n, n)$, where C denotes parental consumption, L parental leisure, E_i the expected earnings of the ith child, B_i the expected bequests and inter vivos gifts to the ith child, and n the number of children. Hereafter I refer to E_i as "earnings" and to B_i as "bequests." For simplicity the sequential nature of decisions is ignored and the allocation problem is viewed in terms of a one-period planning model in which parents make a single, once-and-for-all decision over all variables under their control, except in the last section. To highlight the question of how well child schooling represents child quality, I further assume that family size is predetermined so that the utility function is conditional on the number of children and that in the parental preference ordering the earnings of and bequests to children are separable from parental consumption of goods and leisure.

Parental preferences regarding child earnings and bequests are reflected in the parental welfare function $W(E_1, \ldots, E_n, B_1, \ldots, B_n)$, which is assumed to be quasi-concave so that the indifference curves have the usual shape:

$$U(C, L, E_1, \ldots, E_n, B_1, \ldots, B_n, n)$$
$$= V[C, L, W(E_1, \ldots, E_n, B_1, \ldots, B_n), n]. \quad (A.1)$$

The first definition of quality in the text is the embodied case in which quality is the outcome that is affected by schooling and other investments in the children—for example, earning capacities, but not returns on bequests. In this case earnings are valued differently from other income. An interesting example of the differentiation between income from earnings and that from other sources is provided in the case in which the parental welfare function is separable between the distribution of earnings (= qualities) among the children and the distribution of bequests among the children:[15]

$$W(Q_1, \ldots, Q_n, B_1, \ldots, B_n)$$
$$= W^*[W^Q(Q_1, \ldots, Q_n), W^B(B_1, \ldots, B_n)], \quad (A.2)$$

where Q_i refers to the expected quality of the ith child.

15. I focus on this example because it is tractable, is illuminating, and allows for the possibility of a range of associations between schooling and quality from perfectly negatively to perfectly positively correlated.

In the second definition in the text, quality is equated with income from whatever source. That is, quality is equated with wealth or purchasing power, with no special concern about embodiment in the capacities of the individual through schooling and other investments in the individual. Parents are concerned only about the distribution of expected wealth among their children, not about the composition of that wealth between earning capacities and assets. The parental welfare function in this case is:

$$W(E_1, \ldots, E_n, B_1, \ldots, B_n)$$
$$= W^{**}(E_1 + rB_1, \ldots, E_n + rB_n) = W^{**}(Q_1, \ldots, Q_n), \quad \text{(A.3)}$$

where r is the interest rate.

The appropriate (depending on the definition of quality) parental preference function is maximized subject to two constraints. First, the earnings production function gives the expected child earnings as determined by the child's endowment (G_i), schooling (S_i), and other investments in the child (X_i):[16]

$$E_i = E(G_i, S_i, X_i). \quad \text{(A.4)}$$

The second constraint is the full-income constraint on total use of the household's time and return on assets, given market prices. For the present purpose, the essential point is captured by concentrating on the partial budget constraint containing only the total value of resources devoted to children (R), given the price per year of schooling (P_S) and the price for the other nonschooling investments for the production of child quality (P_X):[17]

$$R = R^B + R^E = \sum_{i=1}^{n} B_i + \sum_{i=1}^{n} P_{S_i} S_i + \sum_{i=1}^{n} P_{X_i} X_i. \quad \text{(A.5)}$$

As is indicated in this expression, the total resources devoted to children include those in the form of bequests (R^B) and those dedicated to producing child earning capacities (R^E).

The first-order condition with respect to schooling for the ith child is

$$(\partial W/\partial Q_i)(\partial Q_i/\partial S_i) = \lambda P_{S_i}, \quad \text{(A.6)}$$

where λ is the Lagrangian multiplier for the partial budget constraint. Similar expressions hold for the other purchased inputs.

To satisfy this condition, there is a two-stage process, with the stages dependent on the definition of quality and the associated parental welfare function.

16. This expression could be generalized to include "public goods" within the family, but the present formulation more simply captures the basic point of this paper.

17. Parents are assumed to provide from their budget all of the resources for child quality producing inputs, except for the endowments; also time costs are ignored. More complicated formulations could be made with different assumptions, but the essential points would be preserved.

In the separable quality–bequest case in which quality is embodied in individuals, first R is allocated between R^B and R^E and then (a) R^B is allocated among the n children and (b) R^E is allocated among the n children. If the parents have equal concern (and therefore symmetrical preference curves) so that the welfare function is symmetric in its treatment of all children (see note 4), the result is equal bequests but not necessarily equal earnings and qualities, since different children have different genetic endowments. In the wealth case in which quality is total income, the first stage allocates R among the n children, and the second allocates resources devoted to each child between bequests and expenditures that affect earnings. If parents have equal concern, this generally does not result in equal bequests (assuming positive values) or in equal earnings, since the optimal division between bequests and earnings differs across children, depending on the children's relative endowments.

Parents satisfy the first-order condition in relation (A.5) (and similar ones for the other inputs) to determine the distribution of schooling, other investments in their children, earnings, bequests, and therefore qualities among their children. Whether the intrafamilial association between children and quality is positive, negative, or zero depends partially on how broadly quality is defined and, in the case in which quality is embodied in individuals and the parental welfare function is separable, whether parents following reinforcing, compensating, or neutral strategies in their allocation of R^E.

If parents define quality to be total income or wealth, so that the wealth model is appropriate and bequests are all positive, further details about the welfare function are irrelevant for the present discussion. This is because parents can adjust their distribution of bequests to attain their desired distribution of R among their children after they determine the most efficient distribution of schooling and other investments and therefore of earnings by investing in each child until the expected marginal return to schooling equals the marginal cost of funds. As a result there is no systematic association between schooling and quality; parents follow a neutral strategy.[18]

If quality is defined to be embodied in earning capacities and the parental welfare function is separable, which strategy parents follow depends on the two partial derivatives in the left side of relation (A.6)—the partial derivative of parental welfare with respect to child quality (earnings) and the partial derivative of quality (earnings) with respect to schooling—and on the price of schooling on the right side of relation (A.6). The first of these partial derivatives reflects the properties of the parental welfare function, and the second reflects properties of the quality (earnings) production function. If parents have great inequality aversion, even if the impact of schooling on quality (earnings)

18. I assume here that preference weights in the parental utility function do not depend directly or indirectly on schooling.

is positive they may adopt a compensating strategy to assure that their less endowed children are not of too much less quality than their better endowed children.[19] If so, the intrafamilial correlation between child quality and schooling is negative. If parental inequality aversion is not so strong, but still exists, its existence tends to weaken (i.e., make less positive) the association between quality and schooling that originates from the positive impact of schooling on quality in the quality production function alone.[20] If the quality production function has technology that allows substitution between schooling, endowments, and other investments in the production of quality, parents have more flexibility in determining the distribution of qualities among their children and, assuming some concern about the equity of that distribution, may choose to allocate schooling to compensate partially for the distribution of endowments or of other investments. Finally, if schooling prices depend positively (negatively) on child endowments, parents tend to find it more (less) costly to invest more in better-endowed children and, in their maximizing allocations, invest less (more) in such children, which reduces (increases) the quality–schooling association.

Thus on an intrafamilial basis, the association between schooling and quality may be positive, zero, or negative. The association is zero if quality is equated with total wealth or income and all bequests are positive. If quality is embodied in individuals and if the parental welfare function is separable between quality and other forms of intergenerational transfer, the quality–schooling association is likely to be smaller the greater is the technological substitution between genetic endowments and schooling in the quality production function, the greater is parental inequality aversion regarding the distribution of quality among their children, and the more that schooling prices depend positively on endowments.

Specific Functional Forms for the Case of a Separable Welfare Function with Embodied Quality

In the case in which quality is equated with earnings and the parental welfare function is separable between earnings and bequests, the foregoing notions can be illuminated further by considering specific functional forms for the parental welfare function and for the quality production function. The relevant points are clearest if parental inequality aversion in the parental welfare function and the elasticity of substitution in the quality production function both are assumed to be constant so that the functions have constant elasticities of substi-

19. In the extreme Rawlsian case of absolute inequality aversion, the parents devote all of R^E to the least endowed child until his or her quality is equal to that of the next least endowed child (and then all of the rest to bring those two up to the third least endowed, etc.).

20. As parental inequality aversion approaches zero, the properties of the quality production function become relatively more important.

tution (CES), which encompasses the spectrum from concern only about equity to concern only about productivity on the side of parental preferences and from zero to perfect substitution on the side of quality production.

Let the parental welfare function regarding the distribution of quality among their children have constant inequality aversion:

$$W^Q(Q_i, \ldots, Q_n) = (\Sigma a_i Q_i^c)^{1/c}. \tag{A.7}$$

The a_i refer to the weights placed on the quality of the ith child; if parents exhibit equal concern, the a_i equal a constant a for all i. Inequality aversion can be defined as

$$\alpha = 1 - c. \tag{A.8}$$

As α approaches zero from above, inequality aversion approaches zero and the parental welfare indifference curves approach straight lines, reflecting that parents with equal concern[21] invest in their children to maximize the sum of their qualities in a pure investment model with no concern about the distribution of qualities among the children (e.g., U_I in fig. 2) with a pure reinforcing strategy. $\alpha = 1$ is the unitary or Cobb–Douglas case in which the parental welfare function is the geometric sum of the qualities with parents balancing equity against investment returns in terms of the total quality of their children with a neutral strategy. As α approaches infinity, inequality aversion also approaches infinity, and the parental welfare indifference curves approach the Rawlsian L-shaped case in which only the quality of the child with the least quality counts (e.g., U_D in fig. 2) and the parents adopt a pure compensating strategy.

For this parental welfare function, the partial derivative of welfare with respect to the quality of the ith child is

$$\partial W^Q / \partial Q_i = (W^Q)^a a_i Q_i^{-a}. \tag{A.9}$$

If the elasticity of substitution is assumed to be the same among all inputs,[22] the CES form of the quality production function is

$$Q_i = (a_G G_i^b + a_S S_i^b + a_X X_i^b)^{1/b}. \tag{A.10}$$

The elasticity of substitution between any two inputs is

$$\sigma = 1/(1 - b). \tag{A.11}$$

This has the standard interpretation: $\sigma \to 0$ implies no substitution or Leontieff production, $\sigma = 1$ implies a log-linear or Cobb–Douglas relation, and $\sigma \to \infty$

21. Parents without equal concern in this case maximize the weighted sum of qualities, with the weights given by the a_i.

22. The extension to incorporate different elasticities of substitution among different inputs would be straightforward but would not add significantly to what follows.

implies infinite or perfect substitution with linear isoquants. The partial derivative of quality with respect to schooling is

$$\partial Q_i / \partial S_i = Q_i^{1/\sigma} a_S S_i^{-1/\sigma}. \tag{A.12}$$

The second cross-partial derivative with respect to schooling and endowment is

$$\partial^2 Q_i / (\partial S_i \partial G_i) = Q_i^{(2-\sigma)/\sigma} a_S a_G (S_i G_i)^{-1/\sigma} / \sigma. \tag{A.13}$$

In general, this is nonnegative (approaching zero from above as $\sigma \to \infty$).

Substitution of relations (A.9) and (A.12) into relation (A.6) and dividing by the identical expression for the jth child gives

$$Q_i / Q_j = (S_i / S_j)^{1/(1-\alpha\sigma)} (a_j P_{S_i} / a_i P_{S_j})^{\sigma/(1-\alpha\sigma)}. \tag{A.14}$$

If there is equal concern (so $a_j = a_i = a$) and if each child within the family faces identical schooling prices (so $P_{S_i} = P_{S_j}$), this expression implies that schooling is a perfect proxy for quality if and only if $\alpha\sigma = 0$. If there is substitution in quality production ($\sigma > 0$) and some parental inequality aversion (so $\alpha > 0$), relation (A.14) implies a less than perfect correlation between schooling and quality within the family, even with equal concern and with schooling prices not dependent on endowments. As $\alpha\sigma$ increases in value, the correlation becomes smaller and schooling becomes a poorer proxy for quality. If $\alpha\sigma = 1$, the correlation is zero. If $\alpha\sigma > 1$, the correlation is negative and schooling is an inverse proxy for quality. Thus the greater is parental inequality aversion and the greater is substitution in the production of quality (given $\sigma > 0 < \alpha$), the poorer a proxy for quality is schooling. This is because the greater σ is, the more schooling for a particular child can technologically be substituted for limited endowment and other investments, and the greater α is, the more the parents want to make such substitutions.

If there is not equal concern, the conditions for schooling to be a perfect proxy for quality are even less likely to be satisfied unless the unequal concern weights depend positively on endowments. This should be intuitively clear, since with unequal concern parents weight more heavily identical levels of quality for some children than for others. Consider, for example, three-children families in which the quality of the first child is weighted more heavily by the parents than are the qualities of the other two. In this case even if the parents have no inequality aversion ($\alpha \to 0$) and schooling prices are independent of endowments ($P_{S_i} = P_{S_j}$), relation (A.14) implies that schooling is *not* a perfect proxy for quality because of unequal concern if the elasticity of substitution is nonzero.

If schooling prices depend on child endowments, the effects on the quality–schooling association are straightforward from relation (A.14). A positive dependence of schooling prices on endowments weakens the quality–schooling association and vice versa.

Interfamilial Versus Intrafamilial Schooling–Quality Associations

If quality is equated with total income or wealth, all bequests are positive, all households face the same marginal cost of funds for schooling, and there is no association across households between child endowments and total allocation of resources to children, then there is no association between quality and schooling on an interfamilial basis. Each household tends to invest in schooling until the expected marginal rate of return equals the same marginal cost of financing, with greater schooling investments in those children with greater endowments if there is complementarity between endowments and schooling. Under these conditions, if wealthier parents allocate more resources to their children's quality than do less wealthy parents, on the average the added resources take the form of added bequests. If wealthier families devote more resources to children and face lower marginal costs of funding or tend to have children with better endowments,[23] however, there would be some positive interfamilial association between schooling and child quality.

If quality is embodied in children and wealthier families devote more resources to children, the possibility of lower marginal funding costs or better child endowments for wealthier families would tend to make the association between schooling and quality greater. On the other hand, there are three factors that work in the opposite direction.

First, the expressions above for intrafamilial comparisons of relative quality and schooling levels incorporate additional factors if they are derived for interfamilial analysis; these additions probably lessen the quality–school correlation. Lagrangian multipliers and the parental welfare levels may vary across families, so for interfamilial comparisons, relation (A.14) must be replaced by

$$Q_i/Q_j = (S_i/S_j)^{1/(1-\alpha\sigma)}[(a_j\lambda_i P_{S_i} W_j^\alpha)/(a_i\lambda_j P_{S_j} W_i^\alpha)]^{\sigma/(1-\alpha\sigma)}. \quad (A.15)$$

The more complicated expression on the right side probably reduces the schooling–quality correlation below what would be attained without the complications (as in the intrafamilial case).

Second, underlying the imperfect representation of quality by schooling are variations in endowments, which are not under the control of the parents. These are likely to be greater among unrelated individuals across families than among siblings because of stronger genetic associations among kin. Therefore, schooling is likely to be a poorer proxy for quality across families than within families.

This point can be illustrated by considering expressions for schooling and quality ratios across individuals as a function of the endowment ratios. To keep the algebra simple, I consider an example in which the quality production func-

23. The latter would occur if there is intergenerational serial correlation in endowments that affect wealth.

tion in relation (A.10) is assumed to have unitary elasticity of substitution, though the inequality aversion parameter in the parental welfare function of relation (A.7) can take on any value. Manipulation of the first-order condition in relation (A.6), the parallel first-order condition for X, and the quality production function in relation (A.10) gives

$$S_i/S_j = (G_i/G_j)^{(1-\alpha)a_G/\gamma} H_S, \qquad (A.16)$$

$$Q_i/Q_j = (G_i/G_j)^{a_G/\gamma} H_Q, \qquad (A.17)$$

where $\gamma = 1 - (1 - \alpha)(a_S + a_X)$ and H_S and H_Q depend on parental welfare levels, Lagrangian multipliers for the partial budget constraint, unequal concern, schooling prices, other prices, and quality production function and parental preference parameters. These relations indicate that, ceteris paribus, the relative quality between i and j generally differs from the relative schooling because the exponents of the relative genetic endowments differ in the two relations. The smaller is the genetic difference, the smaller is the impact of the different exponents and the higher is the correlation between schooling and quality. In the limit, if genetic endowments are identical (e.g., identical twins), the differential exponents have no effect and quality and schooling are perfectly correlated (ignorning H_S and H_Q, the components of which are discussed above and both of which become one with intrafamilial comparisons, constant prices, and equal concern). Thus the generally larger genetic variations across individuals from different families as compared with genetic variations within families are likely to result in weaker positive correlations between schooling and quality for interfamilial than for intrafamilial comparisons.

Third, schooling prices relative to prices of other investments are likely to vary more across families (particularly across localities) than within families. Since these prices enter differently into H_S than into H_Q [i.e., with an exponent of $(1 - \alpha)a_G/\gamma$ in H_S and with an exponent of a_G/γ in H_Q], if relative prices differ across children, the last multiplicative terms in relations (A.16) and (A.17) vary differently across different children. This tends to weaken the association with endowments of both schooling and quality, and therefore of their association with each other.

Imperfect Information about Endowments at Time of Marginal Schooling Decisions

If endowments are imperfectly perceived by a random factor at the time of marginal schooling decisions, the schooling–quality association is weakened.[24]

24. Under the assumption that schooling cannot be adjusted completely when subsequently endowments are better known because of irreversibilities in schooling investments, transaction costs, and other commitments.

For a specific illustration, in addition to the assumptions of the preceding section, assume that perceived endowments at the time of the marginal schooling decisions (G_i^*) are related to actual endowments (G_i) as follows:

$$G_i^* = G_i e^{u_i}, \tag{A.18}$$

where u_i is a random stochastic term. If investments are made in children on the basis of the perceived endowments, relation (A.16) becomes

$$S_i/S_j = (G_i e^{u_i - u_j}/G_j)^{(1-a)a_g/\lambda} H_S. \tag{A.19}$$

If actual quality depends on investments in children and on their actual endowments, then the counterpart to relation (A.17) is

$$Q_i/Q_j = (G_i/G_j)^{a_G/\gamma} H_Q e^{(u_i - u_j)(a_X + a_S)a_G(1-\alpha)/\gamma}. \tag{A.20}$$

If $u_i - u_j$ is nonzero, the relation between S_i/S_j and Q_i/Q_j is weakened, since the relation of each to G_i/G_j is modified by different products involving $u_i - u_j$.

9

Schooling and Other Human Capital Investments: Can the Effects be Identified?

JERE R. BEHRMAN

Parents make considerable investments in the human capital of their children, and the children themselves also make considerable investments. In many cases schooling is a major investment, but there also are considerable non-schooling investments in the children's health, nutrition, and general development. In some poorer societies in which schooling is quite limited, these nonschooling investments often appear to be much more considerable in magnitude than the schooling investments.[1]

Under what conditions can the impact of the schooling investments be identified from the impact of the nonschooling investments? And if such identification is difficult or impossible, how should one interpret estimates of the returns to schooling?

This note addresses these questions. It analyzes investments in children within the standard neoclassical framework with one expected outcome per child that has been used in seminal studies of schooling by Becker (1962, 1967, 1981), Mincer (1974) and others.[2] Such studies have provided the theoretical bases for widespread interpretations of the rate of return to schooling—most notably, the Mincerian interpretation of the estimated coefficient of schooling in semilog earnings functions as the private rate of return to schooling. There-

Reprinted from *Economics of Education Review* 6, no. 3 (1987): 301–5. Copyright 1987, with kind permission from Pergamon Journals Ltd., Headington Hill Hall, Oxford OX3 OBW, UK.

1. Acharya (1981), King and Evenson (1983) and Lindert (1980) summarize some of the evidence on the considerable nonschooling investments in children.

2. Becker's (1962, 1967) and Mincer's (1974) analyses of human capital investments use a neoclassical framework with expected earnings as the outcome of interest for each child. Becker's (1981) more recent intergenerational model uses a neoclassical framework with expected full income as the outcome of interest. Expected full income, of course, should incorporate marriage market outcomes, as emphasized by Boulier and Rosenzweig (1984) and Behrman and Wolfe (1987). It also may incorporate, at least partially, some other outcomes of interest to investors in children, such as their health and cultural knowledge. If there are outcomes which cannot be incorporated into a single measure, E below may be replaced by a vector. The analysis below still may hold exactly if the elements in this vector are weighted equally by investors in different children. To the extent that the weights for the elements in the vector differ across different investors, the results are weakened. However they still apply for the influential one-outcome cases noted in the text.

fore it is important to ask, whether even within the neoclassical framework with one expected outcome per child, is it likely that the effect of schooling can be identified if schooling is but one of a number of human capital investments in children?

The analysis below suggests that the answer to this question is likely to be negative. Patterns of other human capital investments in children probably make it difficult to identify the returns to schooling in standard studies using individual data or in those using sibling data. Moreover the resulting bias in the estimated impact of schooling is very difficult to measure or to avoid empirically because of the usual absence of data on both nonschooling investments in children and on subsequent adult outcomes for those same children decades later and because multicollinearity may make difficult identification of the relevant parameters even if such data were available.

Maximizing Investments in Children

Consider a two-period model. In period one investments are made in a child.[3] In period two that child has become an adult and experiences outcomes which reflect the investments in him or her made in period one. Assume that the investments made in period one are those that maximize the preferences (U) of the investor regarding the expected adult outcome (E) for the child in period two:

$$U = U(E, \ldots). \tag{1}$$

The expected adult outcomes (E) are produced by schooling (S), other investments in the child (X), and endowments (G):[4,5]

$$E = E(S, X, G). \tag{2}$$

3. In order to highlight the concern of interest about multicollinearity between investments in schooling and in other human capital, I avoid complications that would arise from making the time period of such investments endogenous and abstract from discounting. This is not to deny that endogeneity of the length of the first period may not be critical for other important analyses, as is illustrated in Boulier and Rosenzweig (1984) and Mincer (1974).

4. These are endowments in the Becker (1981) sense. That is, they include genetic endowments and other factors which affect the expected outcome of interest for the child, but which do not divert full income from other commodity consumption (as do S and X). Therefore they affect E, but do not enter into the budget constraint in relation (3) below.

5. The assumption that the production function is the same across children, once endowments are incorporated into it, is standard in this literature (e.g., Becker 1962, 1967, 1981; Behrman et al., 1982, 1986, both in this volume; Behrman and Taubman, 1986, in this volume; Behrman and Wolfe, 1984, 1987; Mincer 1974; Psacharopoulos, 1985; Taubman, 1977). Since endowments are included in the function, such a specification allows different outcomes for the same human capital investments for children with different degrees of inherent intelligence or perseverance or with different role models in the home, etc.

Investments in S and X (each of which may be represented for simplicity by one variable instead of a vector of variables) cost P^s and P^x per unit, so that the budget constraint on the allocations of resources devoted to this child (R^c) is:

$$R^c = P^s\, S + P^x\, X + \ldots \qquad (3)$$

Assume that the investor in this child maximizes satisfaction in relation (1) subject to the production relation (2) and the budget constraint (3), and that all of the relevant functions have the standard desirable properties for an interior solution. The first-order conditions imply:

$$\frac{E_S}{P^s} = \frac{E_X}{P^x}, \qquad (4)$$

where E_S and E_X are the partial derivatives of E with respect to S and X, respectively.

Depending on the prices relevant for investments in this child and the form of the production function for the expected outcomes of interest, this first-order relation can imply a strong association across investments in a child.

Illustrative Case with Perfect Correlation between Schooling and Other Investments in Children

For example, consider a CES (constant elasticity of substitution) production function for relation (2):

$$E = (a_G G^b + a_S S^b + a_X X^b)^{1/b}, \qquad (2A)$$

where the elasticity of substitution between any two inputs is $\sigma = 1/(1 - b)$.

This is a general and very widely-used functional form, that allows the full range of substitution among the inputs, from zero to infinite substitution.

With this production function, relation (4) can be rewritten as:

$$X = \left(\frac{P^s a_X}{P^x a_S}\right)^{\sigma} S. \qquad (4A)$$

If the production function in (2) is identical across children (so a_X, a_S and σ are identical across children) and the relative prices of investment are identical across children, this relation implies that schooling and nonschooling investments in children are perfectly correlated across children even though the children differ in their endowments. This perfect correlation holds across all children for which these assumptions are satisfied, whether they are in the same or different families. Relation (4A) also holds whether the investors are children, their parents or someone else. Because of such perfect correlation, it would be impossible empirically in this case to identify the contribution of schooling alone to the outcome (E). If schooling alone is included as a right-side variable for the determination of some outcome of interest (e.g., earnings, fertility, health), moreover, the estimated impact of schooling is biased upward because it incorporates the impact of all human capital investments, not just schooling.

Differing Relative Prices across Children
and Less Than Perfect Correlations between
Schooling and Other Investments in Children

The assumption made above concerning the constancy of relative prices across children merits some comment. To the extent that the relative prices reflect market prices, it is commonly made in this literature without comment. But in addition, there are important time prices, which have played an important role in such analysis since Becker's (1965) seminal article. Some readers may be reflecting at this point that such time prices may vary considerably, as evidenced by the considerable variation in observed market wages for parents.

But remember that it is *relative* prices that count. Time costs probably enter into both the numerator and the denominator of relation (4A): primarily that for the child in the numerator and those for both the child and the child's parents in the denominator. If there is strong enough positive intergenerational familial serial correlations in such time costs, even the time component of *relative* prices may be approximately constant across children (both within and across families). The more child time costs reflect genetic and family-determined environmental endowments, the more constant are relative prices. The available (largely indirect) evidence suggests that family background (including genetic and environmental endowments) may be quite important in determining the marginal value of time (e.g., Behrman *et al.,* 1980; Behrman and Wolfe 1984; Corcoran *et al.,* 1978; Leibowitz, 1977; Olneck, 1977). Therefore the combination of constant market prices and intergenerational familial correlation in time costs may mean that relative prices are much closer to constant across children than might appear to be the case, *prima facie.* Thus, though some variation in relative prices across children probably exists so that the correlation between schooling and other human capital investments is not perfect, such relative price variation may be small enough so that the correlation is high, and the identification of schooling effects difficult.

Concluding Remarks

The implications of this simple analysis for identifying the returns to schooling in standard estimates and interpretations are strong. Recent time and nominal budget studies of intrahousehold allocations suggest that the resource expenditures on nonschooling investments in children tend to be large relative to those devoted to schooling in a wide variety of contexts (e.g., Acharya, 1981; King and Evenson, 1983; Lindert, 1980). Such investments include resources devoted to child health and nutrition and nonschooling forms of training. The failure to control for these (usually unobserved) nonschooling investments in numerous standard estimates of the impact of schooling on earnings, fertility, and many other outcomes, therefore, may cause substantial upward biases in the estimated impact of schooling because of multicollinearity between schooling and the excluded nonschooling investments. Thus the strong policy recommendations for increasing schooling investments based partly on the standard estimates, with rates of return for primary schooling in Latin America, for example, cited to be 44% (this estimate is reported in Psacharopoulos 1981, 1983; also Colclough, 1982; World Bank, 1980, 1981) may be quite misleading.

The identification problem and the upward bias cannot be eliminated, moreover, by use of adult sibling data to control for unobserved childhood family background (as in Behrman *et al.,*1980; Behrman and Wolfe, 1984; and Olneck, 1977) since the association between schooling and the unobserved other investments holds within the family as well as between families.[6] Under certain plausible assumptions about the form of the production function (e.g., the widely-used and fairly general CES case) and the constancy of relative prices for investment in different children, furthermore, the true impact of schooling could not be identified and the biases could not be eliminated even if all nonschooling investments were observed because of the perfect multicollinearity between schooling and other investments in children. Even if relative prices for investment in children differ across children or if nonCES production functions are appropriate so that the correlations among different investments in children are not perfect, they may be high enough to make estimates of the impact of schooling alone difficult to obtain.

The frequent absence of observed data on nonschooling investments and on the relevant relative prices means that it may be hard to avoid upward biases in the estimated impact of schooling as long as there is any positive correlation between schooling and other relevant human capital investments in children. But researchers at a minimum could be sensitive to the identification problem and to this possible bias and indicate its possible effect by presenting alternative estimates (in addition to their standard estimates) with their standard schooling return estimates adjusted by the order of magnitude of the share of

6. In fact, the association probably is stronger within families since the production function for expected outcomes and the relative prices of investments in children are more likely to be similar across children within families than in different families.

schooling in total human capital investments in children. For example, if the share of schooling in total investment in primary schooling age children in Latin America is one half (one quarter), then a lower bound (at least with regard to schooling representing other human capital investments) estimate for the true rate of return to primary schooling in Latin America would be 22 (11)%. As this example illustrates, even if the upward bias in standard estimates of the return to schooling due to the failure to control for unobserved other human capital investments is large, in some contexts the "true" (i.e., corrected for this bias) returns to schooling may be quite high. Thus the probable importance of the identification problem and of the associated bias does not imply that everywhere there is overinvestment in schooling, but only that standard procedures may overstate substantially the returns.

This analysis casts considerable doubt on the myriad of empirical studies purporting to estimate the impact of schooling on various socio-economic outcomes such as earnings, fertility, health and nutrition and on the empirical underpinning for strong advocacy by Colclough (1982), Psacharopoulos (1981, 1983, 1985) and the World Bank (1980, 1981) of increased schooling investments. However, that schooling is a very good and perhaps perfect proxy (in some contexts) for other human capital investments in children suggests that it may be a very good representation of the totality of human capital investments in children. As a result, recent studies of intrahousehold allocation of schooling investments in children (e.g., Behrman *et al.,* 1982, 1986, both in this volume; Behrman and Taubman, 1986, in this volume) are broader in their implications than may have been realized since the schooling allocation may represent very well the allocation of all human capital investments under the control of the parents even though in the data sets used nonschooling investments are not observed.

Acknowledgments

I thank for discussions on related topics, but do not implicate, anonymous referees and my collaborators on related projects: Robert Pollack and Paul Taubman of the University of Pennsylvania, Raaj Sah of Yale University, Barbara L. Wolfe of the University of Wisconsin, and Nancy Birdsall of the World Bank.

Part Four

Associations between Parental Income and Child Earnings

10

Intergenerational Earnings Mobility in the United States: Some Estimates and a Test of Becker's Intergenerational Endowments Model

JERE BEHRMAN AND PAUL TAUBMAN*

Since de Tocqueville, the United States often has been thought of as an open society in which chances in the labor market are independent of one's choice of parents. Others argue that there's "inheritance of poverty" or "inequality of opportunity," and that one's earnings and wealth are conditioned strongly by parental wealth.

Parents' and children's earnings are correlated because of biological and cultural inheritances and problems in borrowing to invest in human capital.[1] However, the higher the value of the mother's labor market participation, the greater is the shadow price of child quantity relative to quality. Assuming negative assortative mating on spouses' market wages as in Becker (1981), higher-earnings fathers are in families with lower shadow prices for child quantity; such families are likely to opt for more quantity implying lower expected children's earnings.

Previous systematic empirical evidence on intergenerational earnings or income associations is very limited. We know of only one recent U.S. estimate based on direct comparisons of actual income or earnings data for both generations.[2] Sewell and Hauser (1975) use data on 1,789 Wisconsin high school

Reprinted from *Review of Economics and Statistics* 67, no. 1 (February 1985): 141–51. Copyright, 1985, by the President and Fellows of Harvard College.

We thank Richard Voith for excellent research assistance and NIH for research support.

1. See Atkinson (1983), Becker (1981), and Conlisk (1974).

2. Corcoran and Datcher (1981) use the Panel Study of Income Dynamics for 413 male household heads age 23–33 in 1978 who had lived with at least one parent in 1967; they report an R of .35 in a regression of son's 1978 ln earnings on parental family income in 1967 and on ten background variables, but do not present a simple intergenerational correlation without the background variables. Atkinson, Trinder, and Maynard (1978) use data on 307 father-son pairs both from York, England; they obtained an R of .17 between father's income in 1950 and son's earnings in 1975–78. deWolff and van Slijpe (1973) use data on 545 males from Malmo, Sweden with parent's income from 1938 and children's income from 1953 and obtain an R of .49. Soltow (1965) considers fathers and sons residing in Sarpsborg, Norway in 1960. He finds an R of .11 and an elasticity of 14% with a sample of 115. There also are some estimates for earlier periods in the United States

seniors in 1957 with nonfarm backgrounds and obtain an intergenerational correlation (R) of 0.17 between parents' income and child's earnings. This low
estimate may reflect the young age of the children (25–28) when current earnings may not reflect well permanent earnings. Moreover, the sample is much
more homogeneous than a representative national sample.

There also are some indirect estimates. Behrman et al. (1980) show that the
R for siblings is an upper bound for the corresponding parent-child R and estimate this sibling R for earnings at age 50 to be 0.33, using 907 fraternal twins
pairs. Olneck's (1977) data on 1973 earnings of 346 pairs of brothers in Kalamazoo, Michigan 1928–1950 yields a sibling R of 0.24. These samples also
are not representative of the overall U.S. population. Another indirect method
is to use as a proxy for father's earnings the mean income in the father's occupational category.[3] However, there is substantial earnings dispersion even
within occupations. If the dispersion is random, there is an underestimate of
the true R.

These estimates suggest that the intergenerational R is small. Another common feature of the studies is "regression" toward the mean, i.e., an elasticity
of offspring's income with respect to parents' income less than one. Economists have developed models to explain both the intergenerational linkages and
regression towards the mean (e.g., Becker, 1967, 1981).

We have collected a new sample which allows us to make another estimate
of the intergenerational correlations of earnings for sons and daughters. It also
permits us to test the Becker (1981) preference model of intergenerational link-
age by using data on years of schooling collected for three generations.

I. Data

Our data set consists of both the adult offspring of the twins and the twins in
the National Academy of Sciences–National Research Council (NAS-NRC)
Twin sample.[4] Data on about 4000 adult offspring were collected in 1977–

---

and for other countries. Becker (1983) summarizes some of these estimates: $R = .71$ for 64 pairs
of U.S. Mormons (father's wealth in 1860, son's wealth in 1870) from unpublished estimates by
Kearl and Pope; $R = .59$ for 202 pairs of U.S. fathers in 1749 and sons in 1779 from unpublished
estimates by Becker with quadratic income terms for father; and $R = .60$ (fathers in 1924–26 and
sons in 1956–57) and $R = .53$ (fathers in 1902 and sons in 1934) based on probate records in
Great Britain in Harbury and Hitchens (1979).

3. Freeman (1981) uses the ln median male income of the three digit father's occupations as
right-side variables with son's ln earnings as the dependent variable; he does not report the R's.

4. The NAS-NRC Twin Sample is described in detail in Behrman et al. (1980). The NAS-NRC
Twin Sample was drawn from a panel of white male veteran twins born between 1917 and 1927
in the United States. If only one sibling in a pair answered, the offspring were surveyed in the
offspring sample.

Table 1 Means and Standard Deviations
of Selected Variables in Offspring Sample

	No. of Observations	Mean	σ
Years of Birth	6352	1953.4	4.8
Sex 1 = Male 2 = Female	4066	1.54	0.5
Schooling	3986	14.7	2.2
Schooling of Father	3739	14.1	2.6
Schooling of Mother	3760	13.8	2.5
1980 Yearly Earnings (in $1000s)	3768	14.3	16.0

Table 2 Means and Standard Deviations
for Selected Variables for Two Groups of Parents

	Parents with Reporting Offspring		Parents with No Reporting Offspring	
	Mean	σ	Mean	σ
Schooling of Father	13.3	3.1	13.2	3.2
Schooling of Mother	12.5	2.8	11.3	4.4
Earnings of Father (in $1000s)	17.5	14.2	15.9	12.9
Age of Father	60.1	2.9	60.1	2.9
Number of Offspring	3.7	1.7	2.6	1.7

1981 by mail and telephone surveys based on addresses provided by members of the NAS-NRC Twin sample.

Table 1 contains some summary statistics from these offspring and their parents. Average age of the respondents was about 28, work experience was 6 years,[5] education was 15 years, and earnings were $14,347 per year. In the 1980 Census the median education of people aged 25 to 35 was 12.9, while in our sample the median education was 15. That the offspring are not a random draw from the population is not surprising since their fathers were above average in education and earnings. To examine selectivity, we calculated means and standard deviations for parents with and without offspring responding (table 2). The respondents tend to come from wealthier families with more educated mothers, but the differences are small.

The NAS-NRC Twin sample is not a random draw of the population, but yields regression results for individuals similar to those from random samples of the same time period (Behrman et al., 1980). To examine this for the off-

5. Experience is calculated as age minus age at time of first full-time job. If the latter age was not given, years of school plus six was substituted. If years of experience are negative as initially calculated, zero is used.

spring, we estimate a standard semilog earnings function for the male non-student offspring:

$$\ln Y = \begin{array}{cc} 7.796 + & 0.082 \ S + & 0.152 \ EXP \\ (62.3) & (10.6) & (14.5) \end{array}$$
$$- \ 0.0062 \ EXP^2 \qquad \bar{R}^2 = 0.23$$
$$(8.35)$$

where Y is earnings in 1981 dollars, S is years of schooling, EXP is work experience, and absolute t-values are in parentheses. The coefficient on years of schooling is significant and similar in magnitude to those obtained in random samples (e.g., Lillard and Willis, 1978). The experience variables have the expected signs and are significantly nonzero. Experience has its peak effect younger than in many other samples. But since the sample has mostly young people, it is not a very appropriate one for finding this peak.

II. Intergenerational Cross-Classifications and Correlations for Earnings

We now present evidence on earnings' intergenerational linkages. We would like to have the present discounted values of lifetime earnings. Instead we must make use of data for each generation drawn from one year. The low offspring average of 28 suggests at least three ways in which current earnings may deviate from the present discounted value of the lifetime earnings of the children:

1. Based on lifecycle profiles, the earnings of the younger sample members are biased downward from their lifetime earnings. We correct by using the coefficients from regressions of earnings on a quadratic in experience to adjust for deviations of an individual's experience from mean sample experience.[6]

2. The earnings of individuals with heavy human capital investments are below their lifetime earnings, but earnings of individuals whose current investment returns exceed their current costs are above. The crossover point (at which the earnings path with on-the-job investment crosses that with no post-schooling investment) generally occurs in less than a decade, so we have individuals on both sides. Therefore we average the earnings of a family's children. Since the very earliest years are the ones that deviate most from lifetime earnings, we also make some calculations excluding those people with less than four years of experience.

3. Due to initial search and matching problems, variances in earnings for those with limited experience may be larger than variances in lifetime earnings. Our use of sibling consortium earnings and the exclusion of those with few

6. The significant coefficients on experience and its square are .15 and $-.0052$ for males and .13 and $-.0063$ for females.

years of experience or very low earnings all should lessen this measurement error.

There are no similar magnitudes of measurement error problems in the parents' earnings data. The parents' ln earnings are unrelated to experience around age 50, when they were surveyed (Behrman et al. 1980).

We made several cross classifications of intergenerational earnings mobility and of R. For brevity we present only the cross classification between father's and son's earnings by deciles (table 3).[7] Reading down a column, we see how the sons are distributed within a father's earnings interval, i.e., for fathers in the fifth decile about 10% of the sons are in the bottom decile, 14% in the second decile, and 10% are in the sons' top decile. The other columns display a similar dispersed shape. The smallest and largest percentages are 2.9% and 17.5% while in a completely mobile society each percentage would be 10%. The median sons' earnings occurs in the fifth fathers' decile except that the richer sons have their medium earnings in the fathers' sixth or seventh decile. High-earnings fathers have sons with more earnings dispersion.

Table 4 contains estimates of weighted intergenerational ln earnings regressions (lns are used for comparability with existing studies).[8] Equations using income yield comparable R^2's. Since we excluded zero earnings and non-responses, there is a potential selectivity problem for daughters. The elasticity in the *full* sample is 0.07, with no significant difference between sons and daughters. The coefficient is significant when the sexes are merged and for sons.

To reduce problems described above, we estimated the intergenerational relations for several subsamples. (1) We exclude observations when offspring's earnings are less than $5,000. This reduces the sample by about 10% and raises the elasticity estimate to 0.15, with no significant difference between sons and daughters. (2) We exclude offspring with less than four years of experience. This eliminates about one-third of the sample and yields an elasticity of 0.11, with no significant difference between daughters and sons. All but the daughters' estimate are statistically significant. (3) We use the consortium earnings. For the full sample and the one in which average earnings are at least $5,000, the elasticities are about 0.15 and 0.17, respectively. Even with these adjustments, we find substantial regression towards the mean.

To examine the intergenerational correlations, we use the square roots of $\bar{R}^2$'s in the next to last column of table 4 since the adjustment for degrees of freedom is small. For the full sample, R is 0.04. R is somewhat higher if the consortium measure is used or if low earners or those with low experience are

7. Tables for fathers and daughters and children's consortium available on request.
8. Each parental family has equal weight.

Table 3 Cross Classification of Father-Son Earnings[a] (percentages of column totals)

Son's Earnings Decile	Father's Earnings Decile									
	1	2	3	4	5	6	7	8	9	10
1	7.8	3.9	10.8	9.7	9.8	11.7	7.8	10.7	10.8	16.5
2	15.7	8.7	11.8	12.6	13.7	6.8	7.8	4.9	10.8	7.8
3	11.8	15.5	11.8	6.8	16.7	6.8	6.9	7.8	5.9	9.7
4	11.8	15.5	13.7	17.5	6.9	9.7	10.8	3.9	4.9	5.8
5	16.7	13.6	10.8	4.9	9.8	8.7	10.8	11.7	5.9	6.8
6	8.8	11.7	10.8	9.7	12.8	14.6	7.8	9.7	11.8	2.9
7	8.8	9.7	7.8	12.6	8.8	9.7	13.7	10.7	8.8	8.7
8	8.8	10.7	7.8	10.7	5.9	5.8	13.7	11.7	10.8	14.6
9	2.9	8.7	7.8	6.8	5.9	14.6	11.8	11.7	16.7	12.6
10	6.9	1.9	6.9	8.7	9.8	11.7	8.8	17.5	13.7	14.6

[a] Earnings adjusted for experience; zero earnings and no answer not included.

Table 4 Weighted Intergenerational Regressions
of Ln Offspring Earnings on Ln Father's Earnings[a]

	Constant	Slope Coefficient	$\bar{R}^2$	R	Sample Size
Full Sample	8.69(23.7)	.07(2.0)	.0016	.04	1994
Sons	8.74(19.1)	.09(2.0)	.0028	.05	1025
Daughters	8.25(15.4)	.09(1.8)	.0024	.05	968
Full Sample Excluding Offspring with Earnings ≤ $5000	8.16(33.3)	.15(6.2)	.0210	.15	1740
Sons	8.08(23.9)	.17(5.1)	.0260	.16	940
Daughters	8.15(25.1)	.13(4.3)	.0213	.15	800
Full Sample Excluding Offspring with Experience ≤ 4 years	8.34(18.5)	.11(2.5)	.0042	.06	1153
Sons	7.27(14.3)	.23(4.7)	.0337	.16	603
Daughters	8.61(12.1)	.06(0.83)	−.0006	—	550
Consortium Sample					
Full	7.90(21.3)	.16(4.4)	.0160	.13	1148
Excluding ≤ $5000	7.87(30.1)	.18(7.1)	.0439	.21	1075

[a]Ln earnings adjusted for experience; zero earnings and no answer omitted. *t*-statistics are given to right of point estimates.

excluded, but the highest value we obtain is 0.21 (the consortium measure excluding low earners). Our values of R indicate almost complete social mobility. The adjusted data still may contain transitory income. Assuming transitory income is not correlated across generations nor with permanent income and that the ratio of the variance in transitory income to the variance in permanent income is 0.3, then the R for permanent income is equal to the observed R times 1.3, which still is small.

Years of schooling often are used as a proxy for "permanent income." Our intergenerational R for schooling is 0.31 (0.33 for sons and 0.29 for daughters). Olneck (1977) reports a schooling R for males 35 to 59 years old with their fathers of 0.45. For the male twins in the NAS-NRC sample, Behrman et al. (1980) obtain an intergenerational R of 0.33. We believe the schooling correlations provide an upper bound to the true earnings' correlation because parental tastes and wealth influence offsprings' schooling much more than their adult earnings capacity (Behrman et al., 1980; Behrman and Wolfe, 1984; Hauser and Daymont, 1977; Olneck, 1977). Some people suggest that we estimate "low" values of R because we are not using income. Using income, estimates are about the same as for earnings.[9]

9. This test would be better if the income data were for later in the offsprings' life cycles when they would have had a greater chance to inherit assets.

The members of this sample come from a highly mobile society. The intergenerational R is below 0.2. Some reasons why such mobility might be high are: offspring of richer parents may choose occupations with more nonwage compensation; many of the offspring grew up in the Viet Nam War era when many children rebelled against their parents' life styles; and the relative prices attached to various inherited and acquired skills may have shifted over time.[10] These results also may reflect a number of public policies undertaken since World War II. Numerous educational loan and scholarship programs were instituted. A variety of transfer programs made money and food available to the poor.[11] For whites born after 1945, there may have been substantial equality of opportunity.

III. Becker's Equilibrium Intergenerational Model

Becker (1981) developed an equilibrium intergenerational model for a society which can explain both correlations in earnings over generations and regression to the mean. This model, which has a parallel structure for both schooling and earnings, has testable implications that we explore for schooling.

Parents have a utility function whose arguments are parental consumption and the expected lifetime earnings capacity (Y_i) of each of N children, where N is exogenous. Parental utility is maximized subject to: (i) the parents' budget constraint in which schooling is the only investment in human capital and (ii) the earnings production function of each child which depends on the child's schooling (S_i) and endowments (e_i),[12] and the expected market luck of the child (u_i).[13] This yields a demand function for S and equilibrium intergenerational relations for S and Y. Following Becker, a linear approximation to the intergenerational schooling relation (in which we have added a random error, w_i) is

$$S_i = aS_p + be_i + bu_i + w_i. \qquad (1)$$

Many samples have data on S_i and S_p, but direct estimation of (1) yields an upward biased estimate of a since the unobserved e_i is positively correlated

---

10. A blacksmith's son may be as strong, but not as well off as his father.

11. It is extremely difficult to determine if intergenerational earnings mobility has shifted over time. Sewell and Hauser's (1975) sample is only a little older than is ours. For generations born earlier, we either have to rely on sibling correlations or on wealth data such as mentioned in note 2.

12. If the earnings production function has constant elasticity of substitution, schooling is a perfect proxy for all other human capital investments (Behrman, 1987b).

13. At times Becker argues that parents cannot forecast u and make their decisions with it at its expected value of zero.

with S_p, assuming b positive. The estimation of this equation is hardly a strong test of Becker's model since there are many reasons for expecting a to be positive.

A stronger test uses the endowment-generating function proposed by Becker to eliminate the unobserved e_i:

$$e_i = \alpha e_p + v_i \quad \alpha > 0, \tag{2}$$

where v_i is a random variable uncorrelated with e_p. Still following Becker, lag (1) by one generation and use (2) to obtain:

$$S_i = (a + \alpha)S_p - \alpha a S_g + b u_i + w_i + b v_i - \alpha b u_p - \alpha w_p, \tag{3}$$

where g denotes grandparents. While estimation of (3) requires data on an extra generation, it provides stronger tests of Becker's model, i.e., if both a and α are positive, this model predicts that the unbiased estimate of the coefficient on S_g is negative. Becker does not provide intuition for this negative sign; however, it emanates from the observation that in the lagged version of (1), for a given S_p a higher S_g is associated with a lower e_p *ceteris paribus*—and, thus, through (2) with a lower e_i. We can use the coefficients on S_p and S_g to obtain estimates of both a and α, though since $(a\alpha)$ is a rectangular hyperbola there may be two estimates of each coefficient.

An estimation problem in (3) is that it contains S_p, u_p and w_p. It is possible that parents' expectations about u_p are zero. But w_p is known by the parents and does not vanish. If S_p and S_g are positively correlated and if a is positive, the ordinary least squares (OLS) estimate of the coefficient on S_g is biased upward and that on S_p downward.

It is possible to eliminate the bias by using an instrumental variable (IV) or a two stage least square (2SLS) estimator. We use as an instrument the father's twin's education.[14] This instrument is appropriate even if the uncle's u is not expected to be zero as long as it is not positively correlated with the father's u. Within a Beckerian framework, if parents foresee a child's future labor market success, there is more of the budget available for both family consumption and for schooling expenditures for all his siblings. If all the adjustment occurs in family consumption, the uncle's education is independent of u_p. If the adjustment is split, the uncle's education goes up when his brother's error is negative; hence, the bias is positive and the OLS and the 2SLS or IV estimates form a lower and upper bound. The aunt's education also can be used as instrument for the mother's education as long as there is assortative mating with respect to

---

14. Chamberlain (1977a) provides an IV interpretation for the use of brother data.

education between spouses. This may well be a weaker instrument because brothers' R for education is only about 0.5 and assortative mating is far from perfect.

IV. Tests of Becker's Intergenerational Schooling Model

Table 5 contains the OLS, 2SLS and IV estimators for male and female children. The results for males are in the table's top half.[15] The first three regressions are the OLS estimates. (1) contains both father's and mother's education as separate variables, both of which have highly significant coefficients. The coefficient on father's education at 0.17 is significantly different from and more than twice the size of that on mother's education. In (2) we add grandparents' education using each gender average.[16] These variables should have negative coefficients according to Becker. We obtain insignificant positive coefficients and obtain the same findings if only one gender of grandparents is used.

Becker assumes a stationary equilibrium over time. In the United States various cohorts have obtained different average education with the peak percentage going to college being reached about 1973 (Mattila, 1982). To allow for trends and cohort effects, we include age and its square in (3). Both these variables are significant and indicate peak educational attainment for those born in 1949. Their inclusion raises slightly the coefficients on mother's and father's education. The coefficient estimates of grandparents' schooling remain highly insignificant, though that for grandmothers' is slightly negative.

The 2SLS estimates shown are obtained by regressing the father's education on his brother's education and all the other "exogenous" variables in their particular OLS regressions and then calculating a purged father's education variable.

Regression (4), (5) and (6) are comparable with (1), (2) and (3). The father's education coefficient in (4) is 0.21. Under the null hypothesis that both coefficients are unbiased, using the standard error from the OLS equation we obtain a t-statistic of 1.7 on the difference of the two estimates. The 2SLS estimate of this coefficient is significantly greater than the OLS estimate at the 10% level, suggesting a downward bias in the OLS coefficient. Becker's model implies an *upward* bias in the OLS equation. In (5) and (6) the grandparents' coefficients are insignificant, though in (5) grandfathers' education switches sign. The co-

15. These results treat each respondent as an observation and do not correct for any within-family residual correlation, which should not cause inconsistency, but the standard errors may be overstated. To be included in the analysis, the respondent must have completed schooling, and the twin must not have indicated that his current wife is not the mother of the child in question.

16. If information was available on one grandparent of a given sex, it was used.

efficient on father's education has risen to 0.23 in (6). The "t" test for the difference between the father's education estimates in (3) and (6) is 1.7.

We attempted to use aunt's education in the 2SLS procedure. Because the estimated questions for father's and mother's education are very similar, the estimated variables are highly collinear and all the coefficient estimates on parents' education are insignificant. Instead, we use an IV approach in which the uncle's education is an instrument for father's and the aunt's for mother's education. The results are in (7) through (9). In (7) and (8), the estimated coefficients of father's and mother's education are higher and lower, respectively, than the corresponding estimates in (1) and (2), with mother's schooling now having an insignificant and negative coefficient. The grandfathers' coefficient estimate is slightly smaller while the grandmothers' coefficient estimate has increased, but remains insignificant and positive. Similar comments apply to (9) versus (3).

If an independent variable contains random measurement error, its OLS coefficient estimate is biased towards zero with the magnitude a function of the noise to signal ratio. We have the offsprings' estimates of their parent's education. As long as the error in the offspring's response is uncorrelated with the parent's error, the R between parent's and child's responses provides an approximate estimate of the noise to signal ratio.[17] This estimate of the noise to signal ratio of 5% to 10% cannot explain the magnitude of the difference between the one and two stage estimates.

Results for females are given in the bottom half of table 5. In (1) both parents' education coefficients are highly significant. The coefficient on father's education is about the same as in (1) for sons, but only about two thirds greater than the coefficient on mother's education. Neither grandparent coefficient is significant, though the grandmothers' coefficient is negative in (2) and (3). The peak education occurred for those born in 1951.

In (4) the coefficient estimate for the purged father's education is 0.27. The downward bias in the OLS regression is significant (t is 2.2). The same general pattern holds in (4) and (5). Once again the OLS estimate is biased downwards, despite the prediction of the Becker model to the contrary.

The IV results are given in (7), (8), and (9). In all instances we find that the IV coefficient estimates are higher than the corresponding results in the OLS regressions, with the differences between the OLS and the IV estimates significant for both father's and mother's education. In the IV estimates the gap between the estimates for father's versus mother's schooling is much smaller (and insignificant) than in the OLS and 2SLS estimates. Only in the IV estimates for

---

17. Offsprings' noise need not have the same expected value as parents' noise.

Table 5   Alternative Intergenerational Schooling Regressions for 1,144 Men and 1,323 Women Offspring[a]

Sex, Estimator and Regressions		Schooling				Age	Age^2	Constant	R^2
		Father's	Mother's	Grandfathers'	Grandmothers'				
Men									
OLS	1	0.17	0.073					11.8	.085
		(7.4)	(2.7)					(34.8)	
	2	0.17	0.067	0.007	0.005			11.8	.086
		(6.9)	(2.4)	(0.3)	(0.2)			(39.4)	
	3	0.19	0.072	0.016	−0.003	0.76	−0.012	−0.49	.173
		(8.0)	(2.6)	(0.7)	(0.1)	(6.1)	(5.1)	(0.3)	
2SLS	4	0.21	0.0052					11.5	.067
		(5.4)	(1.6)					(29.8)	
	5	0.21	0.050	−0.001	0.005			11.5	.069
		(4.9)	(1.6)	(0.1)	(0.2)			(28.5)	
	6	0.23	0.053	0.007	−0.003	0.75	0.011	−0.66	.154
		(5.8)	(1.7)	(0.3)	(0.1)	(5.9)	(4.9)	(0.4)	
IV	7	0.23	−0.040					12.3	.049
		(7.3)	(0.3)					(8.5)	
	8	0.20	−0.070	0.035	0.018			12.7	.057
		(6.0)	(0.0)	(1.4)	(0.7)			(8.8)	
	9	0.22	−0.076	0.048	0.010	0.81	−0.013	0.06	.139
		(6.8)	(0.7)	(2.0)	(0.4)	(6.3)	(5.5)	(0.0)	

Women

Method	#								R^2
OLS	1	0.20 (9.9)	0.12 (5.2)					10.4 (36.3)	.153
	2	0.19 (9.2)	0.12 (4.7)	0.030 (1.5)	−0.019 (0.9)			10.4 (35.8)	.154
	3	0.20 (10.2)	0.12 (4.9)	0.030 (1.5)	0.020 (1.0)			−2.0 (1.4)	.216
2SLS	4	0.27 (8.3)	0.080 (2.9)			0.84 (7.8)	0.014 (7.1)	10.0 (31.0)	.135
	5	0.27 (7.6)	0.083 (3.0)	0.019 (0.9)	−0.024 (1.1)			10.0 (29.5)	.138
	6	0.27 (7.8)	0.090 (3.4)	0.021 (1.0)	−0.023 (1.2)	0.85 (7.8)	−0.014 (7.0)	−2.4 (1.6)	.196
IV	7	0.28 (10.1)	0.25 (3.4)					7.6 (6.4)	.100
	8	0.24 (8.2)	0.21 (2.5)	0.057 (2.8)	0.000 (0.0)			8.1 (6.9)	.112
	9	0.25 (8.6)	0.17 (1.7)	0.060 (3.0)	0.000 (0.0)	0.82 (7.3)	−0.014 (6.7)	−3.1 (1.7)	.164

[a]Absolute t-statistics are in parentheses beneath point estimates. The first stage variables for the 2SLS and IV estimates are discussed in sections III and IV.

women do we find any support for the implication of the Becker hypothesis that grandparents' schooling is relevant; grandfathers' (but not grandmothers') education has significantly positive coefficient estimates in (8) and (9). However, the positive signs are opposite those given by Becker's model.

V. Conclusion

In this paper we present some evidence on the magnitude of the intergenerational correlation in earnings and test a model proposed to explain linkages. The correlation is small though statistically significant, and there is substantial regression towards the mean.

We propose tests of Becker's model of the within-family intergenerational linkages. His strongest prediction is that grandparents' education should enter with a negative sign. We find virtually no supporting evidence for this prediction.[18] He predicts the bias in the OLS coefficients to be *upward* in the two-generational model. We find the OLS coefficients to be biased *downward* vis à vis 2SLS or IV results. Becker's model also predicts biases in the three-generational regression. The results here are mixed, but since grandparents' education variables have insignificant coefficient estimates, little information is conveyed by these findings. Thus we conclude that Becker's model is rejected for this data set.[19]

18. Of 24 coefficients, only 6 are negative, none of which are significant.

19. One interesting finding not directly related to the formal model being tested is the differential effect of mother's education favoring daughters over sons. This differential is observed in every equation presented and is substantial, varying from .037 to .29 all of which are large in comparison with the estimated father's schooling impact. One possible explanation is some genetic difference that exists on the X or Y chromosome. The most likely explanations are that mothers who had more schooling are either role models for their daughters or can provide their daughters with better sex-specific information on the returns to education.

Father's education, in contrast, has the same impact for sons and daughters. This is consistent with either a genetic model and/or an environmental model with education as an indicator of family income. Generally the father's education has a bigger impact than the mother's education. This appears contrary to the predictions of human-capital-based models that focus on the relation of efficiency in raising children to maternal schooling as formulated by Leibowitz (1974) though perhaps it is a result of father's schooling representing income and genetic effects in addition to efficiency and role-model effects. It is also contrary to a pure genetic model, but not to a model in which environment depends upon family income as well as on the family culture.

11

The Intergenerational Correlation Between Children's Adult Earnings and Their Parents' Income: Results from the Michigan Panel Survey of Income Dynamics

JERE R. BEHRMAN AND PAUL TAUBMAN

Economists and philosophers long have thought that the degree of intergenerational mobility, or its complement—the intergenerational correlation in earnings or income—is an important indicator of the healthiness and success of a society. One important reason for this belief is the judgment that equal opportunity is a desirable characteristic of a good society. Equal opportunity within this context means that children from different families have equal options regarding investments in their human resource and their expected incomes.[1]

Theories, a leading example of which is presented below, have been constructed to explain why parents' and children's income or earnings are correlated.[2] Yet surprisingly little is known about the magnitude of this correlation. For example Becker and Tomes (1986), after a thorough search, present evidence from a dozen, nonrandom samples for the period 1960 through 1982 drawn from five countries (U.S., England, Sweden, Switzerland, and Norway). They generally find low intergenerational correlations (a median R of .17) and small elasticities of children's earnings with respect to parents' income (a median of .17).[3] Thus, intergenerational mobility, at least as indicated by the complement of such correlations, appears to be considerable, and at the median only about a sixth of a given percentage change in parents' income appears to be reflected in children's earnings. Such results may be surprising given other studies that find childhood background to be very important in determining adult socioeconomic success (e.g., Behrman, Hrubec, Taubman and Wales, 1980; Olneck, 1977; Behrman and Taubman, 1989).

Reprinted from *Review of Income and Wealth,* 36, no. 2 (June 1990): 115–27.

We thank the National Institute of Health for support for this study, Myung K. Kang for able research assistance, and two anonymous referees for useful comments and suggestions.

1. We are more explicit about how equal opportunity might be defined more precisely in Section 1.

2. For example see Becker (1967, 1981) and Meade (1973).

3. One of the studies is by us (Behrman and Taubman 1985, in this volume) for two recent U.S. generations of whites. Our estimates in this study for the full sample are .20 for the correlation and .07 for the elasticity, though higher values for each are obtained if low-earnings or low-work experience children are excluded.

However, most of the estimates of intergenerational correlations can be criticized on several grounds: the samples are not random; the estimates are based on a single year's earnings for the children which need not be typical of lifetime earnings;[4] the estimates are based on a single year's income for the parents which again may not be typical of lifetime income and may be from the wrong lifecycle stage if liquidity constraints are important;[5] and most estimates do not control for the possible dependence of the elasticity of children's earnings with respect to parents' income on age, gender, and race.[6]

One purpose of this paper is to examine how important these possible problems are and to see how large the intergenerational associations are if we control for these problems. A second purpose of this study is to examine whether the elasticity of children's earnings with respect to parents' income declines as parents' income increases as Becker and Tomes (1986) have proposed (see section 1).

We use the Michigan Panel Survey of Income Dynamics (PSID).[7] The PSID is a random U.S. sample which has the unusual feature that it follows people who in 1968 lived with the surveyed head of household, but who subsequently joined another household. We have identified the offspring who split off and have created parent-child matches.

1. The Model

Economists have argued that one would expect parents' income and children's earnings to be positively correlated. The major reasons for expecting this correlation can be summarized within the framework taken from Becker's Woytin-

4. Jenkins (1987), Solon (1989), and Solon, Corcoran, Gordon, and Laren (1987) all emphasize that the bias from using one year "snapshots" instead of life-cycle "movies" may be large. Solon, for example, suggests that for U.S. workers in the age range 25–32, the factor to be applied to the intergenerational correlation to correct for transitory earnings variations in a one-year sample probably is in the 1.4 to 1.8 range.

5. Flavin (1981), Bernanke (1985), Hayashi (1985) and Zeldes (1989), for example, present aggregate and individual estimates for consumption that suggest that liquidity constraints are important for the U.S. If they are, parents' income at the time of marginal school decisions for the children may be critical rather than parents' income at some other time.

6. There are two studies of which we are aware that include dependence of the elasticities on age, race or gender. Behrman and Taubman (1985, in this volume) find gender differences in elasticities for young white U.S. respondents and Datcher (1982) finds race differences in elasticities for young U.S. males (with control for a number of additional family and community background characteristics). Solon (1989) criticizes a number of estimates [explicitly including Behrman and Taubman (1985, in this volume), and Sewell and Hauser (1975), but presumably implicitly also Datcher and others], because they are based on homogeneous samples (e.g., only whites or only males), and therefore understate actual intergenerational correlations.

7. Solon, Corcoran, Gordon, and Laren (1987) have used a shorter segment (1975–82) of the same panel to estimate sibling correlations.

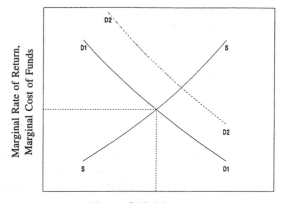

Human Capital Investments

FIG. 1.   Becker's Woytinsky Lecture (1967) Demand and Supply Curves for Investing in an Individual's Human Capital.

sky Lecture (1967). The demand for human capital is downward sloping for any given (exogenously determined) level of endowments due to diminishing returns to such endowments, and shifts to the right as endowments increase. The supply-of-funds curve slopes upwards as the individual exhausts cheaper sources. The equilibrium for a given individual in Figure 1 is found where the relevant demand curve intersects the relevant supply curve. The larger the human capital investments, the higher the children's earnings.

Within this simple model, parents' income and children's earnings are positively correlated on the demand side because parents with above average genetic endowments and income tend to have children with above average genetic endowments and income. If D_1 is the average demand curve and one's parents are on the D_2 curve, then one's demand curve probably lies to the right of D_1, though there may be some tendency towards regression towards the mean. Becker and Tomes (1986) argue that the elasticity of a given child's earnings with respect to parents' income for these demand reasons is nonlinear and diminishing with regard to parents' income. They suggest that low-income parents transfer assets to their children largely as human resource investments since, for small human resource investments, the marginal rate of return in equilibrium on such investments tends to be above the marginal rate of return on investments in financial assets. However, wealthier parents tend to invest much more in their children. As a result, their children tend to obtain an educational level at which the marginal additional resources transferred to children take the form of financial assets.[8]

8. In Behrman, Pollak and Taubman (1994, in this volume), we develop the implications of the Becker and Tomes' model. We demonstrate that for the two-child family there are five cases,

The generations also have positive linkages through the supply-of-funds curve. The supply-of-funds curve shifts down as parental income and wealth rise because those with higher income and wealth can finance more investments from their own sources at cheaper rates (given transaction costs) and have greater access to capital markets. For any given demand curve, the lower the supply curve, the lower the equilibrium marginal rate of return; but the total equilibrium earnings, the area under the demand curve up to the equilibrium point, increases. This supply effect, incidentally, *may* or *may not* offset partially the Becker-Tomes nonlinear impact of parental income on child earnings.[9] Even if it does so over a range, if parents transfer enough resources to their children, the expected marginal rate of return to human resource investments still will be driven down to the (lower) interest rate, so the Becker-Tomes logic will hold equally well as above if parents transfer enough resources to their children.

How does this approach relate to the notion of equality of opportunity? If equality of opportunity means, as economists [10] usually define it, that children with equal abilities have equal options, the critical question is whether children from all families face the same supply-of-funds curve; that is, is this curve independent of family background? If it is, all children with equal endowments have equal equilibrium human resource investments and expected earnings.[11] Therefore the parental income-child earnings correlations would be smaller that if the supply-of-funds curve shifts down with higher parental wealth.

To this point we have focussed on the parental-income-child *earnings* link, which is what we investigate empirically in this paper. However, other intergenerational economic relations such as inter vivos gifts and bequests also affect children's income. The relevant question from the point of view of the interpretation of parental income-child earnings correlations as indicators of equal opportunity is whether such transfers alter child earnings. As suggested by Bowles (1972) and others because of the greater asset income of children who receive greater transfers, these children may choose to work fewer hours

---

depending on the magnitude of parental resources in some cases, the education of at least one child is less than that which would be required to drive the expected rate of return down to the expected rate of return on financial assets. In the two high resource cases the expected rate of return on all human resource investments may be equal to that on financial assets.

9. If the supply of funds curve shifts down, of course, whether equilibrium earnings increase or decrease depend on the demand elasticity in the relevant range (i.e., whether it is greater than or less than unitary). We expect that diminishing returns to endowments mean that at least the demand curve eventually becomes inelastic.

10. For example, see Meade (1973).

11. Behrman, Pollak and Taubman (1989, in this volume) discuss further and explore empirically the implications of this dimension of differential equality of opportunity across recent generations in the U.S.

Table 1   Some Socioeconomic Characteristics of the Offspring
of the Michigan Panel of Income Dynamics in 1984

	Mean	Standard Deviation
Female (%)	50.5	
Age (years)	26.1	5.7
Education (grades)	12.4	2.1
Earnings (thousands $)[a]	14.7	14.5
Married in 1984 (%)	58.4	
Never Married (%)	19.3	

NOTE—If a question was not answered or if earnings were not available, the
person is excluded for the particular variable. The sample sizes range from 2,053
to 3,271.

[a] For those with positive earnings the mean is 17.4 and the standard deviation is
14.1 thousand dollars.

and/or to choose occupations with greater nonpecuniary and lesser pecuniary
returns, which would reduce the parental income-child earnings correlation.[12]
It seems generally to be believed that such offsetting tendencies are only partial, so that in fact a higher parental income-child earnings correlation does
imply less equality of opportunity.

2. The Sample

This study is based on our special adaptation of the Michigan Panel Survey of
Income Dynamics (PSID). The PSID is a longitudinal sample that began in
1968. We have annual observations through 1984. The panel has the unusual
feature that as members of the original responding family set up or joined
new households, the split-offs, including children who had lived with the head
in 1968, became eligible respondents. By 1984 offspring as young as two in
1968 were 18 years old and might have set up separate households. Of course,
the children had to be in the respondent's home in 1968 to be eligible to be a
future sample member. Those above the age of 18 in 1968 still living with
parents may be atypical; therefore, we eliminated those children from the
sample.

Some characteristics of the sample for the children are given in Table 1.
In 1984 the average age of the children was 26.1. The offspring averaged
12.4 years of education and had annual earnings in 1984 of $14,700. Approxi-
mately 51 percent of the sample's respondents are female. To evaluate how
typical these numbers are, we note that in the 1980 *Census,* the mean education
and earnings for 25 to 29 years olds were about 13 years and $11,500 respec-

12. If parents are interested solely in the monetary income of their children (*not* placing a value
on their leisure), then in anticipation of these responses higher-income parents would invest less
in the human resources of their children, ceteris paribus, than they would without such a reaction.

tively. The mean education and earnings from the Census are close to those in our sample. The difference between Census and our sample's mean earnings would be less with correction for inflation from 1980 through 1984.

By splitting the randomly-selected PSID into groups with and without children setting up separate households, we may be creating subsamples of atypical parents. We have examined the characteristics of the two groups of parents and find that they are similar in age, education and earnings with differences in the means of variables of 6 percent or less.

We have data on the individual's earnings, own income, spouse's earnings and income, and income of all members of the household. Both the parents' income and children's earnings data are expressed in 1981 dollars. We concentrate on the ln of parents' income and on the ln of children's earnings since the ln-ln relation most transparently yields the elasticity of interest. To test the Becker and Tomes' (1986) conjecture about this elasticity declining as parents' income increase, in alternative estimates we add a quadratic in ln parents' income. We also explore whether this elasticity is dependent on demographic factors (the children's age, race, and gender). We allow for race and gender differences partly to reflect possible discrimination in the labor market and in the provision of governmental services. We also distinguish between men and women because of women's greater tendency to work part-time and to have lesser earnings because of activities associated with childbearing.

Since the adult children in our sample are relatively young, their earnings may be subject to substantial variation because of initial job searches, sorting, and part-time work while completing schooling or training. These factors would seem to be particularly important for the younger children in the labor force. In Table 2 means and coefficients of variation for ln earnings for different-aged children and parents are given. The means increase monotonically with age for the 21–26 range, and then, generally stabilize. The coefficient of variation tends to be greatest among the children for the youngest children, particularly the 18–21 year olds. After 21, the coefficient of variation for the children tends to settle down (though there are exceptions, such as ages 27 and 33). Therefore, the inclusion of data from the 18–21 year-old children in the analysis below may increase the noise and reduce the apparent intergenerational association.[13] Thus, there may be some tradeoff between using information on more years of children's earnings to reduce both transitory fluctuations and period effects and including additional years at ages at which there is relatively greater variance in earnings as compared with those over 21 years of age. The coefficients of variation for parents' income varies considerably across ages.

---

13. Disaggregation of the data by gender and race reveals that this pattern is similar for whites and blacks and for females and males.

Table 2   Means and Coefficients of Variation for Ln Children's Earnings
and Ln Parents' Income by Age in 1984

	Children			Parents	
Age	Mean	Coefficient of Variation	Age	Mean	Coefficient of Variation
18	9.50 (19,412)	11.20	40	10.02 (30,835)	10.56
19	9.45 (19,935)	12.20	41	10.10 (32,472)	7.61
20	9.34 (18,804)	12.60	42	9.73 (30,781)	20.45)
21	9.19 (14,472)	11.26	43	10.12 (30,147)	6.48
22	9.31 (15,288)	9.70	44	9.50 (22,565)	15.44
23	9.26 (15,585)	10.97	45	10.02 (29,276)	8.10
24	9.28 (15,569)	10.71	46	10.16 (36,417)	9.04
25	9.30 (15,731)	11.26	47	9.94 (32,336)	14.95
26	9.43 (15,842)	8.35	48	9.98 (29,992)	8.85
27	9.09 (14,222)	13.26	49	10.26 (40,067)	8.82
28	9.49 (17,010)	8.93	50	9.79 (28,549)	19.48
29	9.49 (17,450)	8.98	51	9.81 (26,076)	9.02
30	9.47 (17,763)	10.17	52	9.97 (34,785)	13.89
31	9.50 (18,096)	10.04	53	10.10 (31,543)	8.00
32	9.53 (19,763)	9.64	54	10.15 (34,305)	8.40
33	9.40 (18,094)	12.80	55	9.84 (29,313)	13.06
34	9.65 (20,122)	9.64	56	10.14 (39,724)	8.88
			57	10.00 (32,405)	9.11
			58	10.35 (47,158)	9.27
			59	9.86 (28,834)	9.89

NOTE—The means are given for ln earnings for the children and for ln income for the parents, but the means for the values themselves are given in parentheses.

3. Results

In Table 3 alternative simple regressions of ln children's earnings on ln parents' income are given. Regression (1a) is the case in which each variable is measured for 1984 to reduce the relatively greater noise in earnings for the youngest children noted above. Regression (1a) yields a significant elasticity of children's earnings which respect to parental income of .27 and an intergenerational correlation (R) of .26 $[=(.069)^{1/2}]$. Both of these results are similar to the medians of the estimates summarized in Becker and Tomes (1986). Even at the sample average age, when age-earnings profiles are leveling off and showing fairly constant coefficients of variation, such results suggest substantial intergenerational mobility and limited impact of parents' income on children's earnings.

It is not clear that data from 1984 should be used for the parents' income if one is to be restricted to data for a year (but not necessarily the same year) for each of the two variables. After all, in 1984 the children averaged 26 years of age; plausibly some measure of parental income when the children were younger better captures the story outlined in section 1, if liquidity constraints

Table 3   Parents' Income and Child's Earnings, Various Years

	In Parents Income	(In Parents' Income)^2	Intercept	R^2/No. of Obs.
1. Children's Earnings 1984, Parents' Income 1984[a]:				
a.	0.27		6.78	0.069
	(9.8)		(24.6)	1,290
b.	−0.46	0.039	10.12	0.083
	(2.7)	(4.3)	(12.4)	1,290
2. Children's Earnings 1984, Parents' Income When Child 15:	0.60		3.17	0.131
	(4.6)		(2.4)	144
3. Children's Earnings 1984, Parents' Income 1975:	0.37		5.74	0.081
	(10.7)		(16.4)	1,290
4. Children's Earnings 1975–84, Parents' Income 1975–84[b]:				
a.	0.80		1.25	0.287
	(24.4)		(3.7)	1,481
b.	−0.51	0.065	7.79	0.289
	(0.729)	(1.9)	(2.2)	1,481

NOTE—Absolute t values are given in parentheses.
[a] F test for 1b vs. 1a is 8.20, accept null.
[b] F test for 4b vs. 4a is 1.45, accept null.

preclude easy transfer of resources across years. Therefore, we have estimated relations in which the ln children's earnings in 1984 are regressed on ln parents' (real) income calculated separately when the children were ages 14 through 22. Regression (2) in Table 3, which is the alternative which maximizes the intergenerational correlation, uses parents' incomes for the year in which the child was 15 years old. This regression has a slope coefficient of .60 and a R of .36; both are greater than in regression (1a).[14]

In regression (2) incomes are measured in different years for different families and come from different parts of the business cycle. Therefore, we also have estimated regressions with different lags for parents' income. Regression (3) gives the alternative with parents' income for 1975, a year when the children had an average age of approximately 16, about the age of decisions re-

14. For this exploration the same sample of 1,481 children-parent pairs was used for every regression to assure comparability, at the cost of losing a number of observations. The pattern of R's has several local peaks: .06 for age 14, .13 for age 15, .08 for age 16, .09 for age 17, .09 for age 18, .06 for age 19, .06 for age 20, .08 for age 21, and .09 for age 22. Alvin and Thornton (1984) study the comparative role of family background, measured when the child was less than five and as a teenager, on high school performance and years of education completed by age 18. Using a sample of children born in Detroit in 1961, they find smaller impacts of variables measured at widely different times.

garding continuation of education beyond secondary school. The estimates in regression (3) imply larger intergenerational associations than in regression (1A), but less than in (2): the elasticity of children's earnings with respect to parents' income is 0.37 and R is 0.28. Thus, the impact on the intergenerational correlation from controlling for the business cycle as in relation (3) seems to be less than that from controlling for possible liquidity constraints as in relation (2).

What happens to the intergenerational association if we use more years of observations for parents' income and child earnings to average out transitory fluctuations for both generations? Both variables are subject to fluctuations over time due to the business cycle and individual-specific, transitory factors. Solon (1989) claims that the estimates of intergenerational correlations for this age range of the children should increase by 40 to 80 percent with the switch from one year to permanent observations given available estimates of the relative size of the transitory income component. However, including earlier years for children results in more years at the beginning of the children's adult work experience during which variations in their earnings are relatively large. The impact of averaging both variables over 1975–84 in regression (4a) is striking. The elasticity of children's earnings with respect to parents' income is .80, significantly higher than the previous estimates. The R of .54 also is higher than in the other regressions discussed to this point, and the increase in comparison with regression (1a) is even greater than Solon (1989) predicts. Both measures of association are much higher than the values for the medians of the distributions of estimates based on a single year of data in Becker and Tomes (1986). Thus, more permanent earnings and incomes measures increase the estimated intergenerational association substantially.

Now we examine the nonlinear relation between the ln of children's earnings and the ln of parents' income proposed by Becker and Tomes (1986) by including the square of the ln of parents' income in alternative regressions, one for 1984 (regression 1b) and one for the averages over 1975–84 (regression 4b).[15] In both cases there is evidence of some nonlinearity: an F test rejects imposing the constraint that the coefficient of the quadratic term is restricted to zero and the R increases. However, the sign pattern of the estimates suggests *greater* elasticities for higher parents' income, contradicting the Becker and Tomes' conjecture. As we note above in section 1, if the demand curve is sufficiently elastistic and shifts out enough with parental income, such a result is possible within the framework of Figure 1. This effect may be an absolute income effect,

15. This exploration must be qualified since with cross-sectional data we are not exploring what happens for children of *given* ability as parental wealth increases. Nevertheless we think that it is suggestive.

Table 4   Regressions of Ln Children's Earnings on Ln Parents' Income with Multiplicative Controls for Age, Age^2, Gender, and Race for Averages Over One to Ten Years

Time Period Children's Earnings and Parents' Income	Ln Parents'	Ln Parents' Income Multiplied by					
Averaged Over	Income	Age	Age^2	Gender[a]	Race[b]	Intercept	R^2/No. of Obs.
1984	0.011	0.012	−0.00012	−0.007	−0.043	7.37	0.139
	(0.136)	(2.3)	(1.6)	(1.4)	(7.8)	(25.8)	1,290
1983–84	0.16	0.010	−0.00010	−0.010	−0.041	6.18	0.159
	(2.0)	(2.0)	(1.2)	(1.9)	(7.1)	(18.2)	1,364
1982–84	0.17	0.012	−0.00013	−0.012	−0.041	5.86	0.188
	(2.3)	(2.6)	(1.7)	(2.5)	(7.5)	(17.5)	1,393
1981–84	0.25	0.009	−0.00009	−0.012	−0.038	5.42	0.213
	(3.8)	(2.3)	(1.3)	(2.6)	(7.2)	(16.5)	1,413
1980–84	0.26	0.010	−0.00009	−0.013	−0.039	5.21	0.230
	(4.4)	(2.7)	(1.4)	(2.9)	(7.5)	(15.7)	1,426
1979–84	0.29	0.011	−0.00011	−0.014	−0.040	4.82	0.256
	(5.2)	(3.2)	(1.9)	(3.1)	(7.8)	(14.3)	1,440
1978–84	0.40	0.008	−0.00009	−0.015	−0.044	4.16	0.282
	(7.2)	(2.6)	(1.4)	(3.3)	(8.6)	(11.8)	1,458
1977–84	0.51	0.007	−0.00007	−0.015	−0.040	3.30	0.302
	(9.2)	(2.2)	(1.2)	(3.4)	(7.7)	(9.1)	1,467
1976–84	0.57	0.007	−0.00006	−0.017	−0.038	2.75	0.324
	(10.6)	(2.1)	(1.1)	(3.8)	(7.4)	(7.48)	1,471
1975–84	0.60	0.007	−0.00006	−0.012	−0.037	2.42	0.338
	(11.3)	(2.1)	(1.1)	(2.9)	(7.4)	(6.53)	1,481

NOTE—Beneath the point estimates are absolute values of the t statistics.
[a] Dichotomous variable with value of one if child is female, zero if male.
[b] Dichotomous variable with value of one if white, zero otherwise.

so that as the U.S. economy grows, it will become a more rigid society, a disturbing outcome to us. Alternatively it may be a relative income effect in the sense that the elasticities are higher in a cross-section for higher parental incomes, so that there are not implications of increasing rigidity over time. We are not able to identify the importance of the absolute versus the relative income interpretations with our data.

To this point we have ignored the children's gender and the family's race. We have limited our consideration of the age of the children to the question, At which single child age does parental income have the greatest association? However, all three of these characteristics may affect the elasticity of children's earnings with respect to parents' income and the intergenerational correlation.

The regressions in Table 4 allow the elasticity of children's earnings with respect to parents' income to depend upon the child's gender, the family's race, and a quadratic in the child's age.[16] The dependence of the parental income elasticity on such characteristics rarely has been explored, though some other studies have included such characteristics as additive controls.[17] In our case, having the elasticity depend on such characteristics is more consistent statistically with the variation in ln children's earnings than having them enter in an additive fashion; moreover, an F test for the 1984 data does not reject imposing zero restrictions on the additive controls if dependence of the elasticity on such characteristics is allowed.[18]

The regression for 1984 in the first row of Table 4 suggests a much stronger intergenerational correlation, an R of 0.37, than the first two estimates in Table 3 and a larger correlation than those in most studies summarized in Becker and Tomes (1986) (though not larger than the correlation in the third regression in Table 3). The estimates for the quadratic in age imply a maximum elasticity of 0.31 when the children are 50[19] as compared with a value of 0.21, for example, when the children are 21. The estimate for gender implies no significant difference. The estimate for race implies a smaller elasticity for whites than for nonwhites (by $-.043$), perhaps because nonwhites are more constrained by their own familial resources in a variant of the Becker and Tomes' (1986) argument. Thus, these results suggest that controlling for children's age and race makes a significant difference in estimating the intergenerational elasticity, though the same is not the case for gender.

What happens to the estimated intergenerational correlation as we increase the number of years that we average? The results of adding in earlier years are given in the subsequent rows of Table 4. The intergenerational correlation, R, increases substantially in this case by including additional years up to and including the tenth additional year (R increases from .37 for 1984 to .58 for 1975–84). The estimated impact of age, gender, and race on the intergenerational elasticities also changes as we add years. The addition of a number of years to 1984 yields age and race coefficient estimates that appear somewhat less important, but gender effects that appear to be substantially more impor-

16. If interactions among age, race, and gender are allowed in addition, the multicollinearity is so high that it is difficult to sort out effects. Therefore, we do not present estimates with such interactions.

17. See footnote 5.

18. The value of F is .45, with critical values of 3.70 and 2.60 at the 1 percent and 5 percent levels. If the average of the years 1975–84 are used for both variables, an F test rejects imposition of these restrictions ($F = 8.30$). Nevertheless, the formulation with these characteristics only affecting the elasticities is more consistent with sample variance in the ln of children's earnings than is the formulation with only additive characteristics.

19. We do not place great weight on this estimate of the maximum age since the quadratic effect is an imprecise estimate and since our sample includes only young adults and, thus, is not well-suited to precisely estimate the life-cycle association for older adults.

tant (and significant) than in the first row for 1984 alone. We do not have an explanation for the changing relative importance of age, gender and race as the number of years is increased. However, judging by the intergenerational R's and the coefficient estimates of ln parents' income without interactions, the estimates based on more years are of more interest. For the estimates based on 1975–84 in the last row of Table 4, the race impact ($-.037$ for whites) is slightly less than for 1984 alone (though not significantly less). The gender effect ($-.012$ for females) is almost twice that estimated based on 1984 alone, and significantly nonzero for 1975–84, though it is smaller (and significantly so) than the race effect. The quadratic age effects are smaller and less precisely estimated with data for 1975–84 period than for 1984 alone and imply a maximum elasticity at age 58 or .80 as compared with .72 at age 21.[20]

4. Conclusion

We have used the Michigan Panel Study of Income Dynamics to create a linked parent-child file with panel features for both generations. We use this data set to undertake intergenerational earnings/income analysis beyond the usual single year cross-sectional studies. The panel feature allows better representation of life-cycle developments, possible liquidity constraint effects and reduction in measurement error, transitory income, and period effects.

Our estimates suggest higher intergenerational associations than in single cross-sections of the type used in all previous studies in three respects:

First, if only one year of data is used for children's and parents' income, there is a gain to using a year for the offspring's earnings in which the children are old enough to be on a relatively stable segment of their life cycle earnings paths and an earlier year for the parents' income when important educational decisions were being made for the offspring since liquidity constraints apparently are important.

Second, the use of averages over several years may result in higher associations than use of a single year of data because of limiting measurement errors, transitory fluctuations, and period-specific effects. For this data set there seems to be increasing correlations in using up to 10 years in such averaging. The magnitude of this increase is substantial, and larger than that from controlling for parental liquidity constraints.

Third, control for individual and family demographic characteristics increases the intergenerational correlation substantially. The elasticity of children's earnings with respect to parents' income is significantly higher for sons than for daughters and for nonwhites than for whites, with the latter effect larger than for former. This elasticity also increases during the children's initial

20. See note 18.

years of the work cycle, presumably in part because the earnings data for the initial years are noisy for reasons mentioned above.

In our preferred estimates, which incorporate both a decade of data and control for demographic features, we find an intergenerational correlation of .58 – a relatively high value as compared to most previous estimates that are summarized in Becker and Tomes (1986). The elasticity of children's earnings with respect to parents' income is about .80 for white sons at age 58, which is high in comparison with the median from previous estimates. Therefore, intergenerational earnings/income mobility appears to be substantially less between these two recent U.S. generations than implied by most of the estimates summarized by Becker and Tomes. Thus, some of the apparent paradox between the important role of childhood family background claimed in some studies (see the introduction) and low estimates of intergenerational correlations is due to inadequacies in previous estimates of the latter.

Finally, Becker and Tomes (1986) conjectured that the intergenerational elasticities are nonlinear in parents' income for given children with lower slope coefficients for wealthier parents because of relatively rare intergenerational transfer of financial or physical assets for poorer versus richer parents. We find some limited support for this conjecture in the slightly lower elasticity for whites than for nonwhites in the estimates in Table 4 (under the assumption that the former are wealthier). However, we find no support for it in straightforward estimates in which we add the square of the ln of parents' income. True, in such estimates we find some nonlinearity in the elasticity, but this elasticity increases for wealthier parents rather than falling as the Becker and Tomes conjecture would have it. Thus, mobility may decrease as the U.S. grows wealthier if this reflects primarily an absolute, rather than a relative, income phenomenon.

Part Five

"Nature versus Nurture" in Schooling and Earnings

12
On Heritability

PAUL TAUBMAN

Goldberger's recent paper, "Heritability" (1979), contains an excellent discussion of the statistical and logical difficulties encountered in the decomposition of the variance of IQ or income into its unobservable genetic and environmental sources. At the same time, he questions the usefulness of estimates of heritability, i.e., the portion of the variance attributable to unobserved differences in genetic endowments. He argues that heritability conveys no information on how difficult it is to change the level or distribution of earnings' capacity, or on the desirability of tax and transfer policies. Here we are in agreement (see Taubman, 1978*b;* Behrman et al., 1977, ch. 5). But Goldberger goes on to claim that no valid reason has been advanced for the usefulness of estimates of heritability.

I disagree on two grounds. First, many economists are interested in why there is income inequality. Even if heritability has no policy implications, the extent to which inequality is due to genetic differences is an interesting question, since, in the Beckerian model presented below, it indicates how much inequality there would be in a competitive economy with perfect capital markets and no random events.

The second reason is related to inequality of opportunity. Inequality of opportunity is often seen as arising when individuals face different prices for investment in human capital.[1] Usually prices are thought to differ because of variations in parental wealth in the presence of imperfect capital markets. Policies that reduce inequality of opportunity can increase both equity and economic efficiency, in contrast to other transfer policies and training subsidization schemes which increase equity but reduce efficiency. As a consequence, Okun (1975) voiced the hope that most income inequality arises from inequality of opportunity.

Reprinted from *Economica* 48 (November 1981): 417–20.
1. Economists who use this definition include Becker, Okun, and Tawney. Brittain (1977), however, adopts a definition that counts differences in genetic endowments as part of inequality of opportunity.

As is shown below, decomposition of the variance of earnings into genetic and environmental components yields information on the extent to which inequality of opportunity determines inequality of earnings. The decomposition is important for policy purposes, not in what it tells us about heritability but in what it tells us about the variation in (common) environment, which represents variation in opportunities.

Becker (1975) proposed a model in which the distribution of earnings depends on both the distribution of genetic endowments and inequality of opportunity. Let G be genetic endowments, r the return on investments in human capital, K the stock of human capital, Y family income, and D_K and S_K the demand and supply for K. His model is:

$$D_K = D(r, G). \tag{1}$$

$$S_K = S(r, Y). \tag{2}$$

These two equations can be solved for the equilibrium values of r and K (and hence also rK) as functions of G and Y. Suppose that:

$$rK = \gamma G + \delta Y \tag{3}$$

and that earnings E is given by:

$$\ln E = aG + rK + u \tag{4}$$

where u is a random variable. Then we obtain:

$$\ln E = \alpha G + \gamma G + \delta Y + u = (\alpha + \gamma)G + \delta Y + u. \tag{5}$$

where u is a random variable. Then we obtain:

$$\sigma_{\ln E}^2 = (\alpha + \gamma)^2 \sigma_G^2 + \delta^2 \sigma_Y^2 + 2(\alpha + \gamma)\delta\sigma_{GY} + \sigma_u^2. \tag{6}$$

Very few data sets include measures of family income and offspring earnings.[2] But even if figures for E and Y exist, it is still difficult to obtain unbiased estimates of δ in (5) and $\delta^2\sigma_Y^2$ in (6) because of the omitted variable bias that arises if G is correlated with Y.

Behrman et al. (1977, 1980) demonstrate that it is possible to estimate $(\alpha + \gamma)^2 \sigma_G^2$ and the other three contributions on the right-hand side of equation (6) even when G, Y, and u are unobserved. The method uses data collected from identical and fraternal twins and requires certain assumptions to be made, a key one of which is discussed below. Assuming σ_{GY} is zero, we estimate that, for white males around age 50, $(\alpha + \gamma)^2 \sigma_G^2$, $\delta^2\sigma_Y^2$ and σ_u^2 account for 45, 12, and 43 percent of $\sigma_{\ln E}^2$, respectively. In principle, we can estimate the covariance term, but in practice our nonlinear maximum likelihood expression has

---

2. For a recent survey see Atkinson (1979).

never converged when the covariance term is a free parameter. However, in our model we demonstrate that, as σ_{GY} rises, $\delta^2 \sigma_Y^2$ falls. Our direct estimate of the contribution of inequality of opportunity to earnings inequality is 12 percent, and although correction for measurement error and transitory income would increase this figure, we estimate that the overall contribution will be below 20 percent even without the negative influence of a positive σ_{GY}.

It seems likely to me that there was discrimination against certain ethnic and religious groups in our sample of white males. The estimation technique may count such discrimination as genetic, though many people may wish to define discrimination as a dimension of the inequality of opportunity. Presumably for the U.S. population as a whole, this element of inequality is more important than in our sample of white males.

The classical genetic model used by Taubman (1976) to estimate the components of (6) from data on the cross-sibling correlations of identical and fraternal twins is underidentified in a statistical sense. Behrman et al. (1980) have shown how to identify this model using a system of equations. A crucial assumption made to identify the system is that the correlation in common environment for siblings is the same for identical and fraternal twins. If this assumption is not made, it is possible to drive the contribution of G to zero and that of σ_Y^2 to 0·57. The assumption has often been questioned because, for example, the decisions concerning human capital investments in the twins is based, at least in part, on the genetic endowments of the twins. However, this possibility is incorporated explicitly in equation (1), and generates the indirect effect which combines with the direct genetic effect in equation (5). The identifying assumption, thus, is less questionable.

Goldberger (1979) objects to this treatment in equations (1) and (6), preferring instead to regard $\alpha^2 \sigma_G^2 / \sigma_{\ln E}^2$ as the "heritability" component, and to include the effect of γG on rK in the environment term. While this corresponds to the definition of heritability used by classical geneticists,[3] economists are more interested in the contribution of differences in parental incomes or opportunities to the inequality of earnings. This requires combining the direct effect (α) and the indirect (γ) of G on earnings. This also reduces identification problems.

Conclusion

The second section of Goldberger's paper on "Heritability" makes two main points. The first, which has not been discussed here, is that the results are likely

---

3. Behrman, Pollak and Taubman (1982, in this volume) have shown that, in some models consistent with equations (1)–(6), it is also possible to estimate $\gamma^2 \sigma_G^2$. Thus it may be possible to adjust our estimates to obtain figures consistent with the definition used by classical geneticists.

to be misunderstood and misused by people who are against income redistribution programmes. I sympathize with this concern.

Goldberger's other point is that heritability does not provide meaningful information to economists. Regardless of whether economists are interested in heritability, or in describing the sources of inequality, they are interested in differences in earnings attributable to variations in family wealth, since this source of inequality of opportunity can, in principle, be eliminated with no loss in efficiency. Becker has provided a model which distinguishes between the effects of innate ability and of inequality of opportunity on the distribution of income. Data on twins provide a way of estimating the importance of inequality of opportunity.

By eliminating inequality of opportunity, society can improve equity and efficiency. My colleagues and I estimate that inequality of opportunity accounts for less than 20 percent of the variance in earnings for white males. If this estimate is correct, there are important gains to be made from a policy designed to eliminate inequality of opportunity. However, even if all inequality of opportunity were eliminated, most earnings inequality would still remain. Further reductions in inequality will require a trade-off with economic efficiency.

13

Is Schooling "Mostly in the Genes"? Nature-Nurture Decomposition Using Data on Relatives

JERE R. BEHRMAN AND PAUL TAUBMAN

Economists have a long, if erratic, history of studying the determinants of educational attainment.[1] Because economists have usually stressed the role of *acquired* human capital, the nature-nurture debate, frequently explicitly joined in psychology and genetics, has generally remained implicit in economics.[2] This debate questions how much of the variance in an observed outcome—a phenotype such as schooling—can be attributed to the variance in individuals' genotype ("nature") versus the variance in individuals' environment ("nurture").

The nature-nurture framework is a useful one for consideration of the question of how equal educational opportunity is. Inequality of opportunity is used by most economists, including Becker (1967) and Okun (1975), to refer to situations in which family income or wealth differentially limits access to investment in human capital.[3] If the inequality of opportunity is due to inefficiency, for example, that arises from imperfect capital markets, reducing inequality of opportunity offers society the possibility of increasing both efficiency and equity. Indeed Okun (p. 83) hopes that such inequality of opportunity is an important source of inequality of outcomes because it is easier politically to institute changes that raise rather than reduce gross national prod-

Reprinted from *Journal of Political Economy* 97, no. 6 (December 1989): 1425–46. © 1989 by The University of Chicago. All rights reserved.

The work in this paper was supported by the National Institutes of Health and the National Science Foundation. Excellent research support was provided by Al Mathios and Eric Smith. Richard Murnane, Robert A. Pollak, and two anonymous referees provided very helpful comments on an earlier version.

1. Precursors of the human capital school date back at least to the nineteenth century, and interesting related empirical studies such as Gorseline (1932) date back at least to the 1930s. Much of the theoretical and empirical work on education by economists in the last two decades has been shaped by the human capital revolution led by Schultz (1963) and Becker (1964).

2. Some economists and social scientists, however, have been involved in the nature-nurture debate; see, e.g., Jencks et al. (1972), Conlisk (1974, 1984), Meade (1973), Goldberger (1977a), Taubman (1978a, 1981, in this volume), and Behrman et al. (1980).

3. Brittain (1977) is an exception; he defines equality of opportunity as equality of outcome rather than equality of access, given endowments.

uct. The share of the observed variation in schooling that is attributable to across-family variability in environment provides a measure of *in*equality of schooling opportunity.

In this paper we interpret Becker's well-known Woytinsky lecture model of investment in schooling in terms of the nature-nurture debate to explore the extent of inequality of opportunity of schooling for a recent U.S. sample. Becker has supply-of-funds and demand-for-schooling functions whose intersection determines the optimal quantity of schooling and the marginal rate of return. The demand curves vary with endowments, and the supply-of-funds curves vary with family income. We equate endowments with genetic endowments and family income with environment.

Much of the previous work in the nature-nurture area stems from the pioneering effort of Fisher (1918), which has been extended and put into modern matrix notation by Goldberger (1977a). A basic problem in much previous research using the Fisher framework is the assumption that the environmental correlations among relatives not in the same nuclear family (e.g., cousins instead of husband and wife) are zero. In most situations of interest to economists, this assumption is implausible although it may be useful in analyzing plant and livestock controlled breeding experiments. For example, most economists believe that family income influences the quantity and quality of inputs provided to children. Family income is correlated for genetically close relatives.[4] Therefore, siblings and first cousins are likely to have some similarities in their home and school environments, though the degree of similarity is probably greater for siblings than for cousins.

In this paper we explore our version of the Becker model and the nature-nurture issue using a somewhat richer sample than that used for a related exploration in Behrman et al. (1980) and a latent variable methodology similar to the one used in that study. We extend the Fisher model by allowing observed and unobserved differences in the environment of relatives to be correlated. Compared with the model estimated in Behrman et al., the model we estimate here makes different, weaker, and to some extent testable assumptions. Using data that measure completely accurately some of the individuals' environment would make it possible to obtain a lower-bound estimate of the contribution of genotype to the variance of the phenotype and an upper-bound estimate of the contribution of environment.[5] However, random measurement error in the observed environmental variable would bias toward zero the estimated coefficients and the estimated contribution of observed environment to the phenotypic variance. We cannot determine to what extent random measurement error

4. See Behrman et al. (1980), Behrman and Taubman (1986, in this volume), and Kearl and Pope (1986) for some examples and references to the literature.

5. See the discussion at the end of Sec. I.

in our observed environmental variables moves our estimates of the contribution of the genotype away from the lower bounds that would occur with no measurement error.

In Section I we describe the Becker Woytinsky lecture model and the Fisher model and our modifications. In Section II we describe our data. In Section III we report our results. Our estimates suggest that a very large fraction of the variance in educational attainment is attributable to genetic variation. We discuss the features of our analysis and our sample that may have produced these results. Section IV presents a brief conclusion.

I. The Model

In Becker's (1967) model of investment in human capital (hereafter schooling), the equilibrium schooling level is determined by the intersection of the demand and supply curves. The demand for schooling for an individual depends on his or her endowments. Since the productivity of schooling is subject to diminishing returns, the derived demand function for schooling is downward sloping for a given level of endowments. If raising more funds requires paying a higher interest rate, the supply-of-funds curve is upward sloping. The location of an individual's supply-of-funds curve depends on his or her family's wealth due to capital market imperfections: to raise a given amount, those from richer families pay a lower interest rate. The demand curve varies with own ability or endowments, the supply curve varies with family wealth and earnings, and equilibrium schooling varies across families because of underlying variations in family wealth and endowments. We interpret family wealth as environment and the endowment variable as genotype (defined below).

Fisher (1918) proposed a polygenic model to explain the pattern of correlations in outcomes or phenotypes among relatives. (Appendix A describes in more detail the following terms and his model.) In his model, many genes each contribute a small amount to an individual's genotype. We use the standard notation in this literature and define G as the genotypic value, a numerical value associated with an individual's unobserved genetic endowments; N as the environmental value, a numerical value associated with an individual's environment; and Y as the phenotypic value, an individual's observed value of a trait, in this paper years of schooling.

Fisher assumes that Y is a linear and additive function of G and N.[6] By choosing appropriate units for G and N, we can write

$$Y = G + N, \tag{1a}$$

6. This assumption is less restrictive than it may appear prima facie because any power transform of Y can be used as the dependent variable. It does, however, place restrictions on the admissible interactions between G and N.

and, hence, the expected value of the observed variance can be expressed in terms of the expected value of the unobserved variances and covariances, where the expected value symbols are omitted:

$$\sigma_Y^2 = \sigma_G^2 + \sigma_N^2 + 2\sigma_{GN}.$$ (2)

Similarly, we can calculate covariances and the expected values of the unobserved components for relatives such as

$$\sigma_{YY*} = \sigma_{GG*} + \sigma_{NN*} + 2\sigma_{GN*},$$ (3a)

where an asterisk denotes a relative of the original individual.[7]

Fisher derived a formula, reproduced in Goldberger (1977b), that describes a fairly general genetic model and expresses σ_{YY*} as a function of three parameters defined below in (3c)–(3e).[8] This formula yields different combinations of the parameters for various relatives such as father-son, siblings, and cousins.

This model is explained more fully in Appendix A. As in Goldberger's presentation (which is the most accessible), an individual's observed phenotype, Y, is the sum of three unobserved components: the additive genotypic value G_1, the dominance deviation G_2, and the environment N:

$$Y = G_1 + G_2 + N.$$ (1b)

The two G's and the N are assumed to be uncorrelated, so the phenotypic variance is given by

$$\sigma_Y^2 = \sigma_1^2 + \sigma_2^2 + \sigma_N^2,$$ (3b)

where σ_1^2 and σ_2^2 are variances of G_1 and G_2, respectively. Assume that marriage is assortative on the basis of phenotype, that relatives not in the same direct family line do not share common environments, and that the system is in equilibrium (i.e., that none of the variances changes across generations). In this

model the expected phenotypic correlations between relatives can be written as a function of three measures:

$$c_1 = \frac{\sigma_1^2 + \sigma_2^2}{\sigma_Y^2},$$ (3c)

---

7. In (3a) and in eq. (7) below, we assume $\sigma_{G*N} = \sigma_{GN*}$, which is true in an expected value sense. In any event, for our estimates below we set both terms equal to zero.

8. What Fisher's model is missing in epistasy, which occurs if the effect on the phenotype of one gene depends on the realization of another gene.

which is the ratio of total genotypic variance to phenotypic variance,

$$c_2 = \frac{\sigma_1^2}{\sigma_1^2 + \sigma_2^2},$$ (3d)

which is the ratio of additive genotypic variance to total genotypic variance, and

$$m = \frac{\sigma_{YY'}}{\sigma_Y^2},$$ (3e)

which is the correlation of phenotypes of spouses (where Y' denotes spouse's phenotype).

Goldberger presents formulae for phenotypic correlations for some relatives, and those for other relatives can be derived using his appendix. For example, if there is no assortative mating and no dominance or interactive effects, $c_1 = 1$ and $m = 0$. Then first cousins whose fathers are identical twins are genetically equivalent to half sibs and, like half sibs, share one-fourth of their genes; if their environments are uncorrelated, they have an expected phenotypic covariance of $c_1/4$. We give some other examples in the last column of table 1.

One problem for empirical analysis is that there is no accepted formulation of environmental correlations among kin groups, though some previous researchers have tried to model the transmission and correlation of environment across generations (see, e.g., Becker 1981; Cavalli-Sforza and Feldman 1981; Cavalli-Sforza et al. 1982). Cavalli-Sforza and his colleagues develop models for cultural or nongenetic transmission of traits such as religion and drinking milk at dinner. They do not worry about controlling for genetic differences. The Becker formulation leads to no useful estimation developments within Fisher's framework.

Morton (1974) and Morton and Rao (1979) have proposed an estimator that allows parents, offspring, and siblings to have the same unobserved environment, but they assume zero environmental correlation for all other kin groups. Goldberger studies the implications of this model and concludes that to maintain equilibrium this procedure implies negative environmental correlations for these other kin groups. Moreover, there is no good reason to argue that parents have the same common environment as their children since it is the parents' environment when they were children that affects the parents' educational attainment.

Although there are no theoretical formulae analogous to Fisher's genetic formulae to explain how environmental correlations for relatives vary, we do not believe that these correlations are zero and we find it plausible that they differ

Table 1 Cross-Kin Intraclass Correlations (Weighted) for Years of Schooling from NAS-NRC Twin and Adult Offspring Samples

Kin Group*	Age- and Gender-adjusted Data Intraclass Correlation†	Adjustment for Observed Environment (Minus Sign Omitted)	Sample Size	Expected Value of Phenotypic Correlation (Assuming Uncorrelated Environment Except for Spouses)‡
Offspring-grandfather	.16		2,749	$[c_1c_2(1 + m)/2](1 + A)/2$
Offspring-father	.34	.022	2,745	$c_1c_2(1 + m)/2$
Father-grandfather	.42		4,929	$c_1c_2(1 + m)/2$
Offspring-offspring	.34	.063	3,105	$[c_1c_2(1 + A)/2] + [c_1(1 - c_2)/4]$
Identical (MZ) twins	.75	.055	1,233	c_1
Fraternal (DZ) twins	.55	.051	1,160	$[c_1c_2(1 + A)/2] + [c_1(1 - c_2)/4]$
First cousins, MZ fathers	.26	.033	893	$c_1c_2(1 + A)^2/4$
First cousins, DZ fathers	.13	.037	652	$c_1c_2[(1 + A)/2]^3 + [A^2c_1(1 - c_2)/16]$
MZ uncle-nephew/niece	.35	.021	893	$c_1c_2(1 + m)/2$
DZ uncle-nephew/niece	.19	.028	652	$c_1c_2[(1 + A)/2]^2 + [Ac_1(1 - c_2)/8]$
MZ spouse-nephew/niece	.21		420	$mc_1c_2(1 + m)/2$
DZ spouse-nephew/niece	.07		305	$A[(1 + A)/2]^2 + [mAc_1(1 - c_2)/8]$
Father-mother	.34		1,392	m
Grandfather-grandmother	.74		4,937	m
Offspring-spouse	.54		2,122	m
Sisters-in-law (parents' generation)	.22		481	m^2

*Offspring always refers to the third generation; father, mother, aunts, and uncles refer to the second generation; and grandfather or grandmother refers to the first generation. In all cells, we include all individuals who are eligible and we use weights that are inversely proportional to the number of replications (e.g., for grandfather cells, we use one or two grandfathers, depending on the data availability).

† Adjusted refers to the correction for gender and age for the offspring generation described in the text.

‡ $A = c_1c_2m$.

between different groups of relatives.[9] Regarding the latter point, consider, for example, first cousins whose fathers are twins. In the National Academy of Science–National Research Council (NAS-NRC) twin sample, the natural log of father's earnings has a within-pair correlation of .55 and .33 for identical and fraternal twins, respectively. For nearly every variable that has been subject to within-pair correlation analysis, the identical twins have a larger value than fraternal twins.[10] Thus the environments in which first cousins are reared are probably more alike if the fathers are identical rather than fraternal twins.

We model the unobserved environment as correlated with the observed variables Z_1 through Z_n, which have coefficient weights α_1 through α_n, and an additive stochastic term u:

$$N = Z_1\alpha_1 + \ldots + Z_n\alpha_n + u. \tag{4}$$

Substituting (4) into (1b) and imposing equality of α's across relatives, we can estimate the α's along with the parameters in Fisher's equation.

The system can be represented as follows, where for convenience we combine the two genotypic terms in G and treat the Z_i's as a single variable, Z, and we again use an asterisk for a relative of the individual:

$$Y = G + Z\alpha + u \tag{5a}$$

and

$$Y^* = G^* + Z^*\alpha + u^*. \tag{5b}$$

Provided that u and u^* are uncorrelated with Z and G, the expected value of the variance in Y is[11]

$$\sigma_Y^2 = \sigma_G^2 + \alpha^2\sigma_Z^2 + 2\alpha\sigma_{GZ} + \sigma_u^2. \tag{6}$$

The expected cross-kin correlation is

$$\sigma_{YY^*} = \sigma_{GG^*} + \alpha^2\sigma_{ZZ^*} + 2\alpha\sigma_{GZ^*} + \sigma_{uu^*}. \tag{7}$$

We retain Fisher's assumption that $\sigma_{GZ} = \sigma_{CZ^*} = 0$, and we assume for now that $\sigma_{uu^*} = 0$. Then the model in relations (6) and (7) contains the observed σ_Y^2, σ_{YY^*}, σ_Z^2, and σ_{ZZ^*}, the unobserved σ_u^2, and the unobserved σ_G^2 and σ_{GG^*}, expected values of which are given by Fisher's three parameter equations in the last column of table 1. Converting equation (6) to a correlation format (and still

9. The absence of such theoretical formulae is one reason why Chamberlain (1977b) is unenthusiastic about augmenting sibling data with data on other relatives.

10. See Behrman et al. (1980) for other examples and references to other twin studies.

11. The estimate of the contribution of the genetic and environmental components to the variances of Y does not depend on the assumption that u and Z are uncorrelated, but the unbiasedness of the estimate of α does depend on this assumption.

maintaining Fisher's assumption that $\sigma_{GZ} = 0$), we have in expected value terms

$$1 = \frac{\sigma_G^2}{\sigma_Y^2} + \frac{\sigma^2 \sigma_Z^2}{\sigma_Y^2} + \frac{\sigma_u^2}{\sigma_Y^2} = 1 - c_1 - \alpha^2 \frac{\sigma_Z^2}{\sigma_Y^2}. \tag{8}$$

We can use (8) to estimate σ_u^2/σ_Y^2 given estimates of c_1 and α from our maximum likelihood estimates of relations (6) and (7).

There are two problems in using (8) to obtain estimates of σ_u^2/σ_Y^2. First, it is often difficult to obtain a sample for many types of relatives with much representation of the environment. Second, unless α is estimated using a procedure such as ordinary least squares (OLS), the estimated value of σ_u^2/σ_Y^2 may be negative. In fact, some of our estimates of σ_u^2 for offspring using relation (9) and α estimated for all relatives are negative; therefore, in this paper we use the two-step method proposed next.

Under the assumption that $\sigma_{GZ} = \alpha_{Gu} = 0$, we can use data on individuals to obtain unbiased estimates of the coefficients (ignoring measurement error) of the observed environmental variables (the α's) from relation (5). Using these estimates, we can purge the schooling data of observed environmental influences and then estimate c_1, c_2, and m, although c_1 must be rescaled to state it in terms of the original schooling variance. We can use one equation in which each person is a unit of observation or we can use a separate equation for people who appear in each kin group, though the second alternative is not guaranteed to give a positive estimate for σ_u^2. We have eight kin groups, defined below, about whom we have some environmental information and for whom we can estimate our model.

We have assumed that Z and G are uncorrelated. If they are correlated, estimates of α and of the genetic and environmental effects are biased. If Z and G are positive correlated and Z has no measurement error, our estimate of α is upward biased, and we overestimate the environmental and understate the genetic contribution to the schooling variance.

Estimating this system requires samples with data on various relatives and measures of Z that describe early childhood environment. The available measures of Z may be poor proxies for N so that σ_u^2/σ_Y^2 is large, and u and u^* probably are correlated. We investigate below the possibility that u and u^* are not independently distributed.

II. The Data

The analysis in this paper is based on the NAS-NRC twin and adult offspring samples. The NAS-NRC twin sample, described in detail in Behrman et al. (1980), contains about 2,000 twin pairs. The twins are white males born between 1917 and 1927, who were veterans and who answered a 1974 question-

Table 2 Means and Variances of Selected Variables in Offspring Sample

	Number of Observations	Mean	Standard Deviation
Year of birth, from parents	6,278	1,953.3	4.8
Year of birth, from offspring	3,648	1,953.4	4.6
Sex: 1 = male, 2 = female	3,652	1.54	.5
Schooling	3,575	14.7	2.2
Schooling of father	3,341	14.1	2.6
Schooling of mother	3,360	13.9	2.5
Offspring income, 1980	3,206	14,113.6	163.002

naire. Each of these twins was asked in 1978 or 1981 to provide a roster of the names and addresses of his adult offspring (over age 18).[12] The offspring then were sent mail questionnaires in a 1977 pilot survey or in a 1981/82 full survey. Subsequently in 1982, several hundred nonrespondents were interviewed by telephone. The mail and telephone surveys yielded almost 4,000 responding offspring.

This paper uses data from these 4,000 offspring and their parents. Table 2 contains some summary statistics from the offspring sample. The respondents' average age is about 27, their average work experience is about 6 years,[13] their average education is almost 15 years, and their average earnings are about $14,000 per year.

Behrman and Taubman (1985, in this volume) compare the offspring sample with the same cohort in the 1980 census and find that this sample is above average in education and earnings. They also find that the differences in means of various variables between the parents with responding and nonresponding children are small and that a natural log earnings regression estimated using this sample is similar to those obtained from nationwide random samples for recent years.

The twin sample is described in detail in Behrman et al. (1980). The twins are also above average in earnings and education; as with the offspring, a natural log earnings regression yields parameter estimates similar to those obtained from random samples.

The offspring can be sorted into groups of individuals, siblings, and first cousins, with the last of these groups subdivided by the zygosity of the fathers,

12. We checked the latest rosters against supposedly complete offspring data collected in 1974. About 10 percent of the families show an extra offspring in the earlier sample. This discrepancy could reflect reporting errors, early deaths, or children who were born by 1974 but were still preadult in 1981.

13. Experience is calculated as age at survey data minus the age at which the first full-time job began. If the latter age is not reported (the pilot project did not ask for it), we use the standard Mincer (1974) formulation of experience equaling age minus years of school minus six. If years of experience calculated in this way is negative, we use zero.

treating separately those whose fathers are identical (monozygotic [MZ]) twins and those whose fathers are fraternal (dizygotic [DZ]) twins.[14] First cousins whose fathers are identical twins are, from a genetic standpoint, half siblings. This sample also can be sorted into grandfather-grandchild, aunt-nephew/niece, grandfather-grandmother, father-mother, offspring-spouse, and sisters-in-law categories.

To avoid very small cell sizes, we combined offspring data across ages and sex. To do so we regressed offspring's years of schooling on sex, age, and age squared and then used the regression coefficients to adjust the data for estimated age and gender effects.[15]

Many previous attempts to use the Fisher model have merged correlations from different, often small samples. Because we are using two samples coded by the same organization to provide all the correlations, we have greater uniformity in definitions and greater ease in obtaining ZZ^* and ZY^*. However, since the same individuals are used in more than one kin group, the correlations are not independent, our standard errors are biased downward, and t-statistics are biased upward.

III. Results

In many studies, including Taubman (1978a, 1981), Behrman et al. (1980), Behrman and Taubman (1985, 1990, both in this volume), and Becker and Tomes (1986), the correlation coefficient (R) or the coefficient of determination (R^2) is used to measure how much two variables have in common. The standard correlation coefficient is unsuitable here because we have data on several members of a given kin group while the R is for pairs of individuals. A generalization of R for groups each of which has more than two members is the intraclass correlation coefficient, which is the proportion of the total sample variance not attributable to between-group differences in means. This measure eliminates the within-group variation from the numerator. Extensive discussion of this measure can be found in Kendall and Stuart (1958, vol. I).[16]

Table 1 contains our estimates of the weighted intraclass correlations for years of schooling calculated with adjustments for age and gender, and in addition with further adjustments for observed environmental variables using the

14. Behrman et al. (1980, chap. 5) discuss the methods used to establish whether twins are identical or fraternal. We dropped from our analysis the few pairs of twins in our sample whose zygosities are unknown.

15. Estimates calculated separately for males and for females tend to be more erratic than those with the adjusted data in that some of them violate the rank ordering implied by Fisher's formulae in the last column of table 1.

16. The weights for the intraclass correlations depend on the number of people observed per group.

Table 3 Genetic-Environmental Model of Kin Correlations

Coefficient	Parameter or Variable Estimates	t-Value of Coefficient
c_1	.88	406.1
c_2	1.01	21.4
m	.48	7.3
Father is professional or manager	1.05	7.1
Father is skilled worker	−.13	6.8
Father is clerk or salesman	.12	1.6
Family size	−.15	5.5
Log likelihood	−1,118	

PERFORMANCE OF MODEL

Group	Actual Correlation	Predicted Correlation
MZ twins	.75	.75
DZ twins	.55	.41*
Offspring-father	.34	.41
MZ uncle-nephew/niece	.35	.41
DZ uncle-nephew/niece	.19	.21
Offspring-offspring	.34	.43*
MZ cousins	.26	.22
DZ cousins	.13	.13

NOTE—Some categories shown in table 1, e.g., DZ spouse-nephew/niece, were not used because we do not have the environmental measures. The omitted occupational category is unskilled worker. the model was estimated in two stages. The first stage was an OLS regression for individuals using father's occupation and family size. The second used maximum likelihood estimation on the intraclass correlations from which the father's occupation and family size effects were partialed out. In the performance section we have added together the effects of the Fisher model and the effects of the observed variables. The $\dot{\alpha}$ are estimated parameters. The Z's are normalized. $\sigma_w^2 = 1 - \dot{c}_1 - \Sigma_i \dot{\alpha} Z_1 = .09$.

*Differences in these two estimates reflect measurement error in offspring and twin responses.

coefficients in table 3. (These last data are available only for some groups.) We first focus on the data adjusted for age and gender. The correlations vary substantially, ranging from .75 for identical twins to .07 between spouses of fraternal twins and their nephews/nieces.[17]

Some of these combinations have the same expected value in Fisher's formulation (though the expected value of the environmental correlations need not be the same). For example, we have three estimates of the assortative mating parameter, m, ranging from .74 in the grandparents' generation to .34 for

17. Goldberger (1977a) presents IQ intraclass correlations for various kin groups calculated from various samples. These correlations range from .97 for identical twins reared together in the United States to .16 for second cousins in Britain whose fathers generally are not twins.

father and mother, with the offspring-spouse estimate in between at .54.[18] These differences may indicate model misspecification or data problems, or they may reflect differences in assortative mating parameters that we assume are identical.[19] However, the grandparent and offspring-spouse correlations are not used in our estimates of c_1, c_2, and m.

The Fisher formulae predict that the father-offspring and father-grandfather correlations are equal. Our estimated values, .34 and .42, are relatively close, and the difference between them is not statistically significant.

The Fisher formulae also predict that the fraternal twin and the offspring-offspring correlations are equal. We estimate them to be .55 and .34, respectively. In addition to random disturbances, the discrepancy may reflect systematic factors ignored in the theoretical discussion above, for example, variations in family and societal environment for children born at different times and differences in birth order and spacing.[20] As is shown in table 4, the omission of the offspring-offspring correlation has little effect on our estimates.

We now turn to kin groups sorted by the zygosity of the twins. The father-offspring and identical twin uncle-nephew/niece correlations are almost identical. Since the father and his identical twin differ only in their specific environment, these results suggest both little correlation between the father's specific environment and the child's phenotype and either strong assortative mating or a small correlation of mother's environmental contribution with offspring's environment.

We generally find that the correlation falls with genetic distance: as we move from siblings to first cousins whose fathers are identical twins to first cousins

18. The grandparents' education data are reported by the twins. This may lead to inflated correlations. However, the correlation of one twin's response with that of the other twin yields R's of about .9 for grandfather and grandmother, with the R slightly higher for MZ twins. Therefore, random error does not seem to be that important, though systematic error may be.

19. We assume, perhaps incorrectly, long-run equilibrium across generations. This equilibrium assumption is commonly made in genetic and in economic intergenerational models (see Becker 1981; Conlisk 1984). The grandparents of children born between 1917 and 1927 must have completed their education before World War I, an era in which very few people went to college or completed high school. For example, for the population born around 1880, only about 10 percent graduated from high school and only 7 percent went to college. After World War I, there was not only an increase in the average level of educational attainment but also an increase in the correlation between IQ and educational attainment. (See Taubman and Wales [1972] for evidence on these points.) Cross-tabulations with the data used in this study show that in the parents' generation a substantial fraction (18 percent) of the twins who were high school graduates had spouses with no high school education. In the grandparents' generation, in which a smaller fraction of the population entered high school, the percentage of male high school graduates whose spouses had no high school education was much larger (76 percent).

20. Olneck (1977, p. 139) reports no effect of differential birth order and spacing. Behrman and Taubman (1986, in this volume) present evidence of birth order effects in parental preferences underlying schooling investments and give references to other studies of birth order effects.

Table 4   Estimates of Three Parameters
in Fisher Formulae Using Seven Kin Groups

Omitted Kin Group	c_1	c_2	m
MZ twins	1.04	.72	.58
	(27.1)	(8.35)	(4.65)
DZ twins	.88	.72	.96
	(372.0)	(12.7)	(5.70)
Offspring-father	.88	1.04	.46
	(375.3)	(20.0)	(6.54)
MZ uncle-nephew/niece	.88	1.03	.46
	(373.1)	(21.3)	(6.91)
DZ uncle-nephew/niece	.89	1.02	.47
	(381.1)	(21.0)	(6.86)
Offspring-offspring	.89	1.06	.46
	(397.7)	(27.7)	(9.19)
MZ cousins	.89	1.03	.45
	(381.1)	(20.9)	(6.72)
DZ cousins	.89	1.03	.46
	(388.3)	(20.8)	(6.73)

NOTE—Environmental proxies are included in the estimates. The coefficients are the same as those in table 3. t-statistics are below the estimates in parentheses.

whose fathers are fraternal twins, the correlation falls from .34 to .26 to .13. Similarly, the avuncular correlation falls from .35 to .19 as we move from identical to fraternal twin uncles. Similar patterns, though lower correlations, are found for aunts who are the spouses of the identical or fraternal twins.

The next column of table 4 presents the adjustment for the observed environmental differences using the coefficients in table 3 for the kin groupings in which we have observations on the environmental variables. (These coefficients are discussed below.) This adjustment reduces correlations by .02 to .06 with the largest adjustment in the offspring-offspring group as shown in the second column of table 1.

The kin correlations fall as genetic and environmental similarities decline. To identify the separate influences of genetic endowments and environment, we must combine information across kin groups. To estimate the parameters in the modified Fisher model, we have used OLS to adjust the data for observed environmental differences and a nonlinear maximum likelihood routine as described at the end of Section I.[21]

The first model uses father's occupation and family size as observed environmental variables; these are the only environmental measures that are available for all eight kin groups used. Our occupational variable can assume four values: unskilled, clerical or sales, skilled, and professional or managerial.[22]

21. We have imposed the definition $A = c_1 c_2 m$ in the maximum likelihood estimates, as in table 1. Goldberger (1977a) notes that not all researchers have imposed this restriction.

22. Part of the parental occupational differences may arise because of genetic differences

We assume first that the unmeasured environment is a random variable uncorrelated across kin groups. (Later we drop this assumption.) We have the necessary data for individuals, siblings, the two first-cousins groups, the two twin groups, the two avuncular groups, and the offspring-father group.

Our estimated model is given in table 3.[23] Our estimates imply that about 88 percent of the variance in schooling arises from genetic variations. However, this must be rescaled to account for the variance already partialed out. When this is done, c_1 falls to 81 percent. Our estimate of the proportion of the genetic variance that is additive is 101 percent, which does not differ significantly from one, its upper bound.[24] We estimate that the assortative mating coefficient is about .48, which is in the middle of the direct estimates given in table 1.[25] These three genetic parameters are highly significant: the lowest t-statistic is 7.3.[26] The environmental effects indicate that having a father who is a professional or manager rather than an unskilled worker increases a child's education by 1 year. This difference is statistically significant. Surprisingly, significant negative effects occur if the father is skilled. An insignificant positive effect is estimated if the father is a clerk or salesman. The number of sibs has a significant and negative effect; each additional sibling reduces the respondent's education by 0.15 years.[27]

The variance of the random error term is a small positive number of about 9 percent of σ_Y^2. The table also reports predicted and actual correlations. The model generally fits the data reasonably well, but less well for the fraternal twins than for the other groups.

To test the sensitivity of our model, we have reestimated it using all possible combinations of seven kin groups but always adjusting by the OLS equation (estimated with data on individuals), which is presented in table 3. The coefficients and t-statistics in table 4 are similar to those in table 3 except when we omit the MZ or DZ twin groups. Without the DZ twins, c_1 is unchanged, but

---

that may be correlated with genotypic differences influencing schooling. Behrman et al. (1980, chap. 7), who measure occupation more finely, report a small occupation-genetic correlation.

23. In the OLS first-stage equation, $\bar{R}^2$ is .082. We have rescaled the estimate of c_1 for this explained variation.

24. When we reestimate the model restricting c_2 to be one, the estimates do not differ substantially or significantly from those in table 3.

25. See Schoen and Wouldredge (1985) for other estimates.

26. As noted in Sec. II, the standard errors are understated and the t-statistics are overstated because we have not allowed for the nonindependence of the correlations arising from the multiple use of observations on some individuals.

27. Appendix table B1 presents the "environment" equation estimated separately for the various kin groups. There are differences from the results presented in the text, but separate adjustment of the data using the equations estimated for each group has only a small impact on the estimates for c_1, c_2, and m.

there is a sharp drop in c_2 and its t-statistic and a sharp rise in m and its t-statistic. Without MZ twins, c_1 rises to a number insignificantly greater than one, c_2 falls some, m rises some, and t-statistics fall substantially.

Studies using twin data often assume that the unobserved environmental correlation for identical twin pairs has the same expected value as the unobserved correlation for fraternal twin pairs. This assumption has been criticized by Goldberger (1977a) and others. In our sample the observed parental environmental variables are the same for siblings and for both twins in a pair regardless of zygosity. If we exclude the MZ twins from our analysis on the grounds that their environment must be more similar, we obtain results for c_1 slightly beyond its theoretical limit. A mechanical explanation for the importance of the MZ twins is that, as shown in table 1, in Fisher's formulae the entry for the MZ twins is c_1. To fit the data for MZ twins well, this element in the estimated likelihood function has to be somewhat near the MZ entry. Then the other kin groups primarily establish m and c_2.

These estimates of genetic and environmental effects differ from those based on twin data alone that are reported in Behrman et al. (1980). In this paper we attribute much more of the variance to genetic differences and much less to environmental differences.[28] The larger estimated genetic share in the schooling variance in this than in our previous study is surprising since the new kin groups include people who did not have as equal access to financing education as the sample for the earlier study did (i.e., the twins alone) through the GI Bill.[29] It is possible that the stronger genetic influences estimated for the present case reflect the violation of the assumption of a steady-state system across generations, though dropping any group that involves the offspring has little effect on our estimates.

There is another mechanical reason that may explain why our estimates of σ_G^2 are larger using data on many kin groups than the Behrman et al. estimates using data on twins alone. Behrman et al. assumed that covariance in twins' environment is nonzero and used a latent variable methodology to estimate this covariance. In this paper we also estimate the kin covariance, but we use a small number of observed proxies. Our estimate of the twin covariance for environment here is much smaller than the Behrman et al. latent variable estimate or than that in the Panel Study of Income Dynamics (Corcoran and Datcher 1981, p. 188), and the implied residual correlation for the identical twins—and therefore the estimated genetic contribution—is higher since this group apparently plays a major role in estimating c_1.

28. In Behrman et al. (1980), we estimate the genetic contribution to be slightly less than half of the variance in schooling.

29. In Behrman, Pollak, and Taubman (1989, in this volume), we argue that the twins had more equal access to financing than their offspring.

Table 5   Dependent Variable: Education

Variable	Parameter Estimate	t for H_0: Parameter $= 0$
Intercept	14.59	6.1
Number of siblings	−.14	−4.8
Parental income (in thousands)	.030	7.3
Parental age:		
Age of mother	−.10	−1.0
(Age of mother)^2	.002	1.4
Age of father	.50	4.7
(Age of father)^2	−.01	−5.1
Father's religion:		
Catholic	.75	1.2
Protestant	.62	1.0
Jewish	1.48	2.1
None	.17	.19
Own occupation:		
Professional	.74	4.4
Skilled	.11	.7
Clerical and sales	.06	.3
Attitude about job:		
Likes job very much	−.10	−.4
Likes job fairly well	−.08	−.3
Dislikes job very much	−.16	−.3
Prefers to be self-employed	.27	1.8
Prefers to be salaried	.44	2.7
Why selected job:		
Fringe benefits	−.1	−.08
Prospects for eventual success	.44	.4
Prospects for interesting work	.27	1.4
Prospects for independent work	.009	.01
Prospects for challenging work	.19	1.4
Job security	−.14	−1.1
Job offered much free time	.15	1.1
Liked kind of work	−.16	.8
Year of birth	−.11	−6.0
Sex	−.36	−3.4
Marital status:		
Married	−.50	−.3
Remarried	−.67	−.3
Separated	.13	.1
Divorced	−.70	−.3
Age × sex	−.03	−.7

NOTE—The number of observations is 1,362; $\bar{R}^2 = .20$.

It might be argued that family size and parental occupation do not capture much of the environmental correlation across kin groups. For a smaller number of kin groups, we can use a richer representation of the environment. The OLS regression based on individuals in these groups is presented in table 5. The R^2, adjusted for degrees of freedom, for this list of variables is about .2. We at-

Table 6   Fisher Model Using Eight Kin Groups

	Coefficient	t-Value
c_1	.91	376.2
c_2	1.03	24.1
m	.48	8.1
Log likelihood	-1.24×10^4	
σ_u^2/σ_Y^2	.28	

PERFORMANCE OF MODEL

Group	Actual	Predicted
MZ twins	.746	.748
DZ twins	.547	.406
Offspring-father	.343	.432
MZ uncle-nephew/niece	.354	.432
DZ uncle-nephew/niece	.188	.216
Offspring-offspring	.339	.406
MZ cousins	.256	.217
DZ cousins	.134	.114

tempted to use the data adjusted by partialing out the variables listed in table 5 to estimate the Fisher formula parameters using data on individuals, siblings, and the first-cousin groups. The estimates of some parameters, however, are well outside of acceptable bounds.

There remains the question of whether there is correlation among kin in the environmental residuals. To explore this possibility, we have estimated a latent variable model in which we assume that there is a variable, w, that is perfectly correlated for sibling (including both twin) groups, and its correlation across other kin groups falls off as rapidly as the observed environmental variables.[30] We find that there is a significant latent variable and that its coefficient is about .2. The inclusion of this latent variable changes c_1, c_2, and m to .83, .92, and .64 respectively.[31] The first two of these estimates, which are of primary interest for this study, are not substantially different from those in table 3 because of this change, though the assortative mating coefficient estimate (m) is increased. It is possible that a different kin pattern should be imposed on the latent variable, but we have no information that would allow us to specify this pattern.

In table 6 we report estimates of Fisher's model using data on the eight kin groups without adjusting the data for the observed and generally significant environmental variables. The estimates of the common parameters are not much different from those in table 3.

30. Whenever a latent variable is used, a normalization is needed. We normalize the latent variable so that $\sigma_u^2/\sigma_Y^2 = .01\sigma_Y^2$.

31. If we correct for the previous reduction in the variance in Y due to partialing out the observed environment, c_1 falls to .76.

IV. Conclusion

Fisher's genetic model treats environment as an unobserved residual. In this paper we have modified his model by treating environment as partially observed. We estimate a modified Fisher model that is consistent with Becker's Woytinsky lecture. Using the father's occupation and the individual's number of siblings to represent the environment, we have estimated a model of educational attainment with data on a variety of kin groups related through a sample of U.S. male twins. The estimated model fits the data well and attributes a high fraction of the observed variation in educational attainment to genetic differences. This dimension of our results, moreover, seems relatively robust to most alternative specifications that we have explored. If in fact genetic differences do account for a high proportion of the schooling variation, this does not mean that the distribution of schooling cannot or should not be changed. But policy changes directed at the inequality originating in genetic differences probably would have implied losses in economic efficiency.

Appendix A

Here we provide a brief summary of the genetic model. Fisher's polygenetic model is one in which every outcome or phenotype is determined by two factors, a person's genotype and his environment. A person has many genes, each of which contributes a small part to the value of a genotype and phenotype. Each gene has two components, one contributed by the father and the other by the mother. Each gene component has associated with it an unknown numerical value.

The genotype is a function of all the genes that influence the phenotype. The simplest function is a linear one. Fisher's model allows for dominant and recessive genes; for example, a person with one blue-eye gene and one brown-eye gene always has brown eyes, though the person could contribute a blue-eye gene to an offspring. Dominant and recessive genes make c_2 less than one. Fisher's model also allows for the possibility that parents' gene pools are correlated. In his model, assortative mating is based on a person's phenotype; hence, parents' environments also are correlated. The model used in this paper does not allow for the particular realization of one gene to have an effect on the value of another gene. Some genetic models do allow for such "epistasy".

In Fisher's model, the environment is everything else that affects the phenotype. It can include investments in human capital, luck, and so forth. Both genotype and environment have to be multiplied by prices. Hence, we are implicitly assuming that in equilibrium relative prices remain constant, a strong but common assumption in intergenerational analyses.

Table B1 Estimates of Environmental Coefficients for People in Various Kin Groups

		FATHER'S OCCUPATION					
	CONSTANT	Professional and Management	Sales and Clerk	Skilled	FAMILY SIZE	$\bar{R}^2$	NUMBER OF OBSERVATIONS
MZ twins	12.90 (87.6)	.91 (5.1)	1.01 (4.1)	.16 (.7)	−.02 (−3.3)	.0228	1,986
DZ twins	2.32 (81.0)	1.24 (6.8)	1.96 (7.8)	.64 (2.8)	−.02 (−2.9)	.0434	1,822
Offspring	14.97 (106.7)	1.02 (8.5)	.18 (1.1)	−.14 (−1.1)	−.12 (−5.1)	.0740	2,454
MZ cousins	14.05 (41.1)	1.29 (4.4)	−2.5 (−.6)	.16 (.5)	.06 (1.1)	.0808	448
DZ cousins	15.4 (47.2)	.67 (2.3)	.17 (.4)	−.27 (−.7)	−.16 (−3.1)	.0566	368
Fathers	12.67 (115.5)	1.14 (8.7)	1.47 (8.0)	.34 (2.1)	−.03 (−5.5)	.0390	3,440
MZ uncle	13.02 (76.7)	.85 (4.2)	.98 (3.4)	.20 (.9)	−.03 (−3.6)	.0215	1,543
DZ uncle	12.34 (69.7)	1.26 (6.0)	1.83 (6.4)	.61 (2.4)	−.02 (−2.7)	.0428	1,323

14

Measuring the Impact of Environmental Policies on the Level and Distribution of Earnings

Paul Taubman

With the exception of research on recombinate DNA and perhaps test-tube babies, policy research in this country is concerned with proposing and evaluating various changes in the environment. Such policies try to improve an individual's performance, eliminate harmful behavior, and, in general, overcome poor genetic endowments and family background. These policies operate either by providing services directly or by lowering the price of services. Economists have studied environmental policies that relate to many different subjects. This paper will focus on earnings and its relationship with schooling and with inequality of opportunity. These two subjects will be examined separately.

While most policies studied are environmental in nature, one's knowledge of their impacts may be sorely limited if one ignores or does not control for a person's genetic endowments. Perhaps the simplest way of illustrating this point is in terms of the impact of schooling on earnings. It is often argued that the reason the more educated have higher earnings is that the more educated are more able, irrespective of education, and that ability is rewarded in the marketplace. Thus, not controlling for this ability, which is partly attributable to differences in both family environment and genetic endowments, will cause the researcher to obtain a biased estimate of the effect of schooling on earnings.[1]

The argument can be formalized as the bias that arises when a variable is omitted. Let earnings be denoted by Y, years of schooling by S, ability by A, and random events by u. Let the equation to be estimated be:

$$Y = \beta S + \gamma A + u \tag{1}$$

Reprinted from *The Fundamental Connection between Nature and Nurture*, edited by W. Gove and G. Carpenter, with the permission of Lexington Books, an imprint of Macmillan, Inc. Copyright © 1981 by Lexington Books.

This research has been supported by National Science Foundation Grants SOC76p17673. This piece is based on work done jointly with J. Behrman, T. Wales, and Z. Hrubec. Besides them thanks are due to O. Chamberlain, A. Goldberger, Z. Griliches, C. Jencks, and M. Olneck for helpful criticisms.

1. A biased estimate is one whose expected value does not equal its true value.

If one omits the variable A, under standard assumptions the expected value of $\hat{b}$, the least squares estimate of the coefficient on schooling is given by:

$$E(\hat{b}) = \beta + \gamma d \tag{2}$$

where d is given by the auxiliary equation

$$A = dS \tag{3}$$

Thus the estimate of β will be biased unless ability does not have an independent effect on earnings ($\gamma = 0$) or unless ability is not linearly related to schooling ($d = 0$).

This well-known omitted variable problem permeates most empirical, non-experimental research in the social sciences. The two standard approaches to overcoming the problem can best be understood from equations 4 and 5.

$$A = \lambda IQ + v \tag{4}$$

$$A = \delta_1 X + \delta_2 Z \tag{5}$$

In 4 and 5, A, v, and Z are unobserved while IQ and X are observed. Equation 5 states that there is an observed variable such as an IQ test that is a *direct measure* of ability. Equation 4 includes a random variable (v) either because IQ has a test-retest type measurement error and/or because IQ does not correspond exactly to A.

Equation 5 asserts that there is a relationship between ability and some observed variables (X) plus some unobserved variables (Z). The relationship in 5 of the X variables to A can arise *because X causes A* or *because X is correlated with A*. This latter correlation can occur because of a variety of reasons. For example, some identifiable socioeconomic groups may be willing to divert more resources to their children's future than their own present consumption. Then X would be a proxy for the unobserved differential in resources. Alternatively, some variables such as parents' education may be due to their parents' genetic endowments, which will be correlated with a child's genetic endowments, as explained more fully below. The Z variable includes all the causes of A, including genetic endowments, not correlated with X.

Substituting equations 4 and/or 5 into 1, economists and sociologists have included IQ and various Xs as controls in earnings functions. The results have been mixed.[2] In general IQ and a number of other variables, including parental income and education, and the subject's religious upbringing, are statistically significant. However, in a majority of the studies the estimate of β in equation 1 declines by 15 percent or less when such controls are introduced. These studies suggest that there is not a large bias from not controlling for ability. However, in a minority of studies, the bias from not using these controls is

2. For a recent survey, see chapter 1 of Behrman et al. (1980).

25 to 40 percent, which suggests a large bias if ability is not controlled. I am struck by the fact that the minority group is based on samples in which the men had substantial amounts of labor-force experience while the majority group is based on samples in which the men generally had less than seven years' worth of labor-force experience. However, since nearly all samples with measures of intelligence are based on nonrandom, idiosyncratic samples, there may be other reasons for the difference in results.

While these studies just discussed are valuable, they suffer from at least three important defects. The first problem is that A in equation 1 is called *ability*. Many different abilities are rewarded in the marketplace. Very few studies have direct measures of more than a few abilities; and the most widely available proxies of family background, such as parental education, would not seem to be good proxies for many abilities. In other words, the variances of v and Z in equations 4 and 5 may be relatively large. Of course, a bias on the schooling coefficient will occur only if v or Z is correlated with schooling, that is, if the equivalent of d is nonzero. It is not possible, however, to know a priori if all necessary dimensions of A have been controlled.

The second problem is one of possible misinterpretation. Many studies have found that parental education and income and other aspects of family background are statistically significant and have large coefficients in equations for earnings, schooling, etc. There is a tendency to argue that these coefficients indicate the causal effect of increased parental education, etc., on a child's ability and earnings. These results are completely consistent with a model in which better educated or wealthier parents provide a better environment for their progeny. The results are also consistent with a model in which family background is a proxy solely for genetic endowments of the child. If the latter model is the correct explanation, then family background variables do not have a causal interpretation even if they are adequate proxies to control for ability.[3]

The third problem arises if schooling is measured with error. It is well known that random measurement error in an independent variable will bias the coefficient toward zero. Griliches (1978) shows that the magnitude of the measurement error bias per se increases when measures of A are included in the equation because the size of the bias depends on the ratio of the variances of measurement error to the variance in schooling after partialing out the ability variable.

Controlling A through Twins

In this chapter I will use a different approach to control for ability differences. Under certain conditions examined below, it is possible to use data on iden-

3. For a very interesting study on this issue, see Scarr and Weinberg (1977).

tical twins to obtain unbiased estimates of β (in equation 1). A more complicated technique that uses data on both identical and fraternal twins can also be used to obtain unbiased estimates and to test some important assumptions that underlie the similar method.

To understand the argument, a short biological detour is necessary. Genes are located on chromosomes. Each gene at a particular location has two members, one of which is contributed by each parent. The two members can be the same or different, for example, AA or AB. It is known that some genes come in a variety of forms. Each egg and each sperm contain one member, randomly determined, of each gene. When the egg is fertilized by the sperm, the two members combine to form the child's gene. Assume that many genes have small influences on a particular skill. While sibs will receive the same member of one gene from each parent one-fourth of the time, the probability that they will receive the same member from each parent on each gene approaches zero rapidly. In other words, since each egg and each sperm is different, children of the same parents are in general not genetically alike.

There are two twin types, identical (MZ) and fraternal (DZ). Fraternal twins occur when two eggs happen to be released in the same month and each is fertilized by a separate sperm. Fraternal twins are just siblings born at the same time and are not genetically the same.

Identical twins occur when an already fertilized egg happens to split. Both halves of the split egg are genetically alike unless a mutation occurs. Indeed, the definitive way to determine that a twin pair is identical is to demonstrate that they are biochemically alike on a large enough set of factors such as blood type that are solely determined by a person's genetic makeup.

Earlier I noted that genes can come in a variety of combinations. Suppose that I am talking about a particular ability, A_1. For each gene combination that affects A_1 there is associated a particular level of ability that is called the *genotype* (G). A_1 will also be affected by a person's environment, N. G and N combine to produce A_1. The form of the production function is unknown. For the moment, assume that the production function is linear. Since G and N are unobserved, I can express each in units such that

$$A_1 = G_1 + N_1 \tag{6}$$

where I have put subscripts on G on N to indicate that they are the genotype and environment for the first ability.

Classical geneticists generally define or measure G at the mean of all possible environments. From the viewpoint of an economist, it is preferable to assume that parents and their offspring in part choose their environment, and that these choices are conditional on each person's genetic endowments. If this viewpoint is accepted, the G term in equation 6 will be defined to include this impact on environment while the N term will be net of this effect. This difference in definition and interpretation is important in this chapter at only a few points, appropriately noted.

Equation 6 applies to one type of ability. Equivalent equations perhaps with different G and N apply to all abilities. These various abilities can be combined into an overall ability variable that is related to an overall genotype and environment variable as

$$A = G + N \tag{6a}$$

Previously I argued that G would be the same for identical twins in a family but different for fraternal twins in a family. Both types of twins, however, share some environment because they are nurtured in the same womb and generally are raised by the same parents in the same neighborhood till they are at least sixteen years old.[4]

Economists generally think of the environment as investments in human capital though some people may think that such a term is not a felicitous relabeling when applied to love, affection, and time spent by parents with their children. A standard investment in a human capital model for the person f in family k would be 7.[5]

$$I_{jk} = aP_{jk} + cr_{jk} + eY_{jk} + mG_{jk} + nT_{jk} + w_{jk} \tag{7}$$

where I is investment, P is the market price of investment, r is the interest rate on borrowed funds, Y is family income, T is family tastes, and w is a random variable.

The same equation could be written for person j's twin. Then I_{1k} and I_{2k} will be correlated because the variables on the right-hand side of 7 will also be correlated for twins. Indeed, it seems likely, if the investments that influence ability and whose omission biases the estimate of β are undertaken during childhood, that P, r, and Y will be the same for both twins reared together in family k. Within family k, G and T will also be correlated while w will not be correlated. Again I remind the reader that the unobserved N in equation 6 or 6a equals $I_{jk} - mG_{jk}$.

I can, of course, easily measure the one dimension of environment called *years of schooling*. Once I separate out schooling from other unobserved environments, formally I should relabel the G and N in equation 6; however, to simplify notation I will not do so. My model can be stated as equations 1, 6a, and 7.

4. Some twins are separated. For an excellent example of research with this type of sample, see Shields (1962), who also summarizes other studies.

5. The model can be modified to include parental love, affection, and time. In the following discussion they can be considered as part of the T variable.

Randomly order pairs within a family, and denote within-pair differences by Δ. ΔY_k, for example, is $Y_{1k} - Y_{2k}$. Then after substituting 6a into 1, I can write

$$\Delta Y_k = \beta \Delta S_k + \gamma(\Delta G_k + \Delta N_k) + \Delta u \tag{8}$$

For identical twins, ΔG_k is always zero, and from 7 N_k reduces to $(n\Delta T_k + \Delta w_k)$. Ordinary least squares applied to 8 will yield an unbiased estimate of β, provided that (1) ΔS_k is not correlated with $(n\Delta T_k + \Delta w_k)$; (2) S is measured without error; and (3) ΔS_k is not zero for some k.

I will consider the importance of these three provisos in a moment. First, however, I wish to note that if I apply equation 8 to fraternal twins, the ΔG_k terms are not in general equal to zero. Thus ΔG_k is an omitted variable that can cause a bias. Griliches (1978) elegantly demonstrates that under certain conditions the within-pair regressions for fraternal twins may yield a more biased estimate than that obtained from equation 1.

Now let us return to the three provisos. In my sample about one-half of the identical twin pairs do not report the same years of schooling, though most of the discordant pairs differ only by a year or two. As will become evident, this is a large enough sample to estimate the equation.

Measurement error in schooling is a more important problem. Measurement error causes a much greater bias in within-pair equations than in corresponding equations using data on individuals.[6] Thus far I have not been able to determine exactly the measurement error in schooling in my sample. A variety of sources allows me to guess at the magnitude. For example, I have estimates of parents' education from both twins. In any event, I can calculate the extent of the bias for any assumed variance in measurement error.

The third proviso was that ΔS was uncorrelated with ΔN. The major reason for this correlation to be nonzero is that parents consciously allocate more of many types of resources to one or the other of the siblings. That is, parents may like one of the twins more than the other and invest more in him than in his twin. Alternatively, one twin may be thought to be able to make more out of the investments because he is more industrious or has not suffered a debilitating accident.

It is possible to test the proposition that for identical twins ΔS is not correlated with ΔA.[7] Suppose that parents wish to provide more investments of all

---

6. Let true schooling be s and measured schooling be S. The measurement error is v. That is, $S = s + v$. The true equation is $Y = \beta s + u_2$ but using ordinary least squares our estimate of β will be $\Sigma SY/\Sigma S^2$, whose expected value is $\beta/(1 + \sigma_v^2/\sigma_s^2)$. The corresponding estimate from within-pair equations reduces to $\beta/(1 + \sigma_v^2(1 - \rho_w)/\sigma_s^2(1 - \rho_s))$ where ρ is the cross-twin correlation coefficient. For example, $\rho = \sigma s_1 s_2/\sigma s_1 s_2$. We would expect ρ_w to be zero and ρ_s to be positive and large. As long as $\rho_w < \rho_s$, the measurement error bias from the within-pair estimate will be greater than that obtained from individuals.

7. The following tests are taken from Behrman, Hrubec, Taubman, and Wales (1980).

types of human capital to one sib in an MZ twin pair. Then the value of the unobserved ability variable in equation 1 will be higher for this child. If I order the children within a pair by schooling level, the genetically identical child with more schooling would also have more unobserved investments and ability. Thus the within-pair equations ordered by schooling should have a positive constant term.

The second test is much more complicated. It requires setting up a recursive model whose dependent variables are schooling, initial and mature occupational status, and mature earnings. By imposing a number of restrictions on this model, it is possible to test if differences in the noncommon environment that affect differences in earnings directly are correlated with differences in schooling. It is in this model that we make use of the alternative definition of genotype referred to earlier.

There is an additional reason why MZ within-pair equations may not yield unbiased estimates of β. Equation 8 is a combination of equations 1 and 6 or 6a. Equation 6 is a linear production function. It is possible that a nonlinear specification such as

$$Y = G + N + (NG)^\beta \qquad (6b)$$

is more appropriate. If 6b is correct, MZ within-pair equations would contain $(G\Delta N)^\beta$ terms that are not zero. Jinks and Fulker (1970) developed a test of the null hypothesis that 6a is valid. The essence of the test is that if 6b is valid then the variance of MZ within-pair differences in earnings will include $(G\Delta N)^{2\theta}$ terms whose magnitude will vary with G. In other words, the error in the earnings equation will not be homoskedastic. The average earnings of a pair is an imperfect measure of the pairs G. A regression of the MZ absolute differences in Y or the square root of the $(\Delta Y_k)^2$ on $\bar{Y}_k$ is a test for heteroskedasticity. For earnings I find substantial heteroskedasticity but for the ln of earnings, I find homoskedasticity. Thus in our empirical work I will use the ln of earnings.

The Sample

The twin sample I use is described in detail in Behrman et al. (1980) and in Taubman (1976). Briefly, in 1955 the National Academy of Science-National Research Council (NAS-NRC) started a project to construct a twin panel as a resource in studying a variety of questions. The NAS-NRC initially collected birth certificates on nearly all white male twins born between 1917–1927. The twin panel consists of those pairs both of whose members are veterans. My sample consists of those pairs in the panel who answered a 1974 survey. Even this brief description should indicate that the sample need not be a random draw from the population of twins. In addition there are a variety of reasons why twins need not be a random draw of the total population. For example, twins are not reared in a single-sib household.

Compared to white males of the same age cohort or to the veteran sub-sample, the respondents in our sample have above-average earnings. However, my earnings equations yield very similar coefficients to those obtained from random samples of the population drawn in the same time period. I am working on the issue of how generalizable my results are to the population of white males. In the meantime I can only hope that they apply to the larger group.

The sample consists of roughly 1,000 pairs of identical twins and 900 pairs of fraternal twins. For those pairs where both served in the Navy as enlisted men, the person's score on the General Classification Test is also available.

For both the within-pair analysis and the analysis of variance to be described below, it is necessary to distinguish identical and fraternal twin types. In principle this can be accomplished by using a large enough battery of biochemical tests since a pair of identical twins must have the same blood type, RH factor, etc. on all such tests. Such tests have been done for a minority of the pairs. For the most part, however, the twins have been classified on the basis of their answers to the following question: "In childhood were you as alike as peas in a pod or only of ordinary family resemblance?" This may seem like a very delicate item on which to base our analysis, but Jablon et al. (1967) have shown that for this sample, peas in a pod are 95 percent as accurate as biochemical tests. I might add that I was brought up on canned peas, and I do not know how alike peas in a pod are. Indeed I have been told that there is a minor crisis in twin research since many more children and younger adults are as gastronomi-cally deprived as I was and currently respond incorrectly to this question.

The Effect of Schooling on Earnings

In a large number of studies in economics, the semilog specification given in equation 1, amended to include years of work experience, has been used. Table 1 contains a summary of some sample regression results calculated across individuals and within pairs for 1973 earnings, when the men were about 50 years old. When as in line 1 I treat all the individuals in the sample as unrelated individuals, and when I control for no other variables, the coefficient on years of schooling is a highly significant .080, which is unchanged when age is added. This equation's estimated coefficients on years of schooling are similar to those obtained from nationwide random samples collected in 1960 or later (see for example Lillard and Willis 1978 or Jencks et al. 1972). From line 2 we see that holding constant a whole host of observed family background variables and marital status reduces the coefficient by about 12 percent. For those pairs where both were in the Navy, I have data on the General Classifi-

Table 1 Coefficient on Years of Schooling in Equation for ln of 1973 Earnings

Equation Based on		Number of Observations	Coefficient on Yrs./Schooling	t Statistic on Coefficient	Other Variables Held Constant
1.	Individuals	3870	.080	32.4	none
2.	Individuals	3870	.069	25.8	A, B
3.	Navy pairs	404	.051	6.0	A, B, C
4.	Within DZ pairs	914	.059	8.3	B
5.	Within MZ pairs	1022	.026	3.5	B

Other variables held constant, A is: age, number of sibs alive 1940, father's years of schooling, mother's years of schooling, father's occupational status (Duncan score); and the following variables coded as (0,1 dummies) raised in rural area, raised as a Catholic, raised as a Jew, born in the South.
B: married in 1974.
C: score on Navy General Classification Test.

cation Test, which is primarily a vocabulary test and a measure of cognitive skills. Controlling for this test and for the variables in the previous line, and estimating the equation across pair averages reduces the education coefficient to .051, a reduction from line 1 of about 35 percent and from line 2 of about 25 percent.[8]

In line 4 the estimated coefficient from the within-DZ-pair equation is a highly significant .059. This is about 25 percent less than the estimate in line 1 and intermediate between line 2, in which background is controlled, and line 3, in which background plus IQ are controlled. Line 5 presents the within-MZ-pairs results. Here the coefficient on schooling plummets to (a still statistically significant) .026, which is one-third of the estimate in line 1 and one-half of the estimate in line 3. Unfortunately this .026 is almost surely biased toward zero by measurement error.

As shown in note 6, the magnitude of the bias arising from measurement error depends on three elements: the ratio of the variance of the measurement error to the variance of true schooling (σ_w^2/σ_s^2); the cross-twin correlation in true schooling (ρ_s), and the cross-twin correlation in measurement error (ρ_w). If I assume that ρ_w is zero, then I can calculate the measurement error bias for any assumed value of σ_w^2/σ_s^2. If this ratio of the variance is about 20 percent then both the MZ within-pair and the individual equations would yield an unbiased estimate of b of about .09. If, however, this ratio is 10 percent, the corrected estimate from the within-pair and individual equations is about .044 and .088, respectively.

8. The Navy only has test scores for the enlisted men. To correct for selectivity bias a dummy variable with a one for officer was included.

The one piece of evidence on the size of the measurement error in education in this sample comes from the twins' reports on their parents' education. From these independent reports, I can calculate the average σ_w^2/σ_s^2 of the parents' education to be slightly less than 10 percent. It seems likely that each twin knows his own education more accurately than his parents' education. Thus 10 percent seems a likely upper bound.

As noted above, for this magnitude of measurement error, the .026 figure should be adjusted to about .045. While .045 is nearly 100 percent greater than the estimate in line 5, it is also about 50 percent of .088, the line 1 estimate adjusted for the same degree of measurement error. Thus in studying the effects of schooling on earnings in this sample, it is crucial to control for genetic endowments and family endowment. It also appears that measures of cognitive skill and certain aspects of family background provide fairly adequate controls in that the estimate in line 3 is .05, which is quite close to .044. However, the estimate of .05 in line 3 would also be biased toward zero by measurement error. Thus there must be other abilities omitted from equation 3, with the biases from these omitted variables and measurement error approximately offsetting one another.

Based on these results, it appears that identical twins provide the best controls for studying the returns to education. However, a good measure of cognitive skills and a battery of background variables do nearly as well. Since it is probably easier and cheaper to design and collect random samples of individuals than samples of twins with the latter data, this is not a trivial conclusion.

Inequality of Opportunity

While identical twins can be used to control for unmeasured ability, by far the most common use of twin samples has been in nature-nurture studies. Using equation 6a, I can express the observed variance in earnings in terms of the unobserved G and N variables as:

$$\sigma_Y^2 = \sigma_G^2 + \sigma_N^2 + 2\sigma_{GN} \tag{9}$$

Dividing through by σ_Y^2, I have

$$1 = \frac{\sigma_G^2}{\sigma_Y^2} + \frac{\sigma_N^2}{\sigma_Y^2} + 2\frac{\sigma_{GN}}{\sigma_Y^2} \tag{9a}$$

If σ_{GN} is zero, the first term on the right-hand side of 9a is the contribution of nature to the variance in Y while the second term is the contribution of nurture. If σ_{GN} is not zero, there is no nonarbitrary definition of the contribution of nature and of nurture.

As the reader may be aware, there has been an extensive and at times bitter debate in the literature on IQ over the nature-nurture question. This debate has focused both on the statistical question of the properties of the estimates of σ_G^2/σ_Y^2 etc. and on the interpretation or implication of the results. It is the implication question that is, I believe, the basis of the bitterness. Rather than trying to summarize the huge literature on the subject, let me give an interpretation.

An analogy may put this question into perspective. It is known that hemophilia is caused by a genetic defect that prevents the blood from clotting. Several years back a drug was developed that will allow clotting to occur. Thus this genetic disease is curable by a change in the environment. But when this drug was introduced it was very expensive—as I recall, something like $20,000 per year per person. Few families now can afford such an expenditure. Society, of course, can choose to pick up the bill. However, the taxes raised to pay for the drug will distort incentives in the economy and may cause individuals to work and save less. The changes will lower the value of goods and services produced now and in the future. This reduction is called *economic inefficiency.*

Of course some genetic defects can be overcome at a much lower cost. For example, some eye diseases may be genetic in origin and the cure may consist of a pair of eyeglasses. In general, in deciding on the undertaking and scope of various policies, society compares the benefits and the costs. Economic inefficiency is one of the relevant costs.

It is, of course, possible to redistribute income or earnings through transfer schemes or wage subsidies. Many people argue, however, that meaningful redistribution involves too great a loss in economic efficiency. This inefficiency occurs for two reasons. The first is that taxes must be raised to pay for this redistribution and, as argued above, such taxes distort labor-leisure and consumption-saving choices. The second reason for inefficiency is that most transfer schemes provide incentives for people to avoid work. If, however, inequality in earnings arises because of inequality of opportunity (defined rigorously below), then it is possible to redistribute earnings while increasing economic efficiency. On precisely these grounds, Okun (1975) voices the hope that inequality of opportunity is a major source of inequality of earnings. Inequality of opportunity, as used by Okun and by most other economists, means that some people are not able to invest in skill acquisition as much as others because of differences in prices and income or perhaps because of discrimination.

The N in equation 6a can be split into common and specific environments. Twins share some common environment, which differs across families. The difference across families is, I believe, most due to differences in family income and preferences. The contribution of common environment can be used to estimate the importance of inequality of opportunity.

The model that I use to obtain my estimate is given in table 2. Technically I

Table 2 Basic Model with $\ell^* = \ell' = 1.0$, $\lambda \neq 1/2$ (24 parameters)

	G_1	N_1	G_2	G_3	G_4	u_1	u_2	u_3	u_4	S	OC_i	OC_{67}
Reduced form equations												
S	1.85 (15.9)	1.98 (17.5)				1						
OC_i	.68 (5.5)	1.16 (11.7)	1.16 (18.5)			.21 (6.0)	1					
OC_{67}	.69 (6.3)	.78 (8.4)	.37 (5.1)	.82 (13.8)		.29 (8.9)	.14 (5.4)	1				
lnY_{73}	.17 (5.9)	.19 (7.7)	.098 (6.0)	.019 (.8)	.31 (26.2)	.026 (3.4)	.0044 (3.5)	.031 (4.7)	1			
Structural equations												
S	1.85 (15.9)	1.98 (17.5)				1						
OC_i	.30 (1.9)	.75 (5.7)	1.16 (18.5)				1			.21 (6.0)		
OC_{67}	.113 (.1)	.090 (1.0)	.20 (2.3)	.82 (13.8)				1		.26 (7.9)	.14 (5.4)	
lnY_{73}	.12 (3.3)	.13 (5.2)	.087 (5.2)	-.0068 (.3)	.31 (26.2)				1	.016 (2.3)		.031 (4.7)

Other estimates

$\lambda = $ .34 (6.1)

$\sigma_{u_1}^2 = $ 2.17 (22.6)

$\sigma_{u_2}^2 = $ 2.75 (24.4)

$$\sigma_{u_3}^2 = \begin{array}{c} 2.45 \\ (25.1) \end{array}$$

$$\sigma_{u_4}^2 = \begin{array}{c} .127 \\ (23.1) \end{array}$$

Normalizations and restrictions

A,B,C,D,E,F

Functional value: $+ 13431.87$

Restrictions and Normalizations

A is $\sigma_{G_1}^2 = \sigma_{G_2}^2 = \sigma_{G_3}^2 = \sigma_{G_4}^2 = \sigma_N^2 = 1$

B is $\sigma_{N_2}^2 = \sigma_{N_3}^2 = \sigma_{N_4}^2 = 0$

C is $\sigma_{N_1 G_1} = 0$

D is $\sigma_{N_1 G_i} = 0, i = 2,4$

E is $\sigma_{N_i N_j} = \sigma_{G_i G_j} = 0, i = 1 \ldots 4, j = 1 \ldots 4$

F is $\varrho' = \varrho^* = 1$

G is $\lambda_1 = 1/2, i = 1 \ldots 4$

The figures in parentheses underneath the point estimates are absolute values of ratios of parameter estimates to estimated asymptotic standard errors.
S is years of schooling.
OC_i is initial full time civilian occupational status, Duncan scale.
OC_{67} is occupational status in 1967, Duncan scale.
$\ln Y_{73}$ is the logarithm of 1973 earnings.
The actual likelihood function values are given by a functional value noted in the table, aside from a constant.

Table 3   Scores of Variances of Schooling,
Initial and Later Occupational Status, and Earnings, Basic Model

Percent of Total Arising from	S	OC_i	OC_{67}	$\ln Y_{73}$
$\sigma^2_{G_1}$	36%	08%	11%	10%
$\sigma^2_{G_2}$		23	03	03
$\sigma^2_{G_3}$			15	a
$\sigma^2_{G_4}$				32
$\sum \sigma^2_{G_i}$	36	31	29	45
$\sigma^2_{N_1}$	41	22	13	12
$\sigma^2_{u_1}$	23	02	04	01
$\sigma^2_{u_2}$		46	01	a
$\sigma^2_{u_3}$			53	01
$\sigma^2_{u_4}$				42

Source: Table 1.
Totals may not add to 100 percent because of rounding.
[a] Implies less than 0.5 percent.

am using a latent-variance, variance-components model.[9] The key assumption that I make to partition the variance is that the expected value of the cross-twin correlation in environment is the same for identical and fraternal twins. If this assumption is not made, it is possible to estimate the contribution of G to be zero.[10] However, the major reason advanced for this correlation to be greater for the identical twins is that parents and the twins base choices on each child's genetic endowments. Since I define this to be an effect of genetic endowments, this is not a compelling criticism when I estimate the importance of inequality of opportunity.

Table 3 presents the total (the sum of direct and indirect) contributions of the various genetic and environmental variables to each of the four dependent variables. As shown in the table, common environment accounts for 12 percent and 41 percent of the variance of the ln of 1973 earnings and of schooling, respectively. Presumably, parents have much greater impact over schooling decisions of their offspring than over many postschooling decisions. However,

9. For a complete description, see Behrman et al. (1980), chapter 5.
10. See Behrman et al. (1980).

since schooling has only a small contribution to the variance of earnings, the relative size of these two findings is not surprising.

The contribution of across-family inequality of opportunity to the variance in earnings of any other variable is given by the common environment term. The results in table 3 suggest that inequality of opportunity has a substantial impact—44 percent—on the variance of schooling, one type of investment in human capital, but only a very modest impact—12 percent—on the variance in earnings. The results taken at face value would indicate that even if it had been possible to eliminate all the variances in family environment when this cohort was being reared, the inequality in earnings would not have been reduced greatly. There are, however, a variety of qualifications and modifications that must be considered.

These estimates come from a model in which it is assumed that genotype and environment are uncorrelated. In my model common environment or investment in human capital depends on family income. Thus it may appear that this assumption is not tenable in a model that examines earnings. Of course family income need not be the same as the parents' earnings genotype, because in this sample many mothers would not have worked after the twins were born, because of inherited wealth, and because parents' earnings would depend on their environments. Still I would expect the child's genotype and environment to be correlated. In my model this correlation is identified in the statistical sense, but I have never been able to get estimates that converge. The way the model is structured, any nonzero covariance will cause a change only in the estimate of common environment. The greater is the genotype, environment covariance, the smaller would be my estimate of common environment. Thus by assuming this correlation is zero, I am attributing to environment all the effect of the genotype-common environment correlation. It could be argued that the impact of the correlation should be shared between genetic endowments and common environment, and that on these grounds I am overstating the contribution of common environment.

Measurement error usually refers to wrong numbers being written down. Transitory income refers to correct numbers for annual earnings being recorded but annual earnings deviating from the proper concept of normal, permanent, or lifetime earnings. Thus transitory income can be thought of as another type of measurement error.

Using the Michigan Panel of Income Dynamics, Lillard and Willis (1978) estimate that for white males, permanent income constitutes about 80 percent of the variance in annual earnings. Their remainder would include both transitory effects and measurement error. Several considerations suggest that the permanent component of the variation in income may be about 90 percent of the total.[11] Adjusting for measurement error and transitory income, common environment would account for about 15 percent instead of 12 percent of the variance in earnings.[12]

A different sort of concern involves discrimination. Because of discrimination, some people would be denied access to certain positions or training programs and/or receive a wage less than their marginal product. Thus discrimination would appear to meet my definition of inequality of opportunity, though discrimination may be directed at groups with different genotypes. My sample contains only white males. Even within this group, there may have been discrimination against, say, Catholics and Jews. If such discrimination does not change the cross-twin correlation coefficients because, for example, earnings of all affected pairs are changed equally, my estimate of common environment would include some of the effects of discrimination. Still it may be true that for this reason my estimate is too small for the whole labor force.

In this section I provide an estimate of the contribution of inequality of opportunity, defined as the variation in common environment, to the variance in earnings. I estimate inequality of opportunity to account for less than 20 percent of the variance in outcomes, but that who one's parents are accounts for about 60 percent of the variance in outcomes. These estimates are based on one sample that is not a random drawing of the population and that covers only one part of the life cycle. Still, if these findings are confirmed in other studies, the implication is clear. Those who wish to reduce greatly the degree of inequality will have to use compensatory training and transfer programs. With these policies the trade-off between efficiency and equality will have to be faced.

Conclusions

For the past several decades much of the research in the social sciences on the sources of individual differences in schooling, earnings, and many other variables has been based on models in which differences in the environment play the major role. Many people have estimated models in which observed portions of the environment such as schooling are entered as explanatory variables. Often the presumption is that the estimated coefficients on these environmental variables indicate the source or cause of the difference in earnings or IQ. The results obtained from the within-pair equations for identical twins suggest that

11. Their 80 percent figure should be a lower bound for my sample for two reasons. First, their sample includes young people, whose earnings grow most rapidly and irregularly, while my sample includes only men about age 50. The rapid growth of the young counts as transitory income in their methodology. Second, I would expect that transitory income of brothers would be correlated because of choices of similar occupations, on-the-job training, etc.

12. If the permanent component is 20 percent, the estimate for common environment would rise to 17 percent.

this environmental interpretation is overstated. That is, for men aged about 50, I find that 50 percent or more of the coefficient on schooling obtained in an equation estimated for individuals is actually attributable to statistically uncontrolled differences in ability. Since the bias is much smaller when I use within-pair equations for fraternal twins, it is genetic endowments that underlie the differences in this ability. The results from the Navy subsample indicate that the ability that should be controlled in earnings equations includes cognitive skills but there are other dimensions of ability that are correlated with religion and other aspects of family background. (See notes to table 1.)

Many studies have found that measures of family background such as parental education are significant in equations for schooling, earnings, etc. Some people interpret these results as indicating that changes in education will have important intergenerational consequences. My results on the partitioning of the variance of earnings into genetic, common, and noncommon environment components suggest that much more of the observed differences in outcome attributed to parents occur because of genetic inheritance than because of differences in family income or environment. While this statement is consistent with the proposition that a change in average family income of $1 will have a large or small effect on average children's earnings, it suggests that the above intergenerational conclusion may be incorrect.

The conclusion that differences in family income (or common environment) have only a modest impact on the inequality of earnings has another important implication. Suppose that individual's access to capital markets and investments in human capital are limited because of family wealth. Society could eliminate or reduce the importance of family wealth by following a policy of guaranteeing loans or by giving subsidies. The return to society of the elimination of market imperfections can be greater than the social cost of making these loans. Thus elimination of inequality of opportunity can lead to increases in equity and economic efficiency. All other income redistribution mechanisms gain increased equity by sacrificing efficiency. The results from the NAS-NRC twin sample suggest that inequality of opportunity is not a major explanation of inequality of earnings. Society, of course, can still redistribute income to overcome differences in innate ability. The costs of this redistribution will be higher than if inequality of opportunity were important.

References

Acharya, Meena. 1981. *Time-Use Data from Nepalese Villages: Policy Implications.* Washington, D.C.: World Bank. Mimeo.

Adams, James D. 1980. Personal wealth transfers. *Quarterly Journal of Economics* 95, no. 1 (August): 159–79.

Akerlof, George A. 1970. The market for "lemons": Quality uncertainty and the market mechanism. *Quarterly Journal of Economics* 84, no. 3 (August): 488–500.

Alchian, Armen A., and Harold Demsetz. 1972. Production, information costs, and economic organization. *American Economic Review* 62, no. 5 (December): 777–95.

Altonji, Joseph G., and Thomas A. Dunn. 1991. Relationships among the family incomes and labor market outcomes of relatives. In *Research in Labor Economics.* Vol. 12, edited by Ronald G. Ehrenberg, pp. 269–310. Greenwich, Conn., and London: JAI Press.

Alvin, Duane F., and Arland Thornton. 1984. Family origins and the schooling process: Early versus late influence of parental characteristics. *American Sociological Review* 49, no. 6 (December): 784–802.

Anderson, Michael. 1971. *Family Structure in Nineteenth Century Lancashire.* London: Cambridge University Press.

Arrow, Kenneth J. 1963. Uncertainty and the welfare economics of medical care. *American Economic Review* 53, no. 5 (December): 941–73.

———. 1971. A utilitarian approach to the concept of equality in public expenditures. *Quarterly Journal of Economics* 85, no. 3 (August): 409–15.

Arrow, Kenneth J., and Frank H. Hahn. 1971. *General Competitive Analysis.* San Francisco: Holden-Day.

Atkinson, A. B. 1979. Intergenerational income mobility. *IHS Journal,* ser. A, no. 3, pp. 61–73.

———. 1981. On intergenerational income mobility in Britain. *Journal of Post Keynesian Economics* 3, no. 2 (Winter): 194–218.

———. 1983. *Social Justice and Public Policy.* Cambridge: MIT Press.

Atkinson, A. B., C. G. Trinder, and A. K. Maynard. 1978. Evidence on intergenerational income mobility in Britain. *Economic Letters,* 1:383–88.

Banfield, Edward C. 1958. *The Moral Basis of a Backward Society.* Glencoe, Ill.: Free Press.

Barechello, R. R. 1979. The schooling of farm youth in Canada. Ph.D. diss., University of Chicago.

Barnum, Howard N., and Lyn Squire. 1979. *A Model of an Agricultural Household: Theory and Evidence*. Baltimore: Johns Hopkins University Press, for the World Bank.

Barro, Robert J. 1974. Are government bonds new wealth? *Journal of Political Economy* 82, no. 6 (November/December): 1095–1117.

Becker, Gary S., 1962. Investments in human capital: A theoretical analysis. *Journal of Political Economy* 70, no. 5, pt. 2 (October): 9–39.

———. 1964. *Human Capital: A Theoretical and Empirical Analysis, with Special Reference to Education*. New York: Columbia University Press, for the National Bureau of Economic Research.

———. 1965. A theory of the allocation of time. *Economic Journal* 75, no. 299 (September): 493–517.

———. 1967. Human capital and the personal distribution of income: An analytical approach. Woytinsky Lecture. Ann Arbor: University of Michigan. (Reprinted in Becker 1975, pp. 94–117.)

———. 1973. A theory of marriage: Part I. *Journal of Political Economy* 81, no. 4 (July/August): 813–46.

———. 1974*a*. A theory of marriage: Part II. *Journal of Political Economy* 82, no. 2 (March/April): S11–S26.

———. 1974*b*. A theory of social interactions. *Journal of Political Economy* 82, no. 6 (November/December): 1063–93.

———. 1975. *Human Capital: A Theoretical and Empirical Analysis, with Special Reference to Education*. 2d ed. New York: Columbia University Press for the National Bureau of Economic Research.

———. 1976. Altruism, egoism, and genetic fitness. *Journal of Economic Literature* 14, no. 3 (September): 817–26.

———. 1981. *A Treatise on the Family*. Cambridge, Mass.: Harvard University Press. (Enlarged ed., 1991).

———. 1983. Unpublished summary of intergenerational estimates of wealth, income and earnings associations. Chicago: University of Chicago.

Becker, Gary S., Elizabeth Landes, and Robert T. Michael. 1977. An economic analysis of marital instability. *Journal of Political Economy* 85, no. 6 (December): 1141–87.

Becker, Gary S., and H. Gregg Lewis. 1973. Interaction between the quantity and quality of children. *Journal of Political Economy* 81, no. 2, pt. 2 (March/April): S279–S288.

Becker, Gary S., and Kevin M. Murphy. 1988. The family and the state. *Journal of Law and Economics* 31, no. 1 (April): 1–17.

Becker, Gary S., and Nigel Tomes. 1976. Child endowments and the quantity and quality of children. *Journal of Political Economy* 84, no. 4, pt. 2 (August): S143–S162.

———. 1979. An equilibrium theory of the distribution of incomes and intergenerational mobility. *Journal of Political Economy* 87, no. 6 (December): 1153–89.

———. 1986. Human capital and the rise and fall of families. *Journal of Labor Economics* 4, no. 3, pt. 2 (July): S1–S39.

Becketti, Sean, William Gould, Lee Lillard, and Finis Welch. 1988. The Panel Study of

Income Dynamics after fourteen years: An evaluation. *Journal of Labor Economics* 6, no. 4 (October): 472–92.

Behrman, Jere R. 1987a. Is child schooling a poor proxy for child quality? *Demography* 24, no. 3 (August): 341–59. (Reprinted as Chapter 8, in this volume.)

———. 1987b. Schooling and other human capital investments: Can the effects be identified? *Economics of Education Review* 6, no. 3: 301–5. (Reprinted as Chapter 9, in this volume.)

———. 1988*a*. Intrahousehold allocation of nutrients in rural India: Are boys favored? Do parents exhibit inequality aversion? *Oxford Economic Papers* 40, no. 1 (March): 32–54.

———. 1988*b*. Nutrition, health, birth order, and seasonality: Intrahousehold allocation in rural India. *Journal of Development Economics* 28, no. 7 (February): 43–63.

———. 1995. Intrafamily distribution and the family. In *Handbook of Population and Family Economics,* edited by Mark R. Rosenzweig and Oded Stark. Amsterdam: North-Holland Publishing Co.

Behrman, Jere R., and Nancy Birdsall. 1986. Imperfect assortative mating, unobserved human capital, and earnings determinants for Brazilian males. Philadelphia: University of Pennsylvania. Mimeo.

Behrman, Jere R., Z. Hrubec, Paul Taubman, and Terence J. Wales. 1980. *Socioeconomic Success: A Study of the Effects of Genetic Endowments, Family Environment and Schooling.* Amsterdam: North-Holland Publishing Co.

Behrman, Jere R., Robert A. Pollak, and Paul Taubman. 1982. Parental preferences and provision for progeny. *Journal of Political Economy* 90, no. 1 (February): 52–73. (Reprinted as Chapter 1, in this volume.)

———. 1984. Parental age and investments in children's human capital. Philadelphia: University of Pennsylvania. Mimeo.

———. 1986. Do parents favor boys?" *International Economic Review* 27, no. 1 (February): 33–54. (Reprinted as Chapter 3, in this volume.)

———. 1988. Compensating gifts and siblings' earnings and income. Philadelphia: University of Pennsylvania. Mimeo.

———. 1989. Family resources, family size, and access to financing for college education. *Journal of Political Economy* 97, no. 2 (April): 398–419. (reprinted as Chapter 2, in this volume.)

———. 1994. The wealth model: Efficiency in education and distribution in the family. (Chapter 5, in this volume.)

Behrman, Jere R., Mark R. Rosenzweig, and Paul Taubman. 1994. Endowments and the allocation of schooling in the family and in the marriage market. *Journal of Political Economy* 102, no. 6 (December): 1131–1174.

Behrman, Jere R., and Paul Taubman. 1985. Intergenerational earnings mobility in the U.S.: Some estimates and a test of Becker's intergenerational endowments model. *Review of Economics and Statistics* 67, no. 1 (February): 144–51. (Reprinted as Chapter 10, in this volume.)

———. 1986. Birth order, schooling, and earnings. *Journal of Labor Economics* 4, no. 3 (July): S121–S145. (Reprinted as Chapter 4, in this volume.)

———. 1989. "Is schooling "mostly in the genes"? Nature-nurture decomposition with data on relatives. *Journal of Political Economy* 97, no. 6 (December): 1425–46. (Reprinted as Chapter 13, in this volume.)

———. 1990. Intergenerational correlation between children's adult earnings and their parents' income: Results from the Michigan Panel Survey of Income Dynamics. *Review of Income and Wealth* 36, no. 2 (June): 115–27. (Reprinted as Chapter 11, in this volume.)

Behrman, Jere R., Paul Taubman, and Terence J. Wales. 1977. Controlling for and measuring the effects of genetics and family environment in equations for schooling and labor market success. In Taubman (1977), pp. 35–96.

Behrman, Jere R., and Barbara L. Wolfe. 1984. The socioeconomic impact of schooling in a developing country. *Review of Economics and Statistics* 66, no. 2 (May): 296–303.

———. 1987. Who marries whom—and how it affects the returns to schooling. Philadelphia: University of Pennsylvania. Mimeo.

Benedict, Burton. 1968. Family firms and economic development, *Southwestern Journal of Anthropology* 24, no. 1 (Spring): 1–19.

Ben-Porath, Yoram. 1980. The f-connection: Families, friends, and firms and the organization of exchange. *Population Development Review* 6, no. 1 (March): 1–30.

———. 1982. Economics and the family—match or mismatch? A review of Becker's *A Treatise on the Family. Journal of Economic Literature* 20, no. 1 (March): 52–64.

Bergstrom, Theodore C. 1989. A fresh look at the rotten kid theorem—and other household mysteries. *Journal of Political Economy* 97, no. 5 (October): 1138–59.

Bernanke, Ben. 1985. Adjustment costs, durables, and aggregate consumption. *Journal of Monetary Economics* 15, no. 1 (January): 41–68.

Bernheim, B. Douglas, Andrei Shleifer, and Lawrence H. Summers. 1985. The strategic bequest motive. *Journal of Political Economy* 93, no. 6 (December): 1045–76.

Binswanger, Hans P., and Mark R. Rosenzweig. 1982. Behavioral and material determinants of production relations in agriculture. Washington, D.C.: World Bank. (Revised, October 5, 1983.)

———. 1984. Contractual arrangements, employment and wages in rural labor markets: A critical review. In *Contractual Arrangements, Employment and Wages in Rural Labor Markets in Asia,* edited by Hans P. Binswanger and Mark R. Rosenzweig, pp. 1–40. New Haven, Conn.: Yale University Press.

Birdsall, Nancy. 1979. Siblings and schooling in urban Colombia. Ph.D. diss., Yale University.

———. 1985. Public inputs and child schooling in Brazil. *Journal of Development Economics* 18, no. 1 (May/June): 67–86.

Birdsall, Nancy, and Richard Sabot. 1991. *Labor Market Discrimination in Developing Economies.* Washington, D.C.: World Bank.

Blackstone, Sir William. 1765. *Commentaries on the Laws of England.* Oxford: Clarendon Press.

Blake, Judith. 1981. Family size and the quality of children. *Demography* 18, no. 4 (November): 421–42.

Blau, Peter M. 1964. *Exchange and Power in Social Life.* New York: John Wiley & Sons.

Blinder, Alan S. 1973. A model of inherited wealth. *Quarterly Journal of Economics* 87, no. 4 (November): 608–38.

Boulier, Bryan L., and Mark R. Rosenzweig. 1984. Schooling, search, and spouse selection: Testing the economic theory of marriage and household behavior. *Journal of Political Economy* 92, no. 4 (August): 712–32.

Bourguignon, François, Martin Browning, Pierre-André Chiappori, and Valerie Lechene. 1991. Intrahousehold allocation of consumption: Some evidence on Canadian data. Paris: DELTA. Mimeo.

———. 1993. Intra household allocation of consumption: A model and some evidence from French data. *Annales d'economie et de statistique* 29 (January/March): 137–56.

Bourguignon, François, and Pierre-André Chiappori. 1992. Collective models of household behavior: An introduction. *European Economic Review* 36, nos. 2/3 (April): 355–64.

Bowles, Sam. 1972. Schooling and inequality from generation to generation. *Journal of Political Economy* 80, no. 3 (May/June): S219–S225.

Bradley, Omar N., and Clay Blair. 1983. *A General's Life: An Autobiography.* New York: Simon & Schuster.

Brittain, John A. 1977. *The Inheritance of Economic Status.* Washington, D.C.: Brookings Institution.

———. 1978. *Inheritance and the Inequality of Material Wealth.* Washington, D.C.: Brookings Institution.

Bruce, Neil, and Michael Waldman. 1990. The rotten-kid theorem meets the Samaritan's dilemma. *Quarterly Journal of Economics* 105, no. 1 (February): 155–66.

Castañeda, Tarsicio. 1979. Fertility, child schooling, and labor force participation of mothers in Colombia, 1977. Ph.D. diss., University of Chicago.

Cavalli-Sforza, L. L., and W. Bodmer. 1971. *The Genetics of Human Population.* San Francisco: W. H. Freeman & Co.

Cavalli-Sforza, L. L., and M. W. Feldman. 1981. *Cultural Transmission and Evolution: A Quantitative Approach.* Princeton, N.J.: Princeton University Press.

Cavalli-Sforza, L. L., M. W. Feldman, K. H. Chen, and S. M. Dornsbusch. 1982. Theory and observation in cultural transmission. *Science* 218 (October): 19–27.

Chamberlain, Gary S. 1977a. An instrumental variable interpretation of identification in variance-components and MIMIC models. In Taubman (1977), pp. 235–54.

———. 1977b. Are brothers as good as twins? In Taubman (1977) pp. 287–98.

Chamberlain, Gary S., and Zvi Griliches. 1975. Unobservables with a variance components structure: Ability, schooling and the economic success of brothers. *International Economic Review* 16, no. 2 (June): 422–49.

———. 1977. More on brothers. In Taubman (1977), pp. 97–124.

Chiappori, Pierre-André. 1988. Rational household labour supply. *Econometrica* 56, no. 1 (January): 63–89.

———. 1992. Collective labor supply and welfare. *Journal of Political Economy* 100, no. 3 (June): 437–67.

Chiswick, Barry. 1983. The earnings and human capital of American Jews. *Journal of Human Resources* 18, no. 3 (Summer): 313–36.

Chiswick, Barry, and Donald Cox. 1987. *Inter Vivos* transfers and human capital investments. St. Louis: Washington University. Mimeo.

Christensen, Laurits R., Dale W. Jorgenson, and Lawrence J. Lau. 1975. Transcendental logarithmic utility functions. *American Economic Review* 65, no. 3 (June): 367–83.

Clemhout, Simone, and Henry Y. Wan, Jr. 1977. Symmetric marriage, household decision making and impact on fertility. Working Paper no. 152. Ithaca, N.Y.: Cornell University.

Coase, Ronald H. 1937. The nature of the firm. *Economica,* n.s., 4, no. 16 (November): 386–405.

Colclough, Christopher. 1982. The impact of primary schooling on economic development. *World Development* 10, no. 3 (March): 167–85.

Conlisk, John. 1974. Can equalization of opportunity reduce social mobility? *American Economic Review* 64, no. 1 (March): 80–90.

———. 1984. Four invalid propositions about equality, efficiency, and intergenerational transfers through schooling. *Journal of Human Resources* 19, no. 1 (Winter): 3–21.

Corcoran, Mary, and Linda Datcher. 1981. Intergenerational status transmission and the process of individual attainment. In *Five Thousand American Families: Patterns of Economic Progress.* Vol. 9, edited by M. S. Hill, Daniel H. Hill, and James N. Morgan, pp. 169–206. Ann Arbor: University of Michigan, Institute for Social Research.

Cocoran, Mary, Christopher Jencks, and Michael Olneck. 1978. The effects of family background on earnings. *American Economic Review* 66, no. 2 (May): 430–35.

Coulson, N. J. 1964. *A History of Islamic Law.* Edinburgh: Edinburgh University Press.

Cox, Donald. 1987. Motives for private income transfers. *Journal of Political Economy* 95, no. 3 (June): 508–46.

Cox, Donald, and Fredric Raines. 1985. Interfamily transfers and income redistribution. In *Horizontal Equity, Uncertainty, and Measures of Economic Well-Being.* Studies in Income and Wealth, vol. 50, edited by Martin David and Timothy Smeeding, pp. 393–425. Chicago: University of Chicago Press.

Cox, Donald, and Mark R. Rank. 1992. Inter-vivos transfers and intergenerational exchange. *Review of Economics and Statistics* 74, no. 2 (May): 305–14.

Datcher, Linda. 1982. Effects of community and family background on achievement. *Review of Economics and Statistics* 64, no. 1 (February): 32–41.

Davis, Peter. 1983. Realizing the potential of the family business. *Organizational Dynamics* (Summer): 47–56.

Dawkins, Richard. 1976. *The Selfish Gene.* New York: Oxford University Press.

Debreu, Gerard. 1959. *Theory of Value: An Axiomatic Analysis of Economic Equilibrium.* New York: John Wiley & Sons.

Demos, John, and Sarane Spence Boocock, eds. 1978. *Turning Points: Historical and Sociological Essays on the Family,* supplement to *American Journal of Sociology,* vol. 84.

Deolalikar, Anil B. and Wim P. M. Vijverberg. 1983. The heterogeneity of family and hired labor in agricultural production: A test using district-level data from India. *Journal of Economic Development* 8, no. 2 (December): 45–69.

———. 1987. A test of heterogeneity of family and hired labor in Asian agriculture. *Oxford Bulletin of Economics and Statistics* 49, no. 3 (August): 291–306.

DeTray, Dennis N. 1973. Child quality and the demand for children. *Journal of Political Economy* 81, no. 2, pt. 2 (March/April): S70–S90.

———. 1978. *Child Schooling and Family Size: An Economic Analysis.* Technical Paper R-2301 NICHD. Santa Monica: RAND Corp.

deWolff, Peter, and A. R. D. van Slijpe. 1973. The relation between income, intelligence, education and social background. *European Economic Review* 4, no. 3 (October): 235–64.

Easterlin, Richard A. 1973. Relative economic status and the American fertility swing. In *Family Economic Behavior: Problems and Prospects,* edited by Eleanor B. Sheldon, pp. 170–223. Philadelphia: Lippincott.

Easterlin, Richard A., Robert A. Pollak, and Michael L. Wachter. 1980. Towards a more general economic model of fertility determination: Endogenous preferences and natural fertility. In *Population and Economic Change in Developing Countries,* edited by Richard A. Easterlin, pp. 81–135. Universities–National Bureau of Economic Research Conference Series. Chicago: University of Chicago Press.

Eggebeen, David J., and Dennis P. Hogan. 1990. Giving between the generations in American families. University Park: Pennsylvania State University. Mimeo.

Ehrlich, Isaac, and Gary S. Becker. 1972. Market insurance, self-insurance and self-protection. *Journal of Political Economy* 80, no. 4 (July/August): 623–48.

Ernst, Cecile, and Jules Angst. 1983. *Birth Order: Its Influence on Personality.* New York: Springer-Verlag.

Esposito, John L. 1982. *Women in Muslim Family Law.* Syracuse, N.Y.: Syracuse University Press.

Fenoaltea, Stefano. 1984. Slavery and supervision in comparative perspective: A model. *Journal of Economic History* 44, no. 3 (September): 635–68.

Fisher, R. A. 1918. The correlation between relatives on the supposition of Mendelian inheritance. *Transactions of the Royal Society Edinburgh* 52, pt. 2: 399–433.

Flavin, Marjorie A. 1981. The adjustment of consumption to changing expectations about future income. *Journal of Political Economy* 89, no. 5 (October): 974–1009.

Førsund, Finn R., C. A. Knox Lovell, and Peter Schmidt. 1980. A survey of frontier production functions and of their relationship to efficiency measurement. *Journal of Econometrics* 13, no. 1 (May): 5–25.

Freeman, Richard B. 1981. Black economic progress after 1964: Who has gained and why? In *Studies in Labor Markets,* edited by Sherwin Rosen, pp. 247–94. Chicago: University of Chicago Press.

Fuchs, Victor R. 1983. *How We Live.* Cambridge, Mass.: Harvard University Press.

Galton, Francis. 1874. *English Men of Science: Their Nature and Nurture.* London: Macmillan.

Goldberg, Victor P. 1976. Regulation and administered contracts. *Bell Journal of Economics* 7, no. 2 (Autumn): 426–48.

Goldberger, Arthur S. 1977*a*. Models and methods in the IQ debate. Workshop Series no. 7710. Madison: University of Wisconsin—Madison. (Reprinted without the appendix as Goldberger (1979), pp. 327–47).

———. 1977*b*. Twin methods: A skeptical view. In Taubman (1977), pp. 299–324.

———. 1978. The Genetic Determination of Income: Comment. *American Economic Review* 68, no. 5 (December): 960–69.

———. 1979. Heritability. *Economica* 46, no. 184 (November): 327–47.

Gomez, M. 1980. An analysis of fertility in Mexico. Ph.D. diss., University of Chicago.

Gorseline, Donald E. 1932. *The Effect of Schooling upon Income*. Bloomington: Indiana University, Graduate Council.

Gould, William B. 1982. *A Primer on American Labor Law*. Cambridge, Mass.: MIT Press.

Greven, Philip J., Jr. 1970. *Four Generations: Population, Land, and Family in Colonial Andover, Massachusetts*. Ithaca, N.Y.: Cornell University Press.

Griffin, Sally, and Clyde Griffin. 1977. Family and business in a small city: Poughkeepsie, New York, 1850–1880. In Hareven (1977*b*), pp. 114–63.

Griliches, Zvi. 1974. Household and economy: Towards a new theory of population and economic growth: Comment. *Journal of Political Economy* 82, no. 2, pt. 2 (March/April): S219–S221.

———. 1978. A partial survey of sibling models. Cambridge, Mass.: Harvard University. Mimeo.

———. 1979. Sibling models and data in economics: Beginnings of a survey. *Journal of Political Economy* 87, no. 5, pt. 2 (October): S37–S64.

Hannan, Michael T. 1982. Families, markets, and social structures: An essay on Becker's *A Treatise on the Family*. *Journal of Economic Literature* 20, no. 1 (March): 65–72.

Hansmann, Henry B. 1980. The role of nonprofit enterprise. *Yale Law Journal* 89, no. 5 (April): 835–901.

Harbury, Colin D., and D. M. Hitchens. 1979. *Inheritance and Wealth Inequality in Britain*. London: George Allen & Unwin.

Hareven, Tamara K. 1977*a*. Family time and industrial time: Family and work in a planned corporation town, 1900–1924. In Hareven (1977*b*), pp. 187–200.

———, ed. 1977*b*. *Family and Kin in Urban Communities, 1700–1930*. New York: New Viewpoints.

———. 1978. The dynamics of kin in an industrial community. In Demos and Boocock (1978), pp. S151–S182.

Hauser, Robert M., and Thomas N. Daymont. 1977. Schooling, ability, and earnings: Cross sectional findings 8–14 years after high school graduation. *Sociology of Education* 50, no. 3 (July): 182–206.

Hauser, Robert, and William Sewell. 1985. Birth order and educational attainment in full sibships. *American Educational Research Journal* 22, no. 1 (Spring): 1–23.

Hayashi, Fumio. 1985. The effect of liquidity constraints on consumption: A Cross-sectional analysis. *Quarterly Journal of Economics* 100, no. 1 (February): 183–206.

Heath, Anthony F. 1976. *Rational Choice and Social Exchange: A Critique of Exchange Theory*. New York and Cambridge: Cambridge University Press.

Heckman, James J. 1976. The common structure of statistical models of truncation, sample selection, and limited dependent variables and a simple estimator for such models. *Annals of Economic and Social Measurement* 5, no. 4 (Fall): 475–92.

Hill, Daniel H., and Frank P. Stafford. 1974. Allocation of time to preschool children and educational opportunity. *Journal of Human Resources* 9, no. 3 (Summer): 323–41.

Hirschman, Albert O. 1970. *Exit, Voice, and Loyalty: Responses to Decline in Firms, Organizations and States.* Cambridge, Mass.: Harvard University Press.

Hirshleifer, Jack. 1977. Shakespeare vs. Becker on altruism: The importance of having the last word. *Journal of Economic Literature* 15, no. 2 (June): 500–502.

———. 1985. The expanding domain of economics. *American Economic Review* 75, no. 6, suppl. (December): 53–68.

Homans, George C. 1961. *Social Behavior: Its Elementary Forms.* New York: Harcourt Brace & World.

Hurd, Michael D., and B. Gabriela Mundaca. 1987. The importance of gifts and inheritances among the affluent. Working Paper no. 2415. Cambridge, Mass.: National Bureau of Economic Research.

Jablon, S., et al. 1967. The NAS-NRC twin panel: Methods of construction of the panel, zygosity diagnosis, and the proposed use. *American Journal of Human Genetics* 19, no. 2 (March): 133–61.

Jencks, Christopher, and Marsha Brown. 1977. Genes and social stratification: A methodological exploration with illustrative data. In Taubman (1977), pp. 169–234.

Jencks, Christopher, Marshall Smith, Henry Acland, Mary Jo Bane, David Cohen, Herbert Gintis, Barbara Heyns, and Stephan Michelson. 1972. *Inequality: A Reassessment of the Effect of Family and Schooling in America.* New York: Basic Books.

Jenkins, Stephen. 1987. Snapshots versus movies: "Lifecycle biases" and the estimation of intergenerational earnings inheritance. *European Economic Review* 31, no. 5 (July): 1149–58.

Jinks, J. L., and D. W. Fulker. 1970. Comparison of the biometrical, genetical, MAVA, and classical approaches to the analysis of human behavior. *Psychological Bulletin* 73, no. 5 (May): 311–49.

Kalai, Ehud, and Meir Smorodinsky. 1975. Other solutions to Nash's bargaining problem. *Econometrica* 43, no. 3 (May): 513–18.

Katz, Michael B. 1975. *The People of Hamilton, Canada West: Family and Class in a Mid-Nineteenth-Century City.* Cambridge, Mass.: Harvard University Press.

Kearl, J. R., and Clayne L. Pope. 1986. Unobservable family and individual contributions to the distributions of income and wealth. *Journal of Labor Economics* 4, no. 3, pt. 2 (July): S48–S79.

Kendall, Maurice G., and Alan Stuart. 1958. *The Advanced Theory of Statistics,* 3 vols. New York: Hafner.

King, E. M., and R. E. Evenson. 1983. Time allocation and home production in Philippine rural households. In *Women and Poverty in the Third World,* edited by Mayra Buvinic, Margaret A. Lycette, and William Paul McGreevey, pp. 35–61. Baltimore: Johns Hopkins University Press.

Kinkead, Gwen. 1980. Family business is a passion play. *Fortune* (June 30), pp. 70–75.

Klein, Benjamin, Robert G. Crawford, and Armen A. Alchian. 1978. Vertical integration, appropriable rents, and the competitive contracting process. *Journal of Law and Economics* 21, no. 2 (October): 297–326.

Kotlikoff, Laurence J., and Avia Spivak. 1981. The family as an incomplete annuities market. *Journal of Political Economy* 89, no. 2 (April): 372–91.

Kramer, Mark R. 1984. The role of federal courts in changing state law: The employment at will doctrine in Pennsylvania. *University of Pennsylvania Law Review* 133, no. 1 (December): 227–64.

Kuhn, Thomas S. 1962. *The Structure of Scientific Revolutions.* 2d ed., enlarged. Chicago: University of Chicago Press. (2d. ed., 1970.)

Kurz, Mordecai. 1984. Capital accumulation and the characteristics of private intergenerational transfers. *Economica* 51, no. 201 (February): 1–22.

Landa, Janet T. 1981. A theory of the ethnically homogeneous middleman group: An institutional alternative to contract law. *Journal of Legal Studies* 10, no. 2 (June): 349–62.

Landa, Janet T., and Janet W. Salaff. 1982. The socioeconomic functions of kinship and ethnic networks in promoting Chinese entrepreneurship in Singapore: A case study of the Tan Kah Kee Firm. University of Toronto: Institute of Policy Analysis. Mimeo.

Laslett, Peter, assisted by Richard Wall. 1972. *Household and Family in Past Time.* Cambridge: Cambridge University Press.

Leibowitz, Arleen. 1974. Education and home production. *American Economic Review* 64, no. 2 (May): 243–50.

———. 1977. Family background and economic success: A review of the evidence. In Taubman (1977), pp. 1–33.

Lillard, Lee, and Robert Willis. 1978. Dynamic aspects of earnings mobility. *Econometrica* 46, no. 5 (September): 985–1012.

Lindert, Peter. 1977. Sibling position and achievement. *Journal of Human Resources* 12, no. 2 (Spring): 220–41.

———. 1980. Child costs and economic development. In *Population and Economic Change in Developing Countries,* edited by Richard A. Easterlin, pp. 5–79. Universities–National Bureau of Economic Research Conference Series. Chicago: University of Chicago Press.

Luce, R. Duncan, and Howard Raiffa. 1957. *Games and Decisions: Introduction and Critical Survey.* New York: John Wiley & Sons.

Lundberg, Shelly. 1988. Labor supply of husbands and wives: A simultaneous equations approach. *Review of Economics and Statistics* 70, no. 2 (May): 224–35.

Lundberg, Shelly, and Robert A. Pollak. 1993. Separate spheres bargaining and the marriage market *Journal of Political Economy* 101:6 (December), 988–1010.

Lykken, D. T., T. J. Bouchard, Jr., M. McGue, and A. Tellegen. 1990. "The Minnesota Twin Family Registry: Some initial findings," *Acta Geneticae Medicae et Gemellologiae* 39:1 (November), 35–70.

McElroy, Marjorie B. 1985. The joint determination of household membership and market work: The case of young men. *Journal of Labor Economics* 3, no. 3 (July): 293–316.

———. 1990. The empirical content of Nash-bargained household behavior. *Journal of Human Resources* 25, no. 4 (Fall): 559–83.

———. 1992. The policy implications of family bargaining and marriage markets. Durham, N.C.: Duke University. Mimeo.

McElroy, Marjorie, B., and Mary Jean Horney. 1981. Nash-bargained household decisions: Toward a generalization of the theory of demand. *International Economic Review* 22, no. 2 (June): 333–49.

Macneil, Ian R. 1974. The many futures of contracts. *Southern California Law Review* 47, no. 3 (May): 691–816.

———. 1978. Contracts: Adjustment of long-term economic relations under classical, neoclassical, and relational contract law. *Northwestern University Law Review* 72, no. 6 (January/February): 854–905.

———. 1980. *The New Social Contract: An Inquiry into Modern Contractual Relations.* New Haven, Conn.: Yale University Press.

Maine, Henry Sumner. 1861. *Ancient Law: Its Connection with the Early History of Society and Its Relation to Modern Ideas.* London: J. Murray.

Makhya, I. 1978. Adult and child labor within the household and the quantity and quality of children: Rural India. Chicago: University of Chicago. Mimeo.

Manser, Marilyn, and Murray Brown. 1980. Marriage and household decision-making: A bargaining analysis. *International Economic Review* 21, no. 1 (February): 31–44.

Mattila, J. Peter. 1982. Determinants of male school enrollments: A time series analysis. *Review of Economics and Statistics* 64, no. 2 (May): 242–51.

Mauss, Marcel. 1967. *The Gift.* New York: W. W. Norton.

Meade, J. 1973. The inheritance of inequalities: Some biological, demographic, social, and economic factors. *Proceedings of the British Academy,* 59:3–29. London: Oxford University Press, Ely House.

Menchik, Paul. 1979. Intergenerational transmission of inequality: An empirical study of wealth mobility. *Economica* 46, no. 184 (November): 349–62.

———. 1980. Primogeniture, equal sharing and the U.S. distribution of wealth. *Quarterly Journal of Economics* 94, no. 2 (March): 299–316.

———. 1982. What's happening in Cleveland: Is it altruism, reverse bequest, or simply noise? East Lansing: Michigan State University.

———. 1988. Unequal estate division: Is it altruism, reverse bequest or simply noise?" In *Modelling the Accumulation and Distribution of Wealth,* edited by Denis Kessler and Andre Masson, pp. 105–119. Oxford: Oxford University Press.

Michael, Robert T., and Gary S. Becker. 1973. On the new theory of consumer behavior. *Swedish Journal of Economics* 75, no. 4 (December): 378–96.

Michael, Robert T., Victor Fuchs, and Sharon R. Scott. 1980. Changes in the propensity to live alone: 1950–1976. *Demography* 17, no. 1 (February): 39–56.

Mincer, Jacob B. 1974. *Schooling, Experience, and Earnings.* New York: National Bureau of Economic Research.

Modigliani, Franco. 1986. Life cycle, individual thrift, and the wealth of nations. *American Economic Review* 76, no. 3 (June): 197–313.

Morton, N. E. 1974. Analysis of family resemblance. I. Introduction. *American Journal of Human Genetics* 26, no. 3 (May): 318–30.

Morton, N. E., and D. C. Rao. 1979. Causal analysis of family resemblance. In *Genetic Analysis of Common Diseases: Applications to Predictive Factors in Coronary Disease,* edited by Charles F. Sing and Mark Skolnick, pp. 431–52. New York: Liss.

Murrell, Peter. 1983. The economics of sharing: A transactions cost analysis of contractual choice in farming. *Bell Journal of Economics* 14, no. 1 (Spring): 283–93.

Nash, John F. 1950. The bargaining problem. *Econometrica* 28, no. 1 (April): 155–62.

National Association of Realtors. 1986. *The Homebuying and Selling Process.* Washington, D.C.: National Association of Realtors.

Nerlove, Marc. 1974. Household and economy: Toward a new theory of population and economic growth. *Journal of Political Economy* 83, no. 2, pt. 2 (March/April): S200–S218.

Nerlove, Marc, Assaf Razin, and Efraim Sadka. 1987. *Household and Economy: Welfare Aspects of Endogenous Fertility.* Boston: Academic Press.

Oaxaca, Ronald. 1973. Male-female wage differentials in urban labor markets. *International Economic Review* 14, no. 3 (October): 693–709.

Okun, Arthur M. 1975. *Equality and Efficiency: The Big Tradeoff.* Washington, D.C.: Brookings Institution.

Olneck, Michael. 1977. On the use of sibling data to estimate the effects of family background, cognitive skills, and schooling: Results from the Kalamazoo Brothers Study." In Taubman (1977), pp. 125–62.

Pauly, Mark V. 1974. Overinsurance and public provision of insurance: The roles of moral hazard and adverse selection. *Quarterly Journal of Economics* 88, no. 1 (February): 44–62.

Pechman, Joseph A. 1987. *Federal Tax Policy.* 5th ed. Washington, D.C.: Brookings Institution.

Pitt, Mark M., and Mark R. Rosenzweig. 1990. Estimating the behavioral consequences of health in a family context: The intrafamily incidence of infant illness in Indonesia. *International Economic Review* 31, no. 4 (November): 969–89.

Pitt, Mark M., Mark R. Rosenzweig, and Md. Nazmul Hassan. 1990. Productivity, health and inequality in the intrahousehold distribution of food in low-income countries. *American Economic Review* 80, no. 5 (December), 1139–56.

Pollak, Robert A. 1985. A transaction cost approach to families and households. *Journal of Economic Literature* 23, no. 2 (June): 581–608. (Reprinted as Chapter 6, in this volume.).

———. 1988. Tied transfers and paternalistic preferences. *American Economic Review* 78, no. 2 (May): 240–44. (Reprinted as Chapter 7, in this volume.)

———. 1993. Human capital and preferences. Seattle: University of Washington. Mimeo.

Pollak, Robert A., and Michael Wachter. 1975. The relevance of the household production function and its implication for the allocation of time. *Journal of Political Economy* 83, no. 2 (April): 255–77.

Pollak, Robert A., and Terence J. Wales. 1978. Estimation of complete demand systems from household budget data: The linear and quadratic expenditure systems. *American Economic Review* 68, no. 3 (June): 348–59.

———. 1980. Comparison of the quadratic expenditure system and translog demand systems with alternative specifications of demographic effects. *Econometrica* 48, no. 3 (April): 595–612.

Posner, Richard A. 1974. Theories of economic regulation. *Bell Journal of Economics and Management Science* 5, no. 2 (Autumn): 335–58.

———. 1980. Anthropology and economics. *Journal of Political Economy* 88, no. 3 (June): 608–16.

Psacharopoulos, George. 1981. Returns to education: An updated international comparison. *Comparative Education* 17, no. 3:321–41.

———. 1983. Educational research at the World Bank. *World Bank Research News* 4: 3–17.

———. 1985. Returns to education: A further international update and implications. *Journal of Human Resources* 20, no. 4 (Fall): 583–97.

Rawls, John. 1971. *A Theory of Justice*. Cambridge, Mass: Harvard University Press.

Rochford, Sharon C. 1984. Symmetrically pairwise-bargained allocations in an assignment market. *Journal of Economic Theory* 34, no. 2 (December): 262–81.

Rosenzweig, Mark R. 1982. Educational subsidy, agricultural development, and fertility change. *Quarterly Journal of Economics* 97, no. 1 (February): 67–88.

Rosenzweig, Mark R., and T. Paul Schultz, 1982. Market opportunities, genetic endowments, and intrafamily resource distribution: Child survival in rural India. *American Economic Review* 72, no. 4 (September): 803–15.

Rosenzweig, Mark R., and Kenneth Wolpin. 1980. Testing the quantity-quality fertility model: The use of twins as a natural experiment. *Econometrica* 48, no. 1 (January): 227–40.

———. 1985. Specific experience, household structure, and intergenerational transfers: Farm family land and labor arrangements in developing countries. *Quarterly Journal of Economics* 100, suppl.: 961–87.

———. 1988. Heterogeneity, intrafamily distribution, and child health. *Journal of Human Resources* 23, no. 4 (Fall): 437–61.

Roth, Alvin E. 1979. *Axiomatic Models of Bargaining*. Lecture Notes in Economics and Mathematical Systems, no. 170. Berlin: Springer-Verlag.

Rothschild, Michael, and Joseph Stiglitz. 1976. Equilibrium in competitive insurance markets: An essay on the economics of imperfect information. *Quarterly Journal of Economics* 90, no. 4 (November): 629–49.

Samuelson, Paul A. 1947. *Foundations of Economic Analysis*. Cambridge, Mass.: Harvard University Press.

———. 1956. Social indifference curves. *Quarterly Journal of Economics* 70, no. 1 (February): 1–22.

Scarr, S., and R. Weinberg. 1977. Intellectual similarities within families of both adopted and biological children. *Intelligence* 1, no. 2 (April): 170–91.

Schoen, Robert, and John Wouldredge. 1985. Who marries whom: Marriage patterns in California, 1970. Berkeley: University of California. Mimeo.

Schultz, T. Paul. 1990. Testing the neoclassical model of family labor supply and fertility. *Journal of Human Resources* 25, no. 4 (Fall): 599–634.

Schultz, Theodore W. 1961. Investment in human capital. *American Economic Review* 51, no. 1 (March): 1–17.

———. 1963. *The Economic Value of Education.* New York: Columbia University Press.

Sewell, William, and Robert Hauser. 1975. *Education, Occupation and Earnings: Achievement in the Early Career.* New York: Academic Press.

Shields, James, 1962. *Monozygotic Twins Brought Up Apart and Brought Up Together: An Investigation into the Genetic and Environmental Causes of Variation in Personality.* London: Oxford University Press.

Simon, Herbert A. 1957. *Models of Man: Social and Rational.* New York: John Wiley & Sons.

Singh, R. D., G. E. Schuh, and E. W. Kehrberg. 1978. Economic analysis of fertility behavior and the demand for schooling among poor households in rural Brazil. Bulletin no. 214. West Lafayette, Ind.: Purdue University, Agricultural Experiment Station.

Smith, James D. 1975. White wealth and black people: The distribution of wealth in Washington, D.C. in 1967. In *The Personal Distribution of Income and Wealth,* edited by James D. Smith, pp. 329–64. New York: Columbia University Press, for the National Bureau of Economic Research.

Solon, Gary. 1989. Biases in the estimation of intergenerational earnings correlations. *Review of Economics and Statistics* 71, no. 1 (February): 172–74.

———. 1992. Intergenerational income mobility in the United States. *American Economic Review* 82, no. 3 (June): 393–408.

Solon, Gary R., Mary Corcoran, Roger Gordon, and Deborah Laren. 1987. The effect of family background and economic status: A longitudinal analysis of sibling correlations. Ann Arbor: University of Michigan. Mimeo.

Soltow, Lee. 1965. *Toward Income Equality in Norway.* Madison: University of Wisconsin Press.

Stigler, George J., and Gary S. Becker. 1977. De gustibus non est disputandum. *American Economic Review* 67, no. 2 (March): 76–90.

Summers, Clyde W. 1983. Introduction: Individual rights in the workplace: The employment-at-will issue. *University of Michigan Journal of Law Reform* 16, no. 2 (Winter): 201–5.

Tanner, Tony. 1979. *Adultery in the Novel: Contract and Transgression,* Baltimore: Johns Hopkins University Press.

Taubman, Paul. 1976. The determinants of earnings: Genetics, family, and other environments; A study of white male twins. *American Economic Review* 66, no. 5 (December): 858–70.

———, ed. 1977. *Kinometrics: Determinants of Socioeconomic Success within and between Families.* Amsterdam: North-Holland Publishing Company.

———. 1978a. What we learn from estimating the genetic contribution to inequality in earnings: Reply. *American Economic Review* 68, no. 5 (December): 970–76.

———. 1978b. *Income Distribution and Redistribution.* Reading, Mass.: Addison-Wesley.

————. 1981. On heritability. *Economica,* 48, no. 192 (November): 417–20. (Reprinted as Chapter 12, in this volume.)

Taubman, Paul, and Terence Wales. 1972. *Mental Ability and Higher Educational Attainment in the 20th Century.* New York: McGraw-Hill.

————. 1974. *Higher Education and Earnings: A Report Prepared for the Carnegie Commission on Higher Education and the National Bureau of Economic Research.* New York: McGraw-Hill.

Tauchen, Helen V., Ann D. Witte, and Sharon K. Long. 1991. Violence in the family: A non-random affair. *International Economic Review* 32, no. 2 (May): 491–511.

Taussig, Michael K. 1974. Background paper. In *Those Who Served: Report of the Twentieth Century Fund Task Force on Policies Toward Veterans,* pp. 41–129. New York: Twentieth Century Fund.

Tawney, Richard H. 1961. *Equality.* New York: Capricorn.

Thomas, Duncan. 1990. Intra-household resource allocation: An inferential approach. *Journal of Human Resources* 25, no. 4 (Fall): 635–64.

Tomes, Nigel. 1981. The family, inheritance, and the intergenerational transmission of inequality. *Journal of Political Economy* 89, no. 5 (October): 928–58.

Ulph, David. 1988. A general non-cooperative Nash model of household consumption behaviour. Bristol: University of Bristol. Mimeo.

Vanek, Jaroslav. 1969. Decentralization under workers' management: A theoretical appraisal. *American Economic Review* 59, no. 5 (December): 1006–14.

Weitzman, Lenore J. 1981. *The Marriage Contract: Spouses, Lovers and the Law.* New York: Free Press.

Weyrauch, Walter O., and Sanford N. Katz. 1983. *American Family Law in Transition.* Washington, D.C.: Bureau of National Affairs.

Wilhelm, Mark O. 1991. Bequests behavior and the effect of heir's earnings: Testing the altruistic model of bequests. University Park: Pennsylvania State University. Mimeo.

Williamson, Oliver E. 1975. *Markets and Hierarchies: Analysis and Antitrust Implications.* New York: Free Press.

————. 1976. Franchise bidding for natural monopolies—in general and with respect to CATV. *Bell Journal of Economics* 7, no. 1 (Spring): 73–104.

————. 1979. Transaction-cost economics: The governance of contractual relations. *Journal of Law and Economics* 22, no. 2 (October): 223–61.

————. 1981. The modern corporation: Origins, evolution, attributes. *Journal of Economic Literature* 19, no. 4 (December): 1537–68.

————. 1983. Credible commitments: Using hostages to support exchange. *American Economic Review* 73, no. 4 (September): 519–40.

Willis, Robert J. 1973. A new approach to the economic theory of fertility behavior. *Journal of Political Economy* 81, no. 2, pt. 2 (March/April): S14–S64.

Wilson, Charles A. 1977. A model of insurance markets with incomplete information. *Journal of Economic Theory* 16, no. 2 (December): 167–207.

————. 1980. The nature of equilibrium in markets with adverse selection. *Bell Journal of Economics* 11, no. 1 (Spring): 108–30.

Winston, Gordon C. 1982. *The Timing of Economic Activities: Firms, Households, and Markets in Time-specific Analysis.* Cambridge: Cambridge University Press.

World Bank. 1980. *World Development Report, 1980.* Washington, D.C.: World Bank.

World Bank. 1980. *World Development Report, 1980*. Washington, D.C.: World Bank.

———. 1981. *World Development Report, 1981*. Washington, D.C.: World Bank.

———. 1984. *World Development Report, 1984*. Washington, D.C.: World Bank.

Zajonc, R. B. 1976. Family configuration and intelligence. *Science* 192 (April 16, 1976): 227–36.

Zeldes, Stephen P. 1989. Consumption and liquidity constraints: An empirical investigation. *Journal of Political Economy* 97, no. 2 (April): 305–46.

Zimmerman, David J. 1992. Regression toward mediocrity in economic stature. *American Economic Review* 82, no. 3 (June): 409–29.

Author Index

Adams, James D., 29, 41–42
Alchian, Armen, 146
Anderson, Michael, 170–71
Angst, Jules, 96
Arrow, Kenneth J., 31

Barro, Robert J., 3
Becker, Gary S.: on altruist model, 161–68, 173–74, 177–78; on bequests, 66–67; on earnings distribution, 246, 248; on fertility, 7, 183; on household production model, 6, 139–40; on intergenerational earnings correlations, 229–39, 241; on intergenerational endowments model, 18, 215–28; on marital-specific capital, 157, 165; on parental investments, 40, 184, 210, 249–51, 253, 266; and parental preferences, 188; and posteducational transfers, 27; rotten kid theorem by, 9, 66; on schooling, 207; Woytinsky lecture by, 46n. 10, 57, 230–31, 250–51, 266. *See also* wealth model
Bergstrom, Theodore C., 9
Bernheim, B. Douglas, 9, 11–12, 174, 177
Birdsall, Nancy, 56, 90
Blake, Judith, 183
Blinder, Alan S., 67
Bourguignon, François, 13
Bowles, Sam, 232
Brown, Murray, 14, 163
Browning, Martin, 13
Bruce, Neil, 9

Cavalli-Sforza, L., 253
Chiappori, Pierre-André, 13
Coase, Ronald H., 17
Colclough, Christopher, 212
Cox, Donald, 12, 133, 177

Daymont, Thomas N., 104
Demsetz, Harold, 146

Eggebeen, David J., 133
Ernst, Cecile, 96

Fisher, R. A.: on genetic model, 6, 250–51, 266; on kin groups, *261,* 265, *265;* on phenotypic variances, 19; polygenic model by, 251–56, 258–62
Fulker, D. W., 275

Galton, Francis, 89
Goldberger, Arthur S., 62, 245, 247–48, 250, 252–53, 263
Greven, Philip J., 169
Griffen, Clyde, 154
Griffen, Sally, 154
Griliches, Zvi, 40, 271, 274

Hassan, Md. Nazmul, 10
Hauser, Robert M., 104, 215
Heckman, James J., 81
Hirschman, Albert O., 146
Hirshleifer, Jack, 9
Hogan, Dennis P., 133
Horney, Mary J., 14, 163
Hurd, Michael D., 132

Jablon, S., 276
Jinks, J. L., 275

Katz, Michael, 171
Katz, Sanford N., 158
Kendall, Maurice G., 258
Kotlikoff, Laurence, 173

303

Subject Index